THIRD EDITION

Ethics in HEALTH ADMINISTRATION

A Practical Approach for Decision Makers

Eileen E. Morrison, MPH, EdD, CHES, LPC

Professor, Health Administration
Texas State University
San Marcos, Texas

JONES & BARTLETT
LEARNING

World Headquarters
Jones & Bartlett Learning
5 Wall Street
Burlington, MA 01803
978-443-5000
info@jblearning.com
www.jblearning.com

Jones & Bartlett Learning books and products are available through most bookstores and online booksellers. To contact Jones & Bartlett Learning directly, call 800-832-0034, fax 978-443-8000, or visit our website, www.jblearning.com.

Production Credits
VP, Executive Publisher: David Cella
Publisher: Michael Brown
Editorial Assistant: Nicholas Alakel
Associate Production Editor: Rebekah Linga
Senior Marketing Manager: Sophie Fleck Teague
Manufacturing and Inventory Control Supervisor: Amy Bacus
Composition: Cenveo® Publisher Services
Cover Design: Scott Moden
Rights and Photo Research Coordinator: Mary Flatley
Cover and Title Page Image: © file404/Shutterstock
Printing and Binding: Edwards Brothers Malloy
Cover Printing: Edwards Brothers Malloy

To order this product, use ISBN: 978-1-284-07065-1

Library of Congress Cataloging-in-Publication Data
Morrison, Eileen E., author.
 [Ethics in health administration]
 Ethics in health care : a practical approach for decision makers / Eileen E. Morrison.—Third edition.
 p. ; cm.
 Preceded by Ethics in health administration / Eileen E. Morrison. 2nd ed. c2011.
 Includes bibliographical references and index.
 ISBN 978-1-284-04767-7 (paper.)
 I. Title.
 [DNLM: 1. Health Services Administration—ethics. 2. Decision Making—ethics. 3. Ethics, Medical. W 84.1]
 RA394
 174.2—dc23
                                                              2014037883
6048
Printed in the United States of America
19 18 17 16 15   10 9 8 7 6 5 4 3 2 1

DEDICATION

This edition is dedicated to my seventh-grade teacher, Prudence Clark, who believed that I was a writer. It is also dedicated to my family: Grant, Kate, Emery Aidan, and Morrigan Leigh. Their support and inspiration mean so much.

TABLE OF CONTENTS

PREFACE TO THE THIRD EDITION

Health care has undergone a radical change since the second edition of *Ethics in Health Administration*. The Affordable Care Act of 2010 (ACA) promises great changes in healthcare practice and administration. These changes present logistical, fiscal, and ethical challenges requiring deep learning and forward thinking for all those persons who practice health care. Technology also continues its rapid advance and affects the nature and vocabulary of healthcare practice.

Despite change, much remains the same in the U.S. healthcare system. Specifically, the healthcare system must still address the Iron Triangle of access, quality, and cost. It must account for these areas by paying careful attention to the ACA concept of patient-centered care through safety and quality standards. In addition, the healthcare system will need to increase its efficiency, control its waste, and reduce its fraud. Of course, ensuring that the system makes these changes in a manner that delivers the desired outcomes will require appropriately qualified personnel who are ethical in their treatment decisions and practices.

As for healthcare administrators, they must model the level of sound decision-making and ethical practice that they expect from their staff members. In addition, administrators can influence all aspects of healthcare delivery organizations. Therefore, organizations and communities hold them to a high standard of ethical practice. The third edition of *Ethics in Health Administration* offers healthcare administrators the knowledge and applications necessary to build their careers as ethically sound practitioners in the ACA era. Ancora Imparo!

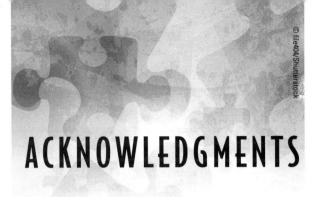

ACKNOWLEDGMENTS

No one writes alone. Authors are inspired, guided, and encouraged by many who care about the work and the person. Therefore, this author acknowledges her debt to the many family, colleagues, and friends who made it possible for her to complete this new edition. She also acknowledges her students, past and present, who continue to inspire and give purpose to her writing. Special gratitude goes to her publisher, Mike Brown, and editors, Chloe Falivene, Nicholas Alakel, and Rebekah Linga. Their encouragement and assistance made the author's writing more accurate, concise, and joyful.

CONTRIBUTORS

The following individuals contributed story ideas that the author used to create the case studies in this text. The author is deeply grateful to each of them.

Karen Bawel-Brinkley, PhD, RN

Associate Professor of Nursing
San Jose State University
San Jose, California

Kim Contreraz, Family Nurse Practitioner

Country Home Health Care, Inc.
Charlottesville, Indiana

Mario Contreraz, RN

Nurse Manager
Indiana Clinical Research Center
University of Indiana Medical School
Bloomington, Indiana

Jan Gardner-Ray, EdD

President
Country Home Health Care, Inc.
Charlottesville, Indiana

Maudia Gentry, EdD

Lecturer
University of North Texas
Dallas, Texas

Ericka Lochner, MBA, RN

Chief Clinical Officer
Kindred Hospital
Corpus Christi, Texas

Elizabeth Morrison-Riggs
Production Supervisor
Norfolk, Virginia

Oren Renick, JD, FACHE
Professor of Health Administration
Texas State University
San Marcos, Texas

Martha J. Morgan Sanders, PhD, RN
National Faculty (Retired)
Nova Southeastern University
Fort Lauderdale, Florida

Michael P. West, EdD, FACHE
Executive Director
University of Texas at Arlington, Fort Worth Center
Fort Worth, Texas

SECTION

I

Foundations for Ethics

It was the best of times, it was the worst of times. It was the
age of wisdom, it was the age of foolishness. It was the epoch
of belief, it was the epoch of incredulity. It was the season
of Light, it was the season of Darkness. It was the Spring of
hope, it was the Winter of despair. We had everything before
us, we had nothing before us.

—Charles Dickens, *A Tale of Two Cities*

■ INTRODUCTION

In light of the challenges of the Patient Protection and Affordable Care
Act of 2010 (ACA), this quote from *A Tale of Two Cities* by Charles
Dickens might be addressing today's healthcare system. The U.S.
healthcare system is facing a change that includes an increase in access
to health care for millions more of the country's citizens. In addition,
there is a new emphasis on patient-centered care, population health,
and prevention. Health care is also benefiting from a rapid change in
the sophistication and application of technology in both patient treatment and healthcare administration. Will these changes mean the best
of times for the healthcare system?

Implementation of the ACA and healthcare changes are not without challenges. They require resolution of the fiscal and logistical issues
of providing more care without adding excessive costs. In addition,
payment systems must adapt to changes in insurance and new government regulation. The ACA also seeks to reduce prices for health care
and control costs. To this end, healthcare organizations must address
efficiency and effectiveness without sacrificing quality of staff or treatments. Coupled with these issues is the business need to satisfy the customers of health care, including patients, providers, shareholders, and
the community. Could this also be the worst of times for health care?
Only the future has the answers.

What is the role of healthcare administration in the ACA era? Healthcare administrators (HCAs) are essential to health care's future success.

Through their leadership and role modeling, they provide the environment where the important work of health care takes place. Even in a time of great change, administrators are the creators of structure and support for the healthcare system. They also serve as the connection to the community and as stewards of the resources invested in health care. Certainly, this grave responsibility will be even more significant in the current era.

How does a healthcare administrator prepare for ethics-based management in such a tumultuous environment? Preparation requires a foundation in systems, human relations, finance, and leadership gained through formal education. It also mandates a deeper understanding of the principles of ethics and appropriate ethical behavior from the individual, organizational, and societal view. This foundation provides the tools to make decisions that are not just fiscally sound, but also ethically appropriate. Ethics needs to be a more than a discussion at meetings; it must be a day-to-day practice.

■ A WORD ABOUT THE TEXT

Just like a healthcare organization, this text has a mission and a vision. Its mission is to provide solid preparation in knowledge of both the theory and principles of ethics. More importantly, it provides a guide to the application of ethics in the real world of health care. The author consulted many scholarly resources in the creation of this text. However, theory alone is not enough. To fulfill this text's mission, the author must also provide practical examples of using ethics in the daily practice of healthcare administration. Therefore, this text combines theory and practice in a reader-centered format. Each chapter contains a feature called "Points to Ponder" that identifies important concepts. There is also a "Key Terms" section to build vocabulary. These key terms are included in bold print in the content section of the text and defined in the glossary.

In addition to information about the topic under study, chapters contain case studies in the form of stories. Some of these stories are fictionalized versions of ideas contributed by healthcare providers from many different healthcare settings. Others are the author's sole creation based on her experience. Each case relates to the chapter so that the reader has a greater understanding of how content relates to real world application.

The model seen in Figure I-1 guides the vision for this text. Since healthcare administrators do not make decisions in a vacuum, the circles represent the impact of influences on decision making. The outer circle represents the theory and principles that are the foundation of ethical decision making. The next circle represents areas external to the

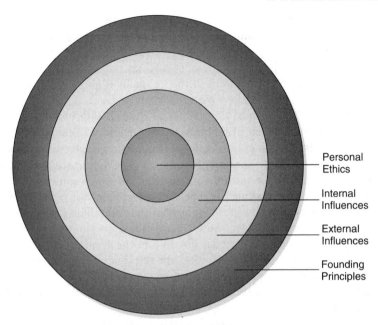

Personal
Ethics

Internal
Influences

External
Influences

Founding
Principles

Figure I-1. A System of Healthcare Administration Ethics

organization that influence the operations of healthcare administration. The model also includes a circle for forces within the organization that also impact decisions and practices. Finally, the inner circle represents the healthcare administrator's personal ethics and its influence on action and career success.

Chapters follow this model by providing information about key issues within these circles. For example, the *Foundations for Ethics* section establishes a foundation in ethics theory and principles. The *Practical Theory* chapter explores founding theories of ethics that guide most of Western ethical thinking. Using this theoretical foundation, the *Autonomy* chapter explores one of the four key principles of healthcare ethics. The *Nonmaleficence and Beneficence* and *Justice* chapters focus on the remaining key principles.

The *External Influences on Ethics* section is the next circle. A new chapter in this edition, *Ethics Challenges in the ACA Era*, provides an overview of the ACA and its connection to ethics-based practice. The chapter examines ethics issues from the perspective of the public, hospitals, practitioners, and insurance companies. The *Market Forces and Ethics* chapter deals with forces including the baby boomers, managed care, and alternative medicine. The *Community Responsibility and Ethics* chapter addresses health care's responsibility to the broader community. It includes information on organizations and laws that require accountability for health care. In addition, sections relate to how healthcare administrators demonstrate their responsibility to the community. Finally, the *Technology and Ethics* chapter presents an in-depth view of technology's impact on ethics.

The healthcare organization's influence on an administrator's ethical decisions is the focus of the *Organizational Influences on Ethics* section. The *No Mission, No Margin: Fiscal Responsibility* chapter presents the challenging area of how fiscal responsibility influences ethical decisions. It also discusses the financial ethics issues related to nonprofit versus for-profit healthcare organizations. The *Organizational Culture and Ethics* chapter features information on ethics committees and models for decision making. The next chapter, *The Ethics of Quality*, addresses quality, which is a major part of the ACA. The *Patient Issues and Ethics* chapter considers how the organization views patients and how it acts to meet their needs. Finally, *Public Health and Ethics*, a new chapter for this edition, explores the responsibility for community health represented by the public health system and its professionals. It includes a discussion of the ethics issues for this important part of the healthcare system.

The Inner Circle of Ethics section (the innermost circle in Figure I-1) presents a more personal look at healthcare administrators' ethics foundations. The *Moral Integrity* chapter investigates this concept and its meaning for the busy healthcare administrator. The *Codes of Ethics and Administrative Practice* chapter discusses codes of ethics and their application to administrative practice. Finally, the *Practicing as an Ethical Administrator* chapter presents information related to the day-to-day practice of an ethics-based healthcare administrator.

Why would a healthcare administrator or future administrator read this text? Through deep reading, this text helps the reader become an administrator who can see the world through "ethical eyes" as well as through financial ones. On the surface, this ability may make daily operations more difficult. Why not just be expedient and follow the money? However, by applying ethics and patient-centered thinking, healthcare administrators can enhance the overall effectiveness of their organizations and better meet the challenges presented by the application of the ACA. Because health care is a trust-based industry, they will also be able to maintain trust by preventing actions that will be viewed as unethical or immoral. In addition, ethics-based administrators enhance their careers. They can become persons of integrity and hold a reputation for using practical wisdom to make decisions that are both fiscally sound and ethically based. In the end, ethics always matters.

CHAPTER
1

Practical Theory

Why is it important to know ethics theory for healthcare administration?

Points to Ponder

1. In the age of the Patient Protection and Affordable Health Act of 2010, also called simply the Affordable Care Act of 2010 (ACA), why do healthcare administrators need to be grounded in ethics?
2. Who are the Big Eight ethics theorists and why are they important for healthcare management?
3. What is your working definition of ethics?

Key Terms

The following is a list of this chapter's key terms. Look for them in bold.

categorical imperative	natural law
consequentialism	normative ethics
conventional	original position
deontology	practical wisdom
ethical egoism	preconventional
eudaimonia	premoral
I-THOU	principled moral reasoning
liberty principle	sense of meaning
maximum principle	utilitarianism
moral development	virtue

■ INTRODUCTION AND DEFINITIONS

A patient looks up as the anesthesiologist puts a mask over her face. A four-year-old boy closes his eyes as the nurse comes close; he knows it is time for his "shot." A daughter walks through the nursing home door; she still hears her mother asking to go home. A health administrator informs the staff about his new policy on infection control. An insurance supervisor explains the copayments for a surgery to a patient. What do these scenes have in common?

First, these scenes deeply connect to the core concept of all of health care—trust. From the patients' view, trust happens on both physical and emotional levels. Patients surrender their bodies and lives for care and expect competence and quality coupled with respect and compassion. From the administration side, trust is the basis for creating policies, procedures, workflow, and other mechanisms to make health care happen. Administrators must trust that healthcare personnel on all levels will provide competent care and want to serve patient needs and within facility guidelines. Administrators must also be constantly aware of the needs of patients while respecting the autonomy of healthcare professionals.

How do these situations connect to ethics for healthcare administrators? To the outside world, administration is about policies, procedures, billing, patient satisfaction, and ACA compliance. While these areas are certainly germane to the practice of healthcare administration, the center of administrative practice is making the best ethical decisions for patients, providers, and the organization. Because of the unique nature of health care, administrators must be able to make both fiscally and ethically sound decisions. They must also be able to defend these decisions to a myriad of audiences, including healthcare professionals, boards of trustees, community members, and government agencies.

In addition, healthcare administrators must make decisions in an environment of system-wide change necessitated by the passage of the ACA in 2010. This law is expected to affect all aspects of health care, from clinical practice to insurance coverage. It will demand much of each person in health care, from surgeons to supervisors. Such profound change also creates new ethics challenges. Given this awesome responsibility and changing environment, is it not appropriate for administrators to have a foundation in ethics and its application?

The first step in obtaining this foundation is to understand ethics and its theories and principles. Therefore, this chapter begins with a section that presents many of the definitions associated with ethics. These definitions should help establish a foundation for studying the theory and principles that follow.

Ethics theory has been a subject of study for many thousands of years, and many brilliant scholars have spent their lives exploring it. It is not possible to study the work of all of these scholars, so this chapter features eight key theorists who were instrumental in creating the foundation of ethics for health care. When students try to read these theorists' works in their original forms, they often find them obtuse and uninteresting. They may also fail to see any application to health administration practice. Therefore, this text seeks to capture the key points of their theories in the context of who the theorists were and the application of their ideas to the current healthcare environment.

To assist the reader in understanding who these theorists were, the chapter section on theory begins with a brief biography of each theorist. A concept summary including the essence of each scholar's key points follows to create a working knowledge of his thinking. Finally, because the application of ethics theory is important, ideas about application of these theories are a part of the discussion for each theorist.

■ DEFINITION OF ETHICS

Defining the concept of ethics and its application is a quest that crosses time and cultures. Perhaps our cave-dwelling ancestors wondered about what was right or wrong as they sat around their campfires. In modern times, the task of defining ethics has fallen to a division of philosophy that is concerned with both meta-ethics (the application of ethics) and **normative ethics** (the study of ethics concepts) (Summers, 2014).

Ethics can be theoretical, community based, organizational, or personal. In turn, it is necessary to define these forms of ethics. For example, from a theoretical base, ethics has a theory orientation, such as deontology or utilitarianism (more on these theories later in this chapter). One can also define ethics as a way to examine or study moral behaviors. With respect to moral behavior and healthcare administrators, Darr (2011) explains that they must think about moral decisions that include, but go beyond, individual patients. He also stresses that ethics involves more than just obeying the law. Law is the minimum standard that society approves for actions or behaviors; ethics is much broader and often much more difficult to codify. Therefore, a person could behave legally, but not ethically. Understanding and addressing the differences between law and ethics may be one of the great challenges faced by health administrators in the complexity of the ACA era.

In addition, the community establishes its sense of what is appropriate ethical behavior for individuals and organizations. Often, administrators are not aware of community standards and suffer personal and career setbacks because of this ignorance. For example, if a person is a hospital administrator in a large city, it might be acceptable to have a drink after work at one's favorite bar. However, in a small town, that same behavior could be unethical, and even be reported to the board of trustees.

Summers (2014) defines ethics in terms of knowing right from wrong and applying ethics theory to one's life (normative ethics). He also stated that this type of ethics challenges administrators to find the correct moral rules to follow. A number of theories discussed later in this chapter represent this definition of ethics. For example, natural law theories, consequentialism, deontological theories, and virtue ethics have their foundation in the study of knowing right from wrong.

Normative ethics is also concerned with organizational ethics, which is commonly defined as "the way we do things here." This form of ethics also assists employees to understand the standards for acceptable behaviors within an organization. Defining ethical standards, behavior, and policy for healthcare organizations is of great importance because these areas influence individual behavior and community perceptions of organizations. However, healthcare organizations do not create operational definitions of ethics—people do. Therefore, specific definition of ethics for an organization must include dialogue to understand differing ideas about ethics and form an operational definition. Can you see why establishing normative ethics for an organization is so important?

There is also a need to define professional ethics. Individual professions establish definitions and guidelines for ethical behavior of their members through codes of ethics. For example, codes of ethics exist for nurses, physicians, physical therapists, occupational therapists, massage therapists, and acupuncturists. In addition, healthcare administrators have guidance from the American College of Healthcare Executives (ACHE) on definitions of ethics, concepts of ethical behavior, and policy development. The ACHE has also developed a self-assessment tool to help busy healthcare administrators keep their ethics on track. Discussion of professional definitions of ethics and codes appears later in this text.

Of course, the practice of ethics really comes down to the person. Practicing healthcare administrators must be aware of theoretical, community, and organizational ethics as they make daily decisions. They also have to be attuned to professional standards. However, in their daily operations as administrators, they ultimately must choose their actions. One might ask, "Isn't ethics just doing what is right at the right time?" The answer is "yes, but. . . ." In healthcare organizations, what is right is not always a simple matter. This is why professionals must develop their personal "ethical bottom line."

Ethical egoism could be part of this bottom line, but may not serve healthcare administrators well. The basis for this type of ethics is the idea that people should center their actions on what will provide their best personal benefit (Summers, 2014). In other words, in this view a person's desires, benefits, and pleasures are considered more important than those of other people. While many people take this position with respect to ethics, it fails to meet the healthcare administrator's obligation to put the needs of the patient first and to be a steward of resources for the community. For an ethics-based administrator in the ACA era, there will be challenges to go beyond ethical egoism as a person and a professional.

In addition, healthcare administrators need to think about the community and its expectations. They need to become more aware of the mission and values of their organizations and the implementation of that mission in the community. In doing so, healthcare administrators need to explore their codes of professional ethics. Finally, they must think about their own values and ask themselves, "What is my true ethics bottom line? On which issues would I be willing to act even if it meant quitting my job?" This thought process should lead to the creation of a personal ethics statement. This document can assist the administrator when making the difficult decisions that will be part of a health administrator's role in the ACA era.

■ ETHICS THEORY AND ITS APPLICATION

While there are many ethics theorists, eight are included here because of their influence on health care. This text calls them the Big Eight: Aquinas, Kant, Mill, Rawls, Aristotle, Buber, Kohlberg, and Frankl. For the purpose of this discussion, the Big Eight is divided into two groups. The first group, which includes Aquinas, Kant, Mill, and Rawls, examined the global issues surrounding ethics and ethical decisions. The second group, which consists of Aristotle, Buber, Kohlberg, and Frankl, studied personal ethics and moral development. This chapter provides a summary of their works and an understanding of their contributions to healthcare ethics.

■ GLOBAL ETHICAL THEORIES

St. Thomas Aquinas (1225–1274)

Biographical Influences on His Theory

St. Thomas Aquinas, the youngest of nine children, was born in Sicily in 1225. His family was wealthy, and Aquinas was well educated in the classic literature of his time. He received his calling to become a member of the Dominican order of the Catholic Church early in his life. However, his family did not support this vocation and tried to prevent him from joining the order. In an effort to change his mind, his family actually held Aquinas prisoner in the family castle for two years. They tried to make him renounce his calling by tempting him with worldly pleasures (including hiring a prostitute to seduce him). Finally, the family relented and allowed him to go to Cologne, join the Dominican order, and continue his study with the major scholars of his day.

Aquinas became a teacher of theology and prolific writer; the greatest of his writings was the *Summa Theologiae*. Part Two of this work was devoted entirely to ethics and combined Aristotelian and

Christian thinking. This work helped to establish the concepts of **natural law** that are part of Aquinas's ethics theory (Davies, 2004).

Concept Summary

Influenced by Christian theology and the writings of Aristotle and others, part of St. Thomas Aquinas's genius was that he brought together faith and reason (Palmer, 2010). According to Aquinas, God is perfectly rational and He created the world in a rational manner (Summers, 2014). God's design for the world included giving humans the ability to reason, wonder about the cause of all things, and make rational decisions. Because humans have this gift of rationality, they have the potential to use moral judgment and to choose good and avoid evil (Darr, 2011; Palmer, 2010). Notice the word "potential"; people do not always do this. Rational people may violate natural law because they are also given the gift of free will. However, if people are true to their rational natures, they will listen to their consciences (i.e., the voice of God) and obey natural law by choosing goodness over evil.

So what is goodness as defined by Aquinas? This theorist provided complex definitions of good and its limitations. His definitions included a belief that acts that preserve life and the human race are part of the definition of good. Something is also good if it advances knowledge and truth, helps people live in community, and respects the dignity of all persons. Aquinas also believed that to find happiness people must not look to pleasures, honors, wealth, or worldly power because these are not the true source of goodness. Instead, true happiness occurs only when one seeks the wisdom to know God. Truly understanding God is the ultimate good that all rational human beings seek (Kerr, 2009).

Theory Applications

It is important to remember that knowledge of ethics builds on the work of previous scholars. Aristotle, Dionysius, and Christian doctrine heavily influenced Aquinas's thinking. How does his philosophy of ethics apply to today's world? If people choose to act against their "rational nature" (as defined by Aquinas), they can do things that are evil for themselves and others. These choices can affect the individual and those around that person. For example, it is not rational to drink to excess and then get behind the wheel of a car. If people make this irrational decision, their actions can cause them harm or even death. This harm can also extend to others who have the misfortune of coming into contact with them in their compromised state. In addition, such acts affect the healthcare system by increasing the costs of health care that might not be necessary if people did not make choices that against their rational nature.

Aquinas's idea of "basic good" seems on the surface to be simple. All a person has to do is respect people's dignity and help them live in community. However, when one translates this concept into the healthcare system and its policies, matters become much more complex. In the ACA era with all of its changes, what does the healthcare system do about people who do not make rational choices? Do they deserve the same level of care as those who make rational choices? How can the business of health care preserve the human race and still have enough money to keep its doors open? These questions relate to the difficult choices (gray areas) that are part of today's healthcare system, where demand for care often exceeds finances.

Immanuel Kant (1724–1804)

Biographical Influences on His Theory

Although Kant became a dominant force in ethics theory, he rarely left his hometown of Königsberg, Prussia, which was a major cosmopolitan center and university town. He began his academic career by studying mathematics, physics, logic, metaphysics, and natural law. After serving as tutor for young children, Kant was finally able to complete his academic credentials and taught philosophy for more than 40 years. He also published works on natural science and even developed a theory about the formation of the solar system. However, Kant's work in moral philosophy is his best-known scholarship. His works included *Groundwork of the Metaphysics of Morals* (1785), *Critique of Pure Reason* (1787), and *Critique of the Power of Judgment* (1790). Because of his extensive writing and teaching, he became the dominant force in German philosophy and an international star in the field (Rohlf, 2010).

Concept Summary

Kant's writing in metaphysics and later on practical philosophy had a major impact on the field of ethics. He went beyond the description of what the world is (theoretical philosophy) to a discussion of what the world should be (practical philosophy). Through his thinking about morals and reasoning, Kant founded an entire area of ethics called **deontology,** or duty-based ethics (Summers, 2014).

For Kant, everything had worth based on its relative value. This means that things like talent, beauty, money, and even happiness are not good in and of themselves. Rather, a person can use any of these assets for good or evil. This is true because attributes (such as intelligence, physical beauty, or bravery) are either gifts of genetics or learned from the environment. They also have their source in the mind or perception. Therefore, a person decides who is smart and who is not, who is beautiful and who is not, and so on. While society may value personal attributes, such as influence, money, or even happiness, it is people who actually use these traits for good or evil. For example, if a person is highly intelligent, immensely talented, or extremely wealthy, he or she might discover a cure for a terrible disease or create a way to change the world. This person might also use that same intelligence, talent, or wealth to become a creative embezzler or a successful serial killer (Blackburn, 2001).

For Kant, the only good that can exist without clarification is something called good will. Good will meant that there was no ultimate end for the person who chooses it. In other words, acting with good will does not give people benefit. They act because they feel that it is the right thing to do. Their inner understanding of their sense of duty motivates them; it is motivation that counts. Therefore, good will is not a means to an end; it just *is* (Blackburn, 2001).

It is important to note that, in the Kantian view, all humans have absolute worth simply by the fact of their existence. Because they have worth, they are not a means to accomplish what an individual wants or to meet a societal goal. Rather, they are an end in themselves. What does this mean in practice? It means that administrators cannot manipulate and use people as a way to get what they want and remain ethical. Instead, they should honor individuals and respect their dignity because they exist as persons. For Kant, it was critical that people value qualities that respect the dignity of others, including freedom, autonomy, and rationality (Palmer, 2010). How does this translate today? It means that people have a duty to choose to act as a moral mediator and base their actions on good will. Good will does not include using people to achieve personal goals or benefits as a part of the decision-making process.

How do people know what is good? First, Kant acknowledged that all people have the ability to think and make their own decisions. In fact, he said, free will is essential to ethical behavior and to understanding what is good. Kant also acknowledged that humans are rational and can use reason to decide what should be the "rules for good." In fact, he provided a tool for understanding how to determine these rules or duties. He called this tool the **categorical imperative**; it represents a way to test actions, determine one's duty, and make moral decisions. For Kant, decisions about duty-based ethical choices include the concept of universal application—that is, becoming a universal law. For example, a person can ask, "Would I want everyone to be able to do this without exception?" If the answer is "yes," then the decision passes test of universalization or the categorical imperative. It then becomes a categorical moral duty and there would be a moral obligation to act in accordance with this duty (Blackburn, 2001; Palmer, 2010).

Some writers think that the categorical imperative is similar to the Golden Rule (a part of many of the world's religions). Kant, however, thought that the categorical imperative differed from the idea of "do to others what you would do to yourself." For example, one could apply the Golden Rule in ways that are not universal if one uses feelings and needs, rather than reasoning, to determine one's actions. Moral duty goes beyond a person and his or her determination of fairness. The test of the categorical imperative also requires that administrators treat everyone as a person and not as a means to an end (Blackburn, 2001; Palmer, 2010; Summers, 2014).

Theory Applications

Kantian, or duty-based, ethics acknowledges the value of all human beings as means unto themselves and gives a test for making decisions about moral duties. Because of the absolute value of human beings, they all deserve respect. All people in one's daily work-life—employees, patients, community members, and others—have absolute value simply by the fact that they exist. Just because they can accomplish more or less in society's eyes does not change their value as human beings. This leads to the idea that, for moral decision making in health care, all persons in similar circumstances deserve the same respectful treatment.

In addition, Kant helps to define the idea of a moral duty as obligations to other people as fellow humans. Therefore, the categorical imperative can also be useful to determine moral duty when developing policy and procedures. For example, when one develops a personnel policy, one can ask, "Why am I really doing this? What is the reason behind it? Is this policy respectful of all people?" The answers to these questions and the categorical imperative should assist in determining if the policy is universal. In other words, should everyone have to comply with this action? To pass the categorical imperative, the action will not treat some employees better than others; instead, it will be required for all and will treat everyone with respect.

Despite Kantian theory's base in good will, one can see that being a strict Kantian might be a problem for the healthcare administrator. To follow Kant in the strictest sense, an administrator should make all decisions based on good will and not on bases such as profit, legal mandate, or pleasing stakeholders. This is not practical or even possible in the political and ACA world of health care. In addition, Kantian moral theory tends to deal in absolutes and does not provide answers to all of the complex issues in today's healthcare system. Here is just one example: If a researcher uses human subjects to help find the cure for cancer, is he or she not using those individuals as a means to an end? Does this negate the worth of human beings and fail the categorical imperative test? One could say that it does, yet there is potential benefit to a larger group from the knowledge gained.

John Stuart Mill (1806–1873)

Biographical Influences on His Theory

John Stuart Mill, one of the most influential ethics theorists in American health care, certainly had an interesting childhood. He was an extremely intelligent child who was heavily influenced by his father's insistence on strict discipline in learning. Mill learned Greek at age 3 and Latin by age 8. At 15, Mill was already disagreeing with current moral theorists. Influenced by Bentham's utility concepts, he began to write his own theory. When he was 20, Mill suffered what was then called a mental crisis that was attributed to the physical and cerebral strain of his strict, self-imposed education. Later in life, he married Harriet Taylor, a feminist and intellectual, who came from a Unitarian background. She was an author in her own right and published articles advocating women's rights. The couple shared philosophies and collaborated on many articles. Some of Mill's major works on ethics included *System of Logic, On Liberty, Utilitarianism,* and *The Subjection of Women.* Mill was ahead of his time in his activism in support of his beliefs. For example, he became a member of the British Parliament to use his political power to help improve the status of women (Wilson, 2007).

Concept Summary

Based on the idea of *telos*, or ends, Mill's theory of utilitarianism forms the ethical justification for many healthcare policies that affect the U.S. public today. This moral philosophy of **utilitarianism** or **consequentialism** had its foundation in the idea that one should base ethical choices on their consequences and not just on intent or duty. Individuals make decisions in life that have consequences that contribute to happiness. When applying utilitarianism, administrators weigh the consequences of those actions and their effects on others' happiness. Then, they can use this reasoning to make decisions based on the good that they can achieve.

Something is good if it produces utility. Just what is that? Mill meant that it gives the greatest benefit (or happiness) to the greatest number of those affected by a consequence or decision. It is wrong if it produces the greatest harm for the greatest number of those affected. Thus the focus of an ethical decision is not on the individual person or on the person's intension, but rather on the best outcomes for all persons. Writers often reduce Mill's theory to the phrase, "the greatest good for the greatest number" (Summers, 2014). In thinking about producing the greatest good, contrary to Kant's theory, a person can be a means to an end. However, this action can occur only when there is a greater good. Ashcroft, Dawson, Draper, and McMillan (2007) provide examples of the greatest good for the greatest number in the healthcare setting, such as public health, quality of life efforts, and the work of healthcare economists.

Mill divided ethical decisions based on utility into two main groups. The first type of decision is to act from utility (act utility), which means that administrators make each decision based on its own merit.

There is an analysis of the consequences for that specific case and, based on this analysis, a person makes a decision. Some writers also call this pure utilitarianism. However, to act from utility or make each decision independently is not always practical in health care because decisions are numerous, complex, and often interrelated. Further, a policy that is created for the greatest good of one person may not have merit for others.

The second type of decision is to rule by utility (rule utility). With this approach, an administrator would use the potential consequences of a decision to determine rules for action. These rules help guide decisions so that, on average, they produce the greatest good for the greatest number or cause the least amount of harm to the smallest number of people. Rule by utilitarian decision making appeals to healthcare administrators because it allows for decisions that will be the best in most cases. It also is part of using the process of cost/benefit or gain/loss analysis to justify a decision.

Theory Applications

Many healthcare administrators perceive Mill's utilitarian principles of ethics to be a practical way to tackle difficult healthcare decisions. Because there is always a scarcity of resources in health care, there has to be a way to make decisions based on universal benefit. Using the balance sheet approach of identifying consequences, determining merit, and making a decision that will benefit the most people who are affected should make ethical decisions easier.

One limitation of Mill's theory is that it might be possible to ignore the needs and desires of the minority in the quest to provide the greatest good for the majority. Since the individual is not the focus of moral decision making and the consequences are the most important element, a person could violate the rights or needs of the individual. Summers (2014, p. 32) refers to these situations as the "tyranny of the majority." An example might clarify this point: Suppose an administrator created a policy and funded a screening program that served all the members of a community. This would seem to benefit the greatest number of people and meet the requirements of rule utility. However, to find the funds for this program, the administrator eliminated funding for a program that served a small group of uninsured patients who needed liver transplants. The funded program might provide the greatest good for the greatest number, but those affected by the defunded program might have good reason to disagree with its value.

John Rawls (1921–2002)

Biographical Influences on His Theory

Rawls was a modern ethics theorist who studied at Princeton and Oxford Universities and served in the military during World War II. While in the service, he read reports about concentration camps and witnessed the aftermath of the bombing of Hiroshima. These experiences had such an impact on Rawls that he declined a commission as an officer and left the army. When he returned home, he finished his doctorate in moral philosophy at Princeton.

Rawls taught at Princeton, Oxford (Fulbright Scholar), and Massachusetts Institute of Technology. In his final academic appointment, he served as a professor at Harvard University for 40 years. His work, including *A Theory of Justice* (1971), centered on defining what a moral society should be through the application of social justice. Because of this work, he had a great influence on modern political, social, and ethical thinking (Wenar, 2012).

Concept Summary

Rawls was interested in defining what makes a moral and just society. His theory relates to social justice or justice as fairness. He studied the philosophers who came before him and found that he both agreed and disagreed with them. For example, some of Kant's arguments appealed to Rawls, but he was opposed to the position of utilitarianism. Based on his study and views, he formulated his own theory of justice that included the concepts of self-interest and fairness. What did he mean? To explain his ideas, Rawls set up a hypothetical scenario in which everyone is equal to everyone else. He called this scenario the "**original position.**" He also asked that a person assume the "veil of ignorance." In other words, the person does not know his or her own future and ignores the characteristics of the people who exist in society, such as age, gender, ethnicity, and socioeconomic status. Given the original position and veil of ignorance, a person would act to protect his or her own best interests. On a societal level, protection of self-interests forms a social contract. What, then, would be in the best interests of individuals and communities (Rawls, 1999; Summers, 2014)?

First, consider what it means to live as a human being. Because humans generally live in social groups, they set up rules that protect their personal interests and those of the society in which they live. To live in society with any kind of peace and justice, people must agree to these rules and practice them. Rawls defined something he called the **liberty principle** (Darr, 2011), which means that all people should have the same basic rights as all others in a society. For example, if the rich have a right to basic education, then so should everyone else.

In Rawls's view, each person has a claim to the basic liberties of a society. To be just, people must also address inequalities in a society, so as to protect those who are in a lesser position in society. This includes children, those in poverty, and those who have medical problems that affect their quality of life (Vaughn, 2010). Rawls included actions to address inequalities in his **maximim principle**. The question then becomes: Why would anyone choose to do this as part of his or her self-interest even when he or she is not in a lesser position in society?

In Rawls's view, everyone has the potential to be in a lesser position. Therefore, when one acts to protect the rights of those who are less well off, one is actually acting in one's self-interest. Further, the problems in a society tend to be suffered more by those who are in disadvantaged positions. For example, persons who are living in poverty are also more likely to be victims of crime or have more severe health problems. In addition, when people in a society are not treated for health problems, that failure to treat everyone can affect the entire society. For example, if a person has a communicable disease and does not receive treatment, that disease can infect others in the society. Finally, governments and individuals judge societies based on how they treat those who are not well off or in optimal health.

Does this mean that everyone in a society has to be equal in all ways, including economic resources? Rawls postulated that differences and advantages could exist in economic and social position in a society if these differences provided benefit for that society. For example, a physician is paid more than others in a society and has greater status. With this difference comes the responsibility of service to the community in which the physician lives. However, such positions of advantage have to be available to all persons in the society. Technically, then, in Rawls's view, anyone who has the ability should be able to attend a university or college and become a person of privilege (Vaughn, 2010).

Rawls also dealt with the idea of providing services or benefits for everyone. He felt that it was morally right to limit services when there is a greater need among certain groups. This can mean that not everything is available to everyone in every instance. For example, if a patient goes to the emergency department with a sprained ankle, there are many services available to diagnose and treat that person. However, the patient might not get immediate treatment or even the use of all of the available treatments if people with life-threatening conditions are simultaneously present in the emergency department. It is in the self-interest of all who have healthcare needs if those with greater needs receive treatment ahead of those with lesser needs. This is true because each person assumes that, if he or she were in a life-threatening position, he or she would receive life-saving treatment.

Theory Applications
Rawls has had a great influence on how political and other leaders think about social justice in the United States. His ideas also influenced how the United States is judged by other nations. For example, how does this country treat its poor or imprisoned citizens? For some observers, treatment of those in a lesser position can be a greater indicator of a

nation's quality than its wealth. In addition, Rawls's thinking about social justice influenced the introduction of such programs as Head Start and Medicaid/Medicare. More recently, one can see applications of his theory in parts of the ACA and its effects on political discussion and future healthcare practice. Likewise, his theory has ramifications for many U.S. institutions such as education, public health, and health care.

Because the basis for many aspects of American society is market justice and not social justice, Rawls's work presents a great challenge to the United States and its healthcare systems. His theory asks that administrators consider even more than the greatest good for the greatest number or the greatest profitability for the greatest bottom line. That is, it asks that healthcare institutions and practitioners consider those in the community who have the least amount of financial resources to invest in health care. The true challenge here is not just demonstrating fairness and compassion, but rather meeting the needs of both those who have adequate resources for health care and those who do not. Within this challenge, there is a need to maintain a healthy bottom line so that doors stay open and salaries are paid. With the major changes in health care anticipated with the full implementation of the ACA, the ideas of justice and fairness introduced by Rawls will not only be a part of philosophical debate, but will also present true challenges for health care.

■ PERSONAL ETHICAL THEORIES

There is need for a brief introduction before reading about the next four theorists. Rather than look at the macro or global picture of ethics, these philosophers addressed individuals and their ethical and moral behavior. They considered how people acquire their perspectives on ethical thinking, moral reasoning, and ethics decision making. The section begins with Aristotle because his work provided a foundation for many of the great ethicists who followed him. Martin Buber is included because he presented ethics in terms of moral relationships, while Lawrence Kohlberg investigated stages of moral development. Finally, Viktor Frankl addressed personal ethics and its relationship to the ultimate meaning of life—a theme that has long been a part of the study of philosophy and ethics. This section continues the previous format. You will learn about these writers' lives, basic concepts, and their influence on healthcare ethics.

Aristotle (384–322 BCE)

Biographical Influences on His Theory
Aristotle's father was the physician for the king of Macedonia, which meant that Aristotle was a child of privilege. At 17, his family sent him to Athens and to study at Plato's Academy. He continued this study by

attending Plato's lectures for 20 years! In 343, the king of Macedonia asked Aristotle to tutor his son, who later became Alexander the Great. Aristotle wrote more than 200 works in the areas of physics, logic, psychology, natural history, metaphysics, politics, and ethics. Today, only 31 of these works exist, but they influenced centuries of thinking about philosophy and ethics. Even though he was famous in his time, Aristotle's renown did not protect him. He was living in Athens in 323 when Alexander the Great died. Since he was a Macedonian and there was so much ill will toward Macedonia in Athens, he feared for his safety and left the city (Shields, 2012).

Concept Summary

Aristotle's work in ethics centered on how people can achieve the highest level of good or virtue. His concept of virtue derives from the Greek word *areté*, meaning "excellence." Virtue, in his view, was not about discussion; it was about the decisions made and the actions taken as a moral person. For Aristotle, a person builds character by taking action and practicing both intellectual and moral virtues. The concepts of **virtue, practical wisdom**, and **eudaimonia** represent key areas in Aristotle's idea of moral person (Palmer, 2010).

Virtue   How did Aristotle describe the concept of virtue? First, virtue requires choices that require action, not just discussion. The bases for these choices are intellect or knowledge and habits. Virtues are also voluntary. One obtains intellectual virtues through education and moral virtues through practice, habit, and moderation. Character and the consistency of how one lives are also reflections of virtue. Examples of virtues include practicing temperance instead of being impulse driven, exhibiting courage in adversity, and helping a friend when there is no reward (Palmer, 2010).

Practical Wisdom   Since building a virtuous character requires action and choice, Aristotle also presented the concept of practical wisdom or *phronesis*. Healthcare administrators face situations that are new, especially in this era of great change. The dynamic nature of health care today means that they might not have an answer about what is right or wrong in all situations. Aristotle suggests that they engage in what he calls practical wisdom. First, administrators need to be stronger than their impulses so they can take the time to use reasoning and research their choices. They should then assess these choices as good or bad and weigh them against each other. Administrators should be guided by their character and rational thinking in this endeavor, and should choose the best option for the current situation. This option is often the middle ground between the choices considered. Practical wisdom can be also applied to groups or even 'whole societies as they attempt to choose the most virtuous action for any given situation. As Aristotle reminded us, "It is not possible to be good in the strict sense without practical wisdom, nor practically wise without moral virtue" (Aristotle, 1908, para 2).

Eudaimonia   Aristotle also introduced the idea of eudaimonia. This concept has been translated as happiness or the idea of flourishing (Summers, 2014). However, Aristotle did not think of happiness in the modern sense. Instead, he meant that a person could be happy if he or she chose to live his or her life as it was intended to be—that is, a life lived by practicing virtues and working to build one's moral character. Such action requires the ability to contemplate and address difficult issues, including how to live together in community. For Aristotle, eudaimonia was unique to humans and was the purpose of their lives (Blackburn, 2001).

Theory Applications

How can Aristotle's ideas apply to the modern healthcare administrator? The modern theory of virtue ethics has been derived from his works and is based on the concept of character. This theory describes how to evaluate actions based on what someone with moral character would do. It also asks that administrators think about why they are making a decision as part of their moral character. In addition, virtue ethics helps define which character traits an administrator should have as a person and as a professional (Ashcroft et al., 2007; Munson, 2008).

One can also see evidence of Aristotle's work in the process of professional socialization. Every profession defines a set of characteristics that describe its ideal practitioner. Defining these characteristics and assuring that they are present in professionals is part of the moral responsibility of the profession itself. In health administration, desired characteristics include honesty, trustworthiness, compassion, and competence. The profession, through its educational process, attempts to inculcate these character traits in its students through lecture, discussion, field experiences, personal example, and other methods. One could say that health administration educators are encouraging their students to engage in a life of eudaimonia. This goal makes sense because students become practitioners, at which point they represent both the profession and their alma mater to the community.

The concept of practical wisdom is especially important in times of great change, and one can apply it in one's professional and personal life. When healthcare administrators make decisions about the best choice for a situation, they can rely on knowledge of ethics and lessons from experience to assist them. They can also use the wisdom of others such as teachers, clergy, and parents to guide contemplation.

Using practical wisdom as part of daily practice helps move an individual along the pathway toward eudaimonia.

Martin Buber (1878–1965)

Biographical Influences on His Theory

Martin Buber was born in Germany and was part of a family of scholars. He spent much of his childhood with his wealthy grandparents—his grandfather was a well-respected rabbi and scholar. In 1933, Buber served as the Director of the Central Office for Jewish Education during a time when Hitler would not allow Jews to go to school. In 1938, he immigrated to Palestine, where he continued his writing and taught social psychology in Jerusalem. One of his most important works on ethics is *I and Thou* (1996). During the 1950s and 1960s, Buber toured the United States and delivered lectures on his ideas about ethics and human relations (Zank, 2007).

Concept Summary

Buber examined how people relate to each other and behave toward each other in moral or immoral ways. He organized a hierarchy of these relationships and showed how they move from what he considered the lowest to the highest ethical levels. At the very bottom of his hierarchy is the "I-I" relationship. In this level, a person is seen as merely an extension of another person. An example might be a child who is expected to become a physician because his father is a physician. The child is seen not as person, but rather as an extension of the father's ambitions. In severe cases, such as a psychopathic personality, a person cannot see anyone except himself or herself. The needs of others simply do not exist, nor does the responsibility of ethical behavior toward them (Buber, 1996).

Buber's next level is the "I-IT" relationship. In this case, people are merely tools to be used for a person's own benefit or for the benefit of the organization. People are not individuals, but rather are the vehicles for accomplishing some goal. Names are not important or even known; people are just "its," or convenient labels.

For Buber, I-IT relationships are morally wrong because they fail to accept people as having individuality and value. People serve only as a means to an end for the person or the organization. Examples of I-IT relationships occur when an administrator uses the term "my people" or "my minions" to refer to the healthcare professionals within the organization. Another example could be when one refers to a patient named Mrs. Smith as "the colon in 405" instead of by her name. Still another example of an I-IT relationship happens when an administrator uses the expression "FTEs" in planning without any regard for the fact that a "full-time equivalent" is a person.

Next in Buber's hierarchy are the "I-YOU" relationships. In this case, people are recognized as individuals with value; each is seen as having unique talents, gifts, and ideas. These differences are not only recognized, but also accepted and respected. An example of this type of relationship can be found in a well-functioning healthcare team in which each member respects the contributions of the others. In health care, patients expect at least an I-YOU relationship as a minimum level of performance from all employees. Employees also expect and appreciate this level of ethical relationship with their supervisors and with one another. When such an environment exists, staff members are more productive and exhibits higher morale.

The highest moral relationship that a person can have is called "I-THOU" (Buber, 1996). It is based on the Greek concept of *agape* (meaning "love for others"), which Buber viewed as the most mature human relationship. In an I-THOU relationship, one recognizes each person as being different and having value, and makes a choice to consider that person beloved or special. Notice the word "choice" used in the preceding sentence. Making the I-THOU choice requires many things from people who make this decision, including increased tolerance of differences, patience, and efforts to make that person's needs equal to their own. A person who is beloved is held in high esteem or unconditional regard.

Because of the commitment that it requires, it is not possible to have an I-THOU relationship with each person whom one meets. However, when a healthcare professional is treating a patient, the patient wants to be the most important person in the encounter. When sick, in pain, and frightened, patients are trusting in a healthcare professional's ability to care for them. They want the level of patience and understanding that professionals would give to beloved or special persons in their lives. They also assume that these health professionals value their needs equally with their own because they chose to have a career in a service-based industry. Likewise, the community assumes that an administrator acts with the highest regard for their needs and serves as a good steward of their resources.

Theory Applications

This short summary offers only a brief look at the basics of Buber's complex thinking about ethics and ethical behavior. However, his definitions of ethical relationships can be useful for the healthcare administrator. For example, when planning a new venture or evaluating a current program, do you think of employees as tools to get the job done or as people who can contribute through their talents? When in conference with a fellow employee, do you try to have at least an I-YOU relationship or do you see this person as an "it"? Finally, when choosing to be in an I-THOU relationship, do you really put that person's needs and wants on equal footing with your own? Are you aware of how the community views your relationship to them? These questions can be helpful in examining the healthcare administrator's personal ethical behaviors and relationships.

Lawrence Kohlberg (1927–1987)

Biographical Influences on His Theory

Lawrence Kohlberg joined the Merchant Marines during World War II. At the end of the war, he was actively engaged in smuggling Jews through the British blockade for settlement in Palestine. Arrested by the British, he served time in an internment camp in Cyprus. Because of this experience, he began to think about how people develop moral reasoning and how ethical thinking is learned.

When Kohlberg returned to the United States, he attended the University of Chicago. where he completed his bachelor's degree in one year! He went on to complete a doctorate at this same university. Kohlberg subsequently became a professor at the University of Chicago and at Harvard University. He began to theorize that **moral development** happened in stages and researched this theory using children and adults. He used a qualitative research model based on categorizing responses to stories featuring moral dilemmas, such as the now famous Heinz's Dilemma. Kohlberg used this story to evaluate people's level of moral development based on their answers and the reasoning behind those answers. His research led to the formulation of a hierarchy of moral development, and his theory has been subsequently verified through studies conducted in the United States and throughout the world.

Kohlberg became an international name in the study of morality and ethics, but his death was a great tragedy. Toward the end of his life, Kohlberg was in great pain from a parasitic infection and suffered severe depression. One January day in 1987, he parked his car on a dead-end street in Winthrop, Massachusetts, left his wallet and in his keys in the car, and walked into the freezing waters of Boston Harbor. The police found his body sometime later in a tidal marsh (Walsh, 2000).

Concept Summary

How does a person learn to practice moral judgment? To understand Kohlberg's answer to this question, one needs some information about developmental stage theory (Kohlberg, 1984). In this theory, people must go through one stage before they can achieve the next highest stage of development. The movement through stages is not always chronological, but movement happens as life presents challenges and people attempt to find solutions for those challenges. Finding solutions helps an individual advance in moral development and reasoning. In addition, Kohlberg believed that a person could not understand moral reasoning that is too far beyond his or her own level. It is possible to be grown-up physically, but not be morally mature, he suggested. Kohlberg also believed that only about 25% of people ever get to the highest level of moral development and that most people remain on what he called Level IV.

What are Kohlberg's stages and what do they mean? There are two stages (Level I and II) that Kohlberg calls **premoral** or **preconventional**. These stages exist before a person has a true sense of moral decision making. In Level I, people make decisions purely to avoid being punished or because a person in higher authority tells them to do it. They center their decisions on what might happen to themselves and nothing else. For example, a child may do things simply to avoid punishment by his or her parents.

Level II is also premoral but its center is the personal outcome of the action. In this case, decisions are made based on selfish concerns and the ability to gain personal reward. This is sometimes called the "What's in it for me?" orientation to ethical behavior or decision making. In this stage, people are valued for their usefulness to the individual and not for any other reason. Generally, Level I and II stage behaviors are common in young children, but they are also present in adults. An example of this behavior is if you choose to act ethically only when it benefits what you want in life or in your career.

Kohlberg's Levels III and IV are what he calls **conventional** or external-controlled moral development stages. In Level III, people make moral decisions based on the need to please people and to be seen as "good." The motivation for making ethical decisions lies in trying to avoid guilt or shame. In this view, there should be rewards for people who do what is good and there should be punishments for those who do not. In this level, people make ethical decisions so that others see them as good employees, good parents, or good friends. They also want to avoid the stigma of the "bad employee" label.

In Level IV, people make moral decisions based on the need to respect rules and laws and maintain a certain order. In this stage, justice is being punished for disobeying the law. Ethics is seen as obeying the law and keeping order in society. Authority is usually not questioned; the idea is that if it is the law, then it must be right. While it is necessary to respect rules and laws in a civil society, there can be extremes. Extreme behavior in this stage explains how Nazi soldiers could actively participate in the Holocaust and still consider themselves to be moral people: They simply claimed that they were being good soldiers, obeying a higher authority, and "carrying out orders."

Levels V and VI of the Kohlberg theory are designated as **principled moral reasoning** because decisions are based on applying universal moral ideas or principles. In Level V, ethical decisions are based on a set of rights and responsibilities that are common to all members of a group or community. These rights encompass the law but go beyond it. Moral decisions are based on respect for oneself and for the rights of others. Level V requires complex thinking about the social contract one has with others and not just about laws (Kohlberg, 1984). For example, when a government or group makes decisions about the use of health-care resources, it must use complex moral reasoning. Therefore, an element of Level V reasoning should be present.

The basis for Kohlberg's Level VI moral reasoning is ideas or principles that are universal. These principles are higher than the authority of law and include ideas of justice and respect for persons and their rights. Ethical decisions are made based on higher-level principles and not just for legal compliance. In addition, those who are functioning at Level VI assume that all humans have worth and value regardless of their societal status (Kohlberg, 1984). For example, Level VI ethical thinking occurred when Martin Luther King, Jr., and others said that segregation, while legal, was unethical. Segregation violated a higher law than that which was created by the courts. These civil rights protesters were willing to disobey the law to bring attention to this issue and to bring about change.

Theory Applications

Kohlberg's theory of moral reasoning helps to provide an understanding of why people make the moral decisions that they do. It might be helpful, as an administrator, to understand that not all persons have the same ethical reasoning. It would also help to understand the basis for people's moral decisions. In addition, if there is too great a difference between the administrator's level of moral reasoning and others' level, those persons might not even understand why the administrator views a decision as ethical. Understanding Kohlberg's ideas can also help administrators analyze their own decisions and determine the moral reasoning behind them. This ability should prove useful when required to defend decisions. An administrator should be able to answer questions such as "Why did you decide to act as you did?" and "What was your reasoning?" (Schissler Manning, 2003).

There is another implication of knowing and understanding Kohlberg's theory—one involving patient/system relations. Think about the role of a healthcare administrator in society's view. Society gives the healthcare system a high level of authority. Along with this authority comes an assumption of trust in the system. This means that patients have faith that the administrator is functioning at a high level (at least on Level IV) of moral reasoning when making decisions about their care and treatment. In other words, they expect the administrator to have the ability to put their needs first and the healthcare organization's profit second. When evidence of actions that do not meet this standard is uncovered, the public can lose trust in the system itself. They can view the healthcare system and its representatives as being unethical and untrustworthy. Once trust is lost, it is difficult to regain and can have a negative impact on the financial future of both the healthcare organization and the healthcare system in general.

Viktor Frankl (1905–1997)

Biographical Influences on His Theory

As a young man, Viktor Frankl demonstrated wisdom beyond his chronological age. While still in high school, he began a correspondence with Sigmund Freud. Frankl also studied Socrates, Plato, Aristotle, Kant, and many contemporary writers in philosophy and psychology (Graber, 2003). However, the most profound influence on Frankl's life and work happened in 1942. In that year, Frankl, along with his new bride, brother, and parents, was arrested and taken to a concentration camp in Theresienstadt. His wife, parents, and brother later died.

Frankl survived the brutality of four different camps before his release. Instead of losing hope, he used this experience to test his theories of human motivation and conscience. His observations confirmed that those who had a **sense of meaning** and purpose kept their humanity even in the midst of this unbelievable suffering. His experience led him to develop a theory about a topic that has been a focus of study for philosophers and ethics for generations: the meaning of life (Eagleton, 2007). The current term for Frankl's lifelong work is *logotherapy* or meaning theory. Frankl authored many books, but the most well known is *Man's Search for Meaning*, which has sold more than 9 million copies and has been translated into dozens of languages.

Concept Summary

Frankl believed that a person is not just a body or a brain. Instead, people are mind, body, and spirit—total human beings. Each person is also unique in the entire universe and entitled to dignity. Each life has meaning, no matter what one's personal circumstances. As thinking persons, people are able to question and wonder about their purpose in life and what their life means. Only humans can ask, "Why am I here and what am I supposed to do?" For Frankl, morality also relates to one's sense of meaning. People make decisions to behave in moral ways for the sake of something they believe, something to which they are committed, or their relationship to their God (the ultimate meaning).

When people do not feel a sense of purpose in their lives, they feel a sense of emptiness, or an existential vacuum. There is a need to fill this vacuum: Some people choose to fill this void with alcohol or drugs, others with work, food, or power. For Frankl, "A lively and vivid conscience is the only thing that enables man to resist the effects of the existential vacuum" (1971, p. 65). What is a conscience? It is a person's ability to go beyond a situation and find meaning in it. Once there is meaning, one can then make choices that are ethical and affect more than one's selfish needs. A conscience is not infinite; it does not have absolute knowledge. It tries to find the best action to take in a situation. Because the conscience is a part of a person, the individual can choose to make decisions that honor those things that are valued and avoid those things that bring harm.

Theory Applications

Can you see a connection here? It almost feels as if we have closed a circle that goes back to the writings of St. Thomas Aquinas, Aristotle, and some of the other theorists mentioned in this chapter. Conscience is again a consideration in ethics. In the case of Frankl's interpretation, one can use it to help understand the meaning of actions and choose the best action possible. Think about the word "choose." By using this word, Frankl implies that because one chooses actions, one is responsible for them. In health care, this statement has profound implications. As a healthcare administrator, you make decisions that can affect the health and quality of life of both patients and employees. Expediency alone should not be the motivation for these choices. One should make choices using as much data as can be obtained and with practical wisdom. Basing decisions on the best data available is a choice that might take more effort, but it also demonstrates your willingness to be responsible for what you do.

Summary

This chapter deals with ethics theory and how it shaped ethics thinking from both a global and a personal view. It serves as a foundation for understanding the remaining chapters in this text. For example, the reader will see connections with these theories as he or she studies the major principles of healthcare ethics. In addition, the reader should be able to recognize the influence of these theorists as he or she explores how the community and organization view the practice of healthcare ethics.

Web Resources

The *Stanford Encyclopedia of Philosophy* is a well-researched source for additional information about the theorists in this chapter. Here are the links to their materials. Sites for theorists not mentioned in that resource are also included here.

St. Thomas Aquinas
http://plato.stanford.edu/entries/aquinas/

Immanuel Kant
http://plato.stanford.edu/entries/kant/

John Stuart Mill
http://plato.stanford.edu/entries/mill/

John Rawls
http://plato.stanford.edu/entries/rawls/

Martin Buber
http://plato.stanford.edu/entries/buber/

Lawrence Kohlberg
http://pegasus.cc.ucf.edu/~ncoverst/Kohlberg's%20Stages%20of%20
  Moral%20Development.htm

Viktor Frankl
http://logotherapy.univie.ac.at/

References

Aristotle. (1908). *Nicomachean ethics, Book IV* (W. D. Ross, Trans.) Available at http://www.sacred-texts.com/cla/ari/nico/nico067.htm

Ashcroft, R. E., Dawson, A., Draper, H., & McMillan, J. R. (2007). *Principles of health care ethics.* West Sussex, UK: John Wiley & Sons.

Blackburn, S. (2001). *Ethics: A very short introduction.* New York, NY: Oxford University Press.

Buber, M. (1996). *I and thou.* New York, NY: Touchstone.

Darr, K. (2011). *Ethics in health services management* (5th ed.). Baltimore, MD: Health Professions Press.

Davies, B. (2004). *Aquinas: An introduction.* New York, NY: Bloomsbury Academic Press.

Eagleton, T. (2007). *The meaning of life: A very short introduction.* New York, NY: Oxford University Press.

Frankl, V. (1971). *Man's search for meaning: An introduction to logotherapy.* New York, NY: Pocket Books.

Graber, A. (2003). *Viktor Frankl's logotherapy: Method of choice in ecumenical pastoral psychology.* Lima, OH: Wyndham Hall Press.

Kerr, F. (2009). *Thomas Aquinas: A very short introduction.* New York, NY: Oxford University Press.

Kohlberg, L. (1984). *The philosophy of moral development: Moral stages and the idea of justice.* New York, NY: HarperCollins.

Munson, R. (2008). *Intervention and reflection: Basic issues in medical ethics* (8th ed.). Belmont, CA: Thomson Higher Education.

Palmer, D. (2010). *Looking at philosophy: The unbearable heaviness of philosophy made lighter.* (5th ed.). New York, NY: McGraw-Hill.

Rawls, J. (1999). *A theory of justice* (rev. ed.). Cambridge, MA: Harvard University Press.

Rohlf, M. (2010). Immanuel Kant. In *Stanford encyclopedia of philosophy* (pp. 1–49). Retrieved from http://plato.stanford.edu/entries/kant/

Schissler Manning, S. (2003). *Ethical leadership in human services: A multi-dimensional approach*. Boston, MA: Pearson Education.

Shields, C. (2112). Aristotle. In *Stanford encyclopedia of philosophy* (pp. 1–53). Retrieved from http://plato.stanford.edu/entries/aristotle/

Summers, J. (2014). Theory of healthcare ethics. In E. E. Morrison & B. Furlong (Eds.), *Health care ethics: Critical issues for the 21st century* (pp.3-46). Burlington, MA: Jones & Bartlett Learning.

Vaughn, L. (2010). *Bioethics: Principles, issues, and cases*. New York, NY: Oxford University Press.

Walsh, C. (2000). The life and legacy of Lawrence Kohlberg. *Society*, *37*(2), 36–41.

Wenar, L. (2012). John Rawls. In *Stanford encyclopedia of philosophy* (pp. 1–37). Retrieved from http://plato.stanford.edu/entries/rawls/

Wilson, F. (2007). John Stuart Mill. In *Stanford encyclopedia of philosophy* (pp. 1–62). Retrieved from http://plato.stanford.edu/entries/mill/

Zank, M. (2007). Martin Buber. In *Stanford encyclopedia of philosophy* (pp. 1–14). Retrieved from http://plato.stanford.edu/entries/buber/

CHAPTER 2

Autonomy

In the age of technology and social media, is autonomy still important?

Points to Ponder

1. What are the key issues for the healthcare administrator (HCA) that relate to informed consent?
2. Why is confidentiality so important in patient care?
3. Is it ever appropriate to withhold the truth from a patient?
4. What is the significance of fidelity to the success of HCAs?

Key Terms

The following are this chapter's key terms. Look for them in bold.

authorization
competence
disclosure
fidelity

informed consent
reasonable person standard
veracity
voluntariness

■ INTRODUCTION AND DEFINITIONS

Principles of ethics have their foundation in ethics theory and assist with making decisions about one's personal and professional choices. In health care, there are four commonly used ethics principles: autonomy, beneficence, nonmaleficence, and justice. This chapter presents information about the principle of autonomy and its application to healthcare practice. Current concepts of autonomy are derived from the Greek definition of autonomy as self-rule and self-determination (Summers, 2014). While protecting autonomy may be more difficult in the age of electronic medical records and social networks, Kant, Frankl, and others support autonomy because of their belief that people have unconditional worth and deserve respect.

Application of the principle of autonomy must assume that people are free from the control of others and have the capacity to make their own life choices. In health care, people also must have the right to hold views that are incongruent with those of the healthcare establishment. For example, if a patient is a Jehovah's Witness and does not believe in blood transfusions, he or she has the right to refuse such treatment. The word "choice" is a key element in this principle. How does this relate to the healthcare administrator? Administrators must understand that people should be free to choose to be compliant or not compliant with their physician's instructions. Patients and their families must also be able to make informed decisions about signing consent forms for surgery or other procedures without undue influence or punitive repercussions from medical staff.

However, autonomy is more than just making informed choices. It is also concerned with how individuals are viewed and treated within the healthcare system. Therefore, if autonomy is an ethical principle for any healthcare organization, certain standards should prevail. Healthcare organizations must create standards for protecting autonomy and respond to state and federal legislation on this issue. For example, this chapter includes an examination of 2013 revisions of the Health Insurance Portability and Accountability Act of 1996 (Title II) (HIPAA) rules that have increased awareness of the need to protect autonomy (Department of Health and Human Services, Office of Civil Rights, 2013).

Informed consent is not the only aspect of autonomy that affects the practice of health care and the responsibilities of healthcare administrators. This chapter focuses on autonomy as truth-telling, through a discussion of what telling the truth means in healthcare situations. Autonomy can also be expressed as fidelity: What does it mean to keep one's word to patients and employees?

■ AUTONOMY AS INFORMED CONSENT

Legal and ethical considerations come together when applied in the area of **informed consent** for treatment. Case law and legislation view informed consent as the duty of physicians or their designees to obtain the patient's permission for treatment. This permission should be given only after the patient understands the treatment and supports its implementation. Failure to obtain permission can constitute negligence or even lead to medical malpractice actions. From a larger view, informed consent is an ethical issue because it requires respect for the autonomy of individuals and their right to choose what is done to their bodies.

Sometimes, autonomous consent is implied through a person's actions. For example, a person makes an appointment with his or her dentist and keeps that appointment: Consent for treatment is implied. However, even with this implied consent, there is an ethical (and often legal) duty to obtain specific written consent. In addition, if nonroutine treatments are required, there may be additional procedures to obtain consent. Another example of implied consent happens when a person cannot express consent, but needs treatment. Suppose a traffic accident occurs in which a person is injured. Emergency personnel rush this person to the emergency department, and she is not conscious when she arrives. If the patient's injuries are life threatening, given that a reasonable person would want treatment and there is no surrogate to give consent, the emergency physician can assume consent and treat the patient (Munson, 2008).

What is informed consent? Beauchamp and Childress (2012) present a model that clarifies this term and serves as a basis for discussion. Informed permission to treat contains the preconditions of **competence** on the part of the patient to understand the treatment, and **voluntariness** in his or her decision making. It also requires disclosure on the part of the physician of material information including the recommended treatment plan. Finally, consent means that the patient is in favor of the plan and gives his or her **authorization** to proceed.

The idea of competence is not a simple one in health care. In general, it is assumed that adults are competent to make decisions about their health but that children are not. However, adults can be in situations where they are not deemed competent. This includes incidents when they are unconscious, mentally ill, or under the influence of drugs (Chell, 2014). Exceptions to the child rule exist as well. Children can be deemed competent when they are legally emancipated from their parents. In these nonroutine circumstances, healthcare professionals can need additional guidance about informed consent and the physician's responsibilities through policies, procedures, and training programs that are provided by the institution in which they practice.

Voluntariness means that the person is not under the influence or control of another person when making a decision. Voluntary decisions are as simple as they seem. Practitioners may think that they know what is medically best (paternalism), but patients sometimes make different judgments about their own health. To give voluntary consent, patients should not feel that they have to please their practitioners or be coerced by physicians who may suggest dire consequences will ensue if the patient does not accept the treatment plan. Whether the coercion is actual or perceived, patients under duress do not freely choose to participate in the treatment.

Similarly, if a healthcare professional tries to manipulate a person into consenting to treatment, this negates autonomy. For example, suppose a researcher needs a certain number of subjects to maintain funding for his study. This researcher finds a suitable subject and promises the person that he or she will receive benefits from participating in the study. The subject then signs a consent form, without knowledge of the researcher's true agenda. This manipulation of study information is unethical and removes the voluntary element from the process of informed decision making.

In addition, patients have the right to refuse treatment as part of informed consent. This means that they can choose not to comply with the practitioner's treatment plan. When this occurs, beneficent practitioners or family members may try to force patients to comply or question their competence to make decisions. These situations may exist even when treatment is futile (such as at the end of life) and are especially difficult when children are involved. In some cases, refusal of treatment issues may even involve the courts (Vaughn, 2010).

Disclosure is a major element in both legal and ethical aspects of informed consent. It seems like a simple thing to tell patients information about their condition, methods of treatment, and alternatives for that treatment. However, this process is far more complex than it appears at first glance. Many states dictate what is called a **reasonable person standard** with respect to what should be disclosed to obtain consent. This means that there is an obligation to present enough information so that a "reasonable person" would be able to make an informed decision about the procedure. Adhering to this guideline poses some ethical issues, particularly in sophisticated and often expensive research studies. If a researcher is too zealous in making statements about the anticipated benefits versus the risks of the study, the subjects might choose not to participate. This could lead to expensive searches for subjects or even a loss of funding for the research.

For patients to make informed decisions about their healthcare options, a recommendation must be made by the health professional. Recommendations must include all of the options available for the patient and the practitioner's best assessment of the best choice. Even this part of informed consent is not without difficulty. For example, some alternative treatments, such as the use of herbs or holistic medicine, appear to be effective but are not approved by the Food and Drug Administration or fully recognized by the medical community. If the physician does not support the use of such forms of treatment, he or she might not present these options to the patient. Another complexity of disclosure occurs in the case of managed care. The physician's recommendation cannot be based solely on the covered treatments in the plan. The patient should be informed of the costs of other existing treatments so the patient can decide if he or she is able to pay for them if the treatments are not covered by the health maintenance organization.

Making efforts to ensure the patient understands the disclosures and the treatment plan is an ethics obligation when seeking informed consent. When the medical news is not good and/or the required treatment is painful and risky, patients can become emotional. These emotions, in turn, may affect the individual's ability to make sound decisions. Therefore, requiring a signed consent too soon after such news is given might not be appropriate action. Ignoring the patient's human reaction to his or her state creates the risk of obtaining uninformed consent. Conversely, delaying the consent procedure too long can impede treatment and potentially cause a negative outcome. Dealing with this ethics dilemma of when to ask for consent requires excellent communication and a sense of appropriate timing.

Achieving understanding also requires comprehension. Comprehension may be challenging because consent forms are often full of legal and medical jargon and are written at a relatively high reading level. When one combines the emotions of dealing with illness with the complexity of the consent form, one can see that a true understanding of such forms might not be possible. Another challenge to comprehension is the patient's level of health literacy. Health care has its own language, and most patients do not speak "healthese" fluently. There is also an assumption that patients can do their own healthcare research on the computer or smartphone. However, not all patients have access to information technology or the desire to use it. Therefore, written materials, at the appropriate level of health literacy, are still an important contributor to comprehension.

Cultural differences may also affect the ability to provide informed consent. For example, many patients do not have English as their primary language, in which case comprehension of the information on consent forms becomes even more challenging. Even if these forms are translated into a person's primary language according to National Culturally and Linguistically Appropriate Services (CLAS) Standards (Department of Health and Human Services, Office of Minority Health, 2013), the patient may not understand the medical terms used. Again, healthcare administrators have the responsibility to put policies, procedures, and forms in place that enhance patient understanding as a way to meet the competence aspect of autonomous consent. Checking the readability of such forms and having qualified personnel available to answer any questions is both good business and good ethics.

Finally, healthcare professionals must consider the patient's decision to implement the treatment plan and the appropriate authorization. This final step can require the use of additional personnel to verify that the patient fully understands the consent form and the procedures as described when he or she gave consent to proceed. While the clinic or hospital may use nonphysician personnel during the process of obtaining informed consent, ultimately the responsibility for ensuring that truly informed consent is given lies with the physician. Therefore, he or she must be willing to verify informed consent with the patient.

This discussion shows that the issue of autonomy as informed consent is highly complex. It is important for healthcare administrators to know their level of responsibility for ensuring that consent is truly consent and that patients are given full, understandable answers to their questions. Administrators must also maintain proof of consent and ensure that this proof is confidential and secure. In addition, they address the need for language-appropriate consent forms and translators as needed.

■ AUTONOMY AS CONFIDENTIALITY

One deals with the principle of autonomy when keeping information about a person's identity, family, health status, and treatment procedures private. This aspect of autonomy also extends to information that administrators know about employees and their families.

Healthcare administrators have many duties when it comes to confidentiality, some of which extend into the legal realm because of the Health Insurance Portability and Accountability Act of 1996 (HIPAA). For example, HIPAA includes a Privacy Rule that set standards for protection of medical records and personal health information (PHI), which involves both providers and health plans. It limits disclosures and allows patients to examine and receive a copy of their medical records. The Security Rule under HIPAA sets up standards to protect electronic medical records. HIPAA is concerned with patient record confidentiality in a time at which the reach of technology is rapidly expanding (Department of Health and Human Services, Office of Civil Rights, 2013).

In March 2013, new HIPAA regulations went into effect. These regulations affect the Privacy Rule, the Security Rule, and the handling of breaches of these rules. They pay greater attention to issues related to confidentiality and increase penalties for security violations. While these new regulations may be challenging for healthcare institutions, private practice, and insurance companies, their ethics intent is to increase the protection of confidentiality (Department of Health and Human Services, 2013).

What do patients expect with respect to confidentiality? Patients believe that they have a right to privacy. They want to have control over access to their physical bodies, their health information, and their decisions. When patients choose to surrender some of their privacy, they expect that what they say or what is done to them will be kept confidential (Beauchamp & Childress, 2012). This expectation goes all the way back to the time of Hippocrates, when physicians were cautioned not to disclose what was said in confidence.

Is there absolute confidentiality in healthcare settings? The answer is "no." It is, of course, necessary to share private information about patients to treat their conditions. Nurses, physical therapists, radiation technicians, and many others may need access to patients' information to treat those patients appropriately. However, this access must follow HIPAA rules and requires patient consent. Specifically, only those who have a legitimate need to know patient information should have access to the medical record and health information. Healthcare administrators need to create and enforce appropriate safeguards to ensure the protection of medical information from access by those who do not have a need to know this information.

On the surface, this sounds straightforward, but safeguarding confidentiality in today's healthcare system is not as simple as a locked file cabinet. Technology and the electronic transfer of records increase the risk of inappropriate access to confidential information. In addition, there are problems safeguarding confidentiality beyond those related to technology. Within the structural procedures at a hospital or clinic, certain practices can automatically threaten the patient's confidentiality. For example, what happens when a patient's surgery takes place in an outpatient surgery setting? Prior to this surgery, healthcare professionals need to discuss the patient's medical history, but this discussion may be held in a cubicle. Only a curtain separates the patient from the other occupants in the room, so there is no confidentiality. It is easy to see that the structure of some healthcare settings may make maintaining confidentiality difficult at best. Even so, health administrators and practitioners need to make every effort to ensure there is respect for this part of autonomy.

Actions in the informal organization that can threaten confidentiality can be even more subtle. If staff members do not receive frequent training in confidentiality, discussions about interesting cases can occur in hallways, elevators, the break room, or the cafeteria. Such conversations, while not intended to do harm, can be overheard by anyone, including the patient's family. It is the administrator's responsibility to reduce the likelihood of such conversations by designing and enforcing appropriate policies and procedures, and by providing frequent training. In addition, administrators need to conduct informal observations to evaluate if training is working, through "management by walking around."

Patient confidentiality is not an absolute even when appropriate practices and procedures are in place. On some occasions, the law or ethical practice makes it necessary to break patient confidentiality. For example, legally mandated exceptions include reporting certain diseases, traumatic events such as gunshot wounds, and incidents of child abuse. In the case of mental health providers, there is also a duty to warn others if a client threatens to be violent. Utilitarian theory supports these exceptions to confidentiality, as they represent means to serve the greater good for the greater number or to prevent greater harm.

Other issues of confidentiality also create complex ethical challenges. For example, should employers have a right to employees' or job applicants' medical records? If so, can the employer use the information found there to avoid hiring a person if he or she has an expensive pre-existing condition? Suppose an employer asks for information about employees' use of tobacco and refuses to hire anyone who smokes. Does this practice violate confidentiality and autonomy? What if a patient has a diagnosis of a genetic condition that could affect the health of his or her family members? Should the physician tell the patient's relatives even if the patient does not want the information discussed with them? To whom does the physician owe a duty in such a case? These questions are just a few examples illustrating how complicated confidentiality can be when considered in its full ethical context.

Another area to consider is the confidentiality of private employee information. Depending on an administrator's position in the health facility, he or she may have access to very private information about employees and their families. It is imperative that all administrators recognize the need to maintain confidentiality with employee information and not to share it with those who have no need to know. Because administrators are in a position of authority, violation of employee confidentiality might not only be a breach of trust, but also lead to dismissal. Therefore, it is vital for healthcare administrators to keep private information private.

■ AUTONOMY AS TRUTH-TELLING

Should a person always tell the truth? Kant would say that truth-telling meets the categorical imperative and telling the truth should be universal. Beauchamp and Childress (2012) consider it one of the obligations of health care. Imagine working as a healthcare administrator if one could not assume that people were telling the truth: Administrators would drown in "proof paperwork" because they would have to document every conversation and every meeting. Contracts and verbal agreements would be all but impossible to negotiate.

Truth-telling or **veracity** is a key part of the business of health care. When patients interact with people in the healthcare system, they make an assumption that veracity exists. Likewise, practitioners must assume that their patients give truthful information. Confidence in truthfulness is the basis of trust that underlies decisions for effective treatment and patient healing.

Given the patient's right to truthfulness, one could assume that it is always ethically correct to tell the truth. However, health care presents situations where universal truth-telling might not be the best position. To understand this statement, consider the utilitarian position on truth-telling. One should always weigh the benefit against harm before disclosing the absolute truth. Once this assessment is done, it might be more ethical to be cautious about disclosure or to tell the truth in pieces over time. But what exactly does this mean?

Professionals in health care often have to give bad news about a condition or treatment and even news of impending death. The full information about this news and the timing of full, truthful disclosure can be influenced by the age and emotional state of the patient and the family's desires for such disclosure. For example, if a there is a diagnosis of end-stage cancer for 90-year-old patient, the family might not want her to know the full truth. They might feel that it is more ethical to deceive this patient and have her enjoy what time she has left. If the physician is aware of the family's request, it can pose an ethical dilemma. Does the physician tell the family about the condition and its prognosis, but not the patient? What does this mean to the patient's right to know and to choose what she wants to do with her remaining time? Will the family feel that their trust has been violated if the physician tells the patient the truth?

It seems that there can be different standards about the scope of truth-telling when dealing with the diagnosis and the subsequent prognosis of a condition. Perhaps a patient can be given the full truth about his or her condition and treatment options. However, when it comes to what happens under treatment, practitioners can choose to give information in pieces over time to avoid overwhelming the patient (Beauchamp & Childress, 2012). This decision is justified as ethical because no one ultimately knows how well a person can do under treatment. Predicting treatment results and death may deal with statistical data and not human determination. In dealing with the truth in stages, providers also do not erode the patient's hope—which in and of itself can be a great motivator for treatment compliance and even healing. This type of truth-telling has the potential to challenge the trust between practitioner and patient, but it is motivated by compassion.

Truth-telling is not limited to the clinical aspects of health care. Health administrators are in positions of power. Their power can affect those with whom they work, the patients whom they serve, and the larger community in which they live. This power also carries with it the ethical responsibilities of truth-telling. In fact, the American College of Health Care Administrators (Darr, 2011) specifically addresses the issue of truth-telling with respect to individuals' qualifications and responsibilities to their organizations. Truthfulness is also featured in several areas of the American College of Healthcare Executives' Code of Ethics (ACHE, 2011).

On the surface, being truthful seems like an easy thing to do. However, there can be times when it is extremely difficult to be completely truthful. For example, when there is a possible need to downsize the staff, does the healthcare administrator tell the whole truth? If he or she does, there is a possibility that the best staff will seek employment elsewhere. It is also possible that senior executives do not want full disclosure, so as to protect their fiscal interests. Therefore, administrators might also find themselves engaged in truth-telling in stages, just like the clinical staff.

Even in their daily interactions with staff, administrators must remember the power of words and appreciate how carefully they should be used. An administrator's view of the truth can destroy or enhance performance depending on its delivery. Therefore, one should consider one's words carefully. This admonition applies to both spoken and written communication. Spoken words can have great emotional impact on others, and written words can come back to haunt one's career. In this electronic age, administrators also need to consider the content of e-mails when considering truthful communication. In the business world, e-mail is not just a friendly exchange; it can be evidence of an administrator's truthfulness on any given issue. In addition, administrators should consider the truthfulness and appropriateness of Tweets, posts to Instagram, and other electronic communications even when not in the work setting. One's image is important and maintaining professionalism should always be uppermost in the healthcare administrator's mind.

Silence can also provide a certain truth because it implies consent. Administrators must have the courage to speak their thoughts about an action or a decision, even when it might challenge their career status. Finally, they must be aware that lying, while expeditious at the moment the lie is uttered, might cause the end of their careers. Once the lying begins, administrators have to spend energy keeping track of lies and remembering to tell others the same lies to cover them up. Eventually, the lie and its cover-up are likely to fall apart, at which point they can lead to a loss of integrity and even to the loss of position (Dosick, 2000).

■ AUTONOMY AS FIDELITY

Fidelity means keeping one's word to others, or promise keeping. In ethics, fidelity fits the Kantian view of the categorical imperative because it is universal. People want to have their promises kept by others, so they should, likewise, keep their promises to others. Buber agrees with promise keeping as part of autonomy because it respects the I-YOU relationship. Respect for the individuality of other people implies that it is ethical to honor those persons by keeping promises. Even the utilitarians agree with this aspect of ethics, because promise keeping has the ability to provide the greatest good for the greatest number or avoid the greatest harm.

In business, the idea of fidelity has long been an ethics standard. It used to be said that a man was as good as his word. People made business deals with a handshake, and only scoundrels failed to uphold their promises. Even in today's business settings, fidelity is important because there is an assumption that contracts, both oral and written, will be honored. This assumption permits services to be rendered and payment to be made without undue concern about fraud and abuse. In addition, vendors with which healthcare administrators do business count on fidelity as part of the success of their businesses.

Health care is also a trust-based business. This means that the community expects fidelity. The community considers it a norm that healthcare personnel keep their word to treat patients with dignity and fairness, and provide care that is appropriate and effective. The *Patient Care Partnership* document created by the American Hospital Association (2003) provides information on the promises expected by patients. This organization asserts that fidelity is not only an ethics duty, but also a right for all patients, and emphasizes that healthcare personnel and organizations should honor this right.

The ethical imperative of promise keeping is also part of the mission statement of most healthcare organizations; the community, in turn, interprets this statement as an indicator of the organizations' business position. For example, if an organization touts its mission when advertising its services, it has an obligation to honor those promises. Suppose a hospital uses the mission statement "Grant Hospital: Demand Excellence" in its television, print, and radio campaign. Because of patients' interpretation of the word "demand," the ad campaign could backfire, leading to a flood of patients "demanding" services. When their demands cannot be met, is fidelity lost? This example makes the point that promises should be taken seriously on all levels and healthcare organizations should be able to deliver on their promises.

Fidelity also means that mission statements should be specific enough to be truthful, but not so crass as to offend the community. For example, healthcare administrators would not accept a mission statement that says "Profit Is Number One" because that statement negates the patients all together. Patients and the community think that they should be the organization's number one concern. Likewise, a mission statement should not be something vague, such as "Optimum Health for All People," because that is an unattainable promise. As part of their ongoing duties, administrators should remember to review mission and other statements frequently to ensure that they truly reflect the organization's commitment to service and ethical behavior. In addition, administrators are obligated to make sure all employees understand the meaning of fidelity toward this mission in their daily work behaviors.

Fidelity is also an ethics obligation to employees. If an administrator makes promises about any aspect of the employment relationship, he or she must honor those promises. Likewise, it is important to be careful about perceptions versus actualities. Words are powerful, and employees can easily view them as promises. This is why administrators need to be aware of what they say and when they say it. For example, if an administrator is discussing benefit changes with employees, he or she must have correct information on what those benefits will be, what they will cost, and when they will be in effect. Misinformation can lead to situations where trust can be broken. This is especially true when major changes are occurring, such as during a merger or buyout, or when making changes to accommodate the ACA implementation.

Maintaining autonomy through fidelity is not a simple matter in health care. Violations of promise keeping occur for many reasons. Perhaps the most obvious is the potential conflict between keeping one's word to the patient and being loyal to third-party payers' demands. Is one loyal to those one serves or to those who pay for services? For example, payers typically require gatekeeping and other functions to provide appropriate levels of care at the least amount of expense. However, when managed care organizations that engage in such practices pay bonuses to physicians for controlling this access, an ethical problem can occur. Will the physician be tempted to cut corners on treatment when 10% to 20% of his or her salary is at stake? Should the physician disclose the bonus arrangement to the patient? Gatekeeping and other fiscal arrangements are appropriate for the bottom line but could present real ethics problems for patient fidelity.

Other challenges arise in regard to fidelity to patients. For example, when a healthcare professional works in a prison setting, there can be conflict of fidelity between the interests of the patient and those of the institution. Certainly, when the legal system is involved, there might be a need to violate patient fidelity because of a subpoena or other action. In addition, for public health actions, such as in the prevention of epidemics, fidelity to the overall community can take precedent over fidelity to the individual. This is also true in the military, where different rules exist for physicians and other healthcare professionals. Using knowledge and skills to keep soldiers "combat ready" and regarding them as "government property" can appear to be an issue of fidelity to the organization over that of the individual.

What is the responsibility for fidelity shouldered by healthcare administrators? Certainly, administrators need to be aware of the impact of fidelity and see that promises are kept. This can entail periodic reviews of the mission statement, training efforts, and observation to see if the mission is being met. Administrators also have an obligation to maintain fidelity where any business contract is concerned. This requires understanding the words and the intent of the contract before they sign it. They must also be able to communicate the features of the contract to those affected by that the contract. In the case of third-party payers, this communication effort includes patients as well as employees. Finally, using the Kantian question, "If I were the patient or the employee, would I want this promise kept to me?", can guide administrators in making appropriate decisions about the fidelity aspect of autonomy.

Summary

Autonomy as a principle of ethics assumes a certain level of respect for persons and their ability to take actions that affect their health. It includes issues of informed consent, confidentiality of information, truth telling, and promise keeping. On the surface, autonomy seems to be a basic principle that should remain inviolate; however, in health care it is never this easy. There are situations and relationships that challenge the principle of autonomy and make it difficult to follow on a consistent basis. The administrator's responsibility is to be aware of challenges within organizations and to do whatever is possible to maintain the right of autonomy for patients, employees, and the community.

Cases for Your Consideration

The Case of the Misguided Relative

Think about the chapter information and consider the following questions. Sample responses and commentary will follow the case.

1. Which violations of autonomy happened in this case?
2. Why did Ms. Jamie Jenson make the telephone call?
3. What was the impact of this action on the family?
4. Which actions could the family take?
5. If you were the administrator of this clinic, which action would you take?

Case Information

The Scene: The office of Dr. Randy Williams, internist, in Smalltown, USA. The date of the case predates the HIPAA rules.

The Situation: Mr. Basil Carpenter was suffering from problems with urinary insufficiency and frequent urination so he went to his physician, Dr. Williams. Dr. Williams performed an ultrasound in the office and saw a shadow in Mr. Carpenter's kidney. He explained to Mr. Carpenter that this might be a tumor and that he needed a consultation with a urologist. An appointment with Dr. Samuels would be made as soon as possible.

While Mr. Carpenter was not thrilled to hear this news, he knew that he needed further test results before he should be worried about his situation. He accompanied Dr. Williams to the front office, where instructions were given to Ms. Jamie Jenson, the receptionist. She was to make an appointment with Dr. Samuels so that he could evaluate Mr. Carpenter. She also needed to make a follow-up appointment for Mr. Carpenter. After reviewing the chart, she made the call to Dr. Samuels, scheduled the follow-up, and gave Mr. Carpenter his appointment card.

However, Ms. Jenson was the cousin of Mr. Carpenter's ex-wife and this news was just too good to keep. As soon as Mr. Carpenter left the office, she called her cousin and told her that Basil had a kidney tumor and it might be cancerous. On hearing this news, Basil's ex-wife called their son, Hamilton, and told him that his father had cancer of the kidney and might not live.

Hamilton decided to get further information about his father's status and called Basil's current wife, Sandra. His first question to her was, "Does Dad have his will and finances in order?" Sandra responded, "Why are you asking this?" Hamilton told her that that Ms. Jenson from Dr. Williams's office said that Basil had kidney cancer and was terminal. Sobbing, Sandra hung up the phone just as Basil walked in the door. Only 30 minutes from the time he left Dr. Williams's office, Basil walked into hysteria of unknown origin.

Responses and Commentary on Questions

1. Which violations of autonomy happened in this case?

   This case occurred before the HIPAA rules were in effect. However, it clearly is a case of breach of confidentiality by a nonmedical staff member. Because Ms. Jenson needed to provide referral information, she had the right to access the chart. However, she should keep the information that she found, no matter what the relationship with the patient, confidential. Kant would be very upset because Ms. Jensen violated the categorical imperative for confidentiality. Imagine if this same incident happened to Ms. Jenson instead of Mr. Carpenter. How would she feel? Yet, she did not even consider this question before she called her cousin. Utilitarians would also find this action inappropriate because it has the potential to cause the greatest harm to the greatest number if it were to become a routine in this practice.

   Comment: The self-profit motive enhances the temptation to violate confidentiality when there is access to confidential records.

Suppose Mr. Carpenter was a major celebrity and the condition was erectile dysfunction. The temptation to leak this information to the press for profit might sway a person's sense of ethical obligation. Does this sound like an exaggeration? Certainly not, when one considers the obsession with celebrities in today's electronic age.

2. Why did Ms. Jenson make the telephone call?

Several things could have motivated Ms. Jenson in this case. Perhaps she saw herself as altruistic or used ethical egoism by giving the family important information that Basil or his new wife might not choose to share. Perhaps she saw it as an issue of family loyalty and a duty to honor the family's right to know. She might not have even realized that she was violating Basil's right to confidentiality because no one had ever told her not to do this. Of course, the motive could have been more purulent—she could have succumbed to the need to share gossip that was truly juicy.

Comment: It is important, as an administrator, to consider that everyone who has access to the medical record is important to the chain of confidentiality protection. Often persons who are not on the clinical side of patient treatment are forgotten in this important area. Receptionists, office managers, and even custodians might have more access to sensitive materials than you realize. Training and monitoring of policies and procedures is necessary.

3. What was the impact of this action on the family?

In this case, the family includes an extended network of individuals. First, consider Ms. Jenson, who just put her job in jeopardy to inform her cousin of some family news. Also consider Basil's ex-wife, who was upset enough to contact their son, Hamilton. How was she feeling? Basil is her son's father and his loss could be very painful to her child. Of course, one might also wonder why she called Hamilton when she did not have the whole story about Basil. Perhaps less than altruistic motives were in place.

How about Hamilton's role? He received this shocking news from his mother. Perhaps he was upset and concerned about his financial future. Of course, he also had the option of waiting for the full story before he called Sandra. Again, one could wonder about his motivation and his response to the news, but one cannot deny the effect of this misinformation and the chain of grief that it caused.

Poor Sandra: She waited for Basil's return from Dr. Williams's office and was worried about his health. Then she got that telephone call from Hamilton. The news shocked her but also made her furious. How did Basil's ex-wife know about his condition before she did? What right did Ms. Jenson have to share this information with Basil's ex-wife before she even knew it? Just how bad is the situation? Will she lose her husband and the father of her children? It is no wonder she is crying.

What about Basil? Imagine if you walked into this situation. He had been given potentially frightening news but decided to put it in its proper perspective until more information was known. He knew that he would have to tell his family but did not want to upset them too soon. Despite his sensible nature, he must have had some fears in the back of his mind. He wondered, "What will happen to my family if I am not around?" He walked in the door to find complete chaos. Sandra was crying and he did not have a clue why. Imagine how angry and upset he was.

Comment: Sometimes it is difficult for healthcare personnel to understand how much of an impact their actions have on others. This case is an example where an entire family was affected by the actions of one healthcare team member, but there are many incidents where whole communities can be affected. Healthcare professionals must always be aware of their power and use it ethically.

4. Which actions could the family take in this situation?

At a minimum, Basil should contact Dr. Williams personally and inform him of what took place. This would allow the physician to take appropriate action in his practice and deal with Ms. Jenson. Dr. Williams could also apologize to Basil for what happened and assure him that it would never happen again. If Basil was so inclined, he could contact his attorney to see if there were grounds for suit.

What actually occurred in this case was very interesting. Sandra accompanied Basil to his appointment with the urologist. She told the specialist that she did not want the records released back to Dr. Williams. She also asked that they be stamped as confidential. When she was asked the reason for her request, she informed the urologist of the events. He was upset for the family and promised to honor Sandra's request. He also spoke to Dr. Williams about the situation. Shortly after this, Basil received a telephone call of apology and numerous statements in the mail about new protection of confidentiality policies in Dr. Williams's office.

5. If you were the administrator of this clinic, which action would you take?

First, from the minute you received the information about what transpired, you would have the obligation to investigate. Document what the family tells you about the situation. Remain calm, listen attentively, and provide assurance that you will take action about the situation. Next, speak with Ms. Jenson privately to hear her account of what happened. You might also want to contact your legal counsel to get his or her advice on the best course of action. Once you have all of the information, confer with Dr. Williams about the situation. He could decide on immediate termination or some other form of action with regard to Ms. Jenson.

This action would deal only with the immediate situation, however. To prevent future incidents of this nature, you should review current policies and procedures to make sure they are clear about confidentiality. Review all HIPAA rules and regulations and the new standards for reporting violations of confidentiality to be sure that your organization is complying with those standards. In addition, determine that the current staff understands the policies and their implementation. You might want to have an in-service education meeting to review confidentiality procedures with all staff members. In addition, you might consider doing some nonintrusive observations to see if staff members are actually implementing confidentiality procedures. These actions would help prevent any future legal actions regarding the violations of confidentiality and provide a response for any HIPAA investigations.

The Case of the Valiant Skateboarder

Think about the chapter information and consider the following questions. Sample responses and commentary will follow the case.

1. How does this case illustrate the concept of patient autonomy?
2. What are some ways to protect Aidan's autonomy?
3. If you were the administrator of St. Mark the Ascetic Hospital, which action would you take?

Case Information

"It hurts! It hurts! Nothing has ever hurt like this!" Twenty-one-year-old Aidan Emerys had attempted a frontside boardslide on his skateboard. When there was a problem with his ollie, his fall caused a break in his kneecap and he was admitted to Saint Mark the Ascetic Hospital for knee surgery. Before going to his room, he needed to have blood drawn for laboratory tests and an intravenous line (IV) placed. At St. Mark's, these procedures are done in the intensive care unit (ICU).

In the ICU, Aidan noticed a group of people standing around. A nurse approached and told him that she needed to start an IV in preparation for his surgery. He knew the stick might hurt, but he could take it.

He was a man. However, the nurse said, "I can't get this in. I'll have to try again." The next stick hurt even worse, but Aidan thought he could take the pain if this was the last one. However, he did not appreciate having an audience of people watching his ordeal.

Then the nurse said, "You have bad veins so I am going to have to get someone else to try this." From out of nowhere, another nurse appeared. This nurse tried to insert the IV in another spot, but again it did not work. She said, "I just blew this vein." All Aidan knew was that it hurt beyond his ability to "suck it up." He began to feel nauseous and someone handed him a basin. He was sick in front of the whole audience in the room. However, he was not finished. A new face appeared. This man said, "I am from the lab and I need to have some blood for your tests." He inserted yet another needle in Aidan's arm.

Before leaving the ICU, a nurse told him that she would send another nurse to his room to insert his IV. This person was known for his ability to insert IVs in difficult patients. Aidan was still terrified. He also felt humiliated that he was sick in front of all those people. He thought, "How can I survive in this torture chamber?"

Responses and Commentary on Questions

1. How does this case illustrate the concept of patient autonomy?

   First, it is important to understand that informed consent means that patients give permission for procedures that may invade their privacy and their bodies. These procedures are needed for treatment and healing. However, informed consent still requires respect patients' autonomy as much as possible.

   Think about Aidan's situation. First, there were three attempts to find a suitable vein for an IV. Each attempt was more painful than the previous one, and Aidan was told he was to blame for the lack of success! No one asked him about his level of pain or provided any acknowledgment of his personhood. He was just another case, expected to take the pain and remain cooperative. In addition, he was required to submit to these attempts in front of witnesses. No one told him who these people were or why they were present. How do you think he felt about his ability to exercise self-rule? Did he have any autonomy?

   In addition, a person told Aidan that he had to supply a blood sample for the lab before he could be taken to his room. Imagine how embarrassed Aidan was. He was exhausted from the pain and smelled awful, yet he was supposed to submit his body to more pain for the sake of the laboratory. This was just expected; no compassion or explanation was given. Again, there was a great lack of respect for his autonomy. It is no small wonder that he saw St. Mark's as a torture chamber.

2. What are some ways to protect Aidan's autonomy?

First, remember that Aidan is just another patient and this is just another day in the ICU. The nurses have had difficulty with IVs before, and they have seen people vomit from pain before. This is nothing new. But this is Aidan's first experience with any hospital procedure: For him, this is not just another day. Could his autonomy be protected in this situation?

Even though he signed an informed consent form at admission, Aidan did not know the specifics of what would happen on admission. The first thing that should have happened in the ICU was some introductions. Simply explaining to Aidan who was in the room and why they were there would have reduced the anxiety of being observed by an unknown audience. Then, the nurse could have explained why she was inserting an IV and what she was going to do. This would have given Aidan the opportunity to understand why the pain was necessary.

When the nurse was not successful on her first try, she could have called in her backup. This person should have been the nurse who was especially trained in inserting IVs. Explaining the need to do this without blaming Aidan for having bad veins would have protected his dignity and decreased his unnecessary pain. In fact, he may have even been spared the embarrassment of being nauseous in front of everyone.

Consider the laboratory technician who watched Aidan's ordeal and insisted on getting his samples. He could have taken the time to explain why this additional pain was necessary and been compassionate in his attitude toward Aidan. For example, he could have assured Aidan that he would get the sample as quickly and painlessly as possible so Aidan could be taken to his room for rest. Even a minor attempt at honoring Aidan as a person and preserving his self-respect could have gone a long way.

3. If you were the administrator of St. Mark the Ascetic Hospital, which action would you take?

This case shows the need for policies and procedures that go beyond informed consent. Of course, Aidan did provide written permission for the procedures to be performed, but he did not consent to the treatment that went with them. As administrator, you can work with the appropriate clinical staff, including the director of nurses and clinical laboratories, to define protocols. For example, one protocol could be that only the necessary personnel are present when a patient has a procedure and that all persons in the room are introduced to the patient.

There also need to be protocols for what happens in a difficult case. How many times should a patient be "stuck" to insert an IV? Is three times an acceptable number? At what point should the backup IV expert be called? At a minimum, there should be more communication with the patient and more compassion shown.

This case also makes a great argument for continuing education. The ICU nurses are generally experts at insertion of IVs. However, it does not mean that periodic sessions to renew and sharpen skills are not needed. More importantly in this case, an increased awareness of patient autonomy and the need for communication and compassion is needed. Perhaps some case studies and discussions or even role-plays about how patients feel and how to treat them would prevent the torture chamber image of St. Mark's in the future.

Web Resources

The following websites provide additional information about topics covered in this chapter.

Department of Health & Human Services, Office of Minority Health
http://minorityhealth.hhs.gov

HIPAA Information
http://www.hhs.gov/ocr/hipaa/

Patient Care Partnership (AHA)
http://www.aha.org/aha/issues/Communicating-With-Patients/pt-care-partnership.html

References

American College of Healthcare Executives (ACHE). (2011). ACHE code of ethics. Retrieved from http://www.ache.org/ABT_ACHE/code.cfm

American Hospital Association. (2003). *The patient care partnership: Understanding expectations, rights, and responsibilities* [Brochure]. Chicago, IL: Author.

Beauchamp, T. L., & Childress, J. E. (2012). *Principles of biomedical ethics* (7th ed.). New York, NY: Oxford University Press.

Chell, B. (2014). Competency: What it is, what it is not and why it matters. In E. E. Morrison & B. Furlong (Eds.). *Health care ethics: Critical issues for the 21st century* (3rd ed., pp. 127–139). Burlington, MA: Jones & Bartlett Learning.

Darr, K. (2011). *Ethics in health services management* (5th ed.). Baltimore, MD: Health Professions Press.

Department of Health and Human Services. (2013). New rule protects patient privacy, secures health information [Press release]. Retrieved from http://www.hhs.gov/news/press/2013pres/01/20130117b.html

Department of Health and Human Services, Office for Civil Rights. (2013). Health information privacy. Retrieved from http://www.hhs.gov/ocr/privacy/index.html

Department of Health and Human Services, Office of Minority Health. (2013). The National CLAS Standards. Retrieved from http://minorityhealth.hhs.gov/templates/browse.aspx?lvl=2&lvlID=15

Dosick, R. W. (2000). *The business bible: Ten commandments for creating an ethical workplace.* Woodstock, VT: Jewish Light.

Munson, R. (2008). *Interventions and reflections: Basic issues in medical ethics* (8th ed.). Belmont, CA: Thompson Wadsworth.

Summers, J. (2014). Principles of healthcare ethics. In E. E. Morrison & B. Furlong (Eds.), *Health care ethics: Critical issues for the 21st century* (3rd ed., pp. 47–66). Burlington, MA: Jones & Bartlett Learning.

Vaughn, L. (2010). *Bioethics: Principles, issues, and cases.* New York, NY: Oxford University Press.

CHAPTER
3

Nonmaleficence and Beneficence

Do nonmaleficence and beneficence matter in health care?

Points to Ponder

1. How does the principle of nonmaleficence affect the healthcare administrator's (HCA) role in the organization?
2. How can a healthcare administrator avoid causing harm to employees?
3. Why is the principle of beneficence important for the operation of a healthcare organization?

Key Terms

The following is a list of this chapter's key terms. Look for them in bold.

beneficence   nonmaleficence

■ INTRODUCTION AND DEFINITIONS

This chapter presents two parallel principles of ethics: **nonmaleficence** and **beneficence**. Some ethics writers view these principles as inseparable cousins. Others argue that nonmaleficence is the strongest obligation of the two because it must be present before one can choose beneficence. Whatever the relationship, these two principles are essential in a trust-based healthcare system. Both society in general and individuals assume that health care holds these two principles to be pillars of practice. Beneficence and nonmaleficence were part of medical practice even in the age of Hippocrates, who recognized these duties in his oath of practice.

Just what do these words mean? Nonmaleficence involves an ethical and legal duty to avoid harming others (Beauchamp & Childress, 2012). The source of this word is the Latin maxim *primum non nocere* or "first, do no harm." This principle involves areas of healthcare practice including treatment procedures and the rights of patients. In addition, it has an impact on how administrators treat employees in the work setting.

Heath care requires that personnel and organizations go beyond just avoiding doing harm to people. There is also an obligation to create benefit and contribute to optimal health for individuals and the community at large. Beneficence, or the choice to act with charity and kindness, is part of this obligation. Beneficence includes helping those in trouble, protecting patients' rights, and providing needed treatment. Kantians would agree that these obligations exist because all people have value and deserve respect. However, in day-to-day healthcare decisions, the utilitarian view of beneficence is often used. This involves balancing benefits of a healthcare decision against its harms. Avoiding the absolutes of Kantian logic, healthcare administrators make practice or policy decisions based on this reciprocity.

■ NONMALEFICENCE IN HEALTHCARE SETTINGS

First, do no harm. How can this be part of the principles of ethics in today's technology-centered and changing healthcare system? Does health care not have to cause patients pain and suffering to cure them? Should physicians avoid invasive diagnostic tests if they cause harm? Is there also a need to consider the emotional pain of receiving a diagnosis? Certainly, this "first, do not harm" concept does not mean that healthcare professionals cannot ever cause harm to patients. In fact, sometimes harm is necessary, but actions they undertake should never cause harm without considering those actions' necessity and recognizing the patient as a person. In each case, providers must weigh the benefits provided by the procedure against the suffering it causes.

Both the ethical and legal practices of health care recognize the important of nonmaleficence. To make the best decisions for the practical implementation of this principle, one could use utilitarian logic. This means that benefits of actions are balanced against the potential harms. If there is greater benefit for the patient or the organization, the act is as an ethical one. In fact, healthcare professionals also have a duty to provide appropriate care to avoid further harm to the patient under what some legal texts call a due care standard. This means that the professional has taken all necessary action to select the most appropriate treatment for the condition and provide that treatment with the least amount of pain and suffering possible. Standards of due care also mean that healthcare professions have the necessary licenses to practice their professions and maintain currency through continuing education (Munson, 2008).

In the age of evidence-based medicine, the requirement for professional currency is even more important as part of the due care standards. To meet this requirement, healthcare administrators need to create standards for currency, review the currency of each professional's license, and support continuing education in any way that is fiscally responsible for the organization. In addition, policies for safety and protection of the patient's physical health and dignity must be present and monitored to avoid harm. These policies must include infection control and other environmental practices so that the patient avoids healthcare-acquired infections and other unnecessary harms. When nonmaleficence is an active consideration, patients will receive their care with a trust that unnecessary harm will not be part of their treatment.

Like many other areas of health care, nonmaleficence is complicated when advanced technology is part of the regimen. Issues around withholding or withdrawing life support, extraordinary measures, and death with dignity involve decisions about balancing unnecessary harm with benefit to the patient. For example, healthcare professionals and family members seem to be more comfortable with withholding (i.e., not starting) treatment than with withdrawing it. Somehow, "pulling the plug" seems more harmful to the patient than not starting life support technology. However, the line between extraordinary and ordinary care has become murkier with the advent of advanced life-sustaining technology. The now classic Terri Schiavo case is an excellent example of this level of complexity (Darr, 2011). In the past, healthcare providers did not go to extraordinary efforts and patients did not face potential harm when there was no hope of benefit. Today, family members who are educated in the marvels of modern medicine have changed this view. Influenced by their knowledge of "medical miracles" through the media, families see what used to be extraordinary measures as ordinary and appropriate for their loved ones. Even some physicians who see death as a failure might advocate for care that prolongs some form of life but increases the suffering of the individual.

How does the healthcare administrator's work affect nonmaleficence? Of course, healthcare administrators do not provide direct patient care, but they create an environment for the consideration and application of nonmaleficence in patient care. For example, suppose advance directive policies are in place, but they are not written so that patients understand them. In such a situation, the healthcare administrator may be involved in policy refinement. He or she certainly will be involved in making sure that appropriate implementation occurs.

This responsibility will include periodic staff education so that staff members are clear about their responsibilities and actions. In addition, health administrators might work closely with an ethics committee whose members can offer advice when challenging nonmaleficence situations occur.

Nonmaleficence and Staff

The application of the principle of nonmaleficence is not restricted to patient treatment; rather, healthcare administrators must consider it when dealing with any member of the healthcare staff. For example, health administrators have an ethical obligation to provide a working environment that is safe and does not harm employees. Such an environment also allows for discussion of concerns without fear of reprisal. It should be a positive environment where values are respected and employees can do their best work on behalf of the patients whom they serve (think about I-YOU relationships). In other words, the work environment should be free of harassment, imposition, and discrimination for all employees, regardless of their status in the organization.

Creation of a positive work environment or climate of trust can go a long way toward ensuring the implementation of the principle of nonmaleficence for employees. Even so, situations might occur that can potentially violate this principle. Certainly, downsizing and reductions in the workforce have a potential to cause the staff great personal and professional harm. How can a healthcare administrator implement a reduction in force plan and cause the least amount of harm to employees? The American College of Healthcare Executives (ACHE, 2012) provides assistance through its *Policy Statement: Ethical Issues Related to a Reduction in Force.* This statement urges administrators to consider both the long- and short-term impact of this decision, not only on those who will lose their jobs, but also on those who will remain in the organization. Survivor guilt can often be destructive to a positive workplace and productivity and cause unnecessary harm.

The ACHE (2012) also stresses the need for frequent and accurate communication with all those involved in the layoffs and the provision of as much support as possible for those who lose their jobs. Often, administrators try to avoid communication about layoffs because they fear disruption and loss of productivity. In keeping information from affected employees, administrators are trying to balance their view of benefits versus harm. Therefore, they keep secret their knowledge of what is to happen to a select group. In such a case, the rumor mill may take over and fill the void in accurate communication, making the situation worse. Even though it might seem to make the administrator's burden easier in a difficult situation, silence is truly not golden and can cause unnecessary harm.

It is equally important to remember those who remain with the organization after a layoff. There can be an administrative attitude of "You should think yourself lucky to have a job" and a lack of empathy for the feelings of layoff survivors. This attitude causes unnecessary harm because it fails to acknowledge the human reaction of "Why them and not me?" or survivor guilt. Healthcare administrators should acknowledge what has occurred and allow time for processing the feelings associated with it. Use of channels of communication including meetings, newsletters, and e-mails allows for the feeling part of these situations to be brought to the fore. In addition, communication needs to be ongoing regarding workload expectations and the potential for any future reductions in the workforce.

As part of their jobs, administrators deal with diversity on many levels. Diversity can include the educational diversity represented by the range of credentials—from a GED to an MD/DO—found in healthcare institutions. Staff members are also professionally diverse because they come from many different professional backgrounds, each with its own culture. They can also be ethnically diverse, representing different cultural traditions and experiences with respect to their thinking about ethical practices.

The administrator's ability to recognize this diversity, honor its differing values, and still administer a cost-effective organization will certainly pose a challenge in the ACA era of rapid change. To create a culture of inclusion, healthcare administrators must review policies and procedures with respect to diversity and make sure that they decrease the potential for harm. For example, administrators need to make clear that the organization has zero tolerance for discrimination, harassment in all forms, and sexual imposition. Appropriate steps need to be in place and procedures enforced when violations occur, even though looking the other way might seem easier in the immediate present. Ignoring issues related to diversity can make staff members believe that the administration, through its silence and lack of action, condones inappropriate behaviors that cause harm.

Workplace bullying in health care is another staff issue related to nonmaleficence that must considered when preventing unnecessary harm. Workplace bullying is a form of psychological violence that can cause great harm to staff and their families. It involves aggressive behaviors toward employees including spreading untruths, social isolation, constantly changing work expectations, assigning unreasonable workloads, publicly belittling the opinions of others, and engaging in intimidation. Bullying is manifested when a pattern of such behaviors is evident (Workplace Bullying Institute, 2012). Niles (2013) finds that bullying is common in healthcare settings.

Currently, most U.S. employees do not have any legal protection against this form of aggression, unlike the case with racial and age discrimination or sexual harassment. Niles (2013) reports that 80% of bullying in the workplace remains legal. However, 13 states are considering bills that will address this situation and make bullying illegal. In addition, administrators can use federal laws such as the Occupational Health and Safety Act of 1970 as legal justification for action against bullying (Niles, 2013).

In all too many cases, however, healthcare organizations view bullying as "business as usual," because the majority of bullies are bosses. Bosses may think that bullying is good management or a way to get rid of those who do not agree with their management style. A lack of understanding of effective management behavior is part of the reason why bullying is so prevalent. Some experts believe that more than 35% of employees will experience this type of abuse in the workplace (Workplace Bullying Institute, 2012).

The impact of bullying on staff can be profound. First, the targets of bullying may take responsibility for the bully's behavior. They may work harder, put in longer hours, and try to prove that they are valuable. This can lead to increased stress levels and take its toll on the target's health, accuracy, productivity, and overall family life. Despite the target's efforts, this diligent work usually fails to stop the aggression and can actually make the bully feel more powerful.

Next, targets may begin to experience psychological symptoms such as loss of confidence, depression, and helplessness. Physical symptoms may also occur, including headaches, panic attacks, and hypertension. If targets question or take action concerning the bullying, the organization may accuse them of insubordination. Often even the human resources department does not recognize this phenomenon and labels employees who voice concerns as "disgruntled." In addition, fellow employees may try to avoid being associated with the target, so that they do not become the bully's next victim. They can even join in the aggression to stay on the bully's best side.

As one might imagine, the workplace characterized by bullying soon becomes unhealthy and suffers a decrease in overall productivity. Targets of bullying absent themselves from work more frequently because of physical problems or the need to avoid the bully. They can also lose their motivation to provide high-quality service and just go through the motions at work. These actions contribute to a loss of productivity for the entire group. Morale decreases as others see the bully's actions and wonder if they are next. Finally, turnover rates can increase as the targets choose to resign and move on to new jobs to avoid the situation.

A stereotype of the phenomenon of workplace bullying is that it occurs only in male-dominated professions or corporate settings. In fact, research has shown that the top three professions for this behavior are the female-dominated fields: nursing, education, and social work (Niles, 2013; Workplace Bullying Institute, 2012).

What should administrators' role be in preventing healthcare workplace bullying and the harm that it causes? First, they should assess their own actions and communications with staff. How do they treat people whose personalities do not agree with them? What do they do about taking needed disciplinary action? Do they keep information confidential or are they part of the informal network or grapevine? Administrators need to search their consciences and make sure that they are using civility instead of bullying to accomplish their goals.

Administrators should also be committed to a safe and healthy workplace for all employees. There must be established policies that make it clear that all types of aggressive behavior are inappropriate in the workplace. This includes a range of behaviors, spanning from verbal bullying to sexual harassment and physical violence. Education is critical as well, so that administration and staff can identify unacceptable behaviors and know what to do if they occur. Providing examples through case studies or even role-plays helps to clarify policies and their application. There should also be a confidential way to file a complaint about bullying without fear of reprisal. Organizations should take complaints seriously and promptly investigate in a professional manner to avoid revictimizing the target (Niles, 2013).

■ BENEFICENCE IN HEALTHCARE SETTINGS

Beneficence is another principle of ethics that is expected and fundamental in a healthcare setting. Patients assume that healthcare professionals are there for their benefit and will act with charity and kindness toward them. Without this element of trust, it would be very difficult for practitioners to provide treatment, especially when such treatment often requires embarrassing, painful, or even life-threatening procedures. The high-trust nature of health care creates a higher moral duty for all healthcare personnel (Summers, 2014). In turn, society expects much more from healthcare employees than it does from employees in other fields. Because of these higher standards, healthcare personnel must make an active decision to act with compassion. They are required go beyond the minimum standards of care and consider patients' needs and feelings. In addition, they must communicate compassionately with the patients and families about what is going to happen and why the treatment is necessary.

In healthcare settings, practicing beneficence is often challenging. Healthcare professionals must often deliver bad news, but they need to consider the patient's situation when they do so. Patients are likely to remember even a small act of compassion. For example, active beneficence can be as simple as holding a patient's hand during a painful procedure. However, practitioners are trained not to be overly emotional, and sharing an act of kindness can be difficult for them. In addition, some practitioners fear that they will lose their objectivity by identifying with the patient. Perhaps taking a few minutes to think about Rawls's ideas and envision the patient's position would make active beneficence easier for practitioners.

From an administrator's position, active beneficence can involve having procedures and policies for assuring that patients receive appropriate care post discharge. In addition, administrators may develop policies for compassionate leave when serious family issues arise for staff members. Beneficence can also involve the entire organization through community service projects that have nothing to do with profit, but everything to do with compassion.

Making the decision to be actively beneficent fits well with Buber's I-YOU and, in some cases, I-THOU relationships (Buber, 1996). It acknowledges each patient or employee as a unique individual who has worth. From a business standpoint, deciding to be actively beneficent increases the organization's positive image and level of trust in the community. However, active beneficence is not without a price. It is not easy to practice this principle on a daily basis because it requires a spirit of giving that may not always be rewarded. In reality, reward should not be the motive for beneficence (think about Kant's idea of good will). In the real business of health care, one sees people at their worst, when they are in pain or deep grief. Health professionals also see things happen to people that others in the community never see and do not understand. All too often, suffering and dying are part of professional life in health care. Therefore, the nature of health care requires a balance of moral duty for beneficence and maintaining appropriate professional distance.

The real beneficence challenge is consistently treating patients with compassion even under stressful circumstances. Being consistent in practicing active beneficence requires much effort and a commitment to continuing education to accomplish this goal. Often personnel are emotionally exhausted at the end of the day and experience what has been called compassion exhaustion or burnout. They feel as if they simply cannot give any more—yet the next patient expects the same level of caring received in the previous encounter.

It is important for administrators to remember to provide active beneficence and foster it among staff. Sometimes simple communication can assist with this effort, such as telling staff members how much their efforts are appreciated or publishing in the newsletter (with the patient's permission, of course) a thank-you note from a patient or the family written to the staff. Administrators can also be aware of the amount of overtime hours worked and allow staff members enough flexibility to take a vacation without guilt. Some institutions even use rewards programs with titles like "Caught You Caring"; they provide cash rewards to staff members who have done something that demonstrates active beneficence. A word of caution: While some of these ideas sound like great ways to boost staff morale, patients may not find such a campaign appealing. They may feel that staff should not have to be "caught caring," but rather assume that the staff will be caring at all times.

Beneficence should be a part of the planning function when conducting a cost/benefit analysis for decision making. In this model, there is an attempt to balance community or business benefit against potential costs and harm. This tool follows rule utility and is useful for many types of healthcare organizations with differing financial structures, including public health organizations. However, cost/benefit analysis as a decision-making model is sometimes difficult to implement effectively with respect to beneficence. It requires time for accurate data collection, openness to discussion, and the application of the principles of ethics to financial decisions. In the era of the ACA, with its potential reductions in payments for providers, it will be tempting to put financial concerns ahead of the practice of active beneficence for patients and the community.

Beneficence and Staff

Administrators should strive to have a climate of caring in both the formal and informal organization. While administrators cannot guarantee that their employees will always practice active beneficence, they can work to create a culture that reinforces this behavior. Thoughtful treatment of employees in the organization can do much to create a culture of compassion.

A compassion deficit can occur when patients receive active beneficence, but employees do not. The message received by employees in this circumstance is that they do not matter in the organization; that is, they think that they are all replaceable. It is easy to see that this impression does not foster the motivation to go beyond the minimum requirements in caring for patients or for other employees. In such a case, the organization becomes a place to do one's time and do the minimum until the employee can find a new job or retire.

The healthcare administrator's behavior and attitude can help prevent the formation of such attitudes and their negative impact on an organization. Ensuring position power, in particular, can increase the dignity and growth of staff. For example, an administrator can choose to praise employees in public for their work, rather than just assume that it is their job to do well. If certain improvements need to be implemented, administrators can choose to discuss action plans in private and in a constructive manner. By practicing respect and honoring an individual's work, administrators help to foster a climate of caring (Dye, 2010).

Being an administrator in a culture of compassion requires more than knowledge of budgets and strategic planning. One must practice "respectful stewardship" (Dye, 2010, p. 49). This means that an individual uses his or her administrative influence to ensure completion of necessary work, but this influence is used a manner that promotes self-esteem and demonstrates respect. For example, an administrator can choose to seek out information and ideas from staff before making decisions. While he or she does not have to use every offered idea, asking for and considering others' ideas is part of respect and may even be the best management practice. In addition, offering appropriate information and guidance when tasks need to be done, rather than simply "issuing orders," shows respect. This action can also be cost-effective because the time spent in clarification can prevent costly errors or resentful, passive aggressive behaviors.

Not only should administrators show appreciation for their employees and their work, but they should also be appropriately enthusiastic about their own work. This means that administrators should understand the reasons for their work and demonstrate enthusiasm for the mission of the organization and department. If they cannot, perhaps it is time for a job search.

Lastly, administrators should consider being their own good stewards. They will need to practice frequent self-assessment to build on their strengths and work on their weaknesses. They also need to be willing to own their mistakes and apologize when necessary. As administrators, they need to be lifelong learners and remain open to new knowledge and practices. This is especially true in the current era, as healthcare organizations grapple with the deep change model associated with the ACA. Because being a good self-steward will take effort, administrators need to practice self-protection. This can mean planning quiet time in the day, taking time out for exercise, remembering that family counts too, and planning real vacations for self-renewal. These actions are not only a benefit the administrator, but actually assist the organization. When they take care of themselves, healthcare administrators will have greater energy to provide the kind of leadership that encourages a culture where active beneficence is the norm, rather than the exception.

Summary

Often healthcare administrators think of nonmaleficence and beneficence as paired principles. In reality, nonmaleficence requires only the prevention of harm. This act of prevention can involve creating an environment where safe practices for the treatment of patients exist and where employees are free from harassment in its many forms.

Beneficence is a more robust principle that requires going beyond prevention of harm to choosing ethical action. For example, in active beneficence, one respects the individuality (I-YOU relationship) of all employees and finds ways to nurture them. Active beneficence includes making the effort to be a steward of resources and talent. This action is, in itself, a virtue but it can also have a positive impact on the bottom line. From a business view, it is much more cost-effective to do the small things that are necessary to build employee morale and retention than to pay the price of constant recruitment and rehiring.

Cases for Your Consideration

The Case of Pru, Fenway, and Willow Tree Centers

Think about the chapter information and consider the following questions. Sample responses and commentary will follow the case.

1. How did Fenway cause harm to Pru and to Gladys?
2. How did Ireland cause harm to Pru and to Gladys?
3. What did Gladys do to reduce the harm for her resident?
4. How did Pru's physician act with nonmaleficence?
5. Which management decisions should Gladys take?

Gladys Monroe worked hard to gain a good reputation for her residential care center. Willow Tree Center's name now stood for quality and compassionate care. In fact, the community believed that Gladys treated residents almost as if they were special family members. Gladys was proud of the work she had done. However, this Saturday was different.

Background: One of Gladys's newest residents was an 85-year-old woman named Prudence James. Pru, as she liked to be called, came to the care center because she had uncontrolled diabetes that was affecting her health both physically and mentally. Her husband was Pru's primary caregiver, but he was also an active alcoholic. This meant that her medications and diet were unsupervised, contributing to her current state of health. Finally, Pru's eldest daughter, Ireland, arranged to have her become resident at Willow Tree and obtained a power of attorney for Pru's health affairs. Gladys, working with Pru's physician, was able to get her diabetes under control and Pru was responding well.

Saturday morning started the usual way, with the residents gathering for their breakfast in the common room. Just as they began eating, the side door of the room burst open. In walked a large, elderly man whose face showed great anger. He said, "You've got my wife and I'm taking her home. I am tired of you stealing our money in what you call taking care of Pru."

Gladys explained that Ireland, his daughter, arranged for Pru to be one of Willow Tree Center's residents and that she had her authorization on file.

The angry man became even more agitated, saying, "Pru is my wife, and she's coming home with me. Aren't you, Pru?"

Pru said, "Fenway, stop making to scene. I will go home with you. Gladys, please help me get my things together."

Although Gladys knew that this decision was not a good one for Pru's health and well-being, she did not think she could deny the request. She helped Pru with her belongings and her medications. She even tried to explain the medication to Fenway, but he just said, "Stop trying to scare my wife. We're going home!"

As Pru and Fenway left, Gladys could see that incident had visibly upset the other residents. She reassured them that everything would the taken care of, and they went back to their post-breakfast routine. However, Gladys was concerned and telephoned Ireland to explain the situation to her. When she finished explaining what happened, Ireland said, "This is really not my problem. She belongs to Dad now. Let him handle it his way." Then she hung up.

Gladys could not believe Ireland's response, but she knew that she had to do something else. She feared for Pru's health and well-being. She telephoned Pru's physician, who was well aware of the reason why Pru was a resident at Willow Tree Center. After hearing the report of what happened, he assured Gladys that he would immediately call adult protective services and request a home visit to assess the situation. He also would contact Fenway. Although Gladys felt somewhat better after this telephone call, she was still worried about what would happen to Pru. Later that day, she also wondered if this incident might have a negative effect on her business.

Responses and Commentary on Questions

1. How did Fenway cause harm to Pru and to Gladys?

   The most obvious harm presented in this case was to Pru. Although not all of the background is part of this case, it seems that Fenway contributed to the worsening of Pru's diabetes complications through his negligence. Support for this observation includes his daughter Ireland's belief that the situation was serious enough to warrant removing Pru from her home. In addition, Ireland sought power of attorney over Pru's health affairs. This situation demonstrates that family members also have duty to practice nonmaleficence.

   Fenway also caused Pru great distress by embarrassing her in front of the other residents and Gladys. Pru realized that his behavior could escalate and reluctantly agreed to go home with him. Perhaps she was acting with beneficence because she put her own health and safety at risk to protect others from potential harm. She knew Fenway's temper better than anyone in the facility and chose to leave with him.

Fenway also caused potential harm to Gladys's business. He upset her current residents by making a scene over Pru's situation and disparaged the care that Gladys provided in front of them. In addition, he refused to listen to anything that Gladys said and almost forced Pru to leave Willow Tree Center. His behavior put Gladys in very difficult position, where she had to act both to prevent potential harm to Pru and to protect her business from any legal action.

2. How did Ireland cause harm to Pru and to Gladys?

    Ireland's response was unexpected. She took the initiative to protect her mother's health and safety by placing her at Willow Tree Center and gaining her power of attorney. Yet, when a crisis was at hand, she chose to withdraw from the situation. There could be any number of reasons for her decisions, but her actions placed her mother at risk for physical and emotional harm.

    As for Gladys, she believed that since Ireland had the power to act on her mother's behalf, she would protect Pru. Ireland's response left Gladys with the additional duty of taking steps to go outside the family to seek assistance. It also made her more concerned about the reputation of her business. If she could not count on family members who held legal responsibility, what was she to do?

3. What did Gladys do to reduce the harm for her resident?

    From an administrative position, Gladys had a duty not to intentionally harm her residents. Certainly, in this case, the potential for harm did not come from her, but from the family members. However, she still had an obligation to do as much as she legally could to prevent potential harm to Pru. Gladys had always kept meticulous records on her residents' medical needs and legal status. In addition, she had protocols for dealing with emergencies, and these protocols helped her to have "next steps" in place. While she could not keep Pru at Willow Tree Center against her will, she remained calm and did not escalate the difficulty of Pru's situation. She tried to explain the medication regimen to Fenway, only to receive even more vitriol.

    After Fenway and Pru left, Gladys spoke calmly to her current residents to assure them that she would do everything possible to help Pru. Her composed delivery of the information helped settle her residents, and they returned to their normal morning routine. Gladys then took immediate action using her protocols. She contacted Ireland, who had the legal power to address Pru's situation. However, Ireland's response did not provide any action that would prevent potential harm to Pru. Gladys could have documented the telephone call and left the situation as it was, but she felt a duty to prevent harm. Therefore, she called Pru's physician, who was able to take further action and documented the conversation.

4. How did Pru's physician act with nonmaleficence?

Being well aware of the case, Pru's physician made the decision to contact adult protective services and insist on a home visit. He wanted to have an outside assessment of Pru's current situation. He also hoped that this visit would send a message to Fenway that others were concerned about Pru and wanted her to have a medically, physically, and emotionally safe living environment. In addition, he made the unusual decision to contact Fenway directly and have a "man-to-man" discussion about Pru and her care. This decision might have been risky for his practice, but his conscience would not let him ignore Pru's potential fate.

5. Which management decisions should Gladys take?

Gladys did have policies and procedures in place to address emergencies involving her residents. She also acted appropriately in Pru's case, given the situation. However, a review of those procedures would be in order now. For example, Gladys had always left the side door open so that family members could come to visit during the day and early evening hours. This access worked successfully for years, but in light of Fenway's behavior, changes might be required. Perhaps she could lock the door and install a buzzer to provide better security. In addition, she needed to think about any other ways that she could handle similar situations in the future. Of course, the need for documentation is always present and there is always room for improvement.

The Case of the Beneficent Boss

Think about the chapter information and consider the following questions. Sample responses and commentary will follow the case.

1. Why did Ms. Dee choose to take the actions that she did in Cindy's case?
2. What was the impact of her actions on the staff?
3. What was the impact of her actions on Cindy?
4. What was the impact of Ms. Dee's actions on the bottom line of the New Hope Community Program?

Case Information

Teresa Dee was a human resources director for a small nonprofit organization called the New Hope Community Program (NHCP). NHCP received its funding through United Way and other community sponsors. Its mission was to decrease the relapse rate of substance abusers by providing the knowledge and skills to help clients obtain and keep jobs. Using effective prevention methods to reduce treatment costs for these individuals was also part of the NHCP mission.

Once a client found employment after completing her program, Dee had the responsibility of serving as liaison between the employer and the client. This required frequent follow-up contacts with both parties. She could delegate follow-up duties to appropriate staff, but she tried to do her fair share so that no one was overwhelmed.

One Monday morning, Dee walked out of her office and saw a thin, young, blond, unkempt woman waiting in the reception area. A review of the referral form from St. Dismas Drug Rehabilitation Center revealed that the client's name was Cindy Rumford and that she had only six months' sobriety. She was only 17 years old but already had six arrests for prostitution. Dee's experience told her that Cindy had an uphill struggle ahead at best.

The initial interview was not a positive one. Cindy's appearance and demeanor showed almost no self-confidence and her responses were barely audible. Dee was able to determine that she had not finished high school and had no discernible job skills. She did not know what she wanted to do with the rest of her life. When asked if she was serious about staying sober, Cindy quietly replied, "Well, I guess I can. I want you to help me make it." Such a response was not a good omen for a positive result for this client. Yet, Ms. Dee sensed something in Cindy that warranted further attention. After all, helping people like Cindy was the mission of NHCP.

From that initial intake visit, Dee took particular interest in Cindy. She held a staff meeting to design a plan to meet Cindy's immediate needs for safe housing, clothing, food, and transportation to the program office. After settling on a plan, the staff worked with Cindy so that she had these basic requirements.

Next, Dee explained NHCP's Work for Recovery Program to Cindy. She could sign a contract with the Program to attend classes to complete her GED and learn basic work habits like applying for jobs, maintaining a good business appearance including dress and makeup, and learning skills to interview and communicate appropriately. Once she completed her classes, Cindy was required to work at the Program office for three months.

During Cindy's training period, Dee took special interest in her progress. At first, she seemed to be a passive learner who barely made eye contact with the staff. She did show some interest when an employer came to talk to the class about what he expected from his employees.

The day she passed her GED seemed to begin a real turnaround for Cindy. It was the first time Dee saw her smile.

Cindy's three-month trial employment at the Program began with housekeeping activities. Dee made a point to tell her how well she was doing with her attendance and attention to detail. Gradually, she increased Cindy's responsibilities to include reception and office work. Cindy's confidence seemed to grow with each new responsibility. By the end of her contract-training period, she had become a more confident person with a professional appearance and a ready smile.

Dee contacted those employers whom she knew would be open to giving Cindy an opportunity to continue to build her work skills. After only one interview, a small company hired Cindy as an office assistant. Dee decided to follow up personally on her placement rather than to delegate it to the staff. Although there were a few rough times, Cindy maintained her sobriety and her position. Dee still gets Christmas cards from Cindy thanking her for caring and the difference she made in her life.

Responses and Commentary on Questions

1. Why did Ms. Dee choose to take the actions that she did in Cindy's case?

   Ms. Dee had seen many "Cindys" in her position as human resources director. Some of them completed the program and went on to become sober and productive citizens. Unfortunately, many of them chose to drop out when it became too difficult. Still others completed the program but relapsed when faced with the pressures of the real world. Experience should have made Dee cynical about Cindy's chances. Yet, she chose to act with beneficence. Perhaps she saw something in Cindy's demeanor that others did not see. Perhaps it was just Dee's nature to refrain from generalizing from previous experiences to the current one. Whatever the reason, Dee decided to act with kindness in this case and remain hopeful.

   Ms. Dee was also being true to the mission of her organization and her position as an administrator. Considering its purpose, all of NHCP's activities were rooted in the principle of beneficence. As an administrator, Dee had the obligation to demonstrate its mission in action. Her decision to live the mission rather than just post it on the walls might have added to her already busy workload, but the time she spent with Cindy seemed to make the sacrifice worthwhile. In addition, Dee had the personal satisfaction of knowing that her actions made a difference.

2. What was the impact of her actions on the staff?

   As an administrator in a small organization, Ms. Dee was highly visible to the staff. In addition, her multiple roles ensured that she was not "office bound" but had the opportunity to interact with them on many occasions. Because of this situation, she served as a role model, not just for Cindy, but for the staff as well. It was noticed when she took extra time to praise Cindy for her efforts. It was noticed when she personally followed up on Cindy's status. It was also noticed when she remained positive about Cindy's future in spite of her seemingly long odds. She did not have to preach about the mission of NHCP and what it meant; she lived the mission through her interactions.

Dee's behavior toward staff compared well with her actions toward clients. She listened to their concerns, acted on suggestions that were appropriate and feasible, and gave credit to the staff members who suggested them. She always made a point to acknowledge the work of her team. When there was a staff issue, she held a frank and documented discussion with the individual, which included the development of an action plan for improving the situation. Again, she lived the mission with her staff and her clients.

Because actions really do speak louder than words, Dee set the norm for the organization. Staff members tried to emulate her behaviors and, in turn, used active beneficence in their dealings with their clients. While the relapse rates for all of their clients did not change dramatically, there was a shift to the positive in their yearly statistics. In addition, overall morale seemed to be much more positive and clients seemed more appreciative. The result was that, on most days, the staff was happy to do their meaningful work, and the clients reaped the benefits of their attitudes and actions. Turnover was very low, which saved the organization thousands of dollars in lost productivity, recruitment, and restaffing funds.

Comment: Staff members notice their administrators' behaviors. This should not make one paranoid, but should help to motivate staff. A variation of the Golden Rule works here: Do unto staff well, and it is more likely that the staff will do their jobs well. This means that healthcare administrators must at least understand the jobs that staff do and be willing to "pitch in" when necessary. On a daily basis, if administrators want an environment where beneficence is the norm, then they must choose to practice it in their actions toward others.

In contrast, when administrators treat a client with beneficence but deny beneficence to their staff, they create an environment of inconsistency. The morale of departments can quickly deteriorate when administrators see the staff's efforts as "just doing their jobs." Staff members will also get the message that they are easily replaceable and begin to feel more like minions than professionals. This lack of active beneficence will reinforce an I-IT relationship in the workplace. Because no one really wants to be replaceable, morale will decrease even among even the most dedicated staff. The potential for high turnover and its associated costs will grow, as will the administrator's negative reputation with the higher echelon.

3. What was the impact of her actions on Cindy?

Certainly, Ms. Dee's decision to practice the principle of beneficence made a difference to Cindy. Perhaps Dee was the first person who took a special interest in her well-being. Cindy responded to even the smallest positive comment from Dee. The encouragement bolstered her own determination to stop her cycle of addiction and its consequences.

In addition, Dee made a point to have Cindy's first real-world work experience be with a person who practiced active beneficence. Her new employer continued to foster Cindy's confidence and self-esteem. No one treated her as a "charity case." She became a true employee of the firm and received respect. While there were times when she made errors, her employer gave her assistance to correct any problems. Because of the training and affirmation she received from Dee and the staff, Cindy was able to become a valued employee in her new position. Having a job and the income it provided gave her the opportunity to live a different and healthier lifestyle.

4. What was the impact of Ms. Dee's actions on the bottom line of the New Hope Community Program?

Certainly, one person cannot make or break an organization, but he or she can have a positive impact. In the case of Cindy, Ms. Dee and her staff were able to see that practicing beneficence brought both personal and organizational rewards. While NHCP's success rates were not perfect, the overall environment of beneficence toward clients and staff did produce less staff turnover and better client results. It is true that this decision took more effort and time than "business as usual," but the reward of a positive work environment offset the investment, making it a positive return on investment.

Comment: Sometimes, the small actions make a difference and make a statement. For example, a chief executive officer (CEO) of a major hospital makes a point to pick up any trash seen each morning on the way in from the parking lot. This is a small action indeed, but it carries a large message about pride in an organization. When employees observe or hear about this behavior, they think, "If the CEO can pick up trash, then maybe I should care about this place, too."

Beneficence is cost-effective because actions of charity and kindness far outweigh the costs of time and effort. It seems so easy to do on the surface, yet we all get busy with our daily efforts and crises and sometimes forget that there are humans behind those full-time equivalents. Therefore, the practice of active beneficence requires a daily decision to act within Kant, Frankl, and Buber principles. The organization, your employees, and your career will gain the benefits of this decision.

Web Resources

Classic Version of the Hippocratic Oath
http://www.pbs.org/wgbh/nova/doctors/oath_classical.html

Bullying in the Workplace
http://www.workdoctor.com/problem/

References

American College of Healthcare Executives (ACHE). (2012). *Policy statement: Ethical issues related to a reduction in force*. [Electronic version]. Chicago, IL: Author.

Beauchamp, T. L., & Childress, J. E. (2012). *Principles of biomedical ethics* (7th ed.). New York, NY: Oxford University Press.

Buber, M. (1996). *I and thou*. New York, NY: Touchstone.

Darr, K. (2011). *Ethics in health services management* (5th ed.). Baltimore, MD: Health Professions Press.

Dye, C. F. (2010). *Leadership in healthcare: Essential values and skills (ACHE management)* (2nd ed.). Chicago, IL: Health Administration Press.

Munson, R. (2008). *Intervention and reflection: Basic issues in medical ethics* (8th ed.). Belmont, CA: Thompson Wadsworth.

Niles, N. J. (2013). *Basic concepts of human resource management*. Burlington, MA: Jones & Bartlett Learning.

Summers, J. (2014). Principles of healthcare ethics. In E. E. Morrison & B. Furlong (Eds.). *Health care ethics: Critical issues for the 21st century* (3rd ed., pp. 47–66). Burlington, MA: Jones & Bartlett Learning,

Workplace Bullying Institute. (2012). The WBI definition of workplace bullying. Retrieved from http://www.workplacebullying.org/

CHAPTER 4

Justice

Why does justice have so many definitions?

Points to Ponder

1. What is patient justice? Why is it difficult to practice?
2. What are the different theories concerning distributive justice?
3. How does distributive justice affect a healthcare organization?
4. What does it mean to be a just administrator?

Key Terms

The following is a list of this chapter's key terms. Look for them in bold.

distributive justice

ethicist

justice

market justice

patient justice

staff justice

■ INTRODUCTION AND DEFINITIONS

Administrators need to understand the principle of justice before they can apply it in healthcare settings. When dealing with people, whether they are patients or staff, **justice** is concerned with doing what people perceive to be fair or deserved. This implies an active ethical response in each situation. It means that there is equal treatment for people in equal situations. However, justice does not apply solely to individuals. **Distributive justice** applies to consideration of what is fair and appropriate with respect to allocation of community, state, or national resources. Since groups in American society view distributive justice very differently, this is an area of great controversy for both society in general and the healthcare system in particular. Administrators struggle with different societal and organizational views on distributive justice and must come to a viable compromise for their organizations. This chapter presents information about distributive justice and the differences between social and **market justice**. In addition, it explores various aspects of **patient justice** and **staff justice**.

■ JUSTICE FOR PATIENTS

When individuals enter the healthcare system at any level, they believe that they will receive fair treatment and that the system will meet their needs expeditiously. Patients also expect respectful treatment regardless of their lifestyle or financial circumstances. Egotistically, patients believe that healthcare professionals will do everything they can to heal them. Therefore, patients' primary view of healthcare organizations is that they are places where healing is the primary mission. In their discomfort, fear, and emotional stress, patients must trust in the system as the vehicle for their healing. At least at the initial contact, they are not concerned with the business aspects of health care or the resources that it needs to stay in business.

Even with the passage of the ACA and its promised changes, the U.S. healthcare system might not be able to live up to this idealized patient view. From a treatment standpoint, there can be times when patients will not get the full attention of the system no matter their financial circumstances or diagnosis. For example, in a busy emergency department (ED), a screaming child with an earache might have to wait far longer than his parents determine to be just. This "unfairness" happens when people with more severe emergencies enter the ED at the same time as the child. These critical patients' greater immediate needs give them priority for treatment. While this system of prioritizing is necessary, unless patients understand the reason for the difference in access to treatment, they may view the lack of immediate treatment as unjust.

While patient justice indicates that health care should treat all patients who have the same healthcare issues the same way, it is not always an easy principle to maintain. First, health care is also a business, and not all patients have the ability to pay for its services. Even with the full implementation of the ACA, there will still be an estimated 18 to 20 million uninsured people in the United States. This figure includes exemptions from the requirement for those who are too poor to purchase insurance and those who are eligible for Medicaid, but are not enrolled (O'Brien, 2014). In addition, undocumented immigrants and individuals who choose to pay a fine rather purchase private insurance are included in this estimate. Who will pay for care when these individuals need it?

Even if they can pay for services, some patients stretch the professional's ability to apply the principle of patient justice. Their personalities or life choices might offend the professional's personal values and sense of professionalism. Yet, there is an expectation that these health professionals will act with justice even when patients demonstrate unpleasant behaviors, are filthy, or are verbally abusive. Health professionals must also be just when patients are arrogant and demanding.

Such patient behaviors should not affect justice, but they do. The daily exposure to demanding, unpleasant, or challenging patients puts a definite strain on the ability to act with justice. Some professionals react to this strain by using labeling and dark humor as a protection. For example, healthcare professions may use the terms "GOMER" (get out of my emergency room) and "frequent flier" (a patient who makes repeated visits to the ED) instead of a patient's name. People become "its" instead of humans when justice is strained.

Active patient justice also requires positive consistency. This means that healthcare professionals strive to treat each patient with dignity and justice, as Kant and others would advocate. Doing so requires careful observation and discernment to determine the best way to act with justice for each person. Practical wisdom is appropriate when faced with patient justice challenges. For example, one patient might find a simple touch on the shoulder reassuring, while another might find it offensive. Whether one is a clinician or an administrator, the goal should be to enter into an I-THOU relationship while in the patient's presence. In other words, the patient should be the most important thing at that moment of encounter.

However, the ability to use careful observation and positive consistency is not innate. It must be taught in schools by focusing on the human elements of care and not just clinical or management skills. The workplace must also reinforce positive consistency through role modeling, in-service education, and frequent reminders. In addition, work practices such as shift scheduling and taking meal breaks can decrease "compassion fatigue" and increase the likelihood that patient justice will be the norm in healthcare facilities.

■ DISTRIBUTIVE JUSTICE

Definitions

The principle of distributive justice involves the appropriate and fair distribution of the benefits offered by a society. It also includes the distribution of the burdens for these benefits (Beauchamp & Childress, 2012). Just what does this mean? In health care, the available benefits are not limitless and many resources are scarce.

Distributive justice reflects how society decides who gets the benefits of healthcare resources, how much they get, and who pays for them.

Distributive justice in health care seems simple on the surface. People who need medical services should get them, and those with the same diagnosis should get equal treatment. However, the United States is also capitalistic and has a market-driven economy. Therefore, how it defines who needs assistance and which mechanisms are used for providing that assistance may be complex. For example, if people have risky lifestyles and do not take good care of their health, should they receive health care? Is the population responsible for care if people do not pay attention to their diets? In a market-driven economy, it simply does not make good business sense to pay for care regardless of lifestyle choices. Conversely, is it just to allow people to suffer and die prematurely because they did not follow all of the rules for good health? Who decides which personal behaviors can keep patients from receiving care?

Certainly, access to health care is a factor in preventing and controlling disease. In the United States, there is a strong link between insurance coverage and access to health care. While the ACA has the potential to improve access, the revised system will still rely on the employer-provided insurance system (Sultz & Young, 2014). Employers will still offer insurance, and some will be required to offer this benefit to their employees or pay fines. In addition, those persons who, in the past, lost coverage because they met the coverage limits of their policies, or because they had a preexisting condition, should now be able to have healthcare coverage. However, the costs of premiums, increased copayments, and other changes in the patient's financial responsibilities may present a mixed bag in terms of patient justice. While increased financial responsibility may decrease the unnecessary use of health care for some, thereby saving unnecessary expenditures, it may also mean that patients do not access care when needed. Postponing needed care could contribute to greater acuity of disease when it is treated and lead to additional pain and suffering for individuals.

Theories of Distributive Justice

What is the fair distribution of healthcare resources for Americans? There needs to be a discussion of the differing views of distributive justice and rights prevalent in American thinking to answer this question. The foundation for the varying views on distributive justice comes from different definitions of what is fair from societal traditions. A discussion of some of these views is necessary to connect describe distributive justice in the U.S. healthcare system.

First, think about the utilitarian position. Utilitarians tend to view justice in health care as taking actions that can provide the greatest amount of benefit to people or prevent the greatest amount of harm.

They favor public health activities such as sanitation, air pollution control, and protection against epidemics, which would improve the health for the entire population. They also find the provision of basic services to all as a form of distributive justice.

However, in the purest form, the utilitarian position might support denying access and treatment to the frail elderly or the most gravely ill. In this view, these population groups use a disproportionate amount of scarce healthcare resources and tend to have poor treatment outcomes. Therefore, the resources used for their care might better benefit society if they were devoted to prevention programs and thereby prevent the greatest harm to the greatest number of people. However, this analysis certainly does not appeal to the families of individuals in vulnerable situations or to those forced to deny them care.

Market justice sees the distribution of healthcare resources in a different way. According to this view, health care is a business and operates in a free market, so its resources should go to those who have the ability to pay. If individuals have earned the necessary funds by their work, they should be able to purchase what they want from the system. This idea fits with the idea of fairness as it relates to contribution, which means that individuals should be able to purchase what they desire using the money that they earned. It also relates to the idea that those who put in the effort to earn money should be able to spend it on what they need or want from the healthcare system (Munson, 2008). In addition, people are rational and, through discussion with their physicians, can make economically sound choices for their own care.

In a system characterized by market justice, the business of health care should be able to provide services or deny them so as to make a profit. Physicians and other healthcare providers should also have the right to provide such care or to refuse it based on the individual's ability to pay. There is no moral obligation to provide health care anymore than there is a moral obligation to provide any other commodity (such as a home, a coat, or a hamburger).

Market justice fits well with the bottom line in running any business. In a business, the organization must make payroll and expenses, and stockholders or the community must receive a fair return on their investments. To survive in a competitive environment, there must also be a sound fiscal foundation. While healthcare organizations might feel compassion for people and their situations, they still have to keep the doors of their facilities open. How can one run a business without paying customers?

Because American culture uses a capitalism model, on the surface this approach makes a good deal of sense. However, society also treats health care as a moral good and not just a market good. Therefore, the public expects healthcare institutions to maintain a well-run business and still care for the needs of the community it services. If a hospital's mission statement reads "Profit Is Number One," the media would certainly portray the facility as "Scrooge Hospital." Certainly, federal and state agencies would not look favorably on denying access to patients, especially under the provisions of the ACA. Therefore, the strict market view of distributive justice, while it has some merit, cannot be the only principle for decision making about the use of health resources.

Rawls would argue that distributive justice means that health care must consider need in its definition of distributive justice. That is, people should have fair access to health care when such care is needed. However, not all persons have the same ability to access healthcare services because of economic or other barriers. Society has an obligation to do what it can to eliminate or reduce those barriers, which is the intent of the ACA. Restoring and maintaining health also allows individuals to be full members of society and to contribute to the good of all of its members (Beauchamp & Childress, 2012).

However, the position of fairness based on need does not mean that health care should provide everything to everyone. It does not mean that just because someone wants a "tummy tuck" or Botox injections, he or she should get these procedures. Instead, it means that, regardless of social or insurance status, persons should have access to adequate basic health care. In a capitalistic model, those who have insurance or the financial means should also be able to purchase services beyond this basic level.

Already one can see a problem with this position. The term "adequate basic health care" is incredibly vague. People of high ethical thinking and an understanding of the U.S. economic system have argued about its definition for years. Often this argument leads to a discussion about what basic health care is not, rather than what it is. Certainly, one can see this discussion played out in some of the provisions of the ACA. There are debates about what must be included in the health benefit exchanges, the differences between a bronze plan and a platinum plan, and what constitutes a basic plan (Kaiser Family Foundation, 2013). The ethics of all of these options are all part of the conversation and include various arguments for distributive justice. The question for many is "How will Americans finance health care?"

Social justice can be the foundation for decisions about how to distribute goods and services in a community or an organization. It has its root is Rawls's ideas about the functioning of a just society and is connected to what the United States holds true in the Bill of Rights of the country's Constitution. Social justice looks at the idea of equality—that is, the notion that everyone should receive needed health care and should share in the financial burden of providing that care (Munson, 2008). The efforts of the ACA to provide access to health care for the greatest number of people with the expectation that every person will participate in health insurance shows the application of social justice.

The basis for this law's success is the concept that health care is a right in a just society and that the country's citizens are willing to share in the financing necessary to create this right. This position often seems counter to the United States' foundation in capitalism and individualism, but it is often part of the mission statements of healthcare facilities, ranging from hospitals to public health departments.

Issues for Healthcare Organizations

The application of distributive justice brings concerns at the healthcare organizational level. Given the financial and ethical challenges presented in the great changes associated with the ACA, organizations need to redefine justice or fair treatment for patients. This definition should consider both ethical and fiscal situations. What is the organization's obligation to its community for just care? How will it balance its fiduciary obligation to its stockholders, payers, and others with this obligation? How does a healthcare organization define basic health care for those it serves? How will the provisions of the ACA affect the organization's ability to practice distributive justice? The answers to these questions require an investment of time and resources to formulate an ethically sound position on justice. Organizations might even need to use an **ethicist** or specialist on ethics on a consultant basis to assist in defining positions on these issues. If an administrator serves in a religious-based facility, the answers to these questions can form a major part of its mission statement.

Distributive justice on an organizational level goes beyond theory, discussion, and mission statements. For example, a facility might have invested a good deal of capital and staffing in its oncology services. It might pride itself on this effort and even advertise these services on radio and television. However, its advertisement campaign can backfire if too many of these high-risk patients use the services. What if, even in the ACA era, patients seeking care have no insurance? The community expects the healthcare system to provide just and compassionate treatment, yet organizations must also be fiscally sound even when they receive less revenue for services rendered.

What does this mean for the practicing healthcare administrator (HCA) when serving both high-risk and high-profit patients? First, the organization must construct its definition of just treatment in this case. For some organizations, each service is a business entity, so it must make a profit like all other entities. In this case, administrators would have to balance the number of Medicare, Medicaid, and other patients against the well insured to ensure that there is still a profit margin. Administrators also need to engage in strategic planning so that effective, efficient, safe, and ethical care is the product of healthcare institutions. This goal is difficult to reach, but is a significant consideration in the ACA era.

For some facilities, the service of high-risk patients is the mission. The mission of faith-based institutions, for example, often includes service to these patients. If high-risk patients are part of their mission, facilities must concentrate on balancing the ethics side of the equation with the ability to break even financially. They must find the funds to treat these individuals and may require community-based fundraising strategies.

■ STAFF JUSTICE

The concept of justice also concerns fairness and equity for employees. To address staff justice, administrators should recognize that they have power associated with their position (title power). They also have power in their leadership style (subtle power). When one has a title, it carries both responsibility and accountability. Titles also provide authority that is necessary to do the business of an administrator. For example, title power allows administrators to distribute scarce resources and to practice justice in their decisions. If administrators increase their power by using discretionary funds to reward those employees who curry favor, they do not use fairness in these decisions. In contrast, administrators could develop policies and procedures that use work production or other universal criteria to make decisions about "who gets what." The latter position not only demonstrates applied ethics. but can also have a positive effect on productivity and morale (Schissler Manning, 2003).

The power to create policies, affect the lives of patients, and have certain privileges (Schissler Manning, 2003) is part of the administrator's title power as well. These powers are necessary to provide patient care and conduct the business of health care, but they also offer opportunities to practice ethics-based management. For example, when administrators assume certain positions of authority, their position may grant them certain additional "perks" such as a higher salary, a bonus plan, and a reserved parking space. The privileges that go with the administrative title serve as a reward for one's greater responsibility, but they come with the ethical temptation of enhancing self-interests over the benefit of the patient or staff member. Certainly, practical wisdom and a healthy conscience are essential to avoid these temptations. In addition, administrators must always keep the mission foremost in their minds as they make decisions within the scope of their responsibilities.

Along with title power, administrators have subtle power. The definition for this type of power is not found in a job description; rather, this power stems from how administrators present themselves, what they say, and how they say it. Their presence, words, and actions can be perceived as fair and just—or just the opposite. Effectiveness of communication, group dynamics, and staff members' sense of their own power are all part of subtle power (Schissler Manning, 2003).

Subtle power can also demonstrate administrators' ability to practice ethics and staff justice. For example, the overall climate of the workplace determines expected behavior and the level of civility practiced among staff members and between staff members and patients. In addition, administrators need to be concerned that their behaviors are enhancing fairness and decreasing the likelihood of inequity. For example, since administrators are human, they may like some staff members more than they may like others. It would be tempting to have lunch with the favored members to the exclusion of the others. However, because of subtle power, exclusionary lunches are more than just soup and salad; they provide a connotation of favored status and unequal distribution of benefits and burdens. Whether this is true or not does not matter. There is an image of the "in-group" and the "out-group"— a perception that can lead to staff resentment and alienation (Schissler Manning, 2003).

What can administrators do to practice staff justice? Can they use their subtle power and their position power to create a just work environment? Certainly, staff justice is possible and essential when administrators work in the current healthcare environment with its multiple layers of change. The first advice is that administrators need to read. Policies and procedures are not just pieces of paper; they form an agreement about to conduct the business of the department. Administrators need to review policies frequently to assess their appropriateness for current circumstances. In addition, the administrator needs to ask the following questions about policies; "Are they clear?" "Are they just?" "Do they make things work more smoothly?" "Do the staff members know what they are?"

How can administrators know the answers to these questions? They can do something radical (or sometimes radical in a healthcare setting) and ask the staff members for information. If administrators have instilled a climate of trust, staff members will provide important information on what is working and what is not. Administrators can also enhance their subtle power through "management by walking around" and observation of the work processes. Some healthcare facilities even have the administrators spend one day doing their employees' jobs (nonclinical, of course) so that they truly understand policy in action.

If policies and procedures are no longer appropriate or effective, then administrators must be willing to reword or discard them. Again, the administrator can use staff members' input to assist in reviewing drafts for clarity and practicality. In addition, administrators need to schedule a policy review meeting so that everyone is up-to-date on revised or new policies. This communication step is essential in the current time of rapid change in health care. When staff members have a void in knowledge and understanding, they may fill this void with false or misleading information, which in turn can prove costly to quality patient care and to the bottom line.

Next, administrators must plan. In the ACA era, administrators have to make "right now" decisions, but that should not be their entire administrative style. Immediacy may be necessary but it does not afford the time to think about the justice of the situation. Part of the role for ethics-based administrators is a willingness to consider the big picture when making decisions and an ability to communicate the decisions' connection to the mission of the organization. This is a challenge in the current healthcare environment, but ethics-based administrators must rise to meet it.

Here is a practical and quick planning example. When administrators hold a meeting, they need to think about more than the agenda. They must consider what they are going to say and how it will affect other people. They must deliver news (good or bad) in a way that is fair to all. In addition, administrators must remember that they send a message that goes beyond their words. Therefore, being organized and well spoken carries its own message. Having "talking points" to remember to emphasize certain words is helpful for staying on message. It is also helpful to conduct a mental rehearsal of what HCAs will say so that they appear confident and prepared for the presentation.

As part of fostering staff justice, administrators must also write well. They should think about how staff members, patients, and family members might interpret their written communication. The interpretation of justice should be part of this assessment. For example, if there is a need for different treatment for some people, is there a well-stated explanation for this distinction? Administrators' written communication should be a tool for efficiency and just treatment, and should not create problems in staff relations.

In addition, administrators should remember that their writing lives forever. This is especially true in the electronic age, where people can retrieve communication even after someone deletes it. Therefore, each document serves a permanent record of the administrator's decisions and applications of policy. Administrators should not be constantly worried about verbiage, but they also should not write documents that staff members, patients, or families could interpret as being unjust or unethical. Additionally, in a time of great change, written communications become even more important. It is important to note that change may create an emotional response that contributes to misinterpretation and misunderstanding. Therefore, additional forms of communication (written, oral, and visual) may be needed for clarification and to maintain overall morale.

Ethics-based administrators should not forget the significance of e-mails, Tweets, Facebook posts, and other areas of electronic communication. Currently, society is interested in "right now" communication.

While "right now" has its advantages, it also has some drawbacks and can lead to unjust behavior. For example, suppose an administrator arrives at the office late after a bad start to his or her morning and an even worse commute. He or she opens his or her e-mail and find a message that "irritates the administrator's last nerve." The temptation is to fire off an immediate response that reflects what the administrator thinks of this person or his or her message. There may also be a temptation to Tweet something that reflects the administrator's frustration with the person or the situation. This, however, is a "be careful" situation.

First, people can read and interpret e-mails in many ways. In the previous example, the intent of the e-mail might not be negative. Even if the intent of the e-mail was to cause the recipient discomfort, pettiness and retribution do not reflect well on the administrator. In the case of instant communication, with its subsequent permanence, the best policy may be to "take ten" before responding. Additionally, the administrator could use other forms of communication to clarify the e-mail message. Although it may seem "old fashioned," the administrator could telephone the person and get clarification before "jumping to administrative conclusions." This clarification may avoid ill feelings and prevent documentation of unjust communication with the sender of the e-mail.

The timing of an administrator's communication may also lead to a perception of staff injustice. For example, suppose downsizing is planned in the organization. Administrators should consider the employees' position. If the administrator was the employee being laid off, when would he or she want to receive written notice? Would the administrator want to know at 8:00 A.M. in front of all his or her peers or just before leaving work on a Friday? If this had to happen, would the administrator want it to be on the day before Christmas Eve or after the holidays? Better yet, would the administrator rather receive the news after a discussion with his or her administrator so that it is not an unpleasant and public surprise? These questions are important to consider when practicing staff justice. No matter the nature of the news, administrators should take the time to consider the employees' view before deciding the timing and delivery of the message.

Finally, to practice staff justice, administrators must become keen observers. Management by walking around is not just a catch phrase. Administrators should know what is really happening in their workplaces. To understand how best to observe, it may be helpful to observe an administrator who practices staff justice. In addition, an administrator might ask this person to serve as an informal ethics mentor. Having a person who will serve as a sounding board could help the administrator think aloud and can assist him or her in making just staff decisions.

Reading, planning, writing, and observing are not the only skills that administrators need to exhibit justice, but these skills form a solid foundation for the application of staff justice. Administrators also need to conduct periodic self-assessments. When making decisions that have an impact on staff, they should ask, "Do I have the facts?" and "Am I being fair to all those involved?" Likewise, administrators have to be willing to explain their decisions, rather than using their power as a justification. The role of a just administrator is not an easy one, especially in a time of great change. However, consistently practicing justice does make for a more positive and productive workplace.

Summary

Justice is not an easy concept to implement in a healthcare setting, especially in a time of great change. Healthcare administrators face the challenge of balancing mission and margin in an era of changing legal requirements, increasingly complex and costly technology, changing patient numbers and expectations, and greater scrutiny. In this environment, practicing justice requires more than a well-written policy manual. Administrators must consider the whole range of justice, from the distribution of goods and services to the treatment of employees. This consideration will require the use of practical wisdom on many levels so that the healthcare organization can balance its obligation to the principle of justice with its fiscal responsibility to the organization's ownership and to the community.

Cases for Your Consideration

The Case of the Studious Sophomore

Think about the chapter information and consider the following questions. Sample responses and commentary will follow the case.

1. What were the violations of patient justice in this case?

2. What role did communication play in patient justice?

3. If you were the administrator, what would you have done in this situation?

Case Information

It was still early in the Friday night emergency room shift (11 P.M.) when Monroe Tyler, NP, and Jantelle McGee, RN, escaped to the break room for their pick-me-up espressos. "If I see one more weepy, puking UG [undergraduate], I think I'll scream," said Jantelle. "How can they be that drunk this early in the shift?"

"Just wait until later," said the Monroe. "When the concert gets going, we'll have the whole Molly crew in here. I remember when we had the Ecstasy crowd, but this kind of MDMA is even worse."

"When will they grow up and stop wasting their parent's money?" said Jantelle.

At 11 P.M. that same night, Bunny Sanders was trying to understand Chapter 7 in organic chemistry. She already read the chapter twice and it was bleeding highlighter. She really wanted to throw the book out the window, but organic chemistry was part of the requirements to be a forensic pathologist and that was her career goal.

All of a sudden, Bunny felt her stomach roll. She barely made it to the bathroom before the violent vomiting started. As she knelt in front of the toilet, she felt as if she was coming apart. When she tried to get up, she felt the room spin around in her head began to hurt. The pain in her head made her feel like she was dying! Bunny called her roommate, who took one look at her and went to get the car. The situation clearly required a trip to the ER.

After checking in with the ER receptionist, Bunny waited for someone to see her. Although her wait was only an hour and a half, it felt like days. The pain was getting worse and her dizziness was increasing. Finally, someone called her back to the examination room. The first person she met was Monroe Tyler. After listening to Bunny describe her symptoms, Monroe began to ask about how much she had to drink that evening. He also asked if she went to the concert and if she had been taking any Mollies.

Bunny, still in a great deal of pain, could not figure out why Monroe was asking these questions. She tried to explain that she was in her room studying organic chemistry when her symptoms began. However, Monroe just looked at her and said, "Yah, right." Monroe left Bunny in the examining room for a few minutes. When he returned, he said, "You're just dehydrated. Go home and drink fluids and take some of these." He handed her a sample of a painkiller.

Bunny wondered what had just happened. Why did the doctor ask such strange questions? Why did he not believe her? Bunny's roommate took her back to the apartment and Bunny tried to get some rest. However, two hours later, her roommate heard a noise coming from Bunny's room. When she opened the door, she found Bunny almost unconscious and her body jerking with seizures. The roommate called 911. When the emergency personnel arrived, the roommate insisted that they take Bunny to a different hospital for treatment.

Responses and Commentary on Questions

1. What were the violations of patient justice in this case?

   First, there was no level of respect or courtesy in Bunny's treatment. To begin with, Monroe Tyler did not introduce himself and give her his credentials. Therefore, Bunny assumed that he was a physician. In addition, he gave no rationale for the questions he was asking her. Although these questions may have been important for her diagnosis, she had no way of knowing why Monroe asked them.

In addition, Monroe made assumptions about Bunny based on her age and student status. Because of his previous experience that evening, he generalized her symptoms to fit his assumptions about her and her behaviors. He did not order any tests to rule out other explanations for her symptoms, including migraines or even certain forms of brain tumor. Instead, Monroe sent Bunny her way with a prescription that did not address the true problem she was experiencing.

2. What role did communication play in patient justice?

Communication certainly played an important role in this case. It seems obvious that Monroe did not exercise patient-centered care and appropriate communication. While he had experienced a very busy night in the ER, his fatigue was not an excuse for poor communication and a lack of courtesy. Monroe appeared to have "jumped the gun" on making a diagnosis because he clearly did not have a complete picture of Bunny's symptoms. This lack of accurate communication meant that he disregarded any alternative explanation for the symptoms and failed to conduct any other kind of assessment before he dismissed Bunny with painkillers and a recommendation for hydration.

One can also see the evidence of stereotypical thinking in this case. This kind of miscommunication happens when practitioners or administrators generalize from one set of experiences with patients to all patients. Certainly, Bunny was not a sophomore student who spent her weekends in the bars and at concerts where she could use Mollies. However, because of her age and student status, Monroe treated her as if she were just another irritating undergraduate. The case makes an argument for making a conscious decision to regard each patient as an individual. Certainly, Frankl, Kant, and many other ethics theorists would support the idea of patient respect and just treatment.

Communication was also a factor with Bunny. First, she did not ask any questions about who was treating her. When Monroe did not introduce himself, she just assumed he was a doctor and made no comment. When Monroe asked her questions that she thought were unusual or even insulting, she did not ask why those questions were necessary for diagnosis. Given her age and experience, it would be common for her to assume that Monroe had the right to ask these personal questions, but she still did not understand their purpose. In addition, when given the advice and the painkiller, she did not ask for more information about what the drug was and how to take it. Perhaps at this point her pain level was such that she just wanted to get home and avoid any other contact with this "doctor."

The case illustrates the need for both the patient and the professional to have a dialogue rather than a one-way conversation. Patient justice should also consider the ability of the patient to feel comfortable when asking questions of professionals. In addition, patients, no matter what their age or status, deserve the courtesy of having disclosure concerning who is treating them and why the treatment is given. Even though ER staff work many hours under extraordinary conditions, patient justice requires that each patient receive the basics including respect and accurate communication.

3. If you were the administrator, what would you have done in this situation?

Clearly, this case illustrates the need for policies and procedures related to patient justice and appropriate communication in the ER. Perhaps the situation in the ER warrants more than just a policy review. It may be necessary to look at things like staff scheduling so that staff members who work under high-stress conditions have the opportunity to take more breaks or have shorter shifts. Making sure that those who serve to help patients at their most critical point in life are at their best skill and communication levels may save the facility from causing harm to patients through mistreatment or misdiagnosis.

If the administrator becomes aware of the situation through a complaint from Bunny or her family, he or she should confer with the director of the emergency department and the hospital attorney. The director would then have a discussion with Monroe about the situation and hear his version of what happened. In addition, the attorney may need to take depositions depending on the nature of the complaint. Actions by the director could lead to Monroe's dismissal from the ER staff or other appropriate action. In addition, ER staff training on communication and patient justice would be necessary to avoid future situations where negative attitudes could affect patient care.

The Case of the Just Downsize

Think about the chapter information and consider the following questions. Sample responses and commentary will follow the case.

1. How did Mr. Muggs prepare to handle the situation with justice?

2. If you were a staff member, how would you feel about Mr. Muggs's actions?

Case Information

Jerry Muggs, director of a public health program called the Youth Anti-Smoking Project, had a staff of five extremely dedicated people. They were so dedicated that they often worked long hours without even a thought of overtime. Even the administrative assistant did extra duty by traveling to program sites to provide support to the three health educators. Unfortunately, the state health department had just decided that a reduction in force was required for all programs. Muggs received a transfer to another position, but his whole department was to receive a reduction in force. Existing staff in other programs would deal with smoking prevention for young people. How could he deliver this news and keep his sense of justice? How could he prevent any unpleasant or even violent reactions from the staff?

First, Muggs was somewhat relieved by the fact that this decision would not be a total surprise for his staff. He kept them informed of the communications from the state and its deliberations about downsizing. Still, he knew that the news would be painful. Therefore, he immediately contacted the state office to get up-to-date information on its reduction in force plan. He asked for detailed information about the timetable, benefits, and salary packages. He also received information on the possibility for staff to transfer to other departments. Muggs wanted all information possible so that he could provide current and accurate answers for the staff.

Knowing that not all of the members of his staff were financially independent, Muggs wanted to see what else he could do before he broke the bad news. He researched community agencies that might be of help and even contacted the local university to see if its career center could provide a consultant for outplacement services. Because he could anticipate the emotional response to the news, he created information packets so that staff members could have reference materials to use after the meeting. After several sleepless nights, Muggs scheduled a staff meeting.

During the meeting, Muggs remained calm as he told the entire staff the news and expressed his sadness about it. He allowed some time for reaction before he gave them information about their options. Because he was prepared, he was able to answer their questions and give ideas for additional resources.

During the weeks that followed, Muggs worked with each staff member to assist in any way that he could. The staff, while upset at their change in circumstances, told him how much they appreciated his efforts. Even though this was one of the most difficult times of his administrative career, Muggs felt that he did what he could to handle the situation with justice.

Responses and Commentary on Questions

1. How did Mr. Muggs prepare to handle the situation with justice?

First, Muggs provided information to his staff before the elimination decision. He kept them informed about downsizing discussions to keep the secrecy issue to a minimum. While this was somewhat risky on his part, Muggs knew his staff's level of dedication and trusted them. The decision to create a flow of communication in this important area actually made Muggs's job easier when he had to break the bad news. While it was unwelcome, it was not a total shock.

Muggs also went beyond what he had to do to comply with the wishes of the state. He actually planned his words and actions to anticipate the needs of his staff. Certainly, he was not required to try to get outplacement assistance for them, but he did. Because of Muggs's altruism, the staff was better able to adjust to what they had to do and appreciated his efforts on their behalf. They did not blame him or the state for their fate, but understood that they were part of a larger situation. His preparation made a difficult situation much more palatable.

2. If you were a staff member, how would you feel about Mr. Muggs's actions?

First, remember that losing your job is one of life's most stressful events. Even though you had information about the state's plans, you really did not believe that downsizing would happen to you. You might wonder if there was something wrong with your performance in the department that influenced the state to choose your department from all of the others. Your reaction might mirror the stages of grief identified by Kubler-Ross (1997) and others. Therefore, you might experience denial, bargaining, anger, sadness, and finally, acceptance. For the short term, you would be miserable.

Yet, you would have to respect Muggs's efforts on your behalf. Because he had earned your trust in the past and formed a strong working relationship with the team, you believed him when he explained the circumstances of the reduction in force. You wanted to be angry with him, but somehow you just could not blame him for the decision. You would then be able to try to make the best of a bad situation and move on to the next stage of your career and your life.

Web Resources

Kaiser Family Foundation
http://www.kff.org

Patient Care Rights
http://www.aha.org/advocacy-issues/communicatingpts/pt-care-
   partnership.shtml

References

Beauchamp, T. L., & Childress, J. E. (2012). *Principles of biomedical ethics* (7th ed.). New York, NY: Oxford University Press.

Kaiser Family Foundation. (2013). *Focus on health reform: Summary of the Affordable Care Act.* Available at http://www.kff.org

Kubler-Ross, E. (1997). *On death and dying.* New York, NY: Scribner.

Munson, R. (2008). *Intervention and reflection: Basic issues in medical ethics* (8th ed.). Belmont, CA: Thompson Wadsworth.

O'Brien, R. L. (2014). A new era of health care: The ethics of healthcare reform. In E. E. Morrison & B. Furlong (Eds.). *Health care ethics: Critical issues for the 21st century* (3rd ed., pp. 363–374). Burlington, MA: Jones & Bartlett Learning.

Schissler Manning, S. (2003). *Ethical leadership in human services: A multi-dimensional approach.* New York, NY: Pearson Education.

Sultz, H. A., & Young, K. M. (2014). *Health care USA: Understanding its organization and delivery* (8th ed.). Burlington, MA: Jones & Bartlett Learning.

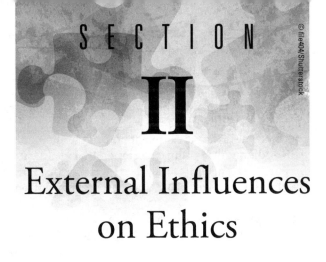

SECTION II

External Influences on Ethics

■ INTRODUCTION

In the era of the ACA, the external environment has an almost unprecedented influence on the operation of healthcare organizations. Because of the nature of its business, the healthcare organization cannot function in isolation. It must understand that its customer base is unique and potentially includes all of the community it serves. In addition, it must understand that the issues that affect the community also affect healthcare facilities.

For example, if the healthcare facility is located in an urban area where social issues of overcrowding, crime, and poverty exist, these circumstances must be included in its business planning. If it is located in a remote rural area, maldistribution of professionals and distance add to its treatment challenges. With the current emphasis on population health and prevention, knowledge of community issues becomes more significant.

The ACA also brings even greater attention to the business of health care and its practices. Patients, their families, and the community in general are now able to access quality information about healthcare institutions and providers. In addition, there is the risk of greater exposure of medical errors and less than high-quality practices through television, the Internet, and other media. Information about quality, cost, and effectiveness is not secret. Therefore, healthcare administrators (HCAs) must be aware of the values and standards needed to balance quality care and fiscal responsibility.

In addition to the ACA requirements, local and state governments and various branches of the federal system provide standards for practice. These agencies include The Joint Commission and the National Committee for Quality Assurance. External agencies are concerned with the provision of care, patient rights, acceptable business practices, credentialing of healthcare professionals, payment for services, and ethical and legal issues. Healthcare administrators must also respond to quality and performance demands from these and other external agencies. However, their standards are often copious, conflicting, and challenging to a business that must maintain profitability and provide patient care. In addition, there is an expectation that healthcare entities will be self-regulating. Therefore, they need to have their own internal standards that serve to articulate appropriate behavior within the organization.

This section discusses how external forces influence behaviors in healthcare entities and their ethics. The *Ethics Challenges in the ACA Era* chapter presents ethical implications of the greatest change in health care in the last 48 years: the Affordable Care Act of 2010. It includes the viewpoints of the public, hospitals, physicians, and insurance companies and offers advice on how to be ethics ready. The *Market Forces and Ethics* chapter explores how market forces—including general market forces, managed care, and the baby boomers—influence the ethics of healthcare administration. In addition, there is a discussion of the ethics issues of integrated medicine (IM).

The *Community Responsibility and Ethics* chapter provides insight into health care's responsibility to the community and the attempts to hold healthcare organizations accountable for meeting that responsibility. It also discusses ethics issues related to advocacy and staff competency.

The *Technology and Ethics* chapter gives a brief overview of some of the current and anticipated advances in technology and includes a discussion of ethical implications for these areas. It pays particular attention to the ethical issues related to information technology and the protection of the patient medical record.

External forces are complex and can conflict. Because healthcare administrators work in a business in which trust is the main commodity, they cannot ignore or de-emphasize the influence of community responsibility. Yet, there is an expectation that healthcare administrators will run their businesses so as to provide high-quality products that meet community needs and create a profit for the healthcare organization. With greater scrutiny from external forces, the temptation to violate ethics for the sake of expediency increases. Successful healthcare administrators will balance ethics with the business of health care; they will be persons of both integrity and business expertise.

CHAPTER 5

Ethics Challenges in the ACA Era

What new ethics challenges will the ACA bring?

Points to Ponder

1. How has the Affordable Care Act (ACA) of 2010 changed the U.S. healthcare system?
2. Which ethics challenges will be present in the ACA era?
3. How will healthcare administrators prepare themselves for implementation of the ACA?

Key Terms

The following is a list of this chapter's key terms. Look for them in bold.

Affordable Care Act (ACA) of 2010
health benefit exchange

individual mandate
mandate
state sovereignty

■ INTRODUCTION AND DEFINITIONS

The U.S. healthcare industry is facing a flurry of changes that will have profound effects on its delivery of care and fiscal position. Currently, the profound of these changes is the **Affordable Care Act (ACA) of 2010**. This act is actually two bills that, when fully implemented, will create a different type of U.S. healthcare system and affect the lives of millions of patients and healthcare providers. These two bills, which were signed into law by President Barack Obama in March 2010, are the Patient Protection and Affordable Care Act and the Healthcare and Education Reconciliation Act. These acts work in tandem to affect the delivery and funding of U.S. healthcare services. In a uniquely American way, the ACA seeks to affect both the delivery and the financing of the country's healthcare system so that Americans will receive greater access to services.

Selker and Wasser (2014) describe the ACA as a national experiment in health policy. This legislation, one of the most debated and hotly contested acts in recent years, challenges the entire healthcare system. Its implementation requires the cooperation of federal and state agencies and all aspects of the healthcare industry, from educational institutions to physician practices. Because of the depth of change and the time required for implementation, the outcomes of the ACA are not entirely predictable.

Given the nature of the ACA, it is not possible to discuss all of its ethical ramifications. Therefore, this chapter will provide a brief history of efforts toward healthcare reform and their outcomes. The key elements of the ACA are summarized, followed by a discussion of the ethical considerations for the act. Differing ethics positions on the ACA legislation are included in the discussion to represent those affected by the act, including the public, states, hospitals, physicians, and insurance companies. While it is not possible to review all 10 titles of the ACA legislation, the individual mandate is included and discussed from an ethics view. Finally, the future of the ACA and its ethics concerns is considered in the chapter, and ethics readiness advice is provided.

■ SETTING THE STAGE: A BRIEF HISTORY

The first attempt to provide health care for Americans began shortly after the Revolutionary War. In 1798, Congress passed legislation requiring ship owners to buy medical insurance for their crews. In addition, they could not deduct the cost of this coverage from the sick crewmembers' pay (Emanuel, 2014). Efforts toward national health reform and universal coverage for Americans began with Teddy Roosevelt in the 1880s, emerging as a national issue during the progressive era. This healthcare insurance coverage model, which was developed by economists, was supported by the American Medical Association (AMA), a professional organization for physicians. Opposition to this reform included those who provided some form of private health benefits (funeral coverage) and labor unions. Ultimately, this early effort was defeated when the United States entered into World War I. American saw the proposed provisions of this legislation as much too "German" at a time when the German army was ravaging Europe (Emanuel, 2014; Parks, 2012; Shi & Singh, 2015).

Debates about the merits of national health care continued through the Franklin Roosevelt presidency. Under his administration, Senators Wagner, Murray, and Dingle introduced a bill for comprehensive healthcare coverage to include hospitalization and physician services. This bill, in which coverage would have been financed through a payroll tax, was never voted on by Congress. In 1945, President Harry Truman urged Congress to pass national healthcare legislation through his National Health Insurance bill. This legislation was deemed socialism, and Congress never voted on the bill (Emanuel, 2014; Shi & Singh, 2015).

In more recent times, the Clinton administration attempted to create healthcare reform (Emanuel, 2014; Shi & Singh, 2015). President Bill Clinton established a national taskforce to develop a proposal for comprehensive health care that involved more than 500 people and 34 committees. When Clinton submitted his Health Security Act bill to Congress, it included state health alliances to increase purchasing power for small businesses and individuals. The intent of this feature was to foster competition among insurance companies. There were also provisions that affected employer coverage of health insurance, Medicare and Medicaid payments, and healthcare inflation. The predicted cost of the legislation and opposition or fragmented support from both political parties contributed to the lack of support for this bill. However, Congress did pass the Children's Health Insurance Plan (CHIP) to increase coverage to children in low-income families.

■ THE AFFORDABLE CARE ACT OF 2010

President Obama signed the Patient Protection and Affordable Care Act into law on March 23, 2010. The law, now called the Affordable Care Act of 2010 (ACA), is almost 1000 pages long and contains 10 titles relating to such issues as quality and effectiveness, the role of public health, chronic disease prevention, and revenue. The intent of this law is to increase access to health care, improve its quality, and lower costs. The ACA also seeks to increase the use of preventive services and address workforce issues (Emanuel, 2014). In addition, it attempts to increase access to health care through a **mandate** that most Americans have health insurance and by providing **health benefit exchanges**. The ACA includes increased coverage of prevention services by Medicare, fraud and abuse prevention, and tax credits to small businesses to help them offer health insurance to their employees. In addition, there are consumer protections including the removal of caps on coverage and denials for preexisting conditions (U.S. Department of Health and Human Services, 2013).

The ACA is a complex law, with many provisions that affect both the individual and the system. The Kaiser Family Foundation (2013) and the American Public Health Association (APHA, 2012), Gruber (2011), and Emanuel (2014) provide detailed summaries of this act. Before beginning an analysis of the ethics implication of the ACA, however, it is important to have a general idea of its nature and form. Working with the state and federal governments, insurance companies, and others, the ACA provides increased access to health care in a number of ways. For example, it mandates that all Americans and legal immigrants have health insurance coverage or pay a fine (O'Brien, 2014), a requirement that is intended to increase access to health care. Likewise, by expanding Medicaid, providing health benefit exchanges, and guaranteeing coverage to patients with preexisting conditions, the act increases access to health care.

The 2010 legislation also included insurance reform. It mandates that health insurance plans offered on the health benefit exchanges provide a minimum set of benefits and that insurers cover preventive services including services for women. To protect consumers, the act requires that insurers do not increase costs based on gender or health standing and prohibits lifetime limits on coverage.

To improve access to health care, the ACA offers both small employers and qualified members of the public the opportunity to receive subsidies or tax credits when purchasing health insurance coverage through health benefit exchanges. Run by states or the federal government, these exchanges or marketplaces feature qualifying health plans that offer a variety of healthcare coverage options. In addition, to these benefits and protection, the ACA includes reviews of premium rates and reform of excessive payments for Medicare Advantage (APHA, 2012).

With respect to health system reform, the ACA focuses on quality and efficiency in a number of ways. It provides incentives for providers to coordinate patient care through accountable care organizations (ACOs). There are also incentives for providing quality services and penalties for practices that demonstrate poor quality and high cost. Examples of poor quality indicators include excessive readmissions and healthcare-acquired infections (HAIs). The ACA addresses the workforce needed to treat the increase in patients that may occur when access to health care increases, by providing educational support for healthcare professionals, grants to address the nursing shortage, and increased emphasis on primary care education.

The ACA not only brings attention to areas of health care such as long-term care and the clinical side of health care, but also addresses community needs, education, and public health, For example, the emphasis on population health—long an issue for public health—is demonstrated through prevention coverage and wellness programs. In addition, the multiyear, staged implementation of the ACA will accommodate needed changes in the overall healthcare system, including prevention practices. However, the final stages of ACA implementation will not occur until 2020 (O'Brien, 2014).

In the summer of 2013, the U.S. Supreme Court ruled on challenges to the constitutionality of the ACA. At stake were the **individual mandate** and state compliance with Medicaid expansion. If the Court declared these two major provisions unconstitutional, it would have had a major impact on the act. Some believed that a negative Supreme Court ruling would strip the ACA of its fiscal power and result in its failure.

Ultimately, the Supreme Court decided that the individual mandate was constitutional under the power of Congress to levy taxes. However, the Court found that Medicaid expansion was unconstitutional because the states did not have enough notice for informed consent and the threat of withholding funds by the Secretary of Health and Human serves states forced states to comply. The remedy was to limit the Health and Human Services Secretary's power to withhold Medicaid funds for noncompliance (Emanuel, 2014; Musumeci, 2012). Although the Supreme Court settled this challenge in a way that left the act largely intact, the ACA continues to face challenges in both Congress and the courts.

■ APPLICATION OF ETHICS TO THE ACA

The Public

The application of ethics theory and principles to the ACA as a whole depends on society's view of the Act. Therefore, a discussion of this application must consider divergent viewpoints, beginning with the public. O'Brien (2014) discusses the premise that access to health care is a basic human right and that the U.S. Declaration of Independence supports this supposition. He also presents the view that most Americans and faith traditions support the idea that health care is a right. Because the ACA increases insurance coverage for citizens and legal immigrants, and works to increase the number of providers of health care, it is moving toward a more just healthcare system. This law is also consistent with Rawls's idea that, in a just society, everyone should have access to basic freedoms. Because the ACA addresses inequalities and benefits those in a lesser position in society, Rawls would also find that this act supports social justice (Summers, 2014).

In addition, access to health care provides the opportunity for greater health for all Americans regardless of their socioeconomic status. Since disease and infirmity do not restrict themselves to a single population group, the ability to protect and treat those in a lesser position (those who are ill) serves the self-interests of all Americans. For example, there is the ability to address childhood obesity through a combination of community health and healthcare system efforts; these efforts may potentially lead to less incidence of diabetes, heart disease, and premature death as the children grow to adulthood. A decreased incidence of these costly problems would, in turn, mean lower costs to all Americans in terms of treatment, disability, family issues, loss income, and contributions to the tax base. As this example demonstrates, health issues are not limited to just those who have ill health; they affect all Americans.

Mill's theory of utilitarianism or consequentialism could also be cited in support of the ACA. The idea that ethical decisions create the greatest good for the greatest number or prevent the greatest harm for the greatest number seems consistent with this act. Although violations of individual or corporate rights (such as the right to be uninsured) for the greater good exist, the benefits of the ACA appear to outweigh the burdens it creates. For example, requiring insurance companies to cover patients with preexisting conditions violates insurance companies' right to deny coverage to potentially expensive patients. A lack of coverage produces harm to those patients, however, in that they have no protection against healthcare costs or must obtain insurance coverage at much higher premiums. The new regulation produces a greater good by giving patients the opportunity to obtain insurance coverage at a reasonable cost. However, in this example, there is a violation of market justice because insurance companies must bear higher costs for providing insurance, may have to increase premiums to other customers, and face the possibility of reduction in their overall profit.

Furlong (2014) demonstrates the ethics implications of the limitations of the ACA. While this law improves insurance coverage for millions of people, some groups will not benefit from its provisions. These groups include undocumented immigrants, non-enrolled Medicaid-eligible patients, and persons who are except from the individual mandate because health insurance is too great a financial burden. Kantian ethics could support the position that denying these groups does not respect their basic dignity as human beings. Thus there is a violation of Kant's categorical imperative. Health care has the moral duty to respect people and not to use them as a means to an end.

Furlong (2014) also uses utilitarian ethics to show that the potential lack of insurance coverage for these vulnerable groups is not ethical. These populations can be more vulnerable to healthcare problems than other groups, but they are not receiving the greatest good provided by access to insurance. In fact, they may receive the greatest harm because of their lack of potential access to care and protection against the financial burden of being uninsured.

In addition, the lack of insurance coverage for these population groups can translate into a lack of social justice (Rawls). When uncovered populations are ill, they seek care through emergency room services and may not have the ability to pay for this care. Therefore, hospitals must find ways to recoup their expenditures on uncompensated care by charging higher rates to those patients who have insurance or by other means. In the end, providing care for those who need it is a social justice requirement. The larger ethics issue becomes who will pay for care of populations not covered by the individual mandate of the ACA.

Summers (2014) lists autonomy, beneficence, nonmaleficence, and justice as the four main principles of ethics used in health care. One's position on the ACA and its effects greatly influences the application of these principles. For example, there is a link between the principle of autonomy or self-rule and the ACA. The act seeks to expand access to health care through insurance coverage. Having insurance increases choices when seeking health care and the ability to be educated about health issues, make decisions about health practices, and obtain assistance when needed. The freedom from the pain and suffering that can accompany untreated disease can also add to people's ability to live their lives based on freedom of choice; that is, they can practice self-rule and not rule by disease.

In reality, the health benefit exchanges, as part of the ACA, do not give the individual true autonomy in decision making about health-care coverage. First, the system assumes that all potential customers have access to a computer and the Internet. This can be an erroneous assumption, considering that low-income individuals may not have the resources to purchase a home computer or the time and transportation needed to spend hours at a public library using a computer there. In addition, the complexity of the insurance plans listed on health benefit exchanges, with their various levels of coverage (from basic to catastrophic to platinum) and deductibles, copayments, and other features, may limit both understanding and the ability to make choices. This complexity requires advisors (navigators) to assist individuals with making these decisions, but in doing so, clients must rely on the independence and integrity of these guides. In the end, the limitations of paternalism versus autonomy may still exist under the ACA.

One can also consider beneficence and nonmaleficence from different views. Providing greater insurance coverage to more Americans, expanding public programs, offering tax credits, and improving cost and quality in health care seem to benefit individuals and the community as a whole. Such efforts act with kindness and charity toward those who were unable to afford health insurance and serve to remove the undue burden on employers that are now required to provide health insurance. Investments in training for the healthcare workforce and in improving research also serve to increase the benefits from the expanded coverage. These investments provide better-qualified professionals and reduce the potential for harm.

However, Furlong (2014) shows that those populations that are not covered under the ACA do not receive beneficence from this law. Often poor and vulnerable, these populations will not have access to health insurance, and the cost of accessing the system may be prohibitive for them. In addition, the lack of coverage can affect even middle-class citizens with major health issues if they are not eligible for Medicare benefits. Members of these uninsured populations may simply go without care or receive care in the emergency department of a hospital. While laws deal with the issues of providing or denying emergency room care, someone must pay for the costs of uncompensated care. Under the ACA, hospitals will still have to absorb the costs of care for the uninsured or pass these costs on to insured patients. Is this action, though necessary, a demonstration of beneficence?

While some would find the denial of insurance coverage to certain population groups completely acceptable, there is a potential for harm to the whole population from this practice (Furlong, 2014). For example, the uninsured live and work in communities alongside those who have access to care. If enough members of the uninsured groups contract a communicable disease that goes untreated, this disease could spread to the whole community. Thus there is a need to weigh the benefits of true universal coverage against the harm to society of not having it.

Finally, the principle of justice seems to be a key feature in the ACA. In terms of distributive justice, the 2010 law supports the idea that access to health care should be fair and available to those in need (O'Brien, 2014). By encouraging employer coverage, providing health benefit exchanges, expanding public programs, and increasing consumer protections within insurance companies, the ACA addresses many issues related to distributive justice. It also addresses critical areas like shortage areas, workforce issues, research needs, and quality incentives. All of these areas are geared toward improving the distribution of scarce healthcare resources (i.e., making them more widely available) and creating a just healthcare system.

Both O'Brien (2014) and Furlong (2014) point out the limitations of distributive justice with the ACA. Under its provisions, some 18 to 20 million Americans will still not be insured, indicating that the system will not be just for everyone. In addition, some employers are required to insure their employees or face fines for not doing so. Employers who are affected by this provision do not perceive this requirement as just. In addition, individuals will face fines if they choose to go uninsured. While the fines may be relatively small, the issue of justice focuses on having a fine at all. Individuals may, therefore, view this part of the ACA as an infringement on their personal independence.

While the ACA does address the four principles of ethics in its intent and provisions, it is easy to see that there is not universal agreement concerning its ethical nature. It remains controversial, and experts continue to argue its ethics using different theoretical and principled views. Because of its complexity, it is wise for healthcare administrators to study selected sections of the ACA with respect to ethics and principles and to remain in "learning mode." These actions will help them be "ACA ready" as the implementation of provisions continues.

The States

The ACA posed ethical problems for the states with respect to their autonomy. Historically, there has been a struggle for power in the United States between the federal government and the states dating back to the Bill of Rights and the 10th Amendment (U.S. National Archives, 2014). In the case of the ACA, the expansion of Medicaid requirements created questions about **state sovereignty**. For example, states were threatened with the loss of matching federal funds if they chose not to expand their Medicaid enrollment criteria. In 2012, the U.S. Supreme Court ruled that this action was coercive and not constitutional. The Court did, however, allow reasonable incentives to encourage states to expand Medicaid (Kaiser Family Foundation, 2013). While the Supreme Court decision seemed to support states' autonomy, ethical issues for the states persist.

The states have different fiscal responsibilities than does the federal government. For example, states are required to balance their budgets, which means that they must find new revenue sources or make budget cuts to cover new expenditures. If the states increase the number of their residents who are eligible for Medicaid benefits, they must find matching funds in their budgets to cover the costs of this expansion of services. While the federal government will provide incentives for a limited time, states are concerned about finding funds to cover new enrollees and Medicaid over the long term. In the future, they might have to cut expenses in areas such as education, transportation, or prisons to cover the additional costs. They may also have to increase taxes to pay for the expanded Medicaid benefits. Many citizens in the states do not find a loss of services or an increase in taxes to cover Medicaid recipients acceptable. With more than 16 million Americans added to Medicaid through the ACA-related expansion of this joint state–federal program, the states have both fiscal and ethics challenges to manage (Parks, 2012).

In addition to the autonomy issue, states face problems with social justice. Many of the Medicaid-eligible citizens have low incomes and a need for healthcare services, which they cannot currently afford. Social justice is concerned about balancing the benefits and the burdens on society within its citizenry, and the burden of illness and disability is certainly higher among citizens with low income. However, some members of the citizenry believe that these individuals could take care of their own problems if they would just stop being poor. This is particularly true if citizens perceive that covering the healthcare expenses of the Medicaid-eligible population will reduce their own benefits within the state. Some would consider this position ethical egoism, while others might view it as market justice.

Hospitals

Because they are major part of the healthcare system, hospitals face many ethical issues with respect to the ACA legislation. For example, hospitals must now address all three aspects of the iron triangle: quality, cost, and access. This need also creates ethical issues at several levels. From a quality standpoint, the ethical principles of beneficence and nonmaleficence are essential. Recall that the mission of hospitals is to provide quality care for those who seek services, regardless of the ability to pay or the form of insurance coverage. The mission of hospitals also addresses social justice because these facilities provide care for those who are in a lesser position in society (Summers, 2014). Of course, because hospitals operate as a business, they must practice market justice as well—that is, they need to make a profit while providing healthcare services.

Because they are such a large cost center for health care, hospitals face changes on several levels as a result of the ACA. For example, there is an emphasis on reducing healthcare prices within this act. To do so, the legislation seeks to reduce Medicare payments, the annual increase in hospital patients, and disproportionate share payments. In addition, there is an emphasis on reducing healthcare utilization through retrospective payment for services (Emanuel, 2014). Hospitals are also receiving greater scrutiny with respect to patients' length of stay, medical errors, fraud, and waste (Gruber, 2011). In addition, satisfaction data gathered for Medicare-covered patients will affect compensation to hospitals. Despite this tighter scrutiny, hospitals are ethically bound to provide quality, cost-effect, patient-centered, and accessible care.

Overall, then, the ACA creates an atmosphere of turbulent change for hospitals and their employees. Such changes, which include both increased scrutiny and tightening of financial compensation, place hospitals under an ethical microscope. Hospitals must be concerned about the financial aspects of their operations because their mission requires that their doors stay open to serve patients. Under the ACA, funding levels reflect patient satisfaction and service effectiveness. Because of value-based purchasing related to Medicaid recipients, there is now a connection between patient satisfaction and financial compensation. Therefore, patients' perception of their care, as well as the quality of that care, matters both ethically and financially.

Of course, hospitals are also employers that must provide compensation for their employees. Nevertheless, their responsibility as employers does not negate their ethical obligations. Hospitals must provide quality and beneficent care, even when they are struggling to deal with the financial aspects of their operations. In addition, staff members must be informed about fiscal issues, but not be so concerned that they sacrifice quality patient care to meet financial goals.

A concern for hospitals is an increased temptation to sacrifice ethical behavior in favor of fiscal balance. For example, there may be many ethical temptations ranging from use of "creative accounting" to layoffs to reductions in services. For example, if money is tight, it may be tempting to reduce staffing to the bare minimum or increase shift time to save money. While this decision may be beneficial in the short run for market justice, its ethical ramifications can be profound. A lack of staffing or implementation of longer shift hours reduces the amount of time that staff has with each patient. Unless training is provided to increase both the efficiency of care and patient empathy and communication, this situation could lead to poor-quality care at best, and neglect and abuse at worst.

Because hospitals will face so many ethical dilemmas and temptations in implementing the ACA, they will need to include ethics in their processes and procedures. Administrators must consider the mission statement of the hospital even more during the transition to the ACA. In addition, hospitals may consider expanding their ethics committees to include a review of policies and procedures for potential ethics issues. Training of all clinical and nonclinical staff members on the basics of effective patient satisfaction techniques, prevention of "never events," and ethics-based decision making will be helpful in avoiding issues that could negatively affect the mission of the hospital.

Physicians

Physicians also are concerned about the practice implications of the ACA. Historically, physicians have been independent practitioners; only relatively recently have they become licensed by states. In turn, physicians have long exercised autonomy in their business practices. Nevertheless, they are educated under the Hippocratic Oath and professional codes of ethics that guide them to provide patient care with beneficence, nonmaleficence, autonomy, and justice. Prior to passage of the ACA in 2010, physicians responded to the demands of insurance companies, federal and state agencies, and patient preferences. Under the healthcare reform plan, they will still face these demands. However, the ACA requires that health care be better coordinated and offers incentives for doing so through accountable care organizations and medical home programs. The act also addresses the need for prevention services, mental health care, and population health (Emanuel, 2014; Stoto, 2013).

The most obvious impact of the ACA for physicians is a change in their practice of medicine. Physicians will continue to be subject to scrutiny from insurance companies regarding their practices and procedures. However, they may take advantage of incentives by making changes in their practice orientation and delivery. For example, if physicians choose the accountable care organization model, they will be increasingly involved in providing care that is coordinated with other professionals to reduce duplication of services and waste. In addition, all physicians may be required to provide preventive services in return for reimbursement from the healthcare insurance plans. These changes, while providing benefits to the patient and the practice, threaten the autonomy of physicians. Ultimately, as a result of these changes, physicians may no longer find themselves to be the center of medical practice. Emanuel (2014) predicts that medical schools will soon adopt a different model for educating physicians so that they will work better with teams of healthcare professionals. While this new model may reduce individual autonomy for physicians, it promises to increase their ability to provide care that reduces harm and produces greater benefit to a larger group of people in the community. Physicians would then have an even greater opportunity to meet their ethical obligations in accordance with their code of ethics and with the Hippocratic Oath.

Health Insurance Companies

The ACA greatly affects the health insurance business and increases market justice issues. For example, it requires that healthcare insurers provide coverage for individuals with preexisting conditions and removes lifetime limits on coverage. Just these two provisions will directly—and dramatically—affect how healthcare insurance companies do business, by altering their profitability and their autonomy. In addition, insurance companies are required to cover certain preventive services at no cost to the patient (Parks, 2012). Another major area included in the ACA is the concept of health insurance exchanges. This feature of the act is having a major impact on health insurance companies in terms of the structure and delivery system of their businesses. Notably, the insurance industry does not control these exchanges; instead, they are under the control of either a state government or the federal government. Despite all of these seemingly negative influences on their profitability, health insurance companies hope to make up for the loss of revenue through additional enrollees and through greater effectiveness and efficiency.

In addition to changing the model of delivery for healthcare insurance companies, the ACA charges new fees to these companies. The U.S. Treasury calculates these fees based on the company's market share and net premiums written. These fees began in 2014 and will increase each year until 2018. It estimated that these fees will amount to more than $8 billion in 2014 alone (Parks, 2012).

It is not surprising that the ACA-related changes in the delivery of health insurance and in the cost of doing business pose ethics issues for health insurance companies. In addition to dealing with profound market justice issues, health insurance companies must still be concerned with issues related to employee justice. For example, such a sea change often creates ethics issues for employees. To retain a highly competent workforce, health insurance companies will need to be keenly aware of employee justice issues. They can honor their Kantian duty to respect employees by providing them with information about upcoming changes, considering their workload, and providing preventive services to help them manage the stress of change.

Health insurance companies can also address Mill's concept of providing the greatest good for the greatest number of enrollees and preventing the greatest harm for them. With the ACA, the number of potential enrollees increases, thereby making this ethical position even stronger. In addition, if health insurance companies choose to emphasize preventive services in their marketing programs, they can increase the benefit for enrollees and decrease the potential harm. Certainly, leaders in health insurance will need to engage in Aristotle's practical wisdom. By using this resource, they can make sound business decisions through avoiding impulses and using the best possible data for decision making. Ethical practice must be part of the business of health insurance, just as it must be part of the business of healthcare delivery.

■ SELECTED AREA: THE INDIVIDUAL MANDATE

Under the ACA, U.S. citizens and legal residents are required to have health insurance coverage or pay a penalty. The federal government will assess these penalties based on individuals' tax returns. However, there are exceptions to this requirement, including financial hardship and religious objections. In addition, the mandate does not cover American Indians, incarcerated Americans, and undocumented immigrants (Kaiser Family Foundation, 2013). Gruber (2011) explains that the individual mandate is necessary for the ACA to be a viable solution to issues of healthcare access, quality, and cost. In his explanation, he compares this provision of the ACA with auto insurance. For example, people are required to purchase auto insurance even if they never have an accident. Thus, people who are accident free subsidize those who were not as fortunate in their automotive history. Likewise, the individual mandate requires that all citizens have health assurance coverage, even those who are not likely to need it. This means that the healthy help to pay for the care for those who are not healthy. However, just as in auto insurance, when someone is insured, he or she has access to health care when needed. The idea of requiring people to have health insurance makes fiscal sense.

The mandate for individual coverage also extends to requirements for employers. Employers have different requirements with respect to providing coverage for their employees. For example, employers with 50 or more full-time employees must provide health insurance that meets certain standards or face fines. Small businesses with 24 or fewer full-time employees do not have to offer healthcare insurance, but they qualify for tax credits of up to 35% to assist with providing insurance premiums for their employees. This mandate to employers will assist in providing for coverage of the greatest number of Americans possible (Kaiser Family Foundation, 2013).

Ethics Theory Application

The most obvious ethical theory that would support an individual mandate would be Rawls's social justice (Darr, 2011). If one defines access to health care as a basic liberty, then Rawls would propose that access is part of the liberty principle. In addition, Rawls points out that it is in everyone's self-interest to protect those who are in a lesser position. This is true because anyone in a society could eventually be in such a position with respect to his or her health. Therefore, it would be in one's self-interest to make sure that everyone has healthcare insurance.

St. Thomas Aquinas (Summers, 2014) might also support the individual mandate. He believed that human beings are capable of rationality and have the ability to avoid evil. Rationality would lead them to think that providing access to health care is consistent with doing good and avoiding evil for most of the U.S. population. In addition, assuring healthcare coverage through the individual mandate and other provisions of the ACA fits well with Aquinas's concepts of natural law and its ability to allow people to reach their full potential.

The individual mandate could also pass Kant's categorical imperative test. This tool for ethical decision making asks the question, "Should this action be a universal law and apply to everyone?" The answer to the question determines whether an individual or society has a duty. The ethics question posed in the categorical imperative with respect to health care becomes, "Should everyone in the United States have access to basic health care?" While different groups might answer that question with caveats, most Americans would respond in the affirmative. Providing basic health care then becomes an ethical duty. To honor this duty, there must be a mechanism for paying for the healthcare system and healthcare delivery.

In addition, one could cite Mill's ideas of utilitarianism to support the idea of an individual mandate for health insurance coverage.

In Mill's thinking, producing benefit or reducing harm through one's actions is ethical. Complying with a mandate that produces benefit and contributes to the benefit of others seems to fit well with Mill's concept of utility.

Because the ACA does not fulfill the entire duty by providing access to basic health care for all Americans, it may not completely meet the ethics requirement. For example, Furlong (2014) analyzes the ACA using deontology. Given that the mandate exempts the poor, undocumented immigrants, and others from its provisions, it does not show the same respect for these groups as it does for other human beings. In addition, Furlong shows that in line with Kant's thinking, the exemptions deny the moral duty of respect for all persons, thereby failing to pass his categorical imperative test. Finally, Furlong argues that the exemptions to the mandate also fail with respect to utilitarianism. By exempting some individuals from the mandate for coverage, the ACA does not extend the greatest good to everyone.

■ THE FUTURE OF THE ACA

As with any major healthcare initiative, predictions for the future of the ACA include change. As implementation of the original legislation continues, the healthcare industry must be prepared to address its roadblocks and meet its ethics challenges. In addition, the healthcare system must be always be prepared to provide quality care that is effective, efficient, and patient centered. Which challenges might the system and healthcare administrators face?

Selker and Wasser (2014) regard the ACA as a major part of the history of public policy. Importantly, they suggest that this act will serve as the foundation for universal health care in the future. Both Selker and Wasser (2014) and Parks (2012) report that the government is becoming increasingly significant in providing access to health care in the United States. These authors also predict the U.S. healthcare market will ultimately be reshaped into partnerships between the public and private sectors. McDonough (quoted in Selker and Wasser, 2014) suggests that the journey toward equity and efficiency in healthcare delivery is not complete. Within the goal of universal health care, the national distributive effect will continue.

McDonough (quoted in Selker and Wasser, 2014) suggests that the reform of the U.S. healthcare system will occur in stages that reflect improved access, system reform, and population health. The population health stage will include increased emphasis on prevention and wellness. The last stage of reform will focus on including health in all government policies. Doing so would require that agencies across local, state, and federal governments incorporate health in their policies;

this cooperation, in turn, could lead to national strategies for health improvement.

Emanuel (2014) explains that the ACA will create new institutions and new rules for institutions of health care. While he acknowledges the riskiness of prediction, he cites six major areas of change for health care beginning in 2020. These changes include the transformation of the health insurance industry into an integrated delivery system or into actuarial support services. There will also be increased emphasis on the health of patients with chronic diseases and on better screening and treatment for individuals with mental illnesses. Moreover, Emanuel (2014) predicts that hospitals will no longer be the center of health care because of cost controls, better patient treatment, and the reduction of hospital-related health issues.

Emanuel (2014) further predicts that there will be a great reduction in employer-based healthcare insurance. In the future, he says, most Americans will receive their healthcare insurance through various forms of exchanges and company-based plans. In addition, he foresees a transformation of medical education. This transformation will include reduction of required years of medical education and an increase in clinical training sites other than hospitals. Medical students will be part of a multiprofessional system where they will attend classes with members of the patient-care team. This educational model will foster the different orientation to patient care that is necessary for addressing acute care issues and improving the health of chronic care patients. According to Emanuel (2014), educators from the business area of health care will have an increased role in the education of clinical professionals in this new environment. He calls for greater management skills on the part of physicians and other clinical professionals.

Certainly, the intense changes suggested by Emanuel (2014) will produce ongoing ethics challenges. In an ideal situation, the very nature of health care provides an opportunity to exhibit the highest ethical standards. After all, patients put their trust and their lives in the hands of healthcare professionals. Do they deserve ethics-based care?

For their part, healthcare administrators must balance patient-centered care and fidelity with market justice, which requires the most effective and efficient use of all healthcare resources. From an ethics perspective, this challenge will require astute use of Mill's utilitarian theory balanced with the application of Kant's deontology. Even in a time of relative calm, the balance between these two theories requires a solid application of Aristotle's practical wisdom. Therefore, the challenge in the ACA era will be to continue to use practical wisdom when addressing rapid change and its effects.

One easily made prediction is that the course of the ACA in the future will not be smooth one. Political and organizational objections to its implementation persist, and the response to these objections is not certain. Yet, health administrators must be ethically ready to address the business needs of healthcare organizations and maintain integrity. Helwig (2013) suggests that leaders in the ACA era will require great resiliency in their practices. They must be able to withstand crises and bounce back from adverse situations. He cites several learned behaviors that resilient leaders exhibit, including integrity and the ability to demonstrate the characteristics of the servant leader.

While there is no simple answer to being ethically ready for the full implementation of the ACA, the strategies necessary for conducting any change in healthcare operations apply. Because they influence the application of healthcare change in terms of its acceptance by staff, healthcare administrators have additional responsibility for making change happen efficiently and with the least amount of harm. For this responsibility, healthcare administrators should practice Michelangelo's model of *ancora imparo* (Michelangelo Quotes, 2014, para. 7)—that is, "always learning." Administrators need to be actively involved in their professional organizations, maintain currency in information regarding healthcare reform, and take advantage of appropriate continuing education opportunities. There is much to do and many ethics challenges to face.

■ ETHICS READINESS ADVICE

Healthcare administrators practice their profession amidst the chaos of the real world of practical leadership. In doing so, they must juggle many issues on an almost daily basis. With the implementation of the ACA, this juggling act has been intensified. In turn, it has become even more challenging to balance the practice of ethics-based management with day-to-day decisions. Following is a list of practices that can assist busy healthcare administrators in maintaining their integrity while still making sound business decisions.

1. Remember that not every decision is immediate. It is often more ethically sound to allow time for thought before deciding.
2. Ethics-based decisions require information beyond what appears at the surface. Remember to gather data and information concerning expectations of the ACA provision that you must implement. Knowledge is truly power with the ACA.
3. While is important to be perceived as a competent leader and one who can make decisions, it is also critical to obtain clarification of the issues at hand before jumping to formation of a policy. There are many stakeholders to consider when creating policy, including patients, the medical community, the board of trustees, and the community at large.

4. Frequently review the basic principles and theories of ethics and consider how they apply to the ACA and its implementation. Again, knowledge is power. In this case, it is ethics knowledge that will prepare the healthcare administrator for action.

5. Take time out for personal renewal. Remember that excessive stress and lack of resilience can cause errors in judgment and behavior that contribute to poor decision making. The implementation of the ACA should be a career maker, not a career breaker.

Summary

This chapter provides a snapshot of the intricacies and challenges of the ACA. Even though its implementation is not complete, this act has already begun to change the healthcare system on many levels. The challenge for healthcare administrators will be to make the myriad of business decisions needed to create efficient, effective, and patient-centered institutions. However, because of the nature of the business of health care, administrators cannot overlook the necessity of making ethics-based business decisions. This dichotomy between business and ethics may cause many sleepless nights for ethics-based administrators. However, a deep knowledge of ethics theories and principles and the ability to use practical wisdom in making decisions should reduce the angst for individual healthcare administrators. It is always important to remember that, as the health administrator, one is a servant both to patients and to those who care for patients. Therefore, healthcare administrators must consider both groups when making business decisions that reflect the mission, vision, and values of the institution.

Web Resources

For current information about ACA 2010, visit these websites:

Health and Human Services
http://www.hhs.gov/healthcare/

Kaiser Family Foundation
http://kff.org/

References

American Public Health Association (APHA). (2012). Affordable Care Act overview: Selected provisions. Retrieved from http://www.apha. org/NR/rdonlyres/26831F24-882A-4FF7-A0A9-6F49DFBF6D3F/0/ ACAOverview_Aug2012.pdf

Darr, K. (2011). *Ethics in health services management* (5th ed.). Baltimore, MD: Health Professions Press.

Emanuel, E. J. (2014). *Reinventing American health care*. New York, NY: PublicAffairs Books.

Furlong, B. (2014). Ethics reform: What about those left behind? In E. E. Morrison & B. Furlong (Eds.), *Health care ethics: Critical issues for the 21st century* (3rd ed., pp. 375–390). Burlington, MA: Jones & Bartlett Learning.

Gruber, J. (2011). *Health care reform: What it is, why it is necessary, how it works*. New York, NY: Hill and Wang.

Helwig, K. R. (2013). Resilience: A responsibility that can't be delegated. *Frontiers of Health Services Management, 30*(2), 301–335.

Kaiser Family Foundation. (2013). Summary of the Affordable Care Act. *Focus on Health Reform*. Retrieved from http://kff.org/health-reform/fact-sheet/summary-of-new-health-reform-law/

Michelangelo Quotes. (2014). Retrieved from http://www.goodreads.com/author/quotes/182763.Michelangelo

Musumeci, M. (2012). A guide to the Supreme Court's Affordable Care Act decision. *Focus on Health Reform*. Kaiser Family Foundation. Retrieved from http://kaiserfamilyfoundation.files.wordpress.com/2013/01/8332.pdf

O'Brien, R. L. (2014). A new era of health care: The ethics of healthcare reform. In E. E. Morrison & B. Furlong (Eds.), *Health care ethics: Critical issues for the 21st century* (3rd ed., pp. 363–374). Burlington, MA: Jones & Bartlett Learning.

Parks, D. (2012). *Health care reform simplified: What professionals in medicine, government, insurance, and business need to know*. New York, NY: Apress.

Selker, H. P., & Wasser, J. S. (Eds.). (2014). *The Affordable Care Act as a national experiment: Health policy innovations and lessons*. New York, NY: Springer.

Shi, L., & Singh, D. A. (2015). *Delivering health care in America: A systems approach* (6th ed.). Burlington, MA: Jones & Bartlett Learning.

Stoto, M. A. (2103). *Population health in the Affordable Care Act era*. Washington, DC: Academy Health. Retrieved from http://www.academyhealth.org/

Summers, J. (2014) Theory of healthcare ethics. In E. E. Morrison & B. Furlong (Eds.), *Health care ethics: Critical issues for the 21st century* (3rd ed., pp. 3–46). Burlington, MA: Jones & Bartlett Learning.

U.S. Department of Health and Human Services. (2013). Read the law. Retrieved from http://www.hhs.gov/healthcare/rights/law/index.html

U.S. National Archives. (2014). The Bill of Rights. Retrieved from http://www.archives.gov/exhibits/charters/bill_of_rights.html

CHAPTER
6

Market Forces and Ethics

How do market forces challenge healthcare ethics?

Points to Ponder

1. What is the relationship between market forces and ethics?
2. What were the ethical roots of managed care?
3. Should a healthcare administrator be concerned about ethics and managed care?
4. Are there ethical issues with alternative/complementary medicine?
5. How do the baby boomers challenge the healthcare market and its ethics?

Key Terms

The following is a list of this chapter's key terms. Look for them in bold.

case management
disease management
gatekeeper
HEDIS

integrative medicine (IM)
managed care
practice profiling
utilization review

■ INTRODUCTION AND DEFINITIONS

How do market forces affect the practice of health care? To answer this question, administrators think beyond the walls of a healthcare facility and consider market forces that affect health care. Changes in the economy; local, state, and national political decisions; social changes; and even weather events can affect the use of health care and its financing. There needs to be an understanding of the potential healthcare market to understand why these forces can affect how it works. In actuality, the market for health care encompasses potentially everyone. As in other markets, not everyone is in the marketplace at the same time, but there is always a potential for use of the products offered by health care. In addition, certain population groups have greater predictability for being in the healthcare market. For example, it would be more likely for an 80-year-old person to be an extensive consumer of healthcare services than for a 20-year-old person to have the same level of consumption.

Given that the potential healthcare consumer base is so large, business success requires a greater knowledge of how market forces affect the industry. For example, healthcare facilities must consider what happens when a new research discovery hits the news. Even if the results of a clinical study are not definitive, there may be an almost immediate public response. Patients may inundate physicians' offices with telephone calls asking for the procedure or product. As the discovery becomes more widely accepted, the pressure increases for all practices to offer it as a service to attract healthcare customers. This need to maintain a competitive edge can increase healthcare spending and costs.

In addition to giving an overview of market forces, this chapter explores just a few of the areas that affect the business of health care. Managed care, a powerful market force, has its own section in the chapter. Understanding its history and status can assist the healthcare administrator in applying ethics principles when dealing with this important market force. The increased role of the consumer is also a major market force. Therefore, the effects of the aging of the baby boomer population and the consumer-driven phenomenon of integrative medicine are part of this chapter. Finally, there is information on how to deal with market forces in an ethics-based manner.

■ GENERAL MARKET FORCES

The overall local, state, and national economies affect healthcare markets in several ways. Recent events, such as changes in employment rates, the housing market crisis, and the banking bailouts, have made Americans realize that economics is more than a course people study in college. Economics affects individuals and businesses—and health care is no exception. For example, when people lose their jobs and cannot find work, they do not have the healthcare coverage that often accompanies employment. While COBRA benefits (i.e., continuation coverage that is made available for a defined period after someone becomes unemployed) and the potential for coverage through the ACA offer potential assistance with maintaining coverage, many people may not be able to afford this coverage. If they lack insurance, patients may delay needed treatment for themselves or their families until their health issues become true emergencies. Their decisions not to seek care add to their healthcare costs and the costs for the entire system. The delay of needed treatment could also have serious health and financial consequences, including premature death and bankruptcy.

Economic changes can also have a ripple effect on the business of health care. For example, the addition of state or national taxes to those businesses that supply health care with goods and services adds costs for both the industry and the patient. How does this happen? When suppliers must pay additional taxes, they may have to increase the prices of their products to earn a profit and remain in business. They pass on this increase to their customers. Therefore, healthcare institutions have to pay more for the materials that they need to do business. The healthcare market, in turn, must pass some of this cost to consumers if healthcare providers are to remain profitable. In this case, there can be higher patient charges for treatment. Since third-party payers are an active part of healthcare finance, higher premiums, increased deductibles, or greater copayments are all likely to reflect these increased costs.

These are just two examples of the effect of economic change on the business of health care. They demonstrate that healthcare administrators must be attentive to the issues that affect the larger economy as well as the market forces that are part of their local communities. What are the ethics ramifications of changes in the economy? Ethics thinking and decision making becomes more challenging when there is an increase in the emphasis on fiscal responsibility. For example, the projected changes with the implementation of the ACA will yield greater emphasis on healthcare costs and fiscal responsibility. These changes do not negate the responsibility to meet payroll for the workforce necessary to provide quality care. It does not change the need to purchase materials, or the need to maintain and grow the healthcare business. However, such challenges may lead to compromised ethics-based practices if economic issues become the driving concern for the healthcare system.

Even in the ACA era, ethics issues concerning providing care for the uninsured remain of concern. O'Brien (2014) reports that even when the ACA is fully implemented, there will not be insurance coverage for potentially 30 million people. Because of legal requirements and ethical obligations, the healthcare system will still have to provide care for those uninsured individuals, who will most likely access health care through the emergency care system. There needs to be payment for the costs of these visits. The issue could be addressed by listing the cost as uncompensated care, using charities as funding sources, or setting up patient payment accounts. While the issue of uncompensated care is not new, new considerations may arise given the status of those who are not eligible for coverage under the ACA. Health care will continue to address this cost issue while undergoing major changes required by the ACA guidelines.

Many other issues can affect the healthcare market, including technology, workforce supply, geography, and even changes in weather. While these issues are too numerous to address in one chapter, or even many chapters, it is important to study how market forces connect to ethics issues and behaviors. This chapter gives three examples of market forces to increase understanding about these connections. The examples are managed care, the aging of the baby boomers, and integrative medicine.

■ MANAGED CARE AND ETHICS

Managed care has been part of healthcare delivery in one form or another for more than 70 years (Shi & Singh, 2015) and has become a major influence on the healthcare market. Managed care contributed to moving health care from a social justice or care model to the current emphasis on a market-based model. As a response to the limitations of fee-for-service payment schemes and healthcare inflation, managed care attempted to control costs and decrease inappropriate access. Currently, managed care coverage appears to drive the provision of care. In addition, healthcare administrators (HCAs) must deal with multiple rules imposed by managed care contracts that mandate the healthcare organization to control costs, prevent abuse, and regulate practice patterns. Health care is now a highly competitive business where profit margins are tight and there is a struggle to meet the patient-centered mission while balancing fiscal goals.

The response to managed care from the greater community is not always favorable. Members of the public, while generally liking their individual practitioners, tend to have negative feelings about managed care in general. They find the limitations of choice and coverage, gatekeeper referrals, and other features to be annoying at best. In addition, this system of delivery has been the target of the media, which look for prime-time issues to cover. State and federal politicians also strive to protect voters from potential abuses by managed care through an increasing amount of regulation (National Conference of State Legislatures, 2011).

A market force like managed care, with its great power and impact, also brings significant ethical issues. For example, what happens when the demands of the ACA decrease managed care's ability to control costs and access? How can healthcare organizations provide quality care for increasing numbers of patients who have insurance through a managed care plan? In addition, what is the role of an ethics-based HCA in negotiating contracts and maintaining quality standards in the face of increasing numbers of patients? These are just a few of the potential ethics questions that managed care is raising as it moves into the ACA era.

The first step in dealing with concerns about future managed care ethical issues is knowledge. A healthcare administrator who is fully informed concerning the workings of the ACA in the managed care environment can be successful in forming business relationships and making sound ethical decisions. The next few sections provide an overview of the status of and future concerns related to managed care. These sections serve as an overview to this broad topic; maintaining full currency on managed care requires a commitment to "reading, reading, and reading."

Current Situation

Managed care did not begin as a business. Originally, it was part of a social movement to assist workers with healthcare costs when they became injured on the job. In 1938, the Kaiser Company introduced a prepaid system to cover expenses associated with accidents, with the company's employees contributing funds toward meeting their own healthcare needs. By addressing both preventive and acute care, Kaiser was better able to maintain a healthy workforce and gained a reputation as a benevolent and ethical company. Managed care grew from these roots in social justice to a business model that encompasses different delivery options (Shi & Singh, 2015).

The managed care industry has been successful in using business practices to control access to services and cost of delivery. For example, the use of the primary physician as a gatekeeper for access to hospitals and specialists has reduced unnecessary hospital stays and treatments. Consumers do not have unlimited choices in treatment or physicians unless they are willing to pay more through a special managed care option. Managed care companies instituted **case management** and **utilization reviews** to coordinate patient care and oversee the appropriateness of that care. While these initiatives may not have met with great favor from practitioner or patient, they have helped to control healthcare costs. Finally, **practice profiling**—the bane of many physicians—allows managed care organizations to compare practice patterns between physicians in similar practices for evidence of practice excesses or even fraud and abuse (Shi & Singh, 2015).

Benefits of managed care include a greater emphasis on patient satisfaction and standardization of some medical practices that has led to better patient outcomes. Patients now can receive some procedures at same-day surgery settings, leading to a reduction in hospital stays. In its effort to control costs, managed care has emphasized preventive care and the control of chronic disease (Shi & Singh, 2015). In a response to concerns about quality of care and cost controls, the

National Committee for Quality Assurance (NCQA) began accrediting managed care organizations through a detailed process involving self-study and site visits. This organization has also worked to monitor quality through a set of standardized measurements called the Healthcare Effectiveness Data and Information Set (**HEDIS**). Its collection of quality data allows NCQA to create report cards on managed care plans that are accessible to employers and others. These efforts have benefited both the individual and the community.

Despite all of this good news, managed care may have done all it can to control costs and produce quality care. Even with its evolution to adapt to consumer demands, costs to provide care continue to rise and managed care contracts may not be able to cover these costs. If physician groups, hospitals, and other providers cannot do business based on managed care contracts, there is a temptation to save money by withholding needed services or by undertreating managed care–covered patients. In addition, with the increased access to and use of the Internet, consumers are becoming more perceptive with respect to their benefits under their managed care plans. Moreover, information technology (IT), fraud, abuse, and other concerns have led to more scrutiny of managed care companies and increased legislation, including the Health Insurance Portability and Accountability Act (HIPAA). These and other factors mean that managed care needs to make serious changes to ensure its future survival, especially as it faces the challenges of the ACA.

Future Concerns

The major issue facing managed care today is the implementation of the ACA. Many of this act's provisions directly influence the business of managed care and challenge the industry to meet new standards and remain competitive. For example, to be able to offer an insurance product on a health benefit exchange, managed care organizations must meet government requirements. These include having adequate networks, contracts with navigators, and contracts with community providers. Managed care organizations must also report specified data in easy-to-understand language and maintain their accreditation (Kaiser Family Foundation, 2013).

The ACA also specifies the requirements for basic insurance coverage and tiers of benefit packages that managed care can provide. Managed care plans can no longer place lifetime limits on coverage or deny coverage based on preexisting conditions. In addition, there are changes in deductibles in some markets and limits on the amount of waiting time for coverage. For those managed care plans that serve Medicare- or Medicaid-covered patients, certain prevention services must be covered without cost sharing (Kaiser Family Foundation, 2013; Kongstvedt, 2013).

These are just a few of the ACA provisions that will affect the managed care industry. Although there is the potential of an increased market owing to the greater number of insured individuals, managed care organizations must be ready to provide coverage for this market and still create a profit to maintain their business and please their stockholders. In addition, if a large number of the newly insured individuals have serious or chronic health problems, the finances of the managed care organization may be strained by the challenging of caring for them. Certainly, the situation will require that managed care organizations act with financial prudence when contracting for services with providers and facilities. Ultimately, such organizations will have to provide greater access to health care with lower costs at an equal or better quality level than is offered today. This task will be challenging at best.

The future of managed care organizations may also include a greater emphasis on prevention. To be profitable, such organizations need healthy enrollees who pay premiums but use the healthcare system infrequently. Managed care also needs to focus on how best to care for chronically ill patients who need high-cost treatment. Better use of **disease management** practices can help to reduce overall costs and improve patient satisfaction. Managed care may be beginning a new phase in its development by becoming more innovative in its patient coverage and provider contracting practices. Its future looks challenging from both a business perspective and an ethics perspective.

Where Is the Ethics?

The interaction between managed care and the healthcare system introduces ethics issues that stem from conflicts between patient autonomy, the overall benefit for managed care members, and profit margins. For example, a conflict occurs when patients need expensive services not covered by the contract. Denying such care might cause unnecessary suffering or even premature death, but providing uncovered services to everyone could have a negative impact on the facility's profit margin and viability. Incentive programs, gatekeeping, inclusions or exclusions in plans, marketing, and disclosure of information are also examples of potential ethical problems related to managed care.

Anderlik (2001), Darr (2011), and Perry (2012) discuss incentive programs for healthcare providers and the ethics issues surrounding them. Typically, such incentives consist of incremental or lump-sum payments designed to reward desirable practice patterns. An ethics concern is that these incentives might unduly influence physician practices to the detriment of the patient. For example, a primary care physician might choose to treat a patient, rather than refer that patient to a specialist, so that the physician can meet the requirements for an end-of-year bonus. However, if the patient's needs are beyond the scope of this physician's practice, the patient might not receive appropriate care. Such a decision also leaves the physician open to possible malpractice litigation.

Healthcare administrators can take several actions to address the ethics of incentive programs. First, they can consider the scope of the program. If incentives are too broad, they can prove too tempting and produce a negative long-term effect on patient care. If they are too narrow, patient variability can make them impossible to meet. Healthcare administrators must also consider the incentive's effect on overall practitioner income. If the percentage is too high (for example, 25%), then there is the potential for inappropriate influence on patient care decisions. If it is too low (for example, 5%), then it can fail to control costs. Remember that when there is a link between incentives and improvements in quality or effective practice innovation, incentives can lead to positive change. Healthcare administrators should consider the need to maintain patient trust and create patient benefit when deciding on accepting or implementing an incentive plan.

The gatekeeping function used in managed care can also bring ethical concerns. On the one hand, it serves to coordinate care and provide the best possible outcomes for the patient. It fosters cooperation between providers so that managed care organizations can identify best practices and customize patient care. On the other hand, the gatekeeper can function as a barrier to care. The gatekeeper role puts the physician in the middle between the patient and the payer. He or she becomes the agent for rationing care based on cost-effectiveness. In some cases, the physician's background may not have prepared him or her to make decisions about providing or denying access to specialty care. For example, physicians are not well educated in the area of mental health, yet they can deny these referrals. Some ethicists see the gatekeeper role as inappropriate for physicians because they should be advocates for patient care. Others feel that this role is highly ethical because it serves to hold down healthcare costs for the whole community.

What should healthcare administrators do about the ethics of gatekeeping? Anderlik (2001) suggests that there is no solid research to support strict rationing principles and stringent adherence to clinical protocols. Gatekeeping decisions should consider physicians' clinical judgment, as it is also a viable part of patient care. To support their judgment, physicians need information about costs and benefits of treatments. They should be encouraged not to recommend treatments that can only minimally benefit the patient. In addition, physicians should make a greater effort to educate patients about treatment decisions. This effort can also be part of meeting the new ACA requirement of providing prevention services to patients. Of course, policies that clearly define treatment coverage and the rationale for exclusion of coverage need to be in place. Such policies will assist physicians to make more appropriate gatekeeper decisions.

Competition has led managed care to expand to the Medicare and Medicaid market, which will involve it in more of the ethics challenges associated with the ACA. Because healthy seniors need fewer services, there is an ethics concern that managed care will market to and attract these individuals (called "creaming"). While this strategy makes sense in the short term, it does not make good long-term business sense. As they age, even these healthy seniors will need more and more services that will affect profitability.

With the ACA and its financial and policy restrictions, ethical issues will increase when trying to balance profitability with best practices for patient care. These challenges bring into conflict the need to provide the greatest good for the greatest number of patients (Mill) with the need to provide the best care for the individual patient (Kant). Given that no managed care organization has unlimited funds, there may be a need to ration care by limiting access or by reducing unnecessary procedures. However, the patient and his or her family may see this action as unethical and even heartless. Obviously, the need for effective communication about why a procedure is not the best for a specific patient is paramount. Otherwise, managed care could be perceived to be "killing grandma" to keep its profit margin.

What is the impact of managed care on the already uninsured? The ACA will not provide universal health care. An estimated 30 million people will not be covered under this act (O'Brien, 2014). This lack of coverage does not mean that these people will not seek care. In fact, it is likely that they will visit the emergency room as their primary caregiver. While social justice calls for healthcare practitioners to treat those who are in need, there must be payment for these visits. Facilities inevitably pass on the costs of uncompensated care to patients and their third-party payers. Is this justice for patients or payers? The answer will vary depending on whether one thinks about social justice and the need to care for those in a lesser position (Rawls) or about market justice.

HCAs will be tasked with facing the ethics issues posed by marketing managed care. Darr (2011) points out that if a practice is too successful in marketing the quality of its specialty care, its bottom line may be adversely affected. In such a case, too many high-risk patients could become members of a particular plan and negatively affect its payment structure and profit margin. Does this mean that physicians should have high standards of quality for services and meet those standards, but keep quiet about their success? Darr advocates stressing the overall quality of services. However, there could be a conflict between the individual patient's needs and right to information and the collective good of members and the organization in general.

Anderlik (2001) suggests that marketing can be an ethics problem when an individual makes promises that he or she cannot deliver. Even though there are ACA mandates pertaining to practice plan inclusions, in the highly competitive managed care business salespeople might be tempted to inflate benefits and choice options to close the sale. This might also occur during the discussion and negotiation of provider contracts. In negotiations, the healthcare administrator's role includes doing homework, questioning all claims and presentations, and asking about sources for information. Healthcare administrators should negotiate in good faith, but not give away too much information. Remember the managed care company is there to close the deal, but the administrator is trying to get the best possible contract to benefit the organization.

Healthcare administrators also work for managed care organizations in marketing and advertising. In this role, they should be sure to give appropriate information (Anderlik, 2001). In addition, they should check the accuracy of all materials (print, media, or Internet) before these materials become public so that they present a positive but accurate picture of the managed care organization. Certainly, during the introduction of new product lines that comply with ACA standards, the healthcare administrator should ensure that staff receive training to provide accurate information. While such extensive training can seem like a high-cost decision, it is easily justified if one considers the ethics obligation to patient autonomy and the cost of legal action or negative publicity. Healthcare administrators will also want to evaluate the sales force's presentation of the organization and its products. Administrators can accomplish this through follow-up telephone interviews with employers or other data collection methods. If a problem is found to exist, there is a need for appropriate counseling to avoid future problems.

Finally, healthcare administrators need to consider the issue of informed consent and disclosure of information in managed care plans. When a person enrolls in a managed care plan, he or she is actually consenting to a form of rationing of health care. Therefore, no ethics issues should arise when information about coverage options is presented. However, the decision for enrolling in a program also assumes an informed decision. Therefore, the healthcare administrator should make every effort to ensure that the consumer understands what he or she is signing.

Ethics considerations should also offer some assistance with the issue of consent and disclosure. The patient should come first. While the plan may offer a certain range of services, the patient has the right to know if other effective options are available. However, such information must include a balanced view of options including cost (to be borne by the patient), benefits, and success rates, among other things. Healthcare administrators should also make every attempt to provide user-friendly information about treatment options. For some patients, this can mean updated information on a website. Other individuals might not have computer access or the desire to use this communication tool. For them, the administrator will need well-designed, accurate, and understandable booklets or pamphlets.

Managed care grew from its roots in social justice. This growth has brought with it many ethical issues for both the managed care organization and its business partners. Perry (2013) gives some general guidelines that should prove useful in dealing in managed care situations:

1. Be careful to use accurate marketing and advertising so choice is truly informed.
2. Protect patients' rights to confidentiality. HIPAA rules go a long way here, but they do not address everything.
3. Remember the responsibility to hire competent healthcare staff and ensure their competence.
4. Establish practice guidelines based on evidence and supported by physicians.
5. Have appropriate appeal policies in place that do not punish the person who asks for the appeal.
6. Remember the community and maintain a commitment to education, research, and uncompensated care.

In addition, healthcare administrators will need to rely on the organization's mission and values for their decisions. Asking the question "Does this fit with our mission and values?" frequently should help discern the correct decisions. In addition, the use of organizational ethics committees is helpful in dealing with difficult managed care–related ethics issues.

■ THE AGING OF THE BABY BOOMERS

Another significant market influence is the aging of the U.S. population and the role of baby boomers. According to Shi and Singh (2015), in 2030, when most of the boomers are in retirement, they will represent 20% of the U.S. population. What will be the impact of the aging of this "bolus of boomers"? History gives a clue. When the baby boomers entered first grade, the schools changed to accommodate their large numbers. When they entered college, the colleges expanded. When they began to buy homes, the real estate market changed. Now, they are aging and are likely to require more health care.

Aging boomers tend to be educated, affluent, and quality seeking. They do not believe that aging begins at 65; rather, they think old age does not begin until age 72 (Cohn & Taylor, 2010). While not entirely enthralled by the digital revolution, baby boomers do use social networks and enjoy online videos. They are concerned with national issues such as the federal debt and the fate of Social Security and Medicare. They also tend to be more accepting of younger adults' lifestyles and attitudes toward marriage and divorce.

Because chronic disease is more prevalent with the onset of aging, the need for different types of healthcare service can be anticipated as the baby boomers age. These type of services will require a major change in thinking and healthcare system design that moves from the acute care model to a chronic disease management model. However, even though aging, the baby boomers present unique challenges and opportunities for the healthcare system. Their trends in healthcare interests and needs pose both market opportunities and ethics dilemmas. Some of the baby boomer health trends are highlighted here:

- Having greater knowledge of healthcare products and services. This knowledge can make baby boomers more questioning about treatments and more likely to ask for second opinions. In addition, they have more discretionary income to obtain services and devices that can prolong their independence.
- Being more politically active and sharing their opinions about health care through their advocacy and their votes.
- Living longer than previous generations and seeking independence even as they age. This creates a demand for a diverse collection of home health services.
- Being more conscious of health issues such as nutrition, food quality, and the benefits of an active life. Boomers have a different vision of their retirement years that does not include sedentary lives and boredom.
- Taking more prescription drugs than previous generations, which may lead to issues of overprescribing and dependence.
- Having higher incidences of obesity and being overweight. Therefore, there is increased interest in weight loss products and services (Scheve, 2013).

Not only will this market force of baby boomers bring change to the type and delivery of health care, but it will also bring its own ethics issues. For example, how will the healthcare business maintain its profit margin if baby boomers' demands for care exceed its resources? The boomers represent a powerful voter block. Will their power allow them to take more than their fair share of the health resources at the expense of younger generations? If this becomes the case, will there be violations of justice, nonmaleficience, and beneficence for these younger groups?

What about the human resources issues here? Will the healthcare business experience a "wisdom drain" as boomers retire and many positions are left vacant? Is there a way for healthcare administrators to use this new "leisure class" of boomer retirees to benefit healthcare organizations as a positive force in market justice? These are just a few of the ethics issues that the baby boomer market force will generate in the immediate future. Answers to these and other ethics issue will soon be a part of the healthcare administrator's future.

Given these examples of baby boomer market forces, prudent HCAs need to maintain a current knowledge of cultural and community trends to stay ahead of the curve and maintain their organizations' competitive edge. They need to practice creative thinking to provide services that baby boomers desire and will support financially. Healthcare administrators must avoid tunnel vision so as not to miss market opportunities and meet the ethics challenges created by the baby boom generation as it ages.

■ INTEGRATIVE MEDICINE AND ETHICS

Why IM and Why Now?

In 1993, David Eisenberg and his group at Harvard Medical School stunned the medical community with a report in *The New England Journal of Medicine*. They estimated that there were more than 425 million visits to complementary and alternative medicine (CAM) providers in the United States every year, which exceeded the number of primary care provider visits. The cost of such care amounted to $13.6 billion, most of which was paid directly by the consumers. Although criticized for its methods, this study became one of the most widely cited research efforts of its type and demonstrated a much wider use of these practices than previously suspected (Eisenberg et al., 1993). It launched a major reexamination of a healthcare field that was once considered a fad or quackery.

Eisenberg and colleagues (1998) repeated this study in 1997 with even more startling results. They found more than 629 million users of **integrative medicine (IM)** services, which was an increase of 47% from the previous study. Currently, IM is a multi-billion-dollar business in the United States. In addition, most patients combine IM practices with conventional medical care. However, many CAM users remain reluctant to inform their physicians about its use.

Different terminology has been associated with this consumer-driven healthcare movement. Initially professionals used the term *alternative medicine*, meaning that these services replaced conventional medicine. The term *complementary medicine* actually describes this form of medicine more accurately, as it used in along with conventional medicine. *Integrative medicine*, the most recent term, comprises an eclectic collection of philosophies and practices. This collection assumes a holistic view of the client, features the healing properties of the body, and seeks prevention as well as treatment of disease. IM does not see humans as a collection of cells and body parts with diseases to be treated, but rather as unique individuals who are part of the environment in which they live. IM in the United States encompasses more than 200 different types of practices, many of which have their roots in healing systems that are thousands of years old (Micozzi, 2011).

The consumers of IM tend to be educated, affluent, and female, but its use is not limited to just this group. Clients of IM desire to be partners in their health care and tend to seek health information. They also are aware of the need for prevention and view IM as a way to decrease the likelihood of serious illness or to prolong the quality of their lives. They show their belief in this system of this type of health care by their willingness to pay billions of dollars in out-of-pocket expenses to use IM services.

A major market for IM services seems to exist among people suffering from chronic disease. These populations, who may also be baby boomers, seek relief and/or control over their symptoms and may not find what they need through traditional medicine. Indeed, traditional medicine's lack of definitive treatments for chronic diseases helps to explain the growing appeal of IM (Micozzi, 2011). In addition, those who use IM want to have more control over their health problems and find that IM offers a greater sense of control. Users of IM also want to be partners in their care.

A visit to the National Center for Complementary and Alternative Medicine (NCCAM) website reveals that IM users also include traditional medicine in their treatment. Even though consumers use both systems, they often are not entirely pleased with the traditional system. Their experience is that conventional medicine is often too impersonal, expensive, and rushed. In addition, they find the side effects of conventional medicines undesirable. IM practitioners, in contrast, spend far more time with each client, including him or her in treatment plans, and use more personal modalities. In addition, practitioners stress preventive practices and areas that complement traditional medicine's approach. According to NCCAM (2013a), the CAM/IM five most frequently used practices are natural products, breathing techniques, meditation, chiropractic treatments, and massage. In addition, clients seek relief from an array of chronic health issues including arthritis pain, anxiety, depression, and insomnia through IM practitioners.

With the increased popularity of IM services, some allopathic medicine practitioners are considering some of these options for their patients. However, despite numerous clinical studies by the NCCAM (2013b), many healthcare providers still find this form of healing to be total quackery and even ridicule patients who use it. Resistance to synergism between allopathic medicine and IM has many sources, including different views of healing, reliance on Western scientific evidence, emphasis on the whole person, and reductionism (Micozzi, 2011).

Criticisms of IM practice often a center on its lack of grounding in scientific theory despite NCCAM's studies that demonstrate the safety and efficacy of many of these options. Some allopathic practitioners also question the qualifications of CAM practitioners based on medical school criteria. Others brand practices with thousands of years of effectiveness as fads or as the result of the placebo effect. For example, herbal medicine, despite extensive research in Germany and other countries, continues to be viewed as ineffective and a waste of money, when compared to pharmaceuticals.

However, allopathic medicine's response to CAM/IM is not all negative. Since the National Institutes of Health began supporting serious research in CAM/IM, physicians have slowly begun to show more interest in the area. U.S. medical schools appear increasingly more interested in the field of IM and some now offer courses in this area (Landau, 2011). Medical students know that their future patients could be using these healing practices and are interested in adding IM to their knowledge base. In addition, centers of IM practice such as the University of Arizona, which has Andrew Weil on its faculty, and Eisenberg's Center for Alternative Medicine Research and Education are responsible for both CAM research and education. There is even a *Physicians' Desk Reference for Herbal Medicine* available so that busy practitioners can readily access the latest information on these treatments. In addition, pharmacy and nursing schools are expanding their coverage of IM practices including holistic nursing (American Holistic Nurses Association, 2013).

The NCCAM now provides a wealth of resources for those allopathic practitioners who seek information about CAM practices. These resources include CAM-based research reports, literature links with PubMed, and evidence reports from the AHRQ. The NCCAM's website also includes clinical practice guidelines and information on areas of CAM from A to Z. To facilitate use of CAM in practices, the NCCAM site includes free continuing education videos and patient information sheets.

Some hospitals and specialty centers have added CAM practices to their existing offerings. For example, these facilities may offer music therapy, massage, guided imagery, and acupuncture as a way to provide patient-centered services (NCCAM, 2013c).

Where Is the Ethics?

The integration of two systems of health care with very different views of patients and their needs has the potential for many ethical problems. If future predictions are correct, IM will grow as a part of the healthcare business. It will be important to consider potential ethics issues and prevent them as much as possible. Perhaps most importantly, administrators of a clinic or hospital must have informed clinical practitioners to avoid harm and provide the best care for patients who also use IM.

While professionals might not agree with what patients choose for their healthcare needs, these patients still expect their healthcare providers to honor their autonomy.

Failure to have a basic knowledge of IM practices will prevent allopathic medical staff from providing the most informed care and could have drastic (and negative) results. For example, some herbs affect the blood's ability to clot. If a patient takes these herbs with prescribed blood thinning agents, the results can even be fatal. A well-informed practitioner is able to prevent such problems by obtaining patient information and by knowing the action and drug interactions between herbs and pharmaceuticals. Physicians, nurses, and other practitioners also need to answer questions about IM practices in a fair and evidence-based way. Continuing education programs and resource materials like those provided by the National Center for Complementary and Alternative Medicine provide resources to improve information and practice in IM.

Informed consent is another ethics issue related to IM. Some have argued that healthcare practitioners should discuss IM options as well as traditional medicine with their patients. The classic tool for patient education, the American Hospital Association's *Patient Care Partnership* document (2003), stresses the need for patients to have information on benefits and risks of healthcare decisions. To assist with patient decision making, physicians and other practitioners should be aware of all treatment options and be able to answer questions. Healthcare professionals must also provide objective and accurate advice about CAM/IM modalities so that patient consent is truly informed. As clinical studies reveal more evidence about which IM practices are effective and which are not, practitioners should feel more comfortable discussing these options with patients. The policy of "Don't ask; don't tell" with respect to IM will not work for the future. In fact, questions about the use of IM practices and herbs are becoming a standard inclusion on medical history forms. Their inclusion provides information necessary for protecting both patient autonomy and practice liability.

What if a clinical practice wants to add IM modalities as a revenue stream? There are certainly areas that administrators and clinicians must consider when pursuing this course. First, administrators will want to become familiar with the IM services readily available in their areas and their frequency of usage. They will also need to investigate insurance coverage for IM services. In today's high-tech world, such information is available through web searches and other methods. Because patient safety is an ethics concern, administrators always want to consider the efficacy and quality of any services. This evidence is increasingly available through the research and practitioner sites on the National Center for Complementary and Alternative Medicine webpage. Administrators would then have to take all of the appropriate steps for adding IM services, including finding a champion for the change. It is also wise to start small and build. For example, an administrator could add a massage therapist after evaluating patient satisfaction and profitability of such an addition. Fortunately, Rakel and Faass (2006) have written a detailed book on how best to integrate IM services into traditional practices.

As part of an administrator's ethical duty to protect patient safety, the HCA must contract with or hire IM practitioners who are prepared in their area of service. It is important to know that many of the 200 areas of IM are now certified or licensed. For example, the American Massage Therapy Association has accredited programs throughout the United States. Many states also require a license to practice massage therapy. Likewise, there is a program for school accreditation and individual certification/licensure for acupuncture and naturopathy practice. To make this even easier, firms now exist to verify practitioner certification and make hiring qualified practitioners easier. While certification and licensure are increasing for many of IM areas, not all practitioners have formal credentialing or are even required to have it to practice. Health-care administrators need to use discernment based on their facilities' mission, their research, and consumer information in those cases.

Summary

This chapter explored issues related to the impact of market forces on healthcare systems and the potential ethical problems that these forces can create. It concentrated on three major trends: managed care, the baby boomers, and IM. This is not the whole picture, however. Practicing HCAs, will have to keep their fingers on the pulse of what is happening in their individual healthcare markets. Certainly, they will need to monitor federal, state, and local laws and regulations that will affect their organizations' market growth and viability. As additional issues surface, healthcare administrators will be responsible for addressing them in a patient-centered, ethics-based manner. Administrators should always remember that they are trusted to provide safe, quality care for patients. In addition, the organization's positive image in the community is critical to its success in creating a viable healthcare business. In dealing appropriately with market forces, organizational and personal ethics matter.

Cases for Your Consideration

The Case of the Concerned Managed Care Administrator

1. Which ethical principles did this administrator use in dealing with Mr. Michigan?

2. What was the cost of her practicing ethical behavior and what were the benefits?

Case Information

Mary Ledbetter was one of the claims managers for St. Dismas Health Plan (SDHP). On Monday, she received a case from one of her assistants for review. The case involved a man named Shamus Michigan who had visited his acupuncturist. This professional found a problem in the kidney meridian. Mr. Michigan subsequently had a full body scan at a local clinic and the scan picked up a mass in the kidney area. Mr. Michigan also had a follow-up scan and a MRI. He was diagnosed with cancer of the kidney. Fortunately, he had an encapsulated tumor and a laparoscopic nephrectomy was possible. He filed a claim for reimbursement for his scans with SDHP, and the company denied his claim.

Mr. Michigan became quite upset when he received this news. He told the claims representative that he thought SDHP discriminated against people who used IM practitioners. After all, if it were not for his acupuncturist, he might be dead instead of just losing one kidney. He could not understand the denial of coverage and, after consulting with an attorney, asked for an appeal.

Usually, Ms. Ledbetter would do a quick review of such cases and issue a form letter to the appellant. However, she felt that this case might be different. She contacted Mr. Michigan and asked for more details. At first, he was upset about the denial of his claim, but he listened to Ms. Ledbetter as she explained their policy. SDHP could only pay for procedures ordered by a physician, not ones chosen by the patient. Ledbetter asked Mr. Michigan if he had a physician order for any of the tests. As it turned out, he did. There was a referral from his physician and he had a copy of his letter.

Ms. Ledbetter put Mr. Michigan on hold and checked her policy book. While such a referral was unusual, it certainly seemed appropriate. She told Mr. Michigan to send her a copy of the information that he had for review. When it arrived by fax, she found that Mr. Michigan was correct; he did have proof of a physician order. When she called him back, she was able to give him good news. SDHP would pay for the last two tests, which would lessen his financial burden considerably.

Mr. Michigan still was not entirely happy with the outcome, but after talking with Ms. Ledbetter, he understood the rationale for the decisions. He thanked her for putting in the effort to help him with his situation and said he looked forward to receiving his check in a reasonable period. After their conversation, he called his lawyer and told him not to go forward with the lawsuit.

Responses and Commentary on Questions

1. Which ethical principles did this administrator use in dealing with Mr. Michigan?

At this point in your study, you should be able to identify many ethics principles for this case. Ms. Ledbetter acted with beneficence when she chose to take the extra time to review the case instead of just issuing a form letter. Her follow-up phone call and decision to assist Mr. Michigan were also acts of beneficence. In addition, she supported the principle of nonmaleficence by making sure he received the benefit that was appropriate and did not have any additional financial harm. She also prevented the harm of a lawsuit against SDHP.

Certainly, Ms. Ledbetter acted to respect Mr. Michigan's autonomy by giving him complete information about the denial of his claim. She even went further to inquire if he had proof of a physician's order. This inquiry helped her to arrive at a successful resolution of the problem because the necessary additional information existed. In addition, she treated Mr. Michigan with respect even though he was angry at SDHP. She was not condescending or rude in her conversation, which kept things on a more rational basis. Finally, she practiced justice because, while she did not order payment for a claim she could not support with a policy, she did make sure that Mr. Michigan received the reimbursement for which he was entitled.

2. What was the cost of her practicing ethical behavior and what were the benefits?

The cost of Ms. Ledbetter's use of ethical behavior was minimal compared with the cost of having to deal with a lawsuit. Even if such a suit did not reach the courts, the negative publicity potential would be great. In addition, she kept an SDHP member satisfied, so he did not wish to change health plans. If asked, he could attest to the fairness of his treatment. This was worth a great deal in positive word-of-mouth publicity for the plan. In all, practicing ethical behavior was good business practice in this case.

The Case of the Confused Abuela (Grandmother)

As you read this case, consider the following questions. Responses and comments will follow the case.

1. Which principles of ethics are involved in this case?

2. What were the ethics issues for Porter Sanders?

3. How important was knowledge of IM practices to the successful resolution of this case?

Case Information

Porter Sanders was the assistant administrator of St. Dismas Home Health (SDHH) program. On Monday morning, one of his best home health nurses, Emma Ray, stopped by his office to discuss a concern. Here is the case she presented.

Ms. Ray received a physician order for a home visit assessment of Mrs. Viola Romero, an 86-year-old woman with hypertension, who was also on thyroid medication. Mrs. Romero was living independently in her own home, but the family was concerned. Her behavior seemed to be deteriorating. She often appeared confused, exhibited some unusual aggressive behavior, and cried without provocation. They were worried that she had Alzheimer's disease and contacted her physician, who then ordered Ms. Ray's visit.

During her assessment, Ms. Ray questioned Mrs. Romero about her health history and activities of daily living. She was supposed to be taking medication for her hypertension. Because she had a thyroidectomy, she also needed daily thyroid medication. However, Mrs. Romero had consulted with the local *curandero*, who conducted several rituals including *sahumerio* (incensing) and prayer. This healer advised Mrs. Romero to stop taking all of her medicines because they were poisoning her system. Instead, she suggested drinking a mint herb tea made with the addition of olive oil. In addition, she sold Mrs. Romero a magnetic bracelet to wear every day to balance her energies.

Mrs. Romero believed in the powers of this healer, who had a good reputation in the community, and she wanted to follow her advice. Ms. Ray tried to talk to her about the problems associated with not taking her medications, which could explain her change in behavior and other symptoms. She tried to explain that Mrs. Romero was endangering her safety and her life by not taking these medications. Mrs. Romero accused Ms. Ray of not respecting her beliefs and being on the side of the physician and her family. At the end of the visit, she remained adamant that she did not want to visit the physician or get back on her medications.

After she filed her report to the physician, Ms. Ray asked for Mr. Sanders's advice on the next steps to take. While she wished to respect Mrs. Romero's autonomy and right to choose or refuse treatment, she was concerned that Mrs. Romero was threatening her life. Mr. Sanders agreed and expressed concern about the effect on SDHH if they did not take action on Mrs. Romero's case. After a lengthy discussion, Ms. Ray decided to discuss her findings with the physician and the family.

Once the physician had a full picture of the situation, he told Ms. Ray to advise the family to bring Mrs. Romero in immediately. In his opinion, this curandero was jeopardizing her life. He needed to evaluate her status and get her on the appropriate medication immediately. Ms. Ray then visited the family and explained what happened. They were shocked and greatly concerned. The family said that they would get Mrs. Romero to the physician "if they have to drag her there."

Two weeks later, Ms. Ray received a call from the family. Mrs. Romero kept her appointment at her physician's office but cried the whole way there. Fortunately, her physician was aware of the practices of curanderos and was able to convince her that her medications were not poisons. He encouraged her to use prayer and the bracelet for balance as long as she continued to take her pills. Mrs. Romero did not want to make the physician angry, so she decided to take the pills. Her symptoms disappeared.

Responses and Commentary on Questions

1. Which principles of ethics are involved in this case?

    From the study of ethics, one can see that many principles are involved in this case. One of the most obvious is the conflict between patient autonomy and paternalism. Who knew what was best for this patient? Ms. Ray wanted to honor Mrs. Romero's autonomy and treat her with respect. Mrs. Romero had the right to control her own body and accept or reject treatment, but her actions put her life at risk. However, these actions also compromised her ability to make informed decisions. Therefore, her family had to intervene in this situation. Additionally, as part of autonomy, she had the right to truth-telling. Ms. Ray carefully provided truthful information to convince Mrs. Romero that the curandero's practices were not in her best interests. Because the belief in the power of curanderos was a part of Mrs. Romero's core culture, this was difficult.

    One can also see the dual principles of beneficence and nonmaleficence in this case. First, Ms. Ray had a moral obligation to respect Mrs. Romero's beliefs and not demean them. Even though she disagreed with these practices, she had to treat Mrs. Romero with respect and kindness. However, she also had a moral duty to do no harm. Allowing Mrs. Romero to continue this practice without any intervention could cause her great harm and contribute to her premature death. Mrs. Romero's physician told Ms. Ray to contact the family immediately, and she supported this decision.

    The principle of autonomy was also an issue for the family. They dearly loved their Abuela Viola and wanted to respect her rights. However, they were concerned that her latest actions made her too confused to make appropriate health decisions. On the advice of Ms. Ray and the physician, they took action on the situation and coerced Mrs. Romero into visiting her physician.

2. What were the ethics issues for Porter Sanders?

    Porter Sanders had a different view of the ethics in this situation. While the mission of SDHH stressed that he must respect the cultural practices of his clients, he also needed to consider the impact of Mrs. Romero's actions on his business. If Mrs. Romero was not convinced to see her physician and died as a result, it could pose real problems for SDHH. The family could choose to blame Ms. Ray and SDHH for her death and contact an attorney, the press, or both. Certainly, the publicity of such actions, even though unfounded, could be harmful to the organization.

Mr. Sanders was also concerned with providing the best advice to Ms. Ray. He needed to listen to and consider her viewpoint in this situation. Of course, because the organization functions under physician order, he had to remind her that she needed to provide detailed information to him. To protect patient confidentiality, he had to make sure that Mrs. Romero's records were complete and protected. Likewise, he needed to be sure that Ms. Ray did not discuss this interesting case with her colleagues over coffee. Mr. Sanders relied on Ms. Ray's professionalism and the policies of SDHH to maintain this ethics obligation.

3. How important was knowledge of IM practices to the successful resolution of this case?

Knowledge of IM practices—specifically the practices of curanderos—was critical to the ability to resolve this case. First, Ms. Ray needed to be fully aware of the belief system of her Hispanic client, Mrs. Romero. This knowledge allowed her to communicate more completely and honor her autonomy. She also had to understand the philosophy and practices of curanderos. Many of these healers use practices that support traditional medicine and can actually be helpful. In Mrs. Romero's case, however, the curandero was giving harmful advice. Ms. Ray needed to be able to explain why it was harmful while respecting Mrs. Romero's culture.

Most assuredly, the fact that Mrs. Romero's physician operated an informed practice helped him understand her culture and explain what she needed to do. Without such knowledge, he might have ignored her beliefs (at best) or even ridiculed them. Either of those responses would not have ensured patient compliance with treatment and might have caused unnecessary harm. However, his knowledge and patience with Mrs. Romero led to a positive outcome in this case.

Web Resources

American Holistic Nurses Association
http://www.ahna.org

National Conference of State Legislatures
http://www.ncsl.org

National Institute on Complementary and Alternative Medicine
http://nccam.nih.gov

References

American Holistic Nurses Association. (2013). What is holistic nursing? Retrieved from http://www.ahna.org/About-Us/What-is-Holistic-Nursing

American Hospital Association. (2003). *The patient care partnership: Understanding expectations, rights, and responsibilities.* Atlanta, GA: AHA Services.

Anderlik, M. R. (2001). *The ethics of managed care: A pragmatic approach.* Bloomington, IN: Indiana University Press.

Cohn, D., & Taylor, P. (2010). Baby boomers approach 65—glumly. *Pew Research Social and Demographic Trends.* Retrieved from http://www.pewsocialtrends.org/2010/12/20/baby-boomers-approach-65-glumly/

Darr, K. (2011). *Ethics in health services management* (5th ed.). Baltimore, MD: Health Professions Press.

Eisenberg, D. M., Davis, R. B., Ettnes, S. L., Appel, S., Wilkey, S., Van Rompay, M. V., & Kessler, R. C. (1998). Trends in alternative medicine use in the United States, 1990–1997. *Journal of the American Medical Association, 280,* 1569–1575.

Eisenberg, D. M., Kessler, R. C., Foster, F. C., Norlock, F. E., Calkins, D. R., & Delbanco, T. L. (1993). Unconventional medicine in the United States. *New England Journal of Medicine, 328,* 246–252.

Kaiser Family Foundation. (2013). Focus on health reform: Summary of the Affordable Care Act. Available at http://www.kff.org.

Kongstvedt, P. R. (2013). *Essentials of managed care* (6th ed.). Burlington, MA: Jones & Bartlett Learning.

Landau, M. D. (2011, April 12). Medical schools embrace alternative medicine. *U S. News and World Report.* Retrieved from http://www.usnews.com/education/best-graduate-schools/articles/2011/04/12/medical-schools-embrace-alternative-medicine

Micozzi, M. S. (2011). *Fundamentals of complementary and alternative medicine* (4th ed.). St. Louis, MO: Elsevier.

National Center for Complementary and Alternative Medicine (NCCAM). (2013a). What is CAM? Retrieved from http://nccam.nih.gov/health/whatiscam

National Center for Complementary and Alternative Medicine (NCCAM). (2013b). Research results. Retrieved from http://nccam.nih.gov/research/results

National Center for Complementary and Alternative Medicine (NCCAM). (2013c). Resources for health providers. Retrieved from http://nccam.nih.gov/health/providers

National Conference of State Legislatures. (2011). Managed care state laws and regulations, including consumer and provider protections. Retrieved from http://www.ncsl.org/issues-research/health/managed-care-state-laws.aspx

O'Brien, R. L. (2014). A new era of health care: The ethics of healthcare reform. In E. E. Morrison & B. Furlong (Eds.), *Health care ethics: Critical issues for the 21st century* (3rd ed., pp. 363–374). Burlington, MA: Jones & Bartlett Learning.

Perry, F. (2013). *The tracks we leave: Ethics and management dilemmas in healthcare* (2nd ed.). Chicago, IL: Health Administration Press.

Rakel, D., & Faass, N. (2006). *Complementary medicine in clinical practice: Integrative practice in American healthcare*. Sudbury, MA: Jones and Bartlett.

Scheve, T. (2013). Top 10 baby boomer health trends, *Discovery Health*. Retrieved from http://www.bing.com/search?q=top+10+baby+boomer+health+trends&qs=n&form=QBLH&pc=BNHP&pq=top+10+baby+boomer+health+trends&sc=0-19&sp=-1&sk=&cvid=1dc4cd66063142dbb4814fe88199276c

Shi, L., & Singh, D. A. (2015). *Delivering health care in America: A systems approach* (6th ed.). Burlington, MA: Jones & Bartlett Learning.

CHAPTER
7

Community Responsibility and Ethics

Why does the business of health care need to be responsible to the community?

Points to Ponder

1. Why are there so many rules and regulations in health care?
2. How can a healthcare administrator practice ethics-based administration in light of multiple regulations?
3. Can health care be responsible to the community and still meet its business goals?
4. How is quality assurance part of community responsibility?

Key Terms

The following is a list of key words for this chapter. You will find them in bold in the text.

ACHE   The Joint Commission (TJC)
APHA   MGMA
BFOQs   NCQA
HIPAA

■ INTRODUCTION AND DEFINITIONS

The Joint Commission, CMS, NCQA, HEDIS, FDA, EEOC, AHA, AMA, HIPAA, ACA, IOM—these are just a few of the agencies and laws that demand quality standards in the business of health care. In addition, one can add numerous state and local agencies to this list.

Likewise, the managed care organizations that fund much of health care maintain their own set of standards for practices tied to reimbursement. Administrators can also add consumer groups such as the AARP to the list of those concerned about patients' treatment by the healthcare system. The enormous burden of accountability to the patient community can seem both overwhelming and costly. Yet, there is an expectation that healthcare administrators (HCAs) will successfully meet the requirements and standards of a plethora of agencies and still maintain profitability. This chapter stresses responsibility to the community through the standards of quality assurance organizations, effective advocacy, and staff competency.

The reality of healthcare organizations is that they work under the microscope and magnifying glass of both macro and micro accountability. On the macro level, they are accountable to external regulators such as federal, state, and local governments. Healthcare organizations are also responsible to accreditation bodies. On the micro level, they are accountable to patients, their families, and certainly, their boards of trustees. In his classic work, Worthley (1997, p. 147) provides a set of questions to guide the assessment of health care's responsibility. He asks, "As health care professionals to *whom* are we accountable? For *what* are we accountable? *How* are we held accountable? *Why* are we held accountable? And *what results* from all of this?"

To answer Worthley's questions, one must understand the public's view of the healthcare industry. To paraphrase an old song, "There's no business like the healthcare business." No other business has the amount and type of power over its clientele. Health care can literally kill its customers or heal them. It can cause them unnecessary suffering or relieve their pain. In addition, many of the practitioners in the healthcare business hold a monopoly on the ability to provide services through their certifications and state licensures. This means that not only is the business of health care the most powerful one in the United States, but individuals within this business also hold power over others.

Throughout history, Americans have demonstrated a certain level of mistrust for anyone or anything that wields such absolute power. They have seen the potential for abuse of power held by those who have less than altruistic motives to the detriment of the population. Therefore, communities have sought to protect themselves from the professional power held by health care by taking certain actions. First, communities tried to limit the power held by health care by limiting its boundaries. They used external controls such as accreditation by The Joint Commission to both limit power and determine minimum standards of care. In addition, Medicare/Medicaid regulations and state laws govern various medical practices. Community actions such as lawsuits and adverse publicity can also limit power and negatively affect healthcare organizations and professionals. Therefore, healthcare administrators need to be aware of the community's power to influence an organization's reputation and marketplace confidence.

In addition, communities can protect themselves from the power of health care by changing its structure and payment systems. For example, private and public agencies can establish certain regulations regarding payment for services that control demand and supply, and emphasize practices that protect patients. In turn, these regulations influence the structure of the healthcare system itself. For example, the ACA stresses prevention as part of insurance coverage (Kaiser Family Foundation, 2013). Because these prevention services are now part of insurance coverage, healthcare systems will alter their practice designs to include them. Putting emphasis on services through laws and regulations changes healthcare practices and serves to control the healthcare system's power through its bottom line. There is some logic to the thinking that without such controls, the healthcare system could become even more expensive and demand even more of the U.S. gross national product.

Society also attempts to limit health care by checking the power of individual practitioners. Communities work through professional and state agencies to pass legislation on practice, continuing education requirements, and accreditation of undergraduate and graduate healthcare programs. While these professional regulations may not limit enrollment numbers, they do add academic requirements to assure greater quality of graduates, while also limiting their professional power by defining a scope of practice. On the micro (i.e., organizational) level, strict standards on professional practice including background checks, verification of credentials, policies on employee ethics, and investigation of employee violations of organizational policies serve to protect the public. These standards of staff competency assist the healthcare organization in meeting its responsibility to the community and are part of this chapter's discussion.

Shortell and colleagues (2000) provide additional reasons for the demand for accountability. The United States has a long history of valuing individual rights and the ability of professionals to make decisions about health care. However, the changes that have occurred in the healthcare industry in recent years have created a greater demand for community accountability. These changes include managed care, federal and state laws (ACA and others), and information technologies including the Internet. In addition, public awareness of how health care works has increased because of Internet sites turned up by search engines, news coverage, and television programs. Today, consumers can actually be "in" the operating room and watch what is happening through entertainment programming. They may also see the hospital in action through "reality" and fictional programs. These up-close views of health care, whether accurate or not, influence community demand for accountability for both the outcomes and the costs of healthcare practice.

There is also an increased demand for accountability in health care when communities learn about ethics violations in other industries. For example, when people see chief executive officers (CEOs) testify before Congress about their misdeeds and wealthy Americans face prison time, the community wonders about the ethics of business in general. While these cases have ended up in the legal system, they began with a lack of ethical standards and practices. Given that health care is also a business, will the lack of ethics practice likewise be a part of its quest for profitability? Because there is less overall trust in business in general, there may also be a similar public response to the business of health care.

The potential erosion of trust is particularly bothersome for the healthcare administrator because, as Annison and Wilford (1998) stressed in their classic book on trust, healthcare administrators are leaders in a trust-based business. Without a high level of trust from the community, the business of healthcare would suffer both in its potential for service and in its financial bottom line. Imagine the level of accountability that would be required if the community lost complete trust in the healthcare system.

Given the community concern about quality and trust, whether it comes from a government agency, business contractor, or private citizen group, it is not surprising that health administrators must navigate in an environment of high accountability and constant scrutiny. They must be prepared to operate a profitable business entity in this environment. The first step in this challenging process is to get to know the organization. Administrators should keep in mind that knowing their organizations assists in successfully complying with the myriad of regulations that apply to business and patient operations. The first step in knowing the organization is to have a clearly stated mission, vision, and values. These statements represent the business and ethics foundation of the organization. Once there is an unambiguous understanding of this foundation, the HCA will need to establish both formal and informal structures and practices that will keep him or her accountable for these espoused values.

In addition, healthcare administrators must know who is asking for compliance. In other words, they must understand the standards that govern their business practices and recognize what these standards mean for their particular organization. Obtaining this knowledge can require many hours of deep reading, telephone calls for clarification, and meetings with staff for interpretation and practice applications. However, because knowledge truly is power in this case, the payoff is worth the effort. In addition to state and federal legislation like the ACA, other areas of accountability must be considered. Examples include the standards set by The Joint Commission, HIPAA, and NCQA. What are the ethics issues related to these standards?

■ THE JOINT COMMISSION

The governance of healthcare practice includes strongly held standards that have their roots in community accountability and laws and regulations. One of the most prominent sources of such standards is **The Joint Commission** (TJC). This organization began in 1951 and originally focused on hospital accreditation. Currently, in addition to hospitals, it accredits long-term care facilities including assisted-living centers. It is also involved in the accreditation of ambulatory care facilities, clinical laboratories, rehabilitation facilities, and behavioral medicine organizations including residential treatment centers and foster care. The Joint Commission provides accreditation for home health agencies and healthcare networks as well. It certifies disease-specific programs, palliative care programs, and staffing services. Although participation in this accreditation process is voluntary for facilities, healthcare organizations often view it as essential. In addition, Medicare recognizes TJC inspections and the inspection results have a tie to funding. Many state agencies also contract with TJC to review managed care organizations. In addition, TJC publishes performance reports that the public can access through its Quality Check program. Because of its scope and depth of involvement in healthcare accreditation, this organization has great influence on both the practices and ethical standards for the industry (TJC, 2013a).

There are sets of standards, which can number into the hundreds, for each of the facilities accredited by TJC. TJC provides each organization with detailed manuals to guide the compliance with these standards and documentation of that compliance. In addition to the accreditation standards and processes, TJC offers tools for dealing with patient care issues through its Target Solutions Tools developed by its Center for Transforming Healthcare. Currently, these products include tools for dealing with hand washing, wrong-site surgery prevention, and hand-offs (TJC, 2013b).

This organization has also made an attempt to improve patient safety through its National Patient Safety Goals initiative. This program includes annual patient safety goals for ambulatory care, behavioral health, hospitals, home health, long-term care, laboratories, and office based surgeries. For example, the 2013 goals for hospitals include specific information on patient identification, staff communication, infection prevention, and surgery error prevention (TJC, 2013c).

Early in its existence as an accrediting body, The Joint Commission made announced site visits. These visits were expensive and required many months of preparation. Because the team was coming, staff at the facility cleaned the carpets, painted the walls, and documented the standards. The site visit was a time to get the records in order to meet the minimum written standards. Today, emphasis has shifted to unannounced visits. These TJC visits commonly occur between 18 and 36 months from the previous survey, and their emphasis is on safety and standards compliance. In addition, the team is interested in seeing the organization as it exists under normal conditions and attempts to lower the costs of site visits (TJC, 2012).

The Joint Commission has also developed standards that emphasize the treatment of patients and their rights. For example, for hospitals, the title of this standards set is "Rights and Responsibilities of the Individual" (TJC, 2013d, p. 9). These standards include ethics-based issues such as patient autonomy, informed consent, respect for the rights of patients in treatment, and patients' involvement in their own care. In addition, they stress respect for patients' preferences and beliefs about their care. These and other standards related to the provision of care, its documentation, and evaluation serve to protect the community and improve overall quality of health care.

■ HIPAA

In 1996, Congress passed the Health Insurance Portability and Accountability Act (**HIPAA**) as an attempt to engage in healthcare reform and deal with new issues facing the industry. The act had several objectives, including providing health insurance coverage when there was a job change or when preexisting conditions existed, reducing fraud and abuse, standardizing health information, and ensuring security and privacy of health information. The legislation had several titles to address all of these objectives. For example, the Administration Simplification provisions dealt with rules for compliance with this act and addressed electronic claims submission, including standards of privacy, confidentiality, and maintenance of health information. It mandated that there be a unique identifier for each patient, employer, health plan, and provider in an attempt to protect patient privacy (Shi & Singh, 2015).

This legislation has an impact on almost all healthcare institutions and on vendors that serve those institutions. One can imagine how confusing the initial communications about the law and its mandates were. The Department of Health and Human Services provided numerous documents to assist with HIPAA compliance. In fact, there is now a whole industry that assists healthcare organizations with HIPAA compliance and training.

The positive features of the law were that electronic transfers of data became easier and more cost-effective. Security upgrades improved the confidentiality of patient data. These efforts protected patients' right to know who has seen their medical records and the use of their personal information within a healthcare organization. Currently, there is an increased awareness of the potential for violating confidentiality. This awareness has led to better protection for the patient's information through procedures for taking health histories, avoidance of inappropriate conversations about patients, and methods to prevent marketing firms from accessing patient names and addresses. In addition, simple procedures like the placement of computers can avoid unnecessary violations of confidentiality. Ethics aspects of autonomy and respect for patients are part of the provisions of HIPAA.

In 2013, the federal government enacted the Omnibus Final Rule for HIPAA. The date for implementation of this rule was September 23, 2013. Privacy and security procedures, notices of privacy practices, and issues related to business associates and vender agreements were all part of the new regulations. In addition, the rule included provisions that prohibit health plans from using genetic information for underwriting purposes and increase the amount of fines and the ability to investigate violations.

The Omnibus Final Rule requires patient notification when there is a violation of patient health information leading to a risk of compromise. In addition, if the patient pays out-of-pocket for care and requests that the provider not report treatment information to his or her plan, the provider must honor the request. There are also limits on how much marketing information a physician can provide without written authorization from the patient. Likewise, the physician cannot sell the patient's health information without the patient's written consent. Moreover, healthcare administrators must consider security when using technology to send copies of the patient's health information and charging patients for copies of their records.

The Omnibus Final Rule (American Medical Association, 2013) also requires that notices of privacy practices (NPP) reflect the new requirements. It includes a policy that requires physician review of agreements with any business associates. Business associates are now responsible for their own protection of patient information and for their subcontractors' protections of this information. In addition, the rule introduces four penalty tiers based on published criteria and defines a 30-day cure period for correcting violations.

What do the changes in the HIPAA law mean for health administrators? Of course, they will be responsible for making sure that their organizations comply with HIPAA and the Omnibus Final Rule. Administrators will continue to spend long hours reading the many publications that relate to the new rule and keeping up with its revisions. Healthcare administrators will also have to ensure that they provide staff training and that they document correctly. If there is an investigation to determine compliance with the Omnibus Final Rule, the healthcare administrator may be part of the team that responds to the investigation. HIPAA is part of the healthcare administrator's life and will certainly be important as he or she assists in achieving compliance with the 2013 rule. While addressing these changes may be stressful, one should always be mindful that HIPAA's intent is to protect patient autonomy and reduce potential harm to the patient and to the organization.

■ NCQA

The National Committee for Quality Assurance (**NCQA**) is a not-for-profit organization that was founded in 1990. Its purpose is to improve the quality of care provided by the managed care industry including health plans, managed care organizations, preferred provider organizations (PPOs), and disease management organizations. With the advent of the ACA, NCQA has begun to provide information and resources on accountable care organizations (ACOs), state health care exchanges, and patient-centered medical homes (PCMHs). Its ACA-related initiatives expand the scope and benefits of this quality-centered organization.

A major factor in the success of NCQA is its data collection through quality indicators called the Health Effectiveness Data and Information Set (HEDIS). More than 90% of healthcare plans to use this tool to determine the quality of managed care programs and services. HEDIS covers five domains of health care and includes more than 80 indicators of quality. Each year these indicators are improved to address new issues or to reflect greater detail. For example, the HEDIS 2013 measures include weight assessment and nutritional counseling for children, immunization status for adolescents, and improvements in data collection. There are also HEDIS guidelines for physicians in measuring quality indicators. Health care plans must report their performance on more than 40 of the HEDIS standards to qualify for consideration for the NCQA Seal of Approval (NCQA, 2013).

NCQA accreditation is voluntary. However, according to NCQA's website, many employers rely on the organization's quality assessments when choosing their employees' managed care options. To assist in this process, NCQA maintains an informational website where employers and the public can review NCQA Health Plan Report Cards, which allow for comparison-shopping of health plans based on their quality scores. NCQA also publishes an annual report called *The State of Health Care Quality*. Using HEDIS data, this report provides insight into areas of improvement for health plans and current and future issues for U.S. health (NCQA, 2013).

■ WHAT ARE THE ETHICS ISSUES FOR COMMUNITY ACCOUNTABILITY?

The previous sections reviewed examples of organizations that measure the quality of service provided by the healthcare industry and limit its power over the community. For healthcare administrators, these organizations with their multiple standards might seem overwhelming, and their standards may even contradict each other. Attempting to stay current and to implement healthcare standards might make administrators feel as if they are operating in a fishbowl. The need to provide so much data is also likely to make them feel chained to their computers and as if they have become an electronic paper pusher rather than an administrative professional. Nevertheless, administrators must consider accountability as a necessary element for the powerful healthcare industry. Being accountable is part of the administrator's ethical responsibilities.

Successful administrators will be able to juggle the ethical mandate for accountability with the challenges of maintaining positive staff relations, providing quality patient care, and attending to the bottom line. This juggling act will require an active role as a continuous learner to keep up with any changes in current standards or the addition of new ones, such as the many requirements of the ACA. How do administrators influence how legislation affects their organizations? The answer lies in the power and ethics of advocacy.

■ THE ETHICS OF ADVOCACY

How can administrators run effective, efficient, and patient-centered businesses in spite of external control? How can they be proactive rather than reactive? Certainly, no one would argue that regulations and standards are costly in both time and the fiscal resources required to address them. However, none of this will change if administrators remain passive or just wait for enforcement of standards.

First, health administrators must understand that the larger community does not have a good understanding of the business of health care. The continuing debates over the ACA demonstrate that individuals and lawmakers have differing views of what health care is and what it should be. Therefore, if healthcare administrators want to have positive change in the future, they must be willing to assist in increasing understanding of the true nature of the healthcare business. They must become ethics-based advocates for their particular organizations as well as their profession. The advocate role requires that the healthcare administrator remain current on the latest healthcare issues concerning the community and addressed by legislation, and model the expected behavior. In other words, administrators must do more than talk about healthcare quality; they must be willing to take an active role in achieving it in their organizations.

Being aware and informed first requires that HCAs research the current state of legislation. Given the changing nature of national healthcare laws, administrators may need to subscribe to online updates from their professional associations and attend workshops and professional meetings. HCAs also need to maintain currency in the main healthcare issues facing their communities by attending local meetings. It is smart to maintain a connection with one's local public health department as well, because this agency has data and information about current health trends and future issues. Of course, professional journals abound with information about national trends in health, including health problems, ideas for dealing with these problems, and pending legislation about these problems. Some of these journals are now available through computer, tablet, and smartphone applications to accommodate busy HCAs.

Being an advocate also means getting involved. Maintaining contact with public health departments, as noted previously, helps to keep the HCA current on health issues. Another proactive step is to examine the idea of creating joint initiatives to increase the likelihood of preventing expensive health problems. These might include health assessment projects, health fairs, school programs, and other prevention-centered activities. As long as it is not a conflict of interest, health administrators might consider becoming members of the various groups and associations that represent their healthcare areas. For example, an HCA could be a leader in a local, state, or national chapter of a hospital or long-term care association. Being an active member would involve being on committees, giving presentations, or even holding office to support health care. Finally, healthcare administrators should consider being active members of professional associations. For administrators in the clinical side of health care, this includes membership in organizations devoted to nursing, respiratory therapy, dentistry, mental health, or medical education, among others. Other opportunities are available for advocacy in the local, state, and national chapters of the American College of Healthcare Executives (**ACHE**), the Medical Group Management Association (**MGMA**), and the American Public Health Association (**APHA**). Their websites are listed at the end of this chapter.

Healthcare administrators often ask, "How can I afford the time to do all of this and still have a life?" There is certainly a concern about work/life balance when the demand for accountability is high. However, HCAs should consider the cost of noninvolvement. Not investing in efforts to maintain accountability and ethics-based practice can leave the healthcare organization behind when trends occur that can cause benefit or harm. Given that HCAs are required to keep current regarding both legislation and trends, they will serve as the "go-to people" for information and ideas to deal with change, as well as how change will affect the organization. Being prepared and offering knowledge-based creative thinking will be a true career builder in the era of the ACA.

Finally, HCAs should remember that to "have a life," they should choose their advocacy opportunities wisely. Healthcare administrators do not have to do everything. However, contributing to their profession, reading professional and other literature, scanning the Internet, and maintaining liaisons with public health offices can go a long way toward keeping them knowledge and change ready. HCAs should expect that their careers will often include meetings, reports, and long hours. However, if they are involved in work that is satisfying and positively affects the quality of patient care, HCAs will find that they not only have lives, but that their lives have meaning and purpose.

■ THE ETHICS OF STAFF COMPETENCY

The ethics of staff competency relates directly to the organization's responsibility to the community that it serves. When patients or clients enter a healthcare organization, they make at least one assumption—that those who are treating them know what they are doing. The foundation of health care is trust and faith in the competence of the providers who treat members of the community. Healing is not just about drugs or surgery, but also about faith in one's healers.

As members of a business charged with maintaining the community's health, healthcare administrators must take on the ethical responsibility of ensuring the competence of all staff members who provide or influence patient care. Obviously, this competence requirement includes those who provide direct patient care such as physicians, dentists, nurses, and counselors. It also includes anyone who supports health care, such as supervisors, information services technicians, and housekeeping staff. In short, any person who works in the healthcare setting should be competent to perform the tasks of his or her position. What are the ethics-related practices and issues of ensuring staff competence?

Practices for Competency Assurance

The classic text in healthcare human resources by Fottler, Hernandez, and Joiner (1997) devotes several chapters to staff competence through human resources functions. The ethical responsibilities related to staff competency assurance actually begin with the analysis of the job itself. Niles (2013) suggests that workflow and its analysis allow healthcare administrators to understand requirements for achieving the goals of a department or the organization as a whole. The process of understand workflow begins with a job analysis that provides information about the functions of the specific position and the competencies needed to be successful in that position. Healthcare administrators should conduct a preliminary job analysis on current and future positions to assist the human resources department in its tasks of recruitment, selection, training, and performance appraisal.

For the healthcare administrator, each of the stages of staff acquisition and retention has its own ethical responsibilities and challenges. For example, in the recruitment stage, healthcare administrators should have a thorough understanding of the type of professional whom they want to recruit. This understanding goes beyond job analysis data. HCAs need to be aware of any specific requirements for the position, also called bona fide occupational qualifications (**BFOQs**), so that they can be accurate and honest in their recruiting efforts. In addition, when hiring healthcare professionals, the healthcare administrator must consider more than knowledge and skills. Attitudes, professional ethics, and ability to work with team members are also important for maintaining a positive workplace. Finally, HCAs must have a plan for recruitment and check all advertising and application materials for concurrence with the Equal Employment Opportunity Commission rules, the organization's mission statement, and ethical practices.

During the selection process, many ethics issues can arise. To prepare for ethical situations, healthcare administrators should review all policies and procedures relating to employee selection. They must be careful to treat all applicants fairly and with respect. Even if applicants in no way meet the position criteria, they should receive courtesy. To assure fair and ethical treatment, healthcare administrators need to review and/or train staff members on telephone protocols and review formats for candidate correspondence for ethics assurance. HCAs must remember that they represent the organization when dealing with a candidate for a position.

A current trend in gaining an impression of future staff members is to review their Facebook or other social media pages without their knowledge. While this action may be common practice, it does present ethics issues. Candidates, especially younger ones, may not realize that their Facebook information can be easily accessed and, therefore, may fail to remove embarrassing photos and comments. Therefore, when a healthcare administrator views their pages, he or she could form a biased view of a candidate. In some cases, the practice of accessing candidates' Facebook pages without their knowledge has been used to "weed out" undesirable candidates. Even though it might be expedient for screening, the choice to screen candidates based on viewing their Facebook or other social media pages violates the principles of autonomy, nonmaleficence, and justice. Thus healthcare administrators should not review these sites unless they notify the candidate in advance.

When making decisions on the best person to hire, healthcare administrators can choose to conduct telephone or in-person interviews on an individual or group basis. During an interview, HCAs must practice caution when asking questions. They should link queries to the job analysis, allow time for responses, and remember to let the applicant also ask questions. In addition, HCAs should provide honest and fair answers about their organizations. From an ethics view, they should be aware of the potential for bias during interviews. Bias, while often not intentional, does not provide just treatment for the candidate. Interviews may include numerous opportunities for bias to creep into the hiring process, such as the first impression of a candidate, responses from the candidates who preceded him or her, and the candidate's physical appearance.

Checking references and credentials has become a key ethics responsibility in ensuring staff competence. In the past, some candidates have engaged in such fraudulent practices as writing their own reference letters, altering transcripts, and forging licenses. In today's high-technology world of health care, it is much easier to verify references and credentials. Nevertheless, healthcare administrators should consider that a reference letter can be politely, but not entirely honestly, written. Many HCAs follow up a reference letter with a telephone call. However, if this is the choice, they should be prepared with questions so that they do not waste the reference's time. Healthcare administrators should also listen to both the words and the tone of the reference's responses. Often what a reference does not say or how that person gives an answer provides more information than the actual verbal response. When doing such follow-up, HCAs should make careful notes so that they can provide an accurate account of the conversation. These notes will help in later decision making to choose the person who represents the best fit for the position.

With respect to credentials, healthcare administrators or human resources staff should inform the applicant about requirements and documentation. For example, some organizations require a physical exam, drug testing, and a background check before a position offer can be extended. With respect to documentation, HCAs should stress that candidates must be able to document current licensure, educational background, training, and any certifications needed for the position—and they must stress that they will be checking this documentation. In large organizations the human resources department is likely to assist in the verification process, but in smaller organizations the healthcare administrator may be responsible for this process, With respect to licensure, HCAs must go beyond currency and check for any suspension, modification, or termination of license. They also need to verify U.S. citizenship and authorization to work in the United States.

After the employee is hired, HCAs' responsibility for ensuring staff competence has not ended. First, they must provide an orientation to introduce their new staff members to the values and standards expected in the organization. This process can be somewhat lengthy depending on the complexity of the job responsibilities and the level of the new hire. Some organizations also use a mentor system for orientation, in which they match the new employee with an appropriate mentor. Usually mentors are two or more levels higher than their protégés. Healthcare administrators must take care when matching mentors and new employees, because mentors will serve as role models and sources of influence on both the practices and attitudes of the protégés.

Over the longer term, the organization has an obligation to provide job-related in-service education that goes beyond orientation. During these in-service sessions, there is an opportunity to provide specific training, such as the use of new technology or ACA-related changes in operations. Providing on-site training is also helpful to ensure consistency in the level of professional competence. Healthcare administrators must ensure that they document competence in the required skills and maintain those records. In addition, time will be required to keep staff informed about specific policies and procedures, and to define attitudes that are required for the positions. For example, the implementation of the ACA will bring many changes in policies and procedures that will require informational and educational meetings with staff members. The process used to deliver information on organizational change will vary depending on the size of the organization.

There are differences of opinion regarding the organization's role in maintaining professional currency and continuing education requirements for licensure. Some organizations believe that it is the professional's responsibility to maintain his or her own license and do not offer any assistance with this process. Other organizations feel an ethical responsibility to cover the cost of continuing education units (CEUs), because they require a current license for employment. Many organizations use some combination of the two approaches and provide release time for continuing education, some coverage for fees, or assistance with travel expenses.

If a healthcare organization chooses to support continuing education for its employees, it must practice the principle of justice as fairness in those policies. HCAs must be wary of "meeting hogs" who want more than their share of the travel budget, while less aggressive employees seldom get support. Healthcare administrators will need to have clear policies about the nature of meetings and events to be included in continuing education, the amount and type of support offered, and requirements for this benefit. Some departments choose to award a flat amount per employee per year for CEU efforts. Healthcare administrators should also consider the message that continuing education support gives. It should indicate that all employees are equally valued and that the healthcare administrator is interested in keeping them current in their field. Positive and fair policies can go a long way toward maintaining department morale. It is also important to keep accurate records of which personnel attend CEU programs and what they have attended. This recordkeeping demonstrates the HCA's stewardship of scarce CEU funding.

Experts in business encourage investment in training and employee development as ways to provide increased morale, improve performance, and reduce job burnout (Niles, 2013). Providing appropriate opportunities for job-related education can add to the quality of job performance. Likewise, it increases retention of the highly skilled staff members who are required to meet the organization's mission of quality patient care. From an ethics and fiscal viewpoint, providing both in-service and external educational opportunities appears to be a logical decision.

Ethics and Incompetence

What happens when a staff member demonstrates a lack of competence? When this happens, it is one of the most difficult and emotionally draining problems for HCAs. First, healthcare administrators must understand that incompetence can be due to several reasons, including impairment from psychoactive drugs or health and personal issues. For example, using psychoactive drugs such as alcohol, caffeine, or tobacco can interfere with professional judgment or patient safety. If signs of impairment exist, HCAs must be prepared to take action. In the early stages of impairment, healthcare professionals or coworkers may not recognize symptoms of impairment. In addition, well-meaning coworkers may enable inappropriate behaviors by making excuses, covering up mistakes, and privately complaining but taking no public action. Coworkers might also choose to remain silent because they have engaged in the same behavior themselves, do not want to be a snitch, or do not want to be responsible for someone's loss of livelihood. Some coworkers may fear retribution if the impaired person is viewed as being in a power position.

What should ethical HCAs do about such problems? First, they should remember that it is always better to be proactive than reactive. Policies should be in place that spell out acceptable and unacceptable behaviors in the workplace. For example, in the past it was considered acceptable to have an open bar at organization functions. While it was not a solid career move to overindulge in alcohol at such affairs, many did so without repercussions. In today's healthcare environment, a policy to have an open bar and encourage excessive alcohol consumption would not exist. In considering alcohol use at healthcare organization functions, it is best to avoid serving alcohol altogether or, alternatively, to offer a cash bar with limitations on consumption.

Education is always a good proactive strategy. Healthcare administrators can educate staff on drug and alcohol policies, and on the signs and symptoms of impairment. They should include information about resources that are available to assist the impaired person. For example, many states have special programs for impaired physicians and nurses. In addition, human resources departments can be a good source of information on resources and programs to help troubled employees. In addition, some organizations have employee assistance programs (EAPs) that provide a number of services to assist the impaired employee.

It is also important for the healthcare administrator to remember that not all reports about employee impairment are true. Therefore, it is important to spend time investigating any claims of impairment and to obtain the assistance of the human resources department if one is available. If the healthcare administrator confronts an impaired employee, he or she needs to be prepared for denial and hostility. Therefore, it is wise to have a witness present or to seek assistance from experts such as human resources representatives. One should consider the ethics principles of justice, nonmaleficence, and beneficence when dealing with employees in these circumstances. Duty to the patient should also be a key element in the actions taken for the situation.

Finally, healthcare administrators should be aware that there are other sources for incompetence. Sometimes the aging process, early symptoms of Alzheimer's disease, or other health issues will cause employee impairment. Emotional problems such as a divorce or the death of a loved one can also temporarily impede the ability to make sound judgments. If the healthcare administrator has created a working environment of respect and trust, employees will self-report such problems. If there are self-reports, HCAs should take the time to listen to employees and refer them to the appropriate source of assistance such as compassion leave or EAP services. If coworkers report a change in a fellow employee's behavior, healthcare administrators should investigate the report, while also preserving the employee's self-respect and dignity. Such interactions are never easy. However, handling them well, with regard for all parties, will increase the HCA's value to the organization and honor his or her role as a guardian of patient safety.

What About the Health Administrator's Competence?

Steven Covey (1989), in his now-classic work *The 7 Habits of Highly Effective People*, stresses it. Carson Dye (2000) devotes a whole chapter to it in *Leadership in Healthcare: Values at the Top*. What is it? It is the necessity for self-evaluation and assurance of one's own competency.

As an ethics-based HCA, one does not wait until the annual evaluation to appraise one's own competency. Instead, the ethics-based healthcare administrator chooses to engage in an ongoing self-assessment and in the process of lifelong learning. In the ACA era with its many changes and challenges, this process is not just ethical; it is part of career survival.

How does this translate into the HCA's daily routine? First, in keeping with what one learns from Frankl's work (1971), healthcare administrators need to take time to think about the meaning of their work. This process might include contemplation and determining the answers to the difficult questions that really matter in their careers. Healthcare administrators should ask themselves questions such as "Why am I here?" and "What do I want to do with my life?" They would examine the meaning in their work by asking: "Where can I make a difference?" and "What do I see myself doing in 5 years?" Finally, they would think about this global question: "For what do I want to be known?"

Many HCAs find it helpful to write a personal mission statement based on this process of contemplation. They review this statement at least annually (often on their birthdays) to see if it is still true or needs revision. The personal mission statement also serves as a compass for making career decisions. For example, comparing one's personal mission statement with that of one's organization can provide career insight. Is the organization's mission reasonably compatible with that of the healthcare administrator? It would be difficult to support an organization that goes against one's core values. If a mismatch occurs, a position change may be in order.

Conducting an ethics self-assessment is also helpful to identify the healthcare administrator's true "ethics bottom line." The administrator needs to think about his or her personal definition of integrity. For example, he or she could ask, "Which principles or events would cause me to resign?" Alternatively, the HCA might ask, "Which principles am I willing to state publicly and act upon?" The American College of Healthcare Executives has a self-assessment tool that many have found helpful in this process (ACHE, 2013); this tool provides a structure to assess ethics competency in an organizational context.

Healthcare administrators also need to take the time to develop a personal ethics code. They need to keep this code in a place that allows for easy reference, such as the middle drawer of their desks. It should serve as a daily reminder of their ethics roots. Brave HCAs actually frame their codes and hang them on their office walls. Not only are they willing to articulate their "ethics bottom line," but they also want staff know what it is. This lessens the temptation for hypocrisy and provides staff members with greater understanding of their healthcare administrator.

After completing a self-assessment, healthcare administrators need to build and maintain their professional competency. When HCAs graduate from college, they possess certain knowledge, attitudes, and skills to begin their process of competency building. However, these accomplishments are just the beginning. As healthcare administrators gain experience by addressing managerial challenges and learning from both successes and failures, they increase their levels of expertise and ethics competence. Healthcare administrators may also seek mentors to assist them in building experience-based competence. A mentor should be trustworthy and willing to make time to provide feedback in an honest, but not ego-crushing, manner. Mentors can also provide insight into the arcane healthcare organizational culture and its unwritten rules so that the new healthcare administrator does not step on someone's toes out of his or her own ignorance.

Once healthcare administrators have identified their strengths, they should not be too complacent. Because change in health care is often rapid and profound, the HCA cannot rely on just a few areas of competence or assume that these areas will never change. Just like muscles, if strengths are not properly exercised, they will diminish. Learning and practice will help the healthcare administrator to maintain their strengths. In addition, HCAs must practice humility to work on areas for improvement. When healthcare administrators are new graduates or are in a new position, they have a honeymoon period where complete organizational knowledge is not expected. This is the time to ask questions and listen to the answers to those questions. The honeymoon period is a time of great learning. However, with the current healthcare environment of change and challenge, healthcare administrators will have shortened honeymoons and steeper learning curves to navigate.

Healthcare administrators also need to consider their own continuing education opportunities. Continuing education opportunities exist on a formal or informal basis. For example, HCAs may consider taking continuing education courses through their local professional organization meetings (i.e., ACHE or MGMA) or community resources. If healthcare administrators have strengths in a certain area, they might consider becoming a part-time teacher or workshop leader. Teaching others helps to reinforce what the HCA knows or may make the HCA learn new areas. Some organizations also have programs for administrators where they take on the job of a staff member (nonclinical, of course) for one day or a half-day. Participants in these programs report a great increase in their understanding of staff's contribution to the organization. Staff members, in turn, appreciate the administrator's willingness to understand their role in the organization; this is a win-win situation. Finally, if healthcare administrators are in a position to do so, they can become a mentor to a new HCA or an experienced one who has recently joined their organization. These efforts help to reinforce one healthcare administrator's learning and assist in the career building of another.

Competent HCAs do not isolate themselves from their communities. They take advantage of opportunities to get involved in appropriate organizations as either a member or an officer. Such organizations include local Rotary Clubs, the Kiwanis, or the Boy Scouts or Girl Scouts. Healthcare administrators might also consider being on advisory boards for health administration programs at local universities, public health programs, and other health-related organizations. Remember that healthcare administrators always represent their organizations when serving in the community, so they must pay attention to their words and actions when serving in these external roles. However, putting themselves "out there" to have a better understanding of the real issues facing their communities is worth the extra effort: It improves both the healthcare administrator's image and that of his or her organization.

In light of healthcare administrators' busy schedules, how are they supposed to find time for all of this competence assurance? First, they cannot afford *not* to find time for it. HCAs are role models and cannot expect efforts to maintain competence from staff members that they are not willing to make themselves. Second, making the time investment discussed here can lead to a substantial return on investment. Not only can HCAs build their careers, but they can also have a greater understanding of their meaning in life. Third, healthcare administrators must appreciate that assuring their own competence will lead to a better understanding of their organizations, staff, and community. This knowledge will help them to be more effective in their daily operation as an HCA. Finally, healthcare administrators will be more complete people who have a level of self-understanding and the desire to grow and adapt to the ever-changing environment that is today's health care.

Summary

Healthcare organizations exist in an age of multiple accountability and profound change. Healthcare administrators are charged with assisting the organization and staff members in complying with regulations from a great many external organizations that serve to protect the public's interests. They are also called upon to act as advocates for healthcare organizations and the health administration profession by maintaining current knowledge and being involved in the organization, professional associations, and the community. In addition, healthcare administrators must ensure their own competency and that of their staff members. Because health care is a trust-based industry, competency assurance is vital to maintaining ethics-based practice and competent patient care.

Cases for Your Consideration
....

The Case of the Novice Nurse

Think about the chapter information and consider the following questions. Sample responses and commentary will follow the case.

1. How effective was the orientation process for ICU nurses at St. Dismas Hospital?

2. What would have prevented this situation?

3. How do you think Lawanda's family felt?

4. What are the steps to address this situation and decrease the damage to St. Dismas Hospital?

Case Information

Lawanda Person was a recent graduate of a BSN program. She had only one year of experience in medical–surgical units when St. Dismas Hospital hired her to be a staff nurse in the intensive care unit (ICU). The situation described in this case occurred during the fourth week of her six-week orientation. On that particular day, Lawanda's assignment was two clients who had suffered anterior myocardial infarctions (MI); both were 48 hours post event. One of the clients was still on a ventilator. Lawanda was the medication nurse should a code happen during her shift. This meant that if there were a code, she would be the team member to give physician-ordered medications to the patient.

Just before her shift was to end, Lawanda's ventilated client went into code. The code team arrived and began CPR. The code was proceeding for more than 20 minutes when the nurse behind her handed Lawanda a syringe. Without any further action, she injected the contents of the syringe into the IV line. Immediately, the patient reacted and his heart stopped. The physician pronounced the patient dead at 10:30 P.M. Lawanda felt sad that the patient died, but knew that she had done everything she could to save him.

After the code, the nurse supervisor completed the documentation and checked the procedures. She discovered that the patient had received the wrong medication! Apparently, there was a mix-up in the medication drawer, and the medication came from the wrong bottle. She immediately notified the nurse manager and the physician and began an investigation.

The next day at the beginning of her shift, the nurse supervisor called Lawanda into her office. The supervisor told Lawanda about a medication error during the code in which Lawanda participated. The nurse supervisor said, "You killed a patient last night. You were the one who was in charge of the meds and you did not check them. You are going to lose your license over this." She told Lawanda that she must call and report herself to the state board of nursing. In addition, she might be subject to fines and jail time for the medical error she had made. The nurse supervisor also threatened to put her on suspension. Lawanda reacted to this news with shock and grief, but the supervisor told her to "get some backbone" and finish her shift.

Lawanda went back to the ICU and, at the first chance she could, called her parents to tell them what had happened. They told her that they would do whatever they could to help. However, this did not make her feel better. Lawanda could feel the cold stares of the staff who would not speak to her during the shift. She tried to be attentive to her patients, but the supervisor's words echoed in her head. She was a murderer! She might go to jail! She began to imagine what was going to happen to her during a full investigation of the event and how her mistake was going to cost her everything she had.

Somehow, she made it to the end of her shift and then she made her decision. She went to the medication drawer, took a bottle of potassium and a syringe, and put them in her pocket. On her way out of the lobby, she entered the restroom, locked the door, and gave herself a fatal dose of potassium. The housekeeper found Lawanda's body later that evening and the emergency department responded; it was too late. Someone called the chief executive officer (CEO), who made the necessary notifications including the hospital's attorney. He also called Lawanda's parents. Understandably, they were shocked and angered by the news and accused St. Dismas of "killing our daughter." Soon after this conversation, Lawanda's parents contacted their attorney and alerted the press.

Responses and Commentary on Questions

1. How effective was the orientation process for ICU nurses at St. Dismas Hospital?

   On the surface, it seems that this was not an effective orientation program at all. After all, a patient died as the result of a preventable medication error. However, the program itself perhaps was not completely responsible.

   First, consider the hiring practices that preceded the orientation process. One could argue that St. Dismas, like many other hospitals, was facing a nursing shortage and had to take a chance on a nurse with limited experience. In addition, Lawanda provided full care for two patients even though she had not finished the entire orientation program. Perhaps, this was just too much responsibility for her at this stage of her orientation process. However, the overall costs of taking a chance on Lawanda were great. A patient and a nurse lost their lives, and the hospital faced the potential for negative publicity. In fact, it took several years before it completely regained public trust.

Comment: This case makes a good argument for having a well-designed staff orientation program. Healthcare administrators need to consider not just an orientation to the routine practices for their institution, but also the inclusion of prevention strategies. In addition, legal support personnel could evaluate orientation programs to see if they contain the most significant information. In terms of prevention of medication errors, The Joint Commission provides assistance with error prevention education. This information can also be a feature in orientation programs. Healthcare administrators should also frequently evaluate orientation programs frequently and use data collected to improve programs as needed.

2. What would have prevented this situation?

Healthcare administrators must begin at the beginning. During a code, there is a great deal of stress, even when the organization has clearly defined protocols. However, in the haste to save a life, it is possible to overlook or omit a procedure. Clearly, Lawanda was not the only person to make an error here. The nurse who was responsible for obtaining the drug failed to check and recheck to make sure she had the correct medication as ordered by the physician. When Lawanda received the medication, she should also have verified that it was the correct medication before injecting it. Failure to follow the check–recheck protocols was the cause of making and not catching the medication error.

Consider the actions that occurred after the code. The nurse supervisor performed the correct procedure for documentation and verification of the process. When she found a problem, she followed the correct procedure for notifications. She also began an investigation and the individuals involved were aware of the seriousness of what occurred.

However, the way the supervisor dealt with Lawanda was very inappropriate. First, she assumed a tone of accusation and blame even before the full investigation was completed. The supervisor also threatened Lawanda with jail and loss of license rather than finding the underlying cause of the situation. In her anger over what happened, the supervisor failed to consider the effects her words would have on this novice nurse. Rather than deal with the situation fairly and apprise Lawanda of what could happen and why, she chose to present the worst-case scenario without having complete knowledge of the situation. Then, to add to the problem, she told Lawanda to complete her shift, thereby potentially endangering current patients.

The nurse supervisor did not have proper instruction on how to handle situations when she had to deliver negative information. Lawanda had a right to know the full story of the events. She also had a right to receive this information in a professional manner. In addition, there should have been a policy concerning her status during the ensuing investigation. At a minimum, she should not have been working with patients on the day that she learned of the incident. The potential for causing unintended harm to clients was too great.

Healthcare administrators should also consider the behavior of Lawanda's coworkers. By ignoring her and, even worse, talking about her when her back was turned, they demonstrated a presumption of guilt. Perhaps compassion or support was too much to expect, but they should have treated her in a professional manner. In addition, no one seemed to be watching the medication drawers, which made it very easy for Lawanda to obtain her fatal dose. Do her coworkers have any ethical burden here? Perhaps they should have been educated about appropriate behavior in adverse circumstances.

3. How do you think Lawanda's family felt?

   Lawanda's parents were aware of the situation at St. Dismas only on a surface level. They received one quick phone call from their daughter, who seemed terribly upset by what the supervisor had said. However, she was going to finish her shift, so they had no real indication of how severe those feelings were. Perhaps, they were feeling some guilt for not going to the hospital and insisting that Lawanda come home. However, she was an adult, and they did not want to interfere. They were also angry with the facility staff for their treatment of their daughter. They felt that the manner in which Lawanda was treated caused her suicide.

4. What are the steps to address this situation and decrease the damage to St. Dismas Hospital?

   Because this situation now involved both law and the media, legal counsel for the hospital must be involved in damage control. These personnel can provide St. Dismas administrators with information on how to deal with any action that is taken against them. They also need to address how best to handle the press to protect the hospital's interests. In addition, there must be an internal investigation to determine all of the facts in the situation. After knowing the facts, the hospital should take appropriate actions and document those actions.

   In dealing with the press, it would serve the hospital best to have a designated spokesperson who would be forthcoming with the appropriate level of information. The spokesperson should be cautioned to avoid the use of "no comment" (it simply makes the person or organization appear to be guilty) and instead to direct the inquiry to the appropriate contact person. The hospital should also instruct involved staff members not to speculate or to give interviews to the press. Regaining the public's trust would be an ongoing process for St. Dismas Hospital.

The Case of Patient Safety and BFOQs

Think about the chapter information and consider the following questions. Sample responses and commentary will follow the case.

1. What motivated Sara and Emma to report their supervisor?

2. What should Stan do in this case?

3. How can Stan prevent future situations of staff impairment?

Case Information

Stan Delouse was the assistant director of human resources at Seraphina Compassionate Care Center (SCCC), a specialty hospital for the treatment of cancer. On Monday morning, two of the RNs from the Evergreen Floor greeted him at his door. After introducing themselves as Sara Katz and Emma Smith, they informed him of the reason for their visit. It seemed that Linda Chard, their nurse supervisor, was no longer able to do her duties. She was, they said, "so fat that she does not even leave the desk anymore unless it is to take a smoke break." They described her as being only 5 feet 4 inches tall but weighing at least 250 pounds. While her weight was not a new issue, her latest incident caused them to be concerned enough to report it to human resources.

On Sunday night, one of the patients on Evergreen had a code. Linda was the first one in the room but she could not even begin to provide basic CPR. She was too heavy to reach across the bed and assist the patient. Further, she appeared to be having symptoms of shortness of breath herself. Fortunately, Sara and Emma were there almost immediately and began the correct procedures. The two nurses did not want to be "tattle-tales" but they were very concerned that Linda's health condition was putting patients in jeopardy. In addition, they felt it was unfair that they had to cover the supervisor's duties because her weight and shortness of breath interfered with her ability to do them. They both wanted Stan to address this issue, but they also had some fears of retaliation.

Responses and Commentary on Questions

1. What motivated Sara and Emma to report their supervisor?

First, in this case, Stan can consider an ethics-based motivation for Sara and Emma's actions. They work in a facility that meets the needs of patients who are in varying stages of pain and suffering. Stan could also consider what it took to report on someone who has power and authority over them. On the one hand, Sara and Emma might genuinely be concerned that Linda's health could compromise care and jeopardize the healing of patients. They also might be somewhat concerned with the injustice, as they view it, of having to do Linda's work as well as their own. They are asking for an investigation into the matter.

On the other hand, Sara and Emma might be angry with Linda for something totally unrelated to the situation. Their motivation might be less than ethical and include a desire to cause difficulty for their supervisor. Perhaps, these two nurses are prejudiced against people who are overweight or health professionals with a smoking habit. Stan needs to investigate this information about Linda without making a prejudgment of fault.

2. What should Stan do in this case?

First, Stan should review the job description related to Linda's current position. Were there specific BFOQs that related to the physical ability to do the job? If the answer is yes, that fact makes his job a little easier because Linda was covered under these conditions. However, if physical abilities for the job are not in the job specifications, he might have to contact the legal team to get advice before taking any direct action.

Next, Stan needs to consider the source of his information and its motivation. He should be sure that other issues are not present here and that the information presented is accurate. He might contact the director of nursing (DON) and ask her to stop by his office. Then, Stan could have a confidential conversation about the situation with Sara, Emma, and Linda. He would need to determine if Linda's health issues truly have an impact on her ability to meet the needs of SCCC's patients.

Assuming the answer is yes, Stan needs to handle the situation with a concern for the ethical treatment of staff. First, he needs to prepare himself for a meeting with Linda. Remembering the cost of termination, recruiting, and rehiring, he must try to develop a plan to solve the problem without having to fire Linda. Stan needs to consult with the DON and invite her to come to any meetings that he has with Linda. While asking Linda to come to the human resources office could create anxiety, he cannot afford to ignore the problem. When he meets with Linda, he should begin by telling her the reason for the meeting and stating the facts as he knows them, including the BFOQs for her position. Then, he should take time for compassionate listening.

Because this situation potentially threatens her livelihood, Linda might be angry and defensive. Stan should allow her to react and to give her version of the case. After she completes her comments, Stan should make note of them and ask for her ideas about how to resolve the situation. This action will help her be a part of the solution and not the victim of the situation. Perhaps she really has the answers to her own problems.

Stan should also introduce his plan for solving the problem, which might include support for Linda to enter smoking cessation programs and referrals to weight management services. There should be a reasonable timeline with checkpoints to monitor Linda's progress. If the DON is present, she can assure Linda that she supports the plan. Before Linda leaves the office, she should sign off on the plan and receive a copy. Stan also needs to include a copy in Linda's human resources file.

This meeting might be stressful for all concerned, but it does not solve the problem. Stan still has the responsibility to follow up on the actions and timelines. He should keep in frequent contact with the DON to verify that Linda has taken the agreed-upon actions and is making progress toward solving her health problems. He should inquire about her job performance and check whether it is now meeting standards. There should be progress at each of the checkpoints to solve the problem. However, if there is no resolution, Stan must be willing to take appropriate action up to and including dismissal. The patient must always come first in any healthcare organization.

3. How can Stan prevent future situations of staff impairment?

Employment of competent personnel begins with the job analysis stage. Therefore, this incident might trigger a reevaluation of the nurse manager position and its job requirements. If there are needed additional requirements, Stan will need to change the job description and BFOQs. Stan should also review the policies and procedures for handling situations where impairment occurs, regardless of its source, to be sure that they support appropriate action. Of course, there might be a need for additional staff education in the future on the subject of impairment. Stan should always keep in mind that he needs to balance safety and quality care for the patients with compassion and respect for the humanity of the staff. This is no easy task, but it is one that is essential to an ethics-based healthcare facility.

Web Resources

American College of Healthcare Executives (ACHE)
http://www.ache.org/hap.cfm

American Hospital Association (AHA)
http://www.aha.org

Health Insurance Portability and Accountability Act (HIPAA)
http://www.hhs.gov/ocr/privacy

The Joint Commission
http://www. The Joint Commission.org/

Medical Group Management Association (MGMA)
http://www.mgma.com/

National Committee for Quality Assurance (NCQA)
http://www.ncqa.org/

References

American College of Healthcare Executives (ACHE). (2013). *Ethics self-assessment*. Chicago, IL: Author. Retrieved from http://www.ache.org/newclub/career/Ethics_self-assessment.pdf

American Medical Association. (2013). The Health Insurance Portability and Accountability Act (HIPAA) Omnibus Final Rule summary. Retrieved from http://www.ama-assn.org/resources/doc/washington/hipaa-omnibus-final-rule-summary.pdf

Annison, M. H., & Wilford, D. S. (1998). *Trust matters: New directions for health care leadership*. San Francisco, CA: Jossey-Bass.

Covey, S. R. (1989). *The 7 habits of highly effective people*. New York, NY: Simon & Schuster.

Dye, C. F. (2000). *Leadership in healthcare: Values at the top*. Chicago, IL: Health Administration Press.

Fottler, M. D., Hernandez, S. R., & Joiner, C. L. (1997). *Strategic management of human resources in health services organizations* (2nd ed.). Albany, NY: Delmar.

Frankl, V. (1971). *Man's search for meaning: An introduction to logotherapy*. New York, NY: Pocket Books.

The Joint Commission (TJC). (2012). Facts about the unannounced survey process. Retrieved from http://www.jointcommission.org/assets/1/18/Unannounced_Survey_Process_9_12.pdf

The Joint Commission (TJC). (2013a). About The Joint Commission. Retrieved from http://www.jointcommission.org/about_us/about_the_joint_commission_main.aspx

The Joint Commission (TJC). (2013b). Target Solution Tools. Retrieved from http://www.jointcommission.org/about_us/about_cth.aspx

The Joint Commission (TJC). (2013c). National patient safety goals. Retrieved from http://www.jointcommission.org/standards_information/npsgs.aspx

The Joint Commission (TJC). (2013d). Accreditation guide for hospitals. Oakbrook Terrace, IL: Author.

Kaiser Family Foundation. (2013). Focus on health reform: Summary of the Affordable Care Act. Available at http://www.kff.org.

National Committee for Quality Assurance (NCQA). (2013). About NCQA. Retrieved from http://www.ncqa.org/HomePage.aspx

Niles, N. J. (2013). *Basic concepts of health care human resources management*. Burlington, MA: Jones & Bartlett Learning.

Shi, L., & Singh, D. (2015). *Delivering health care in America: A systems approach* (6th ed.). Burlington, MA: Jones & Bartlett Learning.

Shortell, S. M., Gillies, R. R., Anderson, D. A., Erickson, K. M., & Mitchell, J. B. (2000). *Remaking health care in America: The evolution of organized delivery systems* (2nd ed.). San Francisco, CA: Jossey-Bass.

Worthley, J. A. (1997). *The ethics of the ordinary in healthcare: Concepts and cases*. Chicago, IL: Health Administration Press.

CHAPTER
8

Technology and Ethics

How does technology create ethics issues for health care?

Points to Ponder

1. What is the relationship between technology and health care?
2. Why is information technology so important in healthcare administration?
3. What is the relationship between technology and ethics?
4. How can an ethics-based healthcare administrator balance technology and ethics?

Key Terms

The following is a list of this chapter's key terms. Look for them in bold.

emerging technology
health information technology (HIT)
moral awareness
protected patient information

technology diffusion
technology imperative
telehealth

■ INTRODUCTION AND DEFINITIONS

Technology has become an integral part of the American culture and is often part of people's individual identity. Americans seem to have a love affair with their smartphones, tablets, and laptops. They also enjoy the convenience of technology that gives driving directions and recommends restaurants. Whole industries have developed to allow people to customize their devices and to protect them from harm and data loss. These examples show the influence of technology on the culture of the United States and the growing dependence on its benefits. In fact,

Shi and Singh (2015, p. 160) use the term **"technology diffusion"** to describe technology's influence on values and culture.

A recent example of the expectations for technology and its impact on culture occurred during the October 2013 rollout of the Healthcare. gov website. Despite an investment of more than $300 million, the website failed to handle the traffic of inquiries and people found it slow and frustrating. Not only did this technology failure create difficulties for consumers, but it also produced media coverage and political criticism of the ACA in general (Payne, Smith, & Cohen, 2013). The presence of technology glitches also negatively affected perception of President Obama's competence and his overall approval rating.

American medicine has also embraced technology, making it a driving force in the U.S. healthcare system from both a treatment and an economic standpoint. In the United States, technology diffusion is so extensive that many Americans equate "good medicine" with the amount of technology that is used, even if it is not appropriate. Technology also has an influence on practitioners, who increasingly rely on it and are educated in its use. Decisions to use medical technology in its various forms leads to a **technology imperative** (Shi & Singh, 2015). This imperative means that there is an expectation of using the latest technology regardless of its cost. The technology imperative is particularly prevalent among the specialty areas of medicine. For example, robotic surgery is becoming the norm because of its benefits—and despite its prohibitive costs. However, not everyone needs robotic surgery and not everyone is able to access it.

Advances in technology have improved the quality of care by providing mechanisms for less invasive surgeries, reducing morbidity, and managing pain. In addition, advanced technology holds the promise of patient-specific treatment, more effective pharmaceuticals, and sophisticated surgical techniques. In addition, medical technology contributes to the quality of life of individuals through its ability to treat formerly terminal illnesses, improve the quality of life for those with disabilities, and decrease pain and suffering (Shi & Singh, 2015). At the same time, technology advances have created new ethical dilemmas that may change the definition of humanity and life.

Even with its benefits, the cost of technology is an issue for the business side of health care. Although practitioners and patients enjoy the advantages of the increasing use of technology, these benefits often come at a higher cost of providing care. Technology costs and benefits are issues particularly for hospitals because these institutions invest large amounts of capital to accommodate the need for technology. Administrators must be increasingly aware of more than the cost per patient in their decisions about acquiring new technology. In particular, they need to address concerns about whether medical technology increases or decreases the overall cost of patient care. In addition, information about the rapid improvements in many of these technologies and their quick obsolescence should be part of making purchase decisions. Administrators should remember that purchasing any form of technology is not the end of the cost considerations. Technology support and replacement are often ongoing processes and represent another cost factor. A thorough cost/benefit analysis is necessary when making purchase decisions about technology.

Other issues with the technology imperative extend beyond cost considerations. While technology provides extensive benefits, these benefits might not be readily available in certain geographic areas or to certain populations. For example, rural Americans have just as much need for magnetic resonance imaging (MRI) as their urban counterparts. However, access is not always available because the technology can be just too expensive for rural healthcare facilities to purchase and maintain. Such differences in technology access may be creating two healthcare systems: one for urban dwellers and one for rural residents. When there is the addition of low-income populations to the picture, there can be a loss of potential benefit from the use of technology. Given the additional costs, should technology be limited to only those who can afford it? Can the ACA accommodate the cost involved in providing the latest technology to all the patients who want it?

It is also important to understand the depth of the ethical implications of technology. For example, Shi and Singh (2015) discuss diagnostic technologies such as computerized axial tomography (CAT) scanners and MRI, along with survival technologies such as bone marrow transplants and intensive care units (ICUs). They also include illness management (e.g., renal dialysis), cures (e.g., hip replacements), and prevention (e.g., vaccines) as part of medical technology. The diversity of technology options and the costs of using these technologies raises issues related to utility and justice. In addition, Harman (2006) writes about the ethics challenges of information management, including concerns related to the electronic medical record, data management, confidentiality, and integrated delivery systems. While it is not possible to address the ethics issues for all of the technology used in health care, this chapter will concentrate on **health information technology (HIT)** and the electronic health record (EHR), and comment on **emerging technology** and its impact on ethics.

■ HEALTH INFORMATION TECHNOLOGY

Health information technology is especially important to healthcare administrators because it enables organizations use the Internet to access and use massive amounts of data. This technology allows healthcare organizations to organize and store patient records electronically and communicate patient information with greater ease. Physicians can place orders for laboratory services, prescriptions, and other patient needs more efficiently. In addition, patients can access health information through the Internet (Shi & Singh, 2015; Sultz & Young, 2014). HIT also includes clinical applications such as **telehealth** (i.e., the use of electronic and telecommunication to support patient care) and health information exchanges that allow health information to be accessed across providers and locations (Harmon, 2006).

Health information is not limited to clinical applications. Healthcare administrators use information technology systems in the business side of health care. One can find information systems used in processes ranging from inventory control to the payment of vendors. Accurate information systems also allow the payment from both government and private sources to be more efficient and effective. Other business applications of HIT include methods to ensure accuracy and compliance of coding, billing procedures, design of computer systems, and compliance with state and federal laws. Of particular significance to applications of HIT is the HIPAA Privacy Rule requirements and the Health Information Technology for Economic and Clinical Health (HITECH) Act (McWay, 2010)

The HITECH Act provides incentives for physicians and healthcare organizations to become active users of HIT. It encourages physicians and facilities that treat Medicare- and Medicaid-covered patients to engage in meaningful use of electronic record technology through financial incentives. To receive these funds, the professionals and organizations must prove that they were gathering and using health information in ways that meet meaningful use criteria. These criteria include use of information for tracking patient conditions, care coordination, quality measurement, and patient engagement. Other meaningful use criteria include e-prescriptions, electronic transmission of laboratory results, patient self-management tools, and efforts to improve population health. These uses for HIT hold promise for improving the effectiveness and efficiency of healthcare delivery and the ability of patients to have greater input and control over their healthcare experiences (Sultz & Young, 2014).

The Health Insurance Portability and Accountability Act of 1996 (HIPAA) and its provisions have a profound effect on the way that HIT is used. For example, the Privacy Rule changed the way that patients can access their records by stating that patients have a right to their own health information. While insurance companies, providers, and healthcare organizations still own and maintain the actual patient records, patients have the right to access them (McWay, 2010).

The protection of privacy was a key feature in HIPAA. Healthcare organizations have to provide greater security for patient health records (called **protected patient information**), including their maintenance and destruction. They must also inform patients that they can have a copy of their health records and can charge only a reasonable fee for this copy. In addition, written permission from patients is required before disclosure of health information to other parties such as insurance companies.

These are just a few of the features included in the HIPPA regulations. Healthcare administrators are responsible for knowing and implementing this act's provisions, including use of unique identifiers for patients, safeguards, security with business contracts, and code set requirements. In 2013, a new HIPAA rule streamlined certain processes and expanded privacy requirements to business associates. It also increased the penalties for noncompliance with HIPAA rules and allows for rigorous investigations of violations (HHS Press Office, 2013). While HIPPA serves to protect the patient record and the integrity of HIT, it also brings greater scrutiny to the use and application of patient information in treatment, payment, research, and other areas.

■ ETHICS ISSUES IN HEALTH INFORMATION MANAGEMENT

McWay (2010) describes the ethical challenges for HIT as stemming from changes in the provision of health care, the increase in documentation requirements, and the increase in the sophistication of technology. In addition, the complexity of reimbursement and coding systems contributes to ethics issues in HIT. For example, issues of patient autonomy and confidentiality frequently occur when HIT professionals must code and obtain reimbursement for sensitive patient areas such as mental health and genetic information. Of special concern is access to celebrity information and the temptation to access this information without permission to meet the demands of curiosity or the press. Firewalls, passwords, and other access protections may be in place, but they do not protect patient confidentiality in all cases.

Another ethics challenge for HIT is maintaining the integrity of the health information system. The system itself is complex, in that it can interface with many departments, each of which has its own sensitive patient and/or proprietary information. Systems developers must include features that not only safeguard patient confidentiality, but also protect the organization from harm. This includes harm caused by errors made on the medical record and by hackers who gain unauthorized access to health information. In designing these systems, HIT professionals need to consider complex issues such as infrastructure, technical problems, vendor access, and use of health information by researchers. Protections such as audit trails, policies on usage and unattended terminals, and confidentiality agreements need to be established as well. These protections require staff training and periodic assessment to be effective (Harman, 2006).

In addition to patient confidentiality and integrity issues, HIT professionals must address staff justice. Employees who develop HIT systems, maintain medical records, or code medical information deserve ethics-based management. This means that leaders in health information management need to practice **moral awareness**. Moral awareness includes the ability to be sensitive to potential ethical issues, including those related to HIT fraud and abuse. Likewise, HIT leaders need to have an understanding of the nature and application of organizational policies and be able to enforce them fairly (Harman, 2006). Staff justice also requires fair treatment for promotions, assignment of overtime, and other issues. Certainly, healthcare administrators will need practical wisdom as they work to balance staff needs and the needs of the healthcare organization.

■ ELECTRONIC HEALTH RECORDS

The electronic health record serves as the cornerstone of much of HIT and clinical information systems. The EHR contains important and often sensitive information about the patient's health care experience. In an ideal world, this computerized record would contain information from prebirth to the end of life (Harman, 2006). It can, for example, include data from hospitals, primary and specialty practices, and ancillary services such as pharmacy, laboratory, and radiology. Authorized users such as physicians and other clinicians, researchers, and evaluators of quality standards can access these valuable records.

In addition to the clinical uses of the electronic health record, the business office can use it for insurance billing and filing claims with Medicare, Medicaid, and other government agencies. Insurance companies also use the EHR to assure the provision of treatment to address employee disabilities. Of course, the electronic health record—like its predecessor the paper record—is a legal document that can be used in liability or other court cases (McWay, 2010).

Given all of these features of the electronic health record, one would assume that every clinic and hospital has this form of patient record in place. In fact, the idea of the EHR is not particularly new. The Institute of Medicine (2001) called for a standardized electronic record as early as 1991 and stressed its importance again in 1997. However, even though evidence is building that the EHR can decrease medical errors and lower costs, progress toward automation has been slow. Even with the incentives from the HITECH Act, the majority of hospitals have not converted to the electronic health record. Bishop, Press, Mendelsohn, and Casalino (2013) note that physician practices have also been slow to convert to electronic records. Roberts (2013) reports that 16% of physician practices are evaluating changing their paper records to digital ones or are seeking solutions for converting to digital records. Only 37% of the practices cited in this report had all of their records in digital format, however.

Even though physicians cite convenience, efficiency, patient satisfaction, and safety as advantages of the EHR, the barriers to conversion are a strong disincentive to adopt this technology (Bishop, Press, Mendelsohn, & Casalino, 2013). Barriers for conversion include patient and physician resistance to change, a lack of payment from health plans for electronic records, added work, and costs of conversion. Given the need for electronic health records in HIT, healthcare organizations and clinical practices will need to increase their participation in EHR development and use. Roberts (2013) notes that conversion to electronic health records is essential to participate in government and other payer systems, and to ensure the interoperability of healthcare systems.

When it comes to the electronic health record, specialized patient records are of particular concern. These records include sensitive information that is beyond what is contained in a general health record. Examples of specialized patient records include information about treatment for alcohol and drug abuse, psychotherapy, genetic testing, and HIV treatment. In some cases, home health records may be included in this category because they contain information about a person's home environment. Converting these special patient records to an electronic system creates legal and ethical issues, including a need for increased protections for confidentiality and authorization for release of information (McWay, 2010).

■ ETHICS ISSUES FOR ELECTRONIC HEALTH RECORDS

The most obvious ethical issue for electronic health records is confidentiality. When one considers the amount of personal information found in any health record, it is easy to see that protecting patient confidentiality is task number one. Actions needed to address this ethical issue may require more than a patient's signature on a form. They include development of physical security, systems to assure authorized access to records, and safeguards on clinical and other data entry. Policies dictating appropriate access and retention of records are needed as well. In addition, the electronic record systems need to have on-call technical staff so that any problems that arise are resolved quickly. Finally, the healthcare organization must obtain confidentiality agreements from all employees, contract employees, and business associates.

These are just a few of the steps necessary to maintain patient record confidentiality in the electronic health record era. It is important that patients feel assured that their records are safe and secure, especially when sensitive treatment areas are involved. Healthcare organizations need to go beyond the HIPAA minimum requirements and provide patient-centered communication about the electronic health record including its benefits and security. In addition, computer systems must be updated so that they can handle the changes in the healthcare system and patient care delivery. One major example of change management is the need to prepare systems to accommodate the changes from the ICD-9 coding system to the ICD-10 system. In addition to determining the best costs and developing appropriate policies, healthcare providers will need ongoing training to address computer and system competency for themselves and their staff members. For their part, healthcare providers need to be computer competent so that they can correctly enter, access, and protect patient data.

The advent of the electronic health record also produces increased concern over patients' rights with respect to their health records. When the healthcare system moved from a stance of paternalism to encouragement of patients' involvement in their healthcare decisions, healthcare organizations needed to address both the ethical and the practice aspects of patients' rights. HIPAA and other laws provided regulations that sparked changes in health information management and access to health records. In addition, ethics committees sought to review policies and procedures that addressed patients' right to treatment, denial of treatment, and access to health records (Harman, 2006).

Provider autonomy is another consideration when one contemplates the change from paper to electronic records. Physician practices, hospitals, and other healthcare organizations will need to convert to electronic health records in the near future, even if they think that their current system is working well. For some practices and organizations, converting to the EHR will require a major change in how they practice medicine—and not all practices will want to make such a change.

Financing a change to the EHR involves capital investments for purchasing new equipment, locating and installing new software, upgrading the legacy systems, and providing appropriate training. In addition, these capital investments can place a heavy burden on smaller physician groups, rural healthcare facilities, and public health settings. In addition to funding issues related to the EHR, healthcare administrators (HCAs) must be concerned with the workforce, which has varying degrees of knowledge and acceptance for the change to electronic records.. There will be extensive training costs and time to assure the technology competency of all clinical and administrative staff.

Patient applications of the electronic health record promise increased access to information and to health providers. It may increase patient autonomy as well: Individuals will be able to access their health records electronically and have greater information about their diagnoses and care. If all health records were electronic, patients could use their personal computers to contact their healthcare providers, order medications, and obtain health advice. However, a patient justice issue may exist because not all Americans have access to the Internet. Currently, more than 15% of Americans do not use the Internet because of its difficulty, the expense of owning a computer, or fear of loss of privacy. These non-Internet users tend to be older than 65, an age when health needs begin to increase (Stern, 2013). If the healthcare system becomes electronic, will the non-Internet-using population receive the same quality of care as the Internet-using population?

■ EMERGING MEDICAL TECHNOLOGY AND ETHICS

Science Daily and other electronic sites that investigate future developments in medical technology often highlight the United States' leadership in research and the use of technology. At these sites, one can find studies on everything from freckles to brain tumors. Scientists and researchers are creating new medical devices that feature everything from nano carriers to new uses for sonograms. The future of medicine shows that technology has great potential for improving health, treating disease, and prolonging life. Nevertheless, each of these emerging health and treatment technologies presents unique ethics issues along with their great promise. The following sections present a few examples of the ethics issues that accompany the miracles of new technologies.

Centralized Data Storage of Electronic Health Records

The promise of having easily accessible, centralized data storage (CDS) of health records through cloud computing services or another commercial mechanism shows great promise for health care. These systems allow backup of records in multiple locations through server farms. In addition to making data accessible anywhere at any time, this so-called cloud computing can streamline data storage and make data analysis easier. This form of data storage makes meeting the data demands of the ACA, insurers, and others much easier, and it provides patients with potentially greater access to their personal medical records. Such ease of access is especially important in a fast-paced society where travel is part of many patients' work and leisure.

With the emphasis on population health, there is greater interest in centralized data storage systems (the cloud). These systems allow for data mining that can create greater knowledge of disease prevention and treatment. In addition, enhanced access to medical records of populations of patients allows for better coordination of care and an increased ability to control costs. Use of data storage systems also increases the ability to identify trends among the patients in an individual group practice, which can lead to better outcomes through evidence-based practice (Grimshaw, 2013).

Although they show great promise, CDS systems are not perfect. Healthcare administrators need to be aware of both practical and ethical concerns with respect to these systems. As cloud technology becomes HIPAA and HITECH compliant, even more healthcare organizations are beginning to consider this form of data storage for their patient records (Carr, 2013). The potential benefits of business agility, interoperability, and cost savings are creating greater interest in this possibility among healthcare organizations. Of chief concern from an ethics standpoint is the imperative to protect these records and maintain patient confidentiality. Protection of confidentiality requires clear understanding of the mechanisms for oversight, designing appropriate encryption, and building patient confidence. Healthcare administrators will need to engage in continuing education, vendor contracting, and marketing efforts to assure patient record confidentiality and to maintain patient trust.

While protecting confidentiality of records would seem to be the most prevailing ethics concern, patients are also worried about violations of nonmaleficence. According to Palmer (2013), when patients learn about security breaches involving electronic devices such as theft and hacking, they are less likely to trust those who maintain their records. In turn, patients may choose to omit parts of their health history that are sensitive. While patients may see these omissions as appropriate, such omissions negatively affect the provider's ability to diagnose conditions and select and implement the best care. Healthcare administrators will need to provide staff education to prevent security breaches. In addition, there must be assurance for patients that their information is safe so that they trust their providers enough to confide often deeply personal, yet necessary health information.

Genetics in Medicine

"Profound" does not adequately describe the potential impact of emergent technologies on society and ethics. Progress, while highly valued, comes with a price. Many ethicists believe that such progress could create issues that will change how Americans value each other. They ask, "Why on earth should it be the case that 'what we ought to do,' should follow from what we can do?" (Gastmans, 2002, p. 18). American society will have to decide on the acceptable balance between technology's new ways to live and the ethics of using these options. Justice requires that Americans also address who should benefit from technology—those who can afford it or those who need it?

These societal issues of emergent technology and ethics are part of the growing field of genetics in medicine. Despite the FDA's concerns about the process, the average American who has $100 and is willing to send in a saliva sample can receive a personal genetic profile. This information can include whether the person is genetically prone to certain diseases, some of which are incurable. The ethics questions for the person using this service are: "Do I really want to know this information?" and "What will I do if I know it?" In addition, people do not always understand that when they pay the fee and send in their saliva, they become part of the growing genetics database. The data in this database will be used for future research and other purposes.

Genetics in medicine is a growing field that includes general genetic testing for the risk of disease, reproductive issues, and pharmacogenomics, among other applications. General testing for disease has the ability to alert people about their predisposition to certain diseases— for example, some forms of breast cancer and colorectal cancer, sickle cell anemia, and Huntington's disease. Although this knowledge would be helpful in prevention and treatment of diseases, many Americans do not wish to participate in testing because they fear that insurance companies or employers will gain access to their records or conduct screenings to determine their genetic status. Knowledge of personal genetic information can also lead to genetic discrimination: Employers may fire employees who may have high health costs (and, therefore, increase the employer's health insurance premiums) in the future (Harman, 2006).

Genetic testing is also increasing in relationship to reproductive medicine. This technology assists in determining the outcome of pregnancies. Several categories of such genetic tests exist, including carrier testing to determine the possibility of an individual having a recessive gene for a particular disease. For example, if the couple has a family history of a disease such as cystic fibrosis or Tay-Sachs disease, physicians can order genetic testing and the results can become part of family planning (Hannah, 2013).

Other genetic testing in reproduction medicines includes preimplantation diagnosis by testing embryos before implantation. This testing can determine gender and genetic conditions before a pregnancy occur. In addition, physicians can use genetic tests for prenatal diagnosis by sampling fetal tissue, taking blood samples from the umbilical cord, and conducting fetal visualization. These tests may help to identify fetal conditions such as Down syndrome. Finally, newborns may receive genetic testing as part of public health efforts to identify and treat genetic diseases (Hannah, 2013).

One of the newer uses of genetics in medicine is pharmacogenomics. This application combines knowledge of the human genome with research on pharmacology. It may potentially lead to customized drug dosages for individuals and reduce the possible side effects that they experience. Research on combining genetics and pharmacology also shows promise for patients who take blood thinners such as warfarin. In addition, scientists are conducting research on genetics and the ability to customize cancer treatments and evaluate drugs used in the treatment of mental health disorders (National Human Genome Research Institute, 2013).

Certainly, genetic information and its use create many ethics concerns. From the provider's view, the HIPAA standards specifically address the protection of genetic information. State laws also prohibit genetic discrimination by insurers. In addition, the Genetic Information Non-discrimination Act of 2008 (GINA) does not allow insurers to require a genetic test before enrollment in a plan. Employers cannot use genetic information in their hiring, firing, or job assignment, nor can they purchase genetic information about their employees (McWay, 2010).

Patient autonomy as expressed in confidentiality and privacy is a critical ethics issue with respect to the use of genetic information. Autonomy means that there should be authorization before anyone accesses a person's genetic information. However, even if a patient signs a release, he or she does not always understand what access entails. Concern has also been raised regarding what will happen with a person's genetic data—that is, how the data might be used. The case of Henrietta Lacks provides an excellent example of the reasons for this concern. Although it happened in a different time, the ethics issues of protection of privacy and lack of patient justice could also be part of future genetics research.

Henrietta Lacks was a black woman from a small town in Maryland. In 1951, a physician at Johns Hopkins Hospital treated her for cervical cancer and took samples of her tumor. Lacks did not give permission for the removal of these cells. In fact, she did not even know that the physician took tissue from her (Skloot, 2011). Her tissue samples became part of George Guy's research on cancer. Guy, the researcher who used Lacks's original sample, found that not only did Lacks's cancer cell line grow well in cultures, but the cells also reproduced at a rapid rate. These cells later became the HeLa cell line, which played a key role in research in virology, the cure for polio, and the field of genetics. In fact, this cell line is still in use today. Despite the millions of dollars generated by culture of this cell line, neither Henrietta Lacks nor her family received any financial benefit. In fact, the family did not even know about Henrietta Lacks's contribution to medical research until *Rolling Stone* magazine published an article on the history of the HeLa cell line. For more information about this remarkable story and its ethics, read *The Immortal Life of Henrietta Lacks* by Rebecca Skloot.

■ THE HCA'S ROLE IN EMERGING TECHNOLOGY

Because of its cost and scarcity in some areas of the United States, technology has always posed challenges concerning the balance of money and mission. For example, when dialysis was a new technology, hospitals had to create committees to decide who would receive this expensive treatment and who would not. As technology diffusion increases and becomes even integrated into care delivery and the business of health care, there will be an ever greater need for ethics-based decision making to balance the economic and human concerns associated with technology.

Hospitals, both urban and rural, already feel the need to supply the "latest and greatest" technology to meet the demands of their physicians and consumers. With the advent of the ACA and other changes in the U.S. healthcare system, such capital investments will strain hospitals' and clinics' already tight budgets. In addition, as the number of insured Americans increases and technology advances, decisions about who will get technology and who will pay for it will become even more intense.

Gastmans (2002), an ethicist, discussed the need to apply utilitarian principles when making these decisions. If economics principles are used, the healthcare system should maximize the benefits of technology to provide the greatest good for the greatest number of patients. Advanced technology and high levels of resources to treat the worst-off, while compassionate, might not provide the greatest utility. This is especially true if such use rules out treatment for those who have a greater chance of achieving improved quality of life.

While this argument may be appealing from a business sense, it also causes great concern for patients and their families, particularly in end-of-life situations. Because the goal of health care is supposed to be improving health, organizations will have to develop policies that consider factors such as quality of life, years of life remaining, severity of disease, and cost/benefit trade-offs of treatment. Of course, physicians will challenge technology utilization policies in their role as advocates for their patients. Denial of treatment, no matter how futile that treatment is in terms of health outcomes, will never be a popular solution. However, emergent technologies will increase the need to find an acceptable balance between economics and ethics.

In addition to raising financial concerns, emergent technologies promise to change the conduct of business. Technology assessment skills relative to both clinical and business applications will be essential for administrative effectiveness. Cost-effectiveness analysis, including the expense of hiring tech support staff, maintenance, frequency of obsolescence, as well as the cost of the technology, will become a routine part of decision making. Facilities will also have to assess the level of risk they are willing to assume if the technology does not turn out to be profitable. Ethical healthcare business practice always involves balancing mission and margin. Depending on how healthcare leaders make their decisions, emerging technology may either help or hinder this balancing act.

The healthcare insurance business will also face challenges related to emergent technologies. Under the ACA, insurers can no longer deny coverage for patients with preexisting conditions or place lifetime limits on coverage. These provisions put even greater pressure on insurance policy makers as they ponder decisions about coverage of emerging technology. However, as technology increases in its speed of innovation, more and more procedures will move from "experimental" to "routine." Consumer demand will force insurance companies to increase what is covered in their policies, which will most assuredly increase insurance rates.

On the positive side, emergent technologies promise to create new business opportunities. While these new businesses will provide job opportunities and revenue sources, they will have an ethical obligation to provide value through quality services using appropriately credentialed providers. In addition, ethics will mandate that educational institutions adequately prepare professionals for service in these new entities. To avoid educational fraud, they will have to evaluate their curricula assure that graduates are ready for the ever-changing healthcare market.

Technology promises to change the role of ethics-based healthcare administrators as well. First, HCAs have an ethical duty to make intelligent decisions about the purchase of technology. This means that they must rely on more than the information presented by vendors. They will need to seek out unbiased information from several sources and keep up with current trends. On the surface, this sounds like a simple matter, but it is often difficult to understand the techno-jargon in information sources. To be truly informed, healthcare administrators may need to engage in conference calls with those who already use the technology. They may also need to attend product demonstrations and visit facilities that already use the technology. Healthcare administrators will make the best decisions for their organizations only when they truly understand what they are purchasing, how much it costs to maintain, how quickly it will need to be replaced, and how easy it is to use. Although there may be costs involved, making the best decision not only demonstrates the healthcare administrator's stewardship of resources, but also treads the financially sensible path by limiting excessive spending and waste.

It is important for healthcare administrators to create policies that decide who gets expensive technology and when they get it. Because the mission of health care is to improve health and treat disease and infirmities, administrators need to consider patients and their families when developing technology utilization policies. Physicians and other clinical staff, the ethics committee, and patient advocates may need to be part of such utilization policy development. However, if economics is the sole basis for policies and they do not conform to the organization's articulated mission and ethical principles, healthcare administrators can become vulnerable to potential lawsuits and/or negative community image. Policies on the use of emergent and even current technology must consider all three elements of the healthcare triangle—cost, access, and quality—along with potential harm and benefit to patients. While these decisions will never be easy, they will continue to be part of the evolving practice of health care for many years to come.

Summary

The information is this chapter is just a first step toward understanding the impact of technology on ethics and ethical decision making. Each healthcare organization will continue to struggle with this issue as the ACA moves through its implementation stages and emergent technology continues to create new opportunities and challenges. Healthcare administrators will face the challenge of balancing a lucrative revenue stream with the ethics base of their organizations. The only way to be prepared to assist in this process is to stay vigilant. The HCA should read, surf the Internet, and attend conferences to keep his or her knowledge at the cutting edge. Consider reading more than the healthcare literature to understand what is happening with information technology in the nonhealth business community. Healthcare administrators will also have to consider "what if" situations before their organizations face "must do" decisions. Effective communication and dialogue among practitioners, ethics committee members, and community representatives will enhance the level of preparedness when making decisions about current and future use of health technology.

Cases for Your Consideration

The Case of the Techno Ankle

Think about the chapter information and consider the following questions. Sample responses and commentary will follow the case.

1. Why did Dr. Aidan set up a multi-staff conference?

2. Which ethics theories and principles apply to this case?

3. Will this conference change Dr. Aidan's decisions about technology?

Case Information

Dr. Shane Aidan was frustrated! He was a well-respected orthopedic surgeon, but this case was becoming more and more perplexing. Fiona Macfee, a 40-year-old woman, broke both bones in her ankle as the result of a home accident. The repair of her ankle required two successful surgeries. However, the surgical wound in her ankle would not heal. Consequently, Dr. Aidan ordered a negative-pressure machine to assist in her healing. While he was not an expert in the use of this machine, past experience led him to believe that it would speed healing.

But something was clearly different about this case. Although Fiona had home care through wound specialist nurses, her progress in healing was slow. In addition, Fiona complained about the quality of care provided by the wound care specialists. Dr. Aidan wondered if the specialists were contributing to the lack of healing progress. He was also concerned about the loss of credibility to his practice and even considered the potential of a lawsuit. Consequently, he decided to take control of the technology dilemma.

He called a meeting during Fiona's next appointment. Attendees were representatives from the company that created the technology, wound care specialists from the home health agency, his office staff nurse, and Dr. Aidan. Using Fiona's ankle as a prop, the representatives discussed the purpose of the machine and how to change the dressings correctly. They also observed the wound care specialist as she applied the dressing and offered suggestions. Both Dr. Aidan and his staff nurse asked questions about how the technology applied to Fiona's particular wound, and how to enhance future healing. After serving as the prop, Fiona asked her questions about the treatment and her healing. In the end, all those who attended felt more knowledgeable about the application of this technology to Fiona's case.

Responses and Comments on Questions

1. Why did Dr. Aidan set up a multi-staff conference?

   Consider Dr. Aidan's dilemma. He was relying on technology to assist healing in a difficult case. However, he was not completely familiar with all of the aspects of the latest version of this technology. Therefore, he could not answer all of Fiona's questions or assure her that healing would happen in a timely manner. In addition, he had concerns about the competence of the home health wound care specialists and their contribution to the slow healing. Because of his concerns, he was considering changing agencies. The logical course of action was to get all parties together and do some technology calibration. This might assure that all parties involved in Fiona's care were working together from common knowledge.

   Dr. Aidan might also be concerned about a potential lawsuit and its effect on his practice. The ability to bring all the participants in Fiona's care together would allow them to communicate and create better understanding, which might mediate any future harm. Dr. Aidan hoped that Fiona would view this meeting as quality assurance on her behalf—a perception that might prevent her from consulting an attorney. In addition, Dr. Aidan could verify that the wound care specialists had the most current information on the technology. This knowledge could give Fiona assurance that her home care would contribute to her healing rather than cause further harm.

2. Which ethics theories and principles apply to this case?

    In this case, the theory of deontology is at work. Even though the bones had healed, Dr. Aidan still had a duty to the patient. He needed to make sure that Fiona could resume her normal life. This duty included the complete healing of her surgical wounds. Calling a meeting of the professionals who contributed to Fiona's care and making sure that these professionals had correct information on the technology was one way to demonstrate active deontology. Dr. Aidan also continued to practice his duty to the patient by making sure that her wound care specialists had up-to-date training on the latest technology.

    While deontology is the most obvious theory at play here, also consider utilitarianism. Dr. Aidan was concerned about making the best decision for his practice. Having a meeting at his office during a patient's appointment meant that he incurred costs. For example, he did not see other patients during the meeting, and that was a loss of income. However, if he used a cost/benefit analysis based on utilitarian in principles, he could determine that the cost of holding a meeting was well worth the benefit of preventing future problems with this technology. In addition, he could save thousands of dollars in lost revenue by preventing a lawsuit.

    With respect to principles, beneficence and nonmaleficence were evident. Dr. Aidan wanted to prevent future harm to Fiona by assuring the correct use of wound care technology. He also needed to understand the technology's features better so that he could use it correctly in the future. Before he prescribed this technology, he wished to be sure that it functioned to prevent harm by increasing healing time. In terms of beneficence, Dr. Aidan made the decision to take time out of his practice and have a meeting. While this action was not required, it demonstrated his concern for the patient and her healing. He also hoped that Fiona would view his actions as taking extra steps to benefit her care.

    Another principle to consider in this case is autonomy. The autonomy of the professionals was respected because they were allowed time to ask questions and gain knowledge necessary for the correct use of the technology. However, Fiona's autonomy was not a priority. During the appointment, she acted more as a prop than as a person. However, at the end of the conference, she asked questions, which demonstrated some level of respect for her as a person.

3. Will this conference change Dr. Aidan's decisions about technology?

Dr. Aidan will need to consider his future decisions about the use of technology based on ethics and economics. From an ethics view, he will consider the benefit to the patient compared to the potential harm. As he learned in this case, technology, when used improperly, can add to a patient's problems rather than promote healing. Dr. Aidan will need to learn about each type of technology before he prescribes it. To be able to keep up-to-date with the advances in technology related to his practice, he will have to engage in continuous learning.

From an economics view, Dr. Aidan must be careful not to succumb to the "lure of the latest." That means he will have to weigh the cost of immediately obtaining the newest technology versus the benefit of this technology for his patients. Perhaps it will be more economical to wait until the price declines before purchasing the newest models. He will also have to remember that newer is not always better. Again, he must base his decisions on research rather than on the influence of a well-spoken sales representative.

The Case of the Lemon Baby

Think about the chapter information and consider the following questions. Sample responses and commentary will follow the case.

1. Which principles and theories of ethics are considerations in this case?

2. How does this technology affect the business of health care?

3. How does this technology affect the nature of families?

Case Information

Introduction

The basis for this case is a scenario that the author uses in her ethics classes and it is always popular. In its early use, students thought it was so bizarre that it would never happen. Now, the case is much closer to reality; some clinicians are even providing this service at a basic level. The case illustrates the need to balance the business potential of technology with the ethics issues it creates. It goes back to Gastmans's (2002) question: Just because you can do something, should you?

The Case

The Center for Reproductive Technology has made great strides in clinical applications of genetic engineering for reproductive services. For a fee of $150,000, it can provide a "baby to specs." This means that the potential parents fill out an extensive questionnaire that gives their preference for gender, eye color, hair color and type, potential height and weight, intelligence potential, athletic potential, and other variables. They also complete three interviews including a psychological evaluation and a marriage stability profile. Standard consent forms are also a part of the client acceptance process and include the promise of product satisfaction.

The procedure uses the egg and sperm of the parents, or donors if necessary, and the clinicians then engineer the genes to meet the parents' specifications. The physician subsequently implants the improved embryos in the mother or surrogate mother for delivery. The Center makes every effort to ensure the quality of the product delivered. In fact, it has customer satisfaction rates of 95%, and the Center has turned a very high profit, which it shared with its investors.

The Doctors Smalley took advantage of the services offered through the Center. They had long wanted a male child to carry on the Smalley name. Dr. Herbert Smalley wanted a male baby who had the ability to be a star athlete. Dr. Matilda Smalley wanted a child with high intelligence potential so he could maintain the family tradition of graduating from Harvard University. The procedures went well and their surrogate mother gave birth successfully. The problem was that the child did not fulfill their order.

The Center's chief executive officer, Kit Ptolemy, received a call from Dr. Herbert Smalley, who was enraged at the lack of product quality. He paid $150,000 for a male child with certain genetic traits and potentials. What he got was a female child who did not meet any of the stated characteristics. He demanded an explanation. Mr. Ptolemy calmed him down and told him that he would investigate immediately.

After checking into the situation, Mr. Ptolemy found that there had been a mix-up in the computer system. The improved embryo implanted in the surrogate mother was from another order, which was for a red-haired, blue-eyed, Caucasian female with high beauty and intelligence potential. Because of a computer error, there were no data concerning the location of the Smalley embryo. Someone might have accidently destroyed it. In addition, the system did not have data on the Caucasian baby order. Because the Smalleys were African American, Mr. Ptolemy recognized that they could be angry about this error.

Mr. Ptolemy called the Doctors Smalley back and explained what happened. He offered to reimburse them for their fees. That is when Dr. Herbert Smalley exploded. He told Mr. Ptolemy that he would not raise a white female child in his home even if she were free. He wanted his full refund and, tomorrow morning, he would be bringing the baby back to the Center. She would be their problem, not his.

Responses and Comments on Questions

1. Which principles and theories of ethics are considerations in this case?

   First, look at the business aspects of this case. The Center for Reproductive Technology made a risky financial decision that paid off. It invested huge amounts of capital in technology and staff to be able to provide a service that many wanted and could afford. In fact, Mr. Ptolemy thought that the fee of $150,000 was a bargain in light of the Center's capital investment.

The administration of the Center felt it was meeting their business obligation to provide a quality product as promised. They tried to prevent any unsatisfactory consequences by insisting on extensive interviews with potential parents of this product, including an assessment of their psychological and marital stability. In addition, as part of a capital-based society, they felt that they had an obligation to make a profit and provide a dividend to their investors. To fail in this effort would be bad for business and violate corporate ethics. Up until the time of the Smalley error, the Center was meeting these obligations and saw itself as a thriving business with great growth potential.

From a purely market justice view, the Center was an ethics-based business. It was providing a service to those who could afford it. However, looking beyond the business aspects reveals some serious ethics issues. First, the Center regarded human embryos and full-term babies as "products," not humans. This is a violation of the principle of autonomy, because the Center's view did not value and respect human life. Buber's (1996) idea of moral relationships also applies here. When humans become "its" instead of valued individuals, that perspective can change the way they are treated in society. The Center, through its designer baby technology, is actually contributing to a negative valuing of individuals.

How do other ethics principles apply to this case? Although the Center provided a societal benefit, its policies do not comply with utilitarian ethics. The ability to design children is limited only to those who are wealthy enough to afford such technology. If one believes that designer babies are a social good, then the greatest good is not provided to the greatest number; it is limited to a few. The case also addresses Rawls's principle of differences, as one could argue that these parents are helping to contribute to the future. They are creating genetically superior children, so they felt that they should be given special treatment.

But is this true? Kantians would reject this idea and say that the Center has an ethical duty to obey the categorical imperative. Apparently, its owners do not feel that designer children should be available to all in society—only to those who can pay for it. When one considers what happened in this case, the Center's actions do not meet the categorical imperative.

2. How does this technology affect the business of health care?

   This case goes to the root of the concerns about implementation of future technology in health care and the impact it can have.

The potential for profit will make many technology-based businesses very attractive, especially if traditional healthcare services begin to be less profitable. They hold the potential for changing how administrators think about healthcare delivery. However, many questions need answers before a new technology is used. For example, what is the purpose of health care? Is it centered on increasing or maintaining health, or is it to be a products-based industry? How can health care invest capital in technology and still have enough resources to provide quality services? With the advent of the ACA changes, who will pay for technology? Even with ACA insurance coverage opportunities, will everyone receive expensive technology? What if the technology's products are medically unnecessary, but are profitable? How do healthcare administrators make appropriate decisions about the use of technology?

Technology's potential seems almost limitless in terms of what it can do for and to the human body. This potential can greatly benefit business and society as well. However, there are difficult decisions to make in determining just how far technology should go. From an ethics standpoint, each organization will have to establish a balance between demand for new technology, investment versus profit potential, and ethical considerations.

3. How does this technology affect the nature of families?

Certainly, the Smalleys have a different view of the family than most. They wanted to have the perfect child who would grow up to meet their expectations. Their access to technology that could provide them with the child that they wanted supported their view of the ideal family. They were able to pay for a child that met their vision. Frankly, they felt that it was nobody's business what they did in their own home. Their only problem with this was that the Center did not deliver. The Center's error produced a very unacceptable product—a redheaded, white, female child. The Smalleys had no desire to spend their time and money raising a child who was not the correct gender or the correct race. A full refund and a return of the defective product seemed fair to them. After all, if their Mercedes child was really a lemon, they should be able to return her.

Healthcare administrators can see from this response that the designer baby business can introduce completely new issues about the nature of what it means to be a family. Will there be issues about designer children versus "natural" children so that one will be valued over the other? Can you imagine the issues this change might create for social workers, psychologists, and counselors who will deal with the psychological impact on the family and individuals? What should happen in schools? Are they prepared to educate a group of super-children? Should there be separate classes for designer children so that they do not have to associate with children of lesser value? How will the non-engineered children fare in school and in society in general?

In the author's classes, several groups tried to grapple with what to do with the "rejected products"—that is, children who were born, but did not measure up to the specifications. They acknowledged that the Center might have to take these children back, much like some adoption agencies do today. Therefore, they decided that they could create a spinoff business by running a discounted adoption center that would place these babies in the homes of those who wanted designer babies but could not afford them. This suggestion, while made facetiously, sparked a class debate about what would happen to designer children who did not measure up and the impact on the family and society in general.

Web Resources

American Health Information Management Association
http://www.ahima.org/

How the Cloud Works Video
http://www.youtube.com/watch?v=TTNgV0O_oTg

Science Daily
http://www.sciencedaily.com/news/health_medicine/

References

Bishop, T. F., Press, M. J., Mendelsohn, J. L., & Casalino, L. P. (2013). Electronic communication improves access, but barriers to its widespread adoption remain. *Health Affairs*, *32*(8), 1361–1367. doi: 10.1377/htlhaff.2012.1151

Buber, M. (1996). *I and thou*. New York, NY: Touchstone.

Carr, D. F. (2013, September 10). HIPAA changes driving customers to cloud, Version says. *Information Week*. Retrieved from http://www.informationweek.com/healthcare/electronic-health-records/hipaa-changes-driving-customers-to-cloud-verizon-says/d/d-id/1111487

Gastmans, C. (Ed.). (2002). *Between technology and humanity: The impact of technology on health care ethics*. Leuven, Belgium: Leuven University Press.

Grimshaw. H. (2013, May/June). Virtual conundrum: A member perspective on HIEs. *MGMA Connexion*, *13*(5), 24–28.

Hannah, K. E. (2013). Reproductive genetic testing. National Human Genome Research Institute. Retrieved from http://www. genome .gov/10004766

Harman, L. B. (2006). *Ethical challenges in the management of health information* (2nd ed.). Sudbury, MA: Jones and Bartlett.

HHS Press Office. (2013, January 17). New rule protects patient privacy, secures information. *HHS.gov*. Retrieved from http://www.hhs.gov/news/press/2013pres/01/20130117b.html

Institute of Medicine. (2001). *Crossing the quality chasm: A new health system for the 21st century*. Washington, DC: National Academy Press.

McWay, D. C. (2010), *Legal and ethical aspects of health information management* (3rd ed.). Clinton Park, NY: Delmar.

National Human Genome Research Institute. (2013). Frequently asked questions about pharmacogenomics. Retrieved from http://www.genome.gov/pfv.cfm?pageID=27530645

Palmer, L. (2013). Why patients might not tell you the truth, the whole truth and nothing but the truth. *Executive View*, 9(2), 14–19.

Payne, E., Smith, M., & Cohen, T. (2013, October 22). Report: Healthcare website failed test ahead of roleout. *CNN Politics*. Retrieved from http://www.cnn.com/2013/10/22/politics/obamacare-website-problems/

Roberts, L. W. (2013). The third side of the coin: Achieving true interoperability. *Executive View*, 9(2), 25–30.

Shi, L., & Singh, D. A. (2015). *Delivering health care in America: A systems approach* (6th ed.). Burlington, MA: Jones & Bartlett Learning.

Skloot, R. (2011). *The immortal life of Henrietta Lacks*. New York, NY: Broadway Books.

Stern, J. (2013, September 21). Couldn't live without the Internet? 15 percent of American adults do. *ABC News*. Retrieved from http://abcnews.go.com/Technology/offline-americans-15-percent-americans-live-email-internet/story?id=20386849

Sultz, H. A., & Young, K. (2014). *Health care USA* (8th ed.). Burlington, MA: Jones & Bartlett Learning.

SECTION III

Organizational Influences on Ethics

■ INTRODUCTION

Ethics must become part of the daily operation of healthcare organizations. The culture of a healthcare organization greatly influences how that organization uses ethics in the work of providing health care. In turn, ethics decisions can have an impact on healthcare organizations' cultures. Healthcare administrators' understanding of their organizations' mission, espoused values, structure, and financial status can enhance this symbiotic relationship. In the ACA era, it is also essential that healthcare administrators serve as moral agents and understand how organizations respond to ethical issues. In addition, they must be aware of their power and use it to make ethics-based decisions. This section assists healthcare administrators with their responsibility to be ethics based and explores areas including finance, culture, compliance, and customers.

The *No Mission, No Margin: Fiscal Responsibility* chapter examines the funding structure of health care and considers how its complexity creates ethics issues. Healthcare facilities must maintain a solid bottom line to keep their doors open, pay their employees competitively, and maintain quality service. Unlike in other industries, the basis for the healthcare organization's mission is service to the individual and to the community. This chapter presents ethics issues related to finance, including the differing issues for nonprofit versus for-profit healthcare organizations and new concerns for finance in the ACA era.

The *Organizational Culture and Ethics* chapter discusses cultures embedded in health care and considers how they present ethics concerns. In addition, this chapter features discussion of management culture and its influence on ethics. It also addresses the functions of ethics committees and their assistance in ethics decisions and policy formulation. The chapter presents ethics decision-making models to assist in making sound ethical decisions in the challenging ACA era.

The next chapter, *The Ethics of Quality*, begins with an overview of the concept of quality as it applies to health care. It gives examples of agencies that address quality issues and discusses ethics issues related to quality compliance. The chapter goes beyond compliance to examine ways that external agencies are working toward improving quality in health care. As the chapter title suggests, the ethical implications of quality assurance are a feature of this chapter.

The *Patient Issues and Ethics* chapter examines the ethical issues affecting the patient from the organization's view. The ACA expects health care to be effective, efficient, and patient centered. This expectation increases the pressure on all healthcare organizations to provide services that satisfy patients and meet quality care standards. This chapter examines the evolving patient culture and the ethics of measuring patient satisfaction and its relationship to healthcare administrators.

The *Public Health and Ethics* chapter is new to this edition. It explores the relationship between public health and its influence on health. The chapter presents key ethical issues for public health systems and for public health professionals. It also examines the relationship between public health and the ACA and its ethics challenges. The intent of this chapter is to explore a different organizational perspective and ethics issues related to public health organizations and administrators.

CHAPTER
9

No Mission, No Margin: Fiscal Responsibility

Why is fiscal responsibility an ethics duty?

Points to Ponder

1. How are the financial aspects of health care different from those of other businesses?
2. Why does healthcare profit making affect community trust?
3. How do healthcare organizations balance mission and profit margin?
4. Which key ethics issues exist in the financial side of health care?
5. Can healthcare administrators balance stewardship with fiscal responsibility?

Key Terms

The following is a list of this chapter's key terms. Look for them in bold.

Hospital Consumer Assessment of Health Care Providers and Systems Survey (HCAHPS)
Hospital Value-Based Purchasing Program (Hospital VBP)
Independent Payment Advisory Board (IPAB)

medically necessary
moral hazard
O Team
self-insured
stewardship
upcoding (coding creep)

■ INTRODUCTION AND DEFINITIONS

In 1870, Ralph Waldo Emerson asked, "Can anyone remember when the times were not hard, and money was not scarce?" (Inspiration Station, 2013), His question could be part of today's discussions about the financial challenges of health care. Even in the best of times, the demand for health care often exceeds the financial and provider resources available, especially in the case of the uninsured or underinsured. However, with the projected changes from the Affordable Care Act of 2010, the ability to balance fiscal requirements and patient-centered care create a different set of issues for ethics-based healthcare administrators.

This chapter provides a basic review of the financing of health care that forms the basis for a discussion of funding and ethics. To highlight the fiscal and ethical issues, it also contains a review of the changes in funding proposed by the ACA. The concept of stewardship as it relates to finance and ethics is included as a consideration for ethics-based administration practice. Examples of ethics challenges for healthcare administrators are presented as well.

■ HEALTH CARE IS A BUSINESS LIKE NO OTHER BUSINESS

Health care is a business, but its funding is like no other business. Suppose Henri owns Henri's Taco Stand and Emporium. Henri orders supplies, provides an excellent product, pays his employees, and calculates his profit margin. Of course, being a good citizen and a Texan, he pays his business taxes and makes sure his Taco Stand and Emporium meets all of the state health codes. Henri serves customers who choose and pay for his tacos and is not responsible for serving those who cannot.

Henri's Taco Stand and Emporium is similar to most businesses in that customers have power because they decide to purchase items based on factors like need, perceived value, available finances, and even location of the services. The business owners do have certain obligations that can influence sales and profit, such as delivering a quality product at a competitive price. There are regulations that govern some of the business practices and costs of doing business, such as employee benefits. However, businesses recoup these costs by including them in the selling price of their products.

What happens in the healthcare business? Shi and Singh (2015) discuss the maze-like complexity of healthcare financing, which includes a myriad of public and private sources. From the private sector, there is funding from third-party organizations that sell nonmandated or private health insurance. Employer-funded benefit plans are the most common source for access to these entities. Options for these plans vary from Blue Cross/Blue Shield types of insurance to various forms of managed care (e.g., health maintenance organizations, preferred provider organizations [PPOs], and independent practice associations).

Large employers may decide to be **self-insured** by collecting premiums and pooling these resources to pay healthcare claims. They often use a commercial insurance company to manage their claims process.

This option provides advantages to employers such as the ability to avoid premium taxes and to earn interest on cash held for claims payment. However, there are also risks, such as liability for withholding payments or not providing quality care. In addition, if premium rates are not set correctly, the employer may face adverse financial consequences (Sultz & Young, 2014).

Regardless of the form of employer-provided insurance coverage, employees usually pay part of the cost through premiums, deductibles, and copayments. However, even though employees share in the costs, employers still pay a large share of the actual costs. In times of economic downturns or changing government tax policies, employer funding for employees' health care can be increasingly difficult to maintain.

The public sector (government) also funds health care, and this funding varies by population (Shi & Singh, 2015; Sultz & Young, 2014). Active-duty military persons and their dependents, military retirees, and veterans have funding systems. State and federal government employees and retirees have a different system. Retirees and certain other qualified members have another system. The qualified poor, children, and those with disabilities have still another system. Native Americans and other qualified populations also have a different financing system. Each of these systems has its own regulations, policies, and procedures for including or excluding people and services. In addition, those who provide care must meet each system's quality standards and provide documentation for meeting these standards. Likewise, cost reimbursement can be different in each system, which adds to confusion, time, and needed staffing to accommodate these variations.

How do those persons who are unemployed or not in a covered population pay for their health care? Before the advent of the ACA, these patients fell into categories of the uninsured. Even with the ACA, if these population groups are wealthy, they simply write a check for services rendered. However, many of the uninsured are not so fortunate. Americans who are self-employed, farmers, or early retirees can obtain an individual private health insurance plan. These plans are often expensive because the basis for their cost is the individual's health risk rather than the risk spread across a large group (Shi & Singh, 2015). If individuals do not have any form of insurance plan, they are responsible for their total healthcare expenses. In the event of an accident or major health issue, uninsured patients may not be able to pay their healthcare expenses and may find themselves in bankruptcy court. There may be assistance for the uninsured through uncompensated care from hospitals, clinics, or charity from nongovernment agencies. They can also make financial arrangements with the facility (e.g., payment plans) or charge services to their credit cards.

Before passage of the ACA, even the insured did not always receive full healthcare coverage, For example, dental and eye care was not part of all healthcare insurance plans' coverage but rather required separate insurance policies. Certainly, prevention services such as nutrition counseling, exercise programs, and integrated medicine services were not included in many health insurance plans, even given their potential for lowering healthcare costs. Despite the Mental Health Parity and Addiction Equity Act of 2008 (MHPAEA; U.S. Department of Labor, 2010), mental health and addiction treatment services, which could benefit millions of Americans, also had limited coverage. Such a lack of insurance coverage causes many Americans to go without treatment, especially if payment for these services is not possible given their current financial status.

Even though healthcare insurance is not universal, there is a financial downside to its existence. While protecting consumers from bearing too heavy a financial burden, health insurance also obscures the true cost of their care. This lack of an accurate understanding of healthcare costs creates **moral hazard**, which means that consumers use more healthcare services than they would if they were financially responsible for the total cost (Shi & Singh, 2015, p. 13). In addition, when insurance is available for areas like dentistry and mental health, consumers want to access these services, so healthcare organizations must be able to provide services. Healthcare providers must be available and accessible to consumers, which influences the need for providers and the education of support personnel for those providers.

In addition to the complexity of the payer system, one must consider the demand side to fully appreciate the scope of the healthcare market. In other businesses, the consumer, often influenced by marketing, creates a demand. However, in health care, it is the provider or the payer who influences the demand. For instance, a patient cannot decide that he or she would like to have an MRI. Instead, a referring physician must order this test and the patient's insurance carrier must approve it. Patients must trust the professional's knowledge and decisions about what is best for them. In addition, the drug industry contributes to the creation of demand for healthcare products through its marketing to professionals and extensive advertising campaigns. Patients do not choose their drugs; they require a prescription from a healthcare provider. In addition, direct marketing to patients through the Internet, television, and other media may convince them that they have a particular disease and need a particular drug even before they see their physicians! Of course, the cost of over-the counter drugs, while not usually covered by insurance, adds to patients' healthcare costs as well.

Both the payer (private and public insurance) and the provider of care make the decision about whether a procedure or test is **medically necessary**. Physicians and other healthcare professionals are well prepared to assist patients in making decisions about their health. However, providers and patients often view the inclusion of the payer in deciding medical necessity with great distrust. In addition, professionals typically resent the rules and regulations that seem to question their professional opinion, increase the complexity of practice, and restrict their practice decisions. The idea of a conflict of interest between the needs of the patient and the profits may be a patient concern as well. In another twist, some employers may ask billing information coders to be creative in their coding so that claims will avoid the medical necessity requirements (Harman, 2006).

What does all of this complexity mean for the healthcare system? First, it adds to the overall cost of providing care. There is a need for separate groups of highly knowledgeable employees if the healthcare organization is to receive the maximum payment for services rendered. These individuals must navigate complex rules and regulations and obtain optimal funding for the organization. Do the employment costs for these personnel take away funds from providing care? On the plus side, can this complexity be a source of employment for those who are on the business side of health care?

Second, complexity leads to ethics challenges. The lure of profit or insecurity over reimbursement can lead to both ethics and even legal problems. For example, while practitioners should use the most appropriate ICD-10 code when submitting claims to obtain the maximum return, there can be a temptation to code for the dollar and not for the diagnosis. This practice, called **upcoding** or **coding creep**, can become a legal issue if there is an audit (Harman, 2006). In addition, certain services may receive better reimbursement from insurance companies. The profit motive, of course, would suggest that medical practices order as many of these better-funded procedures as possible. However, the business of health care, while understanding the need to make profit, requires a higher ethical standard. The community and ethics-based organizations require additional measures of business success including practicing beneficence and providing for the population's health (Harman, 2006).

■ THE ETHICS OF NONPROFIT VERSUS FOR-PROFIT ORGANIZATIONS

Healthcare administrators must also consider issues related to the ethics of for-profit healthcare systems versus nonprofit healthcare entities. Historically, health care was delivered through systems that were nonprofit; such systems were often funded through communities or religious organizations (Shi & Singh, 2015). These organizations, while having to make money to maintain their existence, were not profit driven. In fact, the communities that they served maintained a trust in their ability to serve their needs and granted them tax-exempt status. In contrast, in recent years, there has been an increase in commercialization of the healthcare industry through the growth of for-profit healthcare systems. Because these systems have a duty to shareholders as well as to patients and the community, they have additional ethics concerns, including balancing what is best for business with the needs of patients and staff members.

Social justice is one ethics concern that affects both systems. First, those who argue strongly for social justice make the case that everyone deserves to have access to basic health care and that the United States has a duty to provide this care. Even though these organizations may have tax-exempt status, they often have difficulty meeting their duty. The increases in healthcare costs and cutbacks in funding contribute to the fiscal challenges faced by nonprofits. In addition, these organizations often serve patients who are unable to pay for services and have severe health problems. In the current healthcare environment, these organizations have to compete with for-profit systems for patients who can pay for services or who are insured.

From the for-profit perspective, organizations must serve well-insured patients to make a profit beyond the cost of care. Although they also provide charity care, these businesses cannot be overwhelmed by nonpaying patients if they hope to remain profitable. Competitive pressures require these systems to provide care in attractive settings that offer the latest equipment and services—a requirement that increases the cost of doing business and can reduce profit margins.

For-profit organizations also face ethics issues related to market justice. Put simply, they must use resources in ways that meet patient needs and generate revenue. This can lead to emphasis on ordering profitable tests, treatment, or services to increase the business's margin. There is also a concern that the necessity of creating profits can lead to overuse of services and increase the costs of health care. While these decisions may make good business sense, they contribute to the public's diminished trust in hospitals in general. With the advent of the ACA, hospitals—no matter their business model—will face new business and ethics challenges (Shi & Singh, 2015).

■ HEALTHCARE FINANCE IN THE ACA ERA

The Accountable Care Act of 2010 is part of a continuing attempt to control healthcare costs, access, and quality. It represents the largest change in the U.S. healthcare system since the passage of the legislation establishing the Medicare and Medicaid programs. While the ACA promises to reform care delivery through changes in insurance coverage and health insurance exchanges, it has the potential to influence health care in major ways. For example, the ACA will generate revenue through a series of new penalties, taxes, and fees. Larger employers (i.e., those with more than 50 employees) face fees of $2000 to $3000 per employee depending on certain coverage rules. In addition, there will be an application of many new taxes or fees that affect Medicare payroll taxes, high-cost health plans, and even indoor tanning salons. Insurance companies and manufacturers of certain medical devices also will pay annual fees (Sultz & Young, 2014).

In terms of financing changes that directly affect healthcare services, the ACA has created options to address costs and quality (Sultz & Young, 2014). Examples of these changes include accountable care organizations, the Hospital Value-Based Purchasing Program, and the Independent Payment Advisory Board. Each of these features creates the need for changing "business as usual" for health care and poses unique ethics issues in healthcare finance.

The accountable care organization (ACO) is a practice design that provides incentives for healthcare providers to improve the coordination of care for Medicare patients. The program includes an advanced payment model that gives incentives to providers who participate in its shared savings program and improve their coordination of patient care. The ACO involves doctors, hospitals, long-term care facilities and others in this effort. The Centers for Medicare and Medicaid Services (CMS, 2013a) must approve these organizations before they can begin operation.

The intention of ACOs is to lower the cost of care and improve quality by focusing on patients' needs. They are also expected to save money, increase quality by keeping patients well, provide necessary treatments in a timely way, and avoid duplication of care. These organizations require a major change in the way that physicians, hospitals, and long-term care facilities function. For example, success in coordinating care and maintaining patient wellness should reduce the cost per Medicaid patient, with ACOs sharing in this cost-reduction benefit (Sultz & Young, 2014). As more evidence demonstrating the success of the ACO innovation is published, interest among physician practices, hospitals, and long-term care facilities in this structure is expected to grow.

The government-mandated **Hospital Value-Based Purchasing Program** (Hospital VBP) is of great concern to hospitals because Medicare payments represent a large percentage of their annual revenue. The Hospital VBP is an historic change in Medicare reimbursement to providers and facilities because its basis is the delivery of quality of care. Under the ACA, Medicare will evaluate the quality of care using identified measures and award points based on improvement or achievement of these measures. Scores on these measures will lead to value-based incentive payments. Hospitals will also be subject to point deductions and reduced payments if they fail to meet the identified standards. Examples of areas associated with point deductions include hospital-acquired infection rates and excessive readmissions for patients suffering heart attacks and pneumonia. New standards will be introduced each year (CMS, 2007).

Scoring of quality measures uses a formula that compares hospitals against each other in terms of achievement of standards and compares changes from baseline against current performance. Using items from the **Hospital Consumer Assessment of Health Care Providers and Systems Survey (HCAHPS)**, Medicare will also consider clinical care and the patient's experience as part of quality measures (CMS, 2013b). The CMS chose this instrument because it is a standardized survey endorsed by the National Quality Forum. Beginning in fiscal year 2014, subscores on the Clinical Process of Care domain of the HCAHPS will count toward 45% of a hospital's total performance score (TPS). Scores on the Patient Experience of Care domain will account for 30% of the TPS. On the HCAHPS, questions regarding communication with nurses and physician, pain management, cleanliness and noise levels, and discharge information measure the patient experience in a hospital. In addition, patient satisfaction and other HCAHPS scores will be available to the public on a quarterly basis on a website called *Hospital Compare*.

The ACA also includes the **Independent Payment Advisory Board (IPAB)**, a feature that continues to be controversial. Because the reductions in Medicare spending imposed by the ACA will not slow down growth enough to fully protect the U.S. GDP, the act includes a mechanism to recommend policies to reduce Medicaid spending. To avoid pressure exerted by political influences, the IPAB will use outside experts to study the growth of healthcare spending. It will make recommendations on better coordination of care, best practices, waste management, and increasing primary care services. Despite its "death panel" reputation, the IPAB cannot recommend rationing, restricting benefits, or changing eligibility (Sultz & Young, 2014).

■ STEWARDSHIP AND PRACTICAL WISDOM

Simply put, healthcare organizations need to make money. When a healthcare organization shuts down due to lack of funds, the community loses both a source of care and a source of income. However, if the motivation of a healthcare organization is profit alone, it does not serve its higher mission of caring for the sick and injured. Therefore, a true dilemma exists. How do healthcare organizations maintain an adequate profit margin, yet remain true to their patient care mission (Pearson, Sabin, & Emanuel, 2003)?

The ethical struggle for healthcare administrators (HCAs) is to find the balance between the yin of quality care and the yang of profit and market survival. To achieve this balance and maintain an ethics-based organization, HCAs must realistically assess both aspects and make decisions that are appropriate for the organization and the community it serves.

It all begins with mission. Even in challenging times of great change, healthcare organizations need an operationally defined mission that is used consistently at all levels of decision making. The mission, in an ethics-based organization, needs to include quality services within the framework of community needs and mandates (Boyle, DuBose, Ellingson, Guinn, & McCurdy, 2001). Its foundation must include appropriate and adequate resources such as personnel, equipment, supplies, and funds. Healthcare organizations must address their missions while complying with the ACA and other complex—and sometimes conflicting—standards from external agencies. Being mission centered and compliant with standards challenges the balance of patient care and fiscal responsibility.

How does profitability fit in with mission? Even in times of great change, ethics-based organizations must remain centered and remember that profit allows quality patient care to happen. No one is naïve enough to think that profit is not important. A profitable facility provides many benefits to the community, such as employment and tax revenues, and supports quality patient care.

Stewardship of resources for profit and patient care starts with the O Team—the chief executive officer (CEO), chief financial officer (CFO), chief operating officer (COO), and chief information officer (CIO)—and the board of trustees. Stewardship also means that the O Team will make every effort to control waste and abuse of funds. These leaders must view the budget as both a financial document and an ethics statement. To develop an ethics-based budget, the O Team must pay attention to quality care, community needs, and adequate staff compensation. Their budget should also reflect the organization's ethics through the connection between funding and the organization's purpose.

The O Team is not the only group responsible for making the budget a statement of ethics. Orlikoff and Totten (2007) suggest that members of the board of trustees should also act as stewards of their organization's resources. The basis for this stewardship is the idea that trustees represent their communities and are the guardians of healthcare resources. Trustees of healthcare organizations also need to understand the issues that their facilities face, including the changes associated with implementation of the ACA.

Trustees are not alone in their stewardship role. In fact, all administrators should act as stewards of resources, including money, equipment, and personnel. Steward-type administrators protect resources as if they were their own. They are also trusted to ensure the quality, availability, and best use of these resources. Peter Block (2013), in his book

Stewardship: Choosing Service over Self-Interest, discusses the health-care organization's need to spend its money responsibly. This means taking ownership and accountability for what happens in the organization. It also means paying attention to fit—fit between the organization and the community and between staff and the organization. Block suggests that good stewards hold their employees accountable, too. This means treating staff with real respect, trusting them with decisions, and avoiding excessive micromanagement.

Boyle et al. (2001) offer some specific ideas to address steward-ship and working toward balancing mission and profit margins. These include paying careful attention to patient mix. While it can be tempting to exclude uninsured or low-payment Medicaid-covered patients, such exclusions might not play well in terms of an organization's community image. However, inappropriate use of funds should be carefully defined to avoid reducing or eliminating programs that are beneficial such as "Dial a Nurse," online patient education, and community education.

Waste reduction represents another area of stewardship. For exam-ple, when administrators authorize spending, they need to assure that the organization uses those expenditures for essential functions as defined in the mission. In addition, administrators must model behav-ior that they expect from their staff concerning the use of resources. For example, hoarding materials and over-ordering might seem like a good idea but can lead to waste. Administrators need to consider that resources are finite and there is a need for appropriate use whether they are connected to clinical or business practice. Administrators serve as an example in this regard, and their personal actions to reduce waste carry a strong message.

Boyle et al. (2001) also have words of caution for administrators who make capital expenditure decisions. While there is a need for growth for organizational survival and maintenance, administrators should consider the mission when making large investment decisions. Technology can be helpful to assist these executives with projections of maintenance costs, projected obsolescence, and other data. Of course, conducting product research, using competitive bids, and astute ques-tioning of selected vendors are necessary to make appropriate capital expenditure decisions.

Stewardship in balancing profit and mission includes difficult and personally painful decisions. For example, achieving this balance might necessitate staff and salary reductions and program eliminations. While salary reductions and program eliminations might solve short-term financial problems, they carry a steep cost in diminished employee and community trust. Once these decisions are made, it can take many years (if ever) to rebuild trust. Administrators need careful data analysis and a plan for dealing with their impact before making decisions that affect employees' livelihood. Administrators must also use appropriate communication and treat those affected with dignity and beneficence when they implement difficult decisions.

No single formula applies when balancing mission and profit margin. The issue is not that health care has to make money. In fact, the community feels betrayed if an organization closes its doors. The issue lies with the congruence between what the mission is and how the organization acts on that mission through its fiscal responses. When profit appears to be a stronger motivation than patient care, trust can be lost. If Annison and Wilford (1998) are correct, a loss of trust means a loss of the essential element for the existence of a healthcare organization. Decisions about ethics-based financial policies need to begin with the O Team and trustees. However, healthcare administrators need to implement those policies consistently throughout the organization.

■ ETHICS ISSUES AND HEALTHCARE FINANCE

Change is good. When staring into the "twister of change" that faces today's administrators, however, the level of change can feel almost overwhelming. Administrators must be prepared for the ACA, changes in HIPAA requirements, the change to ICD-10 coding, Hospital VBP, and other new demands in the U.S. healthcare system. They must do this while promising more efficient, effective, and accessible care. Ethics challenges are bound to occur. There will be temptations to do what is necessary for reimbursement even if it lessens resources for other areas. In addition, patients may perceive the "twister of change" as lessening the quality of care as organizations struggle to balance mission and margin and please government agencies. This is a time to be ethically vigilant and have greater awareness of the potential for ethics conflict.

Justice

Market justice relates to the financial position and decisions of healthcare organizations. Healthcare organizations are often large employers, which means they serve market justice by earning profits to support employee salaries and operational funds. Maintaining quality standards and advertising success allows a hospital or clinic to attract more affluent or better-insured patients. By attending to the needs of paying patients and making a profit, the organization also has the resources to provide uncompensated care.

Healthcare finance relates to patient justice as well. Every day, administrators make financial decisions that affect the quality and quantity of care that patients can receive. Decisions about staffing, supply, technology, and other areas affect not only the bottom line, but also the quality of care that a patient can receive. Elements of the ACA such as accountable care organizations provide financial incentives for providing coordinated care that promises cost reductions and higher quality. Because patients may not have to experience pain and risks from duplicate or even unnecessary tests, such a healthcare system can practice beneficence and nonmaleficence. Of course, Hospital VBP includes an element of patient justice in that facilities are evaluated using information about patients' experiences. Because Medicare-covered patients' views about their treatment will be part of the financial outcomes for hospitals, their views may create better experiences for all patients.

Finally, staff justice is a consideration in healthcare finance. With the profound changes happening in almost every aspect of the U.S. healthcare system, it can be easy to forget staff needs. Staff justice requires that administrators prepare staff for the upcoming changes from the ACA, ICD-10 coding, HIPAA, and other areas through education and well-understood polices. In addition, ethics-based administrators should remember to recognize the contributions of staff members during this time of great change. Such recognition may help to reduce the financial negatives of high staff turnover and low morale.

Conflict of Interest

Darr (2011) and Nowicki (2011) discuss conflict of interest as an ethical issue related to the financing of health care. When applied to finance, conflict of interest means that there is a clash between one's financial interests and one's professional or personal interests. For administrators, there may also be a conflict between personal interests and public interests (Business Dictionary.com, 2013). These clashes challenge the HCA's ability to be impartial and can exist on both individual and organizational levels.

Darr (2011) asserts that, in health care, conflicts of interest are not always clear. For example, an administrator may believe that his or her financial decisions create a positive outcome, but this may not be the case. Because administrators are in a superior position and often have insider information, they have a fiduciary duty to act in the healthcare organization's best interest. The most obvious conflict of interest arises when administrators own stock in a business that has contracts with their employers. A conflict of interest could also exist if administrators accept contracts from vendors whose owners are their relatives. Healthcare organizations should have well-defined policies concerning the definition of conflict of interest and make sure that employees are educated on these policies.

Conflicts of interest can also happen when organizations receive a large part of their funding from the government. Because a healthcare organization needs the support of politicians to secure this funding, administrators may ignore the best use of funds based on data, instead using their funding to support whatever the politicians favor.

As "moral agents" (Darr, 2011, p. 134), administrators need to have the courage and ethical strength to avoid this conflict of interest.

Conflict of interests can also affect staff members (Darr, 2011). For example, it is common practice to allow vendors to provide gifts such as lunches or dinners for staff members. In some cases, vendors may complete with each other to provide staff lunches. This practice has become so common that staff members often do not recognize that there really is no "free lunch." Such gifts may subtly influence providers to purchase the vendor's goods or services over those offered by competitors. Besides representing a conflict of interest, accepting gifts creates an unfair advantage for the gift giver in the competition to do business with the clinic or hospital. Healthcare organizations need to mirror the practices of their peers in other industries and create policies about the type and costs of acceptable gifts in the process of doing business.

Other potential conflict-of-interest situations might include employment outside of the organization and behavior during personal time. An organization has the right to expect its employees to provide adequate time on task for salary paid. Moonlighting or working two jobs can affect the employee's ability to provide satisfactory performance. In some circumstances, however, outside employment may not adversely affect the organization and can even enhance its image. Therefore, policies need to be developed that clearly identify the organization's position on employment and the potential for conflicts of interest.

Personal behaviors may sometimes create conflicts of interest, such as the use of personal time. While the organization cannot and should not have policies to control all of its employees' behaviors outside of the employment setting, certain behaviors will negatively affect the organization's image. For example, in the past many organizations offered alcoholic beverages at social functions. This practice became a problem when employees did not limit their consumption and were involved in traffic accidents or other serious incidents. Currently, most organizations either refrain from providing any alcohol at functions or restrict its use through cash bars and limited access. In addition, healthcare organizations establish policies regarding the recreational use of alcohol and other drugs and support pre-hire and random screenings. Because this personal behavior has a direct impact on patient care and the facility's image, healthcare administrators must take action to rehabilitate or remove employees who violate such a policy. The interests of the organization take precedence over individual rights in this situation.

Billing Practices

Harman (2006) addresses the ethics of billing practices from the view of the coders who provide diagnosis codes for reimbursement. Standards for coding provided by the American Health Information Management

Association (AHIMA) address the need for accuracy and quality of data for billing. Examples of practices that would violate this code include not clarifying physician documentation, assigning codes based on reimbursement rather than treatment, modifying coding so as to increase reimbursement, and developing coding policies that encourage cheating third-party payers. Harman (2006) provides an action plan matrix to assist coding professionals in dealing with billing ethics issues. He stresses that these personnel must respect professional ethics in their service to patients and to their organizations.

Nowicki (2011) includes billing practices as both an ethical and a legal issue for healthcare finance. Some of these practices, while remaining within the letter of the law, violate basic ethics principles. For example, if an organization delays as long as possible the refunding of overpayments from insurance companies or is slow to pay its vendors, these practices can help its bottom line. These actions may have a negative impact on the level of trust in the community and possibly future contracts if the organization makes this choice.

Fraud and Abuse

According to Sultz and Young (2014), "The Federal Bureau of Investigation estimated that fraudulent billings to the public and private health care programs were 3–10% of the total spending, or $75–250 billion in fiscal year 2009" in the United States (pp. 295–296). Shi and Singh (2015) claim that there is a loss of at least 10% of healthcare spending because of fraud and abuse. In the past, some healthcare organizations ignored this issue because it was difficult to detect and prosecutions were rare.

How does fraud happen? It can occur if there is intentional falsification of codes or costs. It can also occur if organizations provide services that are not medically necessary. In addition, fraud happens when an agency does not provide services and bills for those services. Examples of these practices include billing for dental restorations when the patient is edentulous, recording a higher code when the service was actually a lower code, and having a pattern of the same error without making any effort toward its correction. In addition, if a practitioner provides referrals for patients and receives kickback payments for those referrals, he or she is committing fraud. Shi and Singh (2015) cite fraud and abuse as a major concern for Medicare and Medicaid in particular.

Recent efforts to control fraud and abuse include the Health Care Fraud Prevention and Enforcement Action Team in 2009 and the waste, fraud, and abuse provisions of the ACA. While these and other efforts have increased the attention paid to fraud and abuse prevention and have recovered some of the lost funds, they have also added to the expense of providing health care. The time (e.g., for completing reports), personnel, and money used to ensure compliance, track violations, and resolve any issues simply add to overall healthcare costs. As the complexity of the U.S. healthcare system increases with greater adoption of electronic health information systems and the ACA changes, the potential for fraud and abuse will increase. Ethics-based healthcare administrators will have to be vigilant in protecting the healthcare system from the expensive and unethical practice of healthcare fraud and abuse.

Summary

What should healthcare administrators do to balance profits and mission? First, they should remember that no matter what their position is in the healthcare system, money matters. Administrators will be dealing with financial matters as part of their role, whether it is monitoring the budget, requesting funds, or planning for future needs. There are several steps they can take to make ethics-based decisions on financial issues. Remember that administrators are stewards of the organization's resources, including its finances. As such, they have a fiduciary duty to protect these resources and make the best decisions concerning their use. High levels of accountability and public scrutiny are also part of this duty.

Healthcare administrators should consider the organization's mission as they participate in the various aspects of the budget cycle and monitor expenses against budget codes. In doing so, they must remember that knowledge is power. Therefore, they must read financial documents related to their areas and understand these documents. They must question codes that do not seem to be appropriate and amounts that appear to be in error. It is also important to have correct documentation to support financial decisions and transactions. It is also critical that healthcare administrators understand that saying nothing means that they are agreeing with the financial report.

In a time of great change, it is important for healthcare administrators to serve as role models for stewardship. Even though the healthcare organization may have written policies in place, it is HCAs' actions that create the real policy for their departments or organizations. For example, if administrators create unnecessary waste and abuse resources, they send a loud message that policy does not matter. While it is not necessary for them to become the finance police, administrators need to be aware that they are accountable for their actions. They should be willing to ask for details about requests for funding, whether it is to pay for continuing education units, travel, or new equipment. Whatever healthcare administrators authorize should support the mission of the healthcare organizations that they serve. If expenses cannot be mission justified, administrators must be prepared to say "no." The ethics of finance is not just for the O Team; healthcare administrators make ethics the norm for their organizations.

Cases for Your Consideration

The Case of the Lost Chapel

Think about the chapter information and consider the following questions. Sample responses and commentary will follow the case.

1. What are the organizational ethics issues in this case?

2. How could the organization have done things differently?

3. What was the true bottom line in this case?

Case Information

The Sisters of Mary founded St. Basil the Great Hospital in 1894 with a mission of caring for those with the greatest need. One of the first buildings in the hospital complex was a chapel dedicated to St. Basil, the patron saint of hospital administrators. Over the years, this chapel became a spiritual center for the hospital and the community. It was the site of many weddings and funerals.

In recent years, the hospital was part of a merger with a for-profit hospital chain but, because of community recognition, retained its name. The merged hospital placed great emphasis on fiscal stability and its commitment to provide profit for its shareholders. To that end, the O Team (e.g., CEO, CIO, COO, and CFO) conducted a review of utilization and cost/benefit of St. Basil's buildings. Because it was not used on a daily basis for patient needs, the chapel failed to meet the standards for effectiveness. It also required funds for its maintenance and upkeep. However, the land on which the chapel stood was valuable and could be used as the site of a high-rise parking garage. Because parking was a true need at St. Basil's and the hospital could make a profit from its fees, the O Team voted to demolish the chapel and put up a parking garage.

After some discussion, the board of trustees approved the proposal and approved an immediate call for bids. However, when the news hit the community, a problem arose. The O Team did not consult the community about the potential chapel demolition and garage construction. Community leaders demanded a meeting to discuss what, in their view, was a tragedy. The O Team denied their request and stated their reasons for demolishing the chapel in favor of a parking garage. The community leaders offered to fund the chapel's upkeep to save it from demolition. However, the O Team reminded them that St. Basil's Hospital had an obligation to shareholders, and a parking garage more positively affected the bottom line. Finally, the community leaders tried to save the chapel by having it declared a historical landmark, but their request was denied.

Frustrated, community leaders organized and began an Internet campaign called "Save Our Sanctuary." Their efforts involved the local media, which featured several pieces on the issue, including coverage of a candlelight vigil held to mourn the death of the chapel. The local newspaper also ran two feature-length articles telling the story of couples who had been married in the chapel, and highlighting the potential loss of the community's history.

Members of the O Team, while not happy about the community response, felt that it was well within their rights to make business decisions that would have a positive impact on the hospital's bottom line. They thought the "sound and fury" of the protests would soon blow over, so the bulldozers and other equipment did their work, destroying the 120-year-old chapel. However, their actions were not without a price. They lost the positive relationship that St. Basil had with the community. Because of the hospital's new image of prioritizing profit over decency, many of the local physicians did not admit patients to St. Basil's, and well-insured families chose to use other hospitals for their care needs. Because of the reduction in census numbers for both inpatient and outpatient facilities, the parking lot soon became a liability and not an asset.

Responses and Commentary on Questions

1. What are the organizational ethics issues in this case?

   First, this is a case about balancing mission with profit margin. The O Team was trying to make sound fiscal decisions based on their definition of contribution to mission and revenue generation. Perhaps they were also concerned with the financial issues that they faced trying to comply with the ACA. When the sole considerations were profit and cost containment, the chapel was a liability: It could not produce the revenue of a parking garage and was actually costing money because of its upkeep.

   What the O Team did not consider was the impact of destroying the chapel on St. Basil's image and ultimate financial situation. The O Team lacked the vision to understand that destroying a chapel to put up a parking garage would anger the community. Once they learned of the community's concerns, these leaders simply dismissed them. The O Team believed that the community would soon lose interest—and after all, the stockholders were important, too.

   This case also points out some of the difficulties in mergers between for-profit organizations and religion-based facilities. In the view of the O Team members, they were being fiscally responsible to their shareholders by decreasing waste (the chapel) and increasing profitability (the parking garage). Members of the community, in contrast, perceived their actions as the destruction of part of their history and an insult to their faith traditions. Despite their objections, the community lost the chapel.

This case also is an example of utilitarianism ethics without consideration for Kantian ideas. The O Team based its decision on trying to do the greatest good for the greatest number. The chapel was not used on a daily basis. By replacing it with a parking garage that would provide convenience, they were able to provide a benefit for more customers. In addition, the funds generated by parking fees could be added to the operational budget and help defray costs for areas like uncompensated care. In addition, the O Team provided a greater good by being true to their shareholders and increasing their return on investment potential.

By treating the chapel and the people who used it as a means to an end, however, the O Team violated a basic concept of Kantian ethics. The team members did not even consult with the community. It was only when community leaders asked to be heard that they were given any attention. The O Team treated the community leaders, as Buber would say, as "its" and ignored their protests, feelings, and recommendations. The O Team believed that, in the end, the community leaders would eventually come around and see the parking garage as an asset. As the subsequent events demonstrated, the community felt otherwise.

This case also shows the impact of market justice when there is a lack of balance with patient or community justice. The decision to build the parking garage was perfectly just in the eyes of the O Team. After all, they had a responsibility to their shareholders to make profit. The O Team believed that all resources should be used toward that goal. The chapel was certainly not a revenue stream. However, in the eyes of the community, the O Team failed to act with justice. The O Team was more concerned about profits than with preserving a symbol of faith and community history.

2. How could the organization have done things differently?

First, the O Team was correct in assessing St. Basil's assets and utilization or resources. They wanted to be able to assure the shareholders that property was being used to its best advantage for patient care and profitability. In addition, they certainly had an ethical responsibility to be good stewards of the hospital's resources and to make sound business decisions.

However, what they failed to assess were the priorities of the internal and external communities. The O Team acted with a one-sided view of the situation (tunnel vision) and lacked an understanding of the bigger picture. To begin with, they were now partners with a religion-founded facility. It should have been obvious that a 120-year-old chapel would have some meaning for those who chose to work at St. Basil's and for the community that the hospital served. Conducting some form of information gathering to determine the importance of the chapel and the impact of tearing it down would have added to their understanding of the situation and to a decision that was more acceptable to the community. However, the O Team chose to disregard both their own employees and the community they served.

They also failed to anticipate the long-term impact of their actions on the community. Although they might have realized that some protest would occur, the O Team leaders truly believed that their business decision would have a positive impact on the organization's bottom line. Despite queries from the community and offers of alternative solutions, they chose the parking garage over the chapel. This decision, right or wrong, painted the O Team as heartless administrators who cared little for the community and its history.

There could have been other solutions to this case. First, the O Team, armed with data about the use of the chapel, could have presented the problem to its board of trustees. The O Team could have asked the board to develop a solution to meet the parking needs and the needs for preservation of the chapel. Perhaps the internal and external communities could have been involved in a positive way to raise funds to move the chapel to a different site or find another way to provide parking and revenue. Admittedly, this solution would take more time, but decreasing the long-term negative effect would be worth the effort.

In addition, the O Team could have done a much better job with informing the community of its decision. Providing community members and media with the rationale for the decision might have helped. The O Team could also have planned some type of ceremony honoring the chapel and its meaning to the community. Any communication and action that respected the community could have greater benefit than just going forward with plans. The message to the community was clear: "You do not matter—this is business."

3. What was the true bottom line in this case?

   The bottom line in this case ended up to be the opposite of what the O Team intended. Even though they built the garage, there was a loss of profit. Because census figures were even lower in the aftermath of the chapel incident, St. Basil did not receive a solid return on investment for the parking garage. In addition, it lost a more critical asset: the goodwill of the community. For many years, the community remembered the handling of the chapel incident and declined to support the hospital at the level that it did in the past. As Annison and Wilford (1998) say, once the community loses trust in its healthcare facility, it is difficult to regain.

The Case of the Ghost Patients

Think about the chapter information and consider the following questions. Sample responses and commentary will follow the case.

1. What motivated the former vice president of operations to create ghost patients?

2. Which choices did Mr. Sagesse have in this situation?

3. How did these decisions to use ghost patients affect the organization?

Case Information

Mr. Richard Sagesse prepared for his interview for the position of senior vice president for operations (VPO) at Claremont Hospital. He carefully researched and reviewed all of the financial data on this facility and checked *Hospital Compare* for its quality scores. He found that the facility had a patient-centered mission and a strong net worth. He was impressed with the executive team including the CEO, CFO, and executive vice president (EVP). When Claremont offered him the position, he was delighted and planned for a long career there.

After working at the hospital for only a month, Mr. Sagesse received a visit from Morrigan Keenan, a member of the Hospital VBP Quality Team. She seemed nervous and asked for confidentiality. When Richard assured her that he would keep the conversation confidential, she told him about the hospital's "ghost" Medicare patients. Under the orders of the previous VPO, certain members of the quality staff created HCAHPS data for Medicare patients who did not exist. They used data from patient records to create these ghost patients and added their satisfaction surveys to those that were included in the quarterly reports. Of course, the ghost Medicare patients were highly satisfied with Claremont and their numbers boosted the satisfaction rates that were sent to the CMS database. Morrigan was afraid to tell anyone what was going on because she believed that all of the hospital's upper management knew about the practice. However, she felt that Mr. Sagesse, as a new VPO, was entitled to the information.

Mr. Sagesse was shocked. He had changed his whole life and that of his family for this career opportunity. Now, it seemed as if he had walked into situation that was highly questionable at best. What should he do? Being unemployed was not what he wanted, but could he just ignore the ghost patient situation?

Responses and Commentary on Questions

1. What motivated the former vice president of operations to create ghost patients?

   Consider the situation of the former vice president of operations. Patient satisfaction scores were part of the Hospital VBP reimbursement for

Claremont Hospital. The VPO did not want the loss of critical Medicare reimbursement to happen on his watch. Because patient satisfaction data were soft at best, he was sure that all hospitals altered data in some way. Surely, just a few happy patients added to the mix would not matter. His strategy certainly seemed to be working. In addition, it would not affect the VPO because he was moving on to a better job.

2. Which choices did Mr. Sagesse have in this situation?

What a dilemma! Mr. Sagesse had just accepted this position and now this! He was almost physically ill after meeting with Morrigan Keenan. However, his conscience would not let him ignore this situation. He had to make a plan and carry it out.

Mr. Sagesse's first step was to investigate the situation to determine if it was factual. After all, Morrigan Keegan was his only source of information at this point. He also consulted the ACHE website for any model ethics policies dealing with misuse of information and for the ACHE's ethics decision-making model. In addition, he researched the records of the previous VPO, including previous HCAHPS scores, to determine if any evidence of ghost patients was present.

Under the guise of obtaining current information as the new VPO, Mr. Sagesse's next step was to meet with the Hospital VBP Quality Team. The purpose of this meeting was to allow the team to give him information about their quality control processes and discern any problems that they could identify in the current system. This meeting, he hoped, would allow team members to provide information about the ghost patient situation. In addition, he could order an audit of all HCAHPS scores for the current quarter and for the last two quarters in the hope of identifying any discrepancies.

Depending on the findings, Mr. Sagesse might have to schedule a meeting with the CEO to discuss the situation. Of course, his fear was that this individual might have colluded with the former VPO. However, once the CEO received a formal report on this situation, he could not ignore it. If ghost Medicare patients were actually a part of the CMS reporting, bigger issues existed. There would have to be notification of the Claremont Hospital attorney, the board of trustees, and CMS. There were bound to be repercussions. What a mess!

3. How did these decisions to use ghost patients affect the organization?

If the accusations of the use of ghost Medicare patients are true, they could affect the financial status and credibility of Claremont Hospital. The CMS could order an audit of all the processes used in meeting the Hospital VBP requirements. This audit process would not only be costly for Claremont, but could also lead to penalties from CMS. In addition, if the ghost Medicare patient practice led to negative media coverage, it could damage the reputation of Claremont Hospital. The community, including practitioners and patients, might question the authenticity of its patient-centered mission and choose to obtain health care from other facilities. At a minimum, this practice, while solving a short-term problem, would create a larger future problem for Claremont Hospital.

Web Resources

American College of Healthcare Executives
http://www.ache.org/

Health Care Compliance Organization
http://www.hcca-info.org/

Healthcare Financial Management Association
http:// www.hfma.org

Health Care Information Management Association
http://www.ahima.org/

References

Annison, M. H., & Wilford, D. S. (1998). *Trust matters: New directions in health care leadership*. San Francisco, CA: Jossey-Bass.

Block, P. (2013). *Stewardship: Choosing service over self-interest* (2nd ed.). San Francisco, CA: Berrett-Koehler.

Boyle, P. J., DuBose, E. R., Ellingson, S. J., Guinn, D. E., & McCurdy, D. B. (2001). *Organizational ethics in health care: Principles, cases, and practical solutions*. San Francisco, CA: Jossey-Bass.

Business Dictionary.com. (2013). Conflict of interest. Retrieved from http://www.businessdictionary.com/definition/conflict-of-interest.html

Centers for Medicare and Medicaid Services (CMS). (2007) CMS issues final rule for first year of Hospital Value-Based Purchasing Program [Fact sheet]. Retrieved from http://www.cms.gov/apps/media/press/factsheet.asp?Counter=3947

Centers for Medicare and Medicaid Services (CMS). (2013a). Advanced payment accountable care organization (ACO) model [Fact sheet]. Retrieved from http://innovation.cms.gov/Files/fact-sheet/Advanced-Payment-ACO-Model-Fact-Sheet.pdf

Centers for Medicare and Medicaid Services (CMS). (2013b). *HCAHPS fact sheet* [Fact sheet]. Baltimore, MD: Author. Retrieved from http://www.hcahps.online.org

Darr, K. (2011). *Ethics in health services management* (5th ed.). Baltimore, MD: Health Professions Press.

Harman, L. B. (2006). *Ethical challenges in the management of health information* (2nd ed.). Sudbury, MA: Jones and Bartlett.

Inspiration Station. (2013). Ralph Waldo Emerson quotes. Retrieved from http://www.inspirationstation.info/ralph-waldo-emerson/ralph-waldo-emerson-quotes.html

Nowicki, M. (2011). *Introduction to the financial management of healthcare organizations* (5th ed.). Chicago, IL: Health Administration Press.

Orlikoff, J. E., & Totten, M. K. (2007). Stewardship in action. *Healthcare Executive, 22*(5), 56–59.

Pearson, S. D., Sabin, J. E., & Emanuel, E. J. (2003). *No margin, no mission: Health-care organizations and the quest for ethical excellence.* New York, NY: Oxford University Press.

Shi, L., & Singh, D. A. (2015). *Delivering health care in America: A systems approach* (6th ed.). Burlington, MA: Jones & Bartlett Learning.

Sultz, H. A., & Young, K. A. (2014). *Health care USA* (8th ed.). Burlington, MA: Jones & Bartlett Learning.

U.S. Department of Labor. (2010). The Mental Health Parity and Addiction Equity Act of 2008 (MHPAEA) [Fact sheet]. Retrieved from http://www.dol.gov/ebsa/newsroom/fsmhpaea.html

CHAPTER
10

Organizational Culture and Ethics

What is the culture of an ethics-centered healthcare organization?

Points to Ponder

1. Why is the culture of health care important to patient-centered care?
2. How do the forces of culture influence ethical decision making?
3. What is the function of ethics committees in healthcare organizations?
4. Given the dramatic changes posed by the ACA, how can the culture of health care balance ethics and profits?

Key Terms

The following is a list of key words for this chapter. Look for them in bold.

culture
culture clash
institutional ethics committee

institutional review board (IRB)
pediatric ethics committee
professional socialization

■ INTRODUCTION AND DEFINITIONS

Culture is a term that has both literal and emotional meanings. One can look at the term through its classic definition, which focuses on the values and beliefs of a particular society or group. These values and beliefs affect how the people who live in the society think about their lives and the world in which they live. For example, in American culture, scientific thinking greatly influences the delivery of health care. Capitalism, mistrust of large government efforts, and the ideal of independence are strong cultural values (Shi & Singh, 2015).

American culture tends to favor market justice as part of the distribution of resources in a free economy. In turn, Americans tend to support free market approaches to health care such as employer-based healthcare insurance over government-provided insurance. Essentially, American culture favors the idea that the market works better than the government does in supplying health care. This element of culture explains the varied responses to healthcare reform efforts, including the ACA (Shi & Singh, 2015).

Culture also influences health and disease among Americans. Research in public health as well as other areas has reinforced the wide diversity found among Americans. While there are some common beliefs held by most Americans, the United States is home to a plethora of cultures, as evidenced by the racial categories found on the decennial census conducted by the federal government: White, Black or African American, American Indian or Alaskan Native, Asian, Hispanic, or Some Other Race (Spector, 2013). These groups of people have varying socioeconomic status issues, incidence of illnesses, and healthcare experiences. In addition, their health traditions may be very different in terms of their views of physical, mental, and spiritual health and their acceptance of the dominant American healthcare practices. This cultural diversity, coupled with the need to practice health care in an ethical manner, both contributes to the need for healthcare providers and administrators to be culturally competent and influences organizational culture.

Culture can also be personal. For example, healthcare administrators can define their culture in terms of their relationships inside and outside of the workplace. They can consider their role in the delivery of health care and its difference from the roles of clinicians. There may be differences in the language, norms, traditions, and mindset of business and clinical professionals, but the two cultures must learn to bridge these differences to provide ethics-based, patient-centered care.

Given the complexity of the concept of culture and its potential influence on the practice of health care, an examination of the connection between culture and ethics is appropriate. To conduct this examination in a concise and cohesive manner, the analysis presented here begins with the person at the center of health care—the patient. It then examines the culture of healthcare professionals and ethics. In addition, the discussion focuses on the ramifications of culture for organizations, including the need for ethics committees. Finally, a more person-centered assessment of administrators and ethics is undertaken, including the need to prevent "administrative evil."

■ PATIENT CULTURE AND ETHICS

There is one consistency among patients in the healthcare system: They are all different. While medical schools and evidence-based medical practices may teach that treatment A will produce effect B in patient C, the data on this relationship may not be consistent for all patients. As a consequence, healthcare professionals must often act more like detectives who try to diagnose and treat patients based on an analysis of signs and symptoms (as described by the patient), physical assessment, and laboratory tests (Roizen & Oz, 2006).

No matter how well educated the individual, when a person becomes a patient, he or she enters a world that is uncomfortable, unfamiliar, and often deeply embarrassing. While it is normal for practitioners to ask probing questions about pain levels, bowel movements, and drug use while examining a semi-clad patient, the patient may find these intimate queries difficult to answer. In addition, if the healthcare professional asks these questions in what the patient perceives as a cold or matter-of-fact manner, the patient may not provide full or accurate answers. This lack of candor can, in turn, affect the accuracy of diagnosis. When hospitalization or rehabilitation is required, patients may fear death or disability, or they may be in extreme pain. Against this backdrop, they may act out of their emotions and not their intellect. In such a case, the **culture clash** between them and the healthcare professional is even deeper.

Even though all patients are different, they share at least one commonality: They are all in vulnerable positions when interacting with healthcare professionals. Patients must trust that these individuals will adhere to the ethics of care and focus on healing and best practices for their health. However, health professionals are also busy people who must meet the needs of many individuals in any given day. Pressures to do what is required can lead to errors in practice that can cause harm to patients, such as forgetting to wash one's hands or delivering incorrect medications. The vulnerable nature of the human element in care is exacerbated by the fact that the media, Internet, and other sources are creating a greater awareness of the limitations of health care and creating a more sophisticated patient culture.

Websites such as WebMD and the Mayo Clinic provide discerning patients with ready access to research—that is, sound information about their diagnoses. While dealing with a patient who produces Internet-sourced information during the appointment may be annoying to a well-educated healthcare professional, this interaction is also part of the patient culture. In addition, patients are more likely to prepare for their medical care and hospitalization by using sources such as *You: The Smart Patient* (Roizen & Oz, 2006) and *Don't Go There Alone!* (Kalina, Pew, & Bourgeois, 2004). The Joint Commission and other sources also inform patients that they have rights, which means that they may act on those rights (Roizen & Oz, 2006). Dr. Seuss (1986) has written a patient education book that uses humor to demonstrate the wide cultural divide that often separates patients and healthcare professionals. While not all patients are informed consumers of the products of health care, those who match this description create a different cultural experience for healthcare providers.

What are the ethics implications of an informed patient culture? Informed patients can better protect their ability to collaborate with their healthcare providers and assume greater autonomy. Like previous generations of patients, they still need to have confidence in the wisdom of their healers and trust their diagnoses and treatments. However, informed patients may bring additional ethics challenges for healthcare professionals. These professionals will not always encounter patients who are compliant and who accept their decisions with great deference. Sometimes, health professionals may lose their patience because patients are no longer passive and find their questions annoying and time consuming. Healthcare professionals will need to rely on their dedication to ethical practice that respects patients even when there are time and production demands. They will often have to ask themselves, "Why did I choose this profession and what do I hope to do?"

■ PROFESSIONAL CULTURES AND ETHICS

The most obvious difference in culture among professionals occurs when organizations employ individuals who received their education outside of the United States. While these professionals have a license to practice in the United States, their values, traditions, and practices may be very different from those of their fellow professionals. This situation requires professionals to honor their codes of ethics and obligations to patients by treating one another with respect, justice, and beneficence.

There are also cultural differences among healthcare professionals who are educated in the United States. For example, the faculty members in institutions of higher learning work to educate and graduate professionals who will uphold certain standards and represent their profession with honor. They use **professional socialization** to accomplish this goal. This means that faculty instills values, traditions, knowledge, and skills to create future professionals. Each practitioner comes to the workforce with his or her own concept of professionalism, however, and individuals' definitions can vary.

Groopman (2007) has suggested that physicians and other healthcare professionals think differently. Using data collected through research, he presents information on how clinicians are taught to think and make diagnoses. Clinicians are taught to determine the most likely diagnosis and then the best treatment for that diagnosis. Their professional socialization assists them in making the correct diagnosis and identifying the most appropriate treatment. Unfortunately, clinicians are not always correct. There may be temptations to think erroneously, make snap judgments, or fail to gather sufficient information. Groopman (2007) reminds patients of the cultural differences between clinicians and patients, with the goal that patients be better prepared to contribute to their own health care.

In addition, cultural differences may exist among members of the same profession. Because professional socialization attempts to instill identity and pride in one's profession, biases against others may exist. For example, neurosurgeons may believe that because of their level of expertise in brain surgery, they are superior to pediatricians or family medicine specialists. Likewise, family medicine specialists may consider themselves superior to psychiatrists. This attitude of superiority is not limited to physicians, but can also be present among nurses (operating room nurses versus floor nurses) and other healthcare personnel (dental hygienists versus dental assistants). While such rivalry is often the subject of insider jokes, it can affect the ability of healthcare teams to work together. With the ACA's increased pressures to produce high-quality, cost-effective health care, health professionals will be required to work effectively in teams and communicate well. To do so, they will have to overcome their socialization messages and work together in teams based on respect, beneficence, and justice.

■ ORGANIZATIONAL CULTURE

To understand the impact of culture on an organization, an administrator needs to have a clear definition of the word *organization*. Daft (2012) recalls that organizations have goals, defined structures, and systems for organizing their activities. In addition, they have a connection to the environments in which they exist. Ginter, Duncan, and Swayne (2013) suggest that organizations also have a culture that defines what the organization is for its employees and for the public. This organizational culture includes mission, vision, goals, and expectations. Employees accept these organizational standards, which may be either written or unwritten, and use them to guide their actions. In high-functioning healthcare cultures, these shared norms often center on quality patient care and service to others.

In light of the challenge of a changing healthcare system, it is necessary to create a culture that can adapt to change and still keep its ethics center. In such a culture, employees choose to believe and support the facility's values. They have a common identity that gives them the information needed to work well with one another and meet the organization's mission even in times of stress. History, languages, ceremonies, stories, symbols, and traditions that help to establish a shared identity will establish the more flexible culture needed for 21st-century healthcare organizations (Daft, 2012). A culture that can adapt to change will also assist new employees to learn how thing are done in the organization, both formally and informally, and encourage them to be become integral parts of the organization.

Daft (2012) provides a greater understanding of the mechanisms necessary for cultural change and adaptation by subdividing organizational cultures into mission-based, clan-based, bureaucratic-based, and learning-based cultures. In a mission-based culture, the needs of populations are the focus and rapid change is not the norm. In a clan-based culture, employees' needs are the focus and rapid change is common. In a bureaucratic-based culture, order is present in procedures and the environment remains stable, and the change process moves slowly. Finally, in a learning-based organization, there is an emphasis on adapting to change, values, caring for each other, and "big picture" thinking. Learning-based organizations also resist the temptation to be "culture bound" or to say, "We have always done it this way." They emphasize the value of change as a mechanism for success when the environment is unpredictable.

All of Daft's (2012) examples can be found in today's healthcare organizations and can affect their ability to adapt to change. Healthcare administrators (HCAs) should find the drive to change within the organization's internal mission, but must be rapid adapters to the ever-changing external environment. Of course, professionals within the organization also want to succeed and have a high quality of life—and they expect the HCA to provide the means to enable them to accomplish those goals. In addition, healthcare organizations are often bureaucracies, which can make it difficult to effect needed changes. Finally, the basis of a learning-based organization model, while essential in a time of great change, is often counterintuitive to those who use other models of thinking. Making a cultural change in such an environment will be difficult, but remains necessary to deliver excellent patient care and support the bottom line.

Profound change and its correlated stress can make ethics a cultural issue for all organizations (Daft, 2012). In such an environment, there may be temptations to falsify records, lie to employers, and abuse drugs and alcohol at the workplace. In some organizations, there is an attitude that if no law is broken, then there is no ethics issue. However, especially in times of great change and temptation, organizational culture must influence day-to-day ethical conduct in positive ways through its rituals, ceremonies, and stories. If ethics is a part of the culture's traditions, it reinforces the idea that ethics really matters—it is not just words in a mission statement.

Within this milieu, the O Team must support and model the kind of behaviors it expects from others. As part of upper-level administration, the members of the O Team must be champions for a culture that respects ethics as well as fiscal responsibility. They must also model ethics-based leadership. They must not just "talk" the vision; they must "walk" it as well. The O Team and all others in the administrative role should remember that their actions carry far more weight than their words. Moreover, the healthcare organization's stories, language, rituals, and ceremonies serve to create organizational loyalty and the desire to work toward achieving its mission.

■ HEALTHCARE ORGANIZATIONS' RESPONSE TO ETHICAL CONCERNS

Healthcare organizations must respond to ethics concerns that involve a myriad of issues, ranging from employee misdeeds to violations of patient autonomy and safety. In addition, organizations must address ethics standards and practices included in regulations stemming from both government and private sources. The goal is to be proactive and prevent ethics violations, thereby reducing potential financial and loss of trust issues. As part of this effort, organizations create and enforce policies and procedures to create ethics-based workplaces that focus on quality patient care.

An example of a standard that influences ethics-based practice in health care is the Office of Minority Health's (2013) National Standards for Culturally and Linguistically Appropriate Services in Health and Health Care (National CLAS Standards). The goal of these standards is to provide health care that responds to health needs while respecting cultural beliefs and language preferences, and addressing patient health literacy. The CLAS Standards deal with signage, language assistance, use of interpreters, and diversity among healthcare providers. They also require training for staff and community assessments. Healthcare organizations use materials provided by the Office of Minority Health to improve their interactions with the many cultures that they serve and to address health disparities in the communities that they serve.

Healthcare professionals must sometimes make difficult decisions about patient care that involve the practice of ethics. For example, the advent of some new technologies has created ethics issues and required a mechanism to respond to these issues. Technology has also increased the need for hospitals to have a mechanism to address complex ethics dilemmas, leading to the formation and utilization of ethics committees. For example, in the 1960s, when kidney dialysis was a new technology, the number of patients who needed dialysis vastly outstripped the availability of machines. Hospitals responded by creating ethics committees to decide which patients would receive the needed treatment. These groups, often called "god squads," became powerful decision makers because of their power over life-or-death situations for patients.

In the 1970s, the well-publicized case of Karen Ann Quinlan made hospitals more aware of the ethics surrounding the use of technology to prolong life. Ethics committees needed to develop policies on the withdrawal of life support and other end-of-life issues. Although The Joint Commission (TJC) currently does not specifically mandate the existence of ethics committees as part of its accreditation process, it does suggest that the most common way to provide a process for addressing complex ethics issues is through an ethics committee (Schyve, 2009). Today, ethics committees exist in almost every hospital in some form and have responsibilities that are more global.

Just what does an ethics committee do? To begin with, larger facilities often have three ethics committees. One is charged with general ethics responsibilities for the facility; one with issues related to pediatrics and ethics; and the last with research ethics (called the **institutional review board [IRB]**). The general ethics committee has different titles depending on the hospital's culture. One title is the **institutional ethics committee.** The placement of the committee on the hospital's organizational chart can vary, and its position on the chart usually reflects its importance within the organization. In any event, it needs a prominent place in the hierarchy. This prominence is necessary because, if the administrative and clinical staff do not take the committee seriously, it becomes nothing more than window dressing.

Regardless of the title, these general committees have functions in common, which include education, creation of policies, and patient case review. In the area of education, the committee can provide in-service education programs on identified or upcoming issues to staff, patients, families, and even the larger community. The educational component can also positively influence the way that ethics is valued in the organization by enhancing ethics awareness, creating an ethics dialogue, and reinforcing the vision, mission, and purpose of the facility. In addition, committee members must educate themselves on upcoming issues and orient new members (West & Morrison, 2014).

Another major function of a hospital ethics committee is policy development and review for ethics-related issues. The CEO, chief operating officer, chief of medical staff, board of trustees, or other key administrators can request these reviews. Policies that address recurrent organizational issues often require that ethics committee serve in a consultant role. Examples of these ethics issues include policies on advance directives, withholding treatment, withdrawing treatment, informed consent, and organ procurement. Ethics committees can also be involved in policies relating to allocation of resources and preservation of the vision and mission of the facility. For example, they can recommend policies on community outreach, charitable contributions, and fundraising. In each case, these committees try to assure the fairness of policies for all who are affected by them (West & Morrison, 2014).

Finally, ethics committees review and provide advice on individual patient cases where difficult ethical concerns arise. The system for this review varies from facility to facility. In some cases, committee members are on call (similar to a specialist). Staff, administrators, patients, guardians, or family members all are eligible to pose a question or request an informal review from the ethics committee. Full reviews require the presence of all committee members and follow a formal procedure in making recommendations. Of course, the committee must work within the organizational structure and have a clear understanding of the articulated values and ethics position of the overall facility.

Who should be on the ethics committee? Again, the constitution of the committee will vary by institution. Generally, the CEO or his or her representative, clinical staff members including physicians and nurses, clergy members or persons with an ethics background, and attorneys are all members of an ethics committee. Some facilities also include quality improvement staff, a member of the board of trustees, community members, and social workers. Organizations should take great care when selecting the membership of their ethics committee. Beyond professional qualifications, a potential member should be open-minded, work well in teams, have a knowledge of ethics, and be able to work within a framework. In addition, all members should have a sufficient commitment to ethics so that they are willing to spend the required time in meetings, training, and updating their personal knowledge.

Pediatric ethics committees, also called infant care review committees, have the special charge of dealing with difficult ethical issues that concern the care of newborns, infants, and children. End-of-life procedures, treatment for disabilities, child abuse and neglect, and disagreements between healthcare professionals and the family require particular attention. Recommended members for such a committee include pediatricians, pediatric oncologists, neonatologists, nurses, and social workers. These members are responsible for keeping current on ethics issues related to infants and children, and they may be on 24-hour call (Darr, 2011).

Institutional review boards are specialized ethics committees that deal with issues related to research on human and animal subjects. Research is a major part of the healthcare system because it contributes to the understanding of disease and the improvement of health for millions of people. Unfortunately, it also has the potential for ethics violations that can cause psychological and even physical harm to participants. The roots of the IRB are in the Nuremburg Code of 1949 and in the Belmont Report, which addressed the protection of human subjects in experiments (Darr, 2011). The IRB also serves to protect people from abuses like those that occurred during the Tuskegee Syphilis Experiment in the United States.

The Tuskegee Experiment shows how good intentions do not always produce ethical behaviors. The U.S. Public Health Service conducted this study between 1932 and 1972. The research involved 399 African American men who had syphilis, and researchers used misleading information about the study's purpose and procedures to ensure their cooperation. The real purpose was to follow the men until they died and then collect data from autopsy results. Even when information about a cure for syphilis became available, the researchers did not inform the subjects of that fact and the patients did not receive any medication. The researchers thought that by keeping the patients in the dark, they could provide a benefit to society that was worth the sacrifice of a few lives. They also thought that this knowledge could benefit the African American population by creating greater knowledge of how syphilis affected this racial subgroup (Centers for Disease Control and Prevention [CDC], 2013). The researchers justified their actions by citing utilitarian ethics, but the value of the individuals (Kantian ethics) was not a consideration.

These and other research abuses led to the formation of IRBs in universities, hospitals, and other healthcare institutions. The functions of the IRB in a hospital are to protect research subjects and see that protocols do everything possible to decrease risks to their well-being. This committee must also make sure that consent to participate in any research is given based on a full understanding of the risks and benefits, and that participants' privacy is protected (Darr, 2011). The IRB is responsible for ensuring that researchers follow informed consent procedures stringently to protect potential subjects from coercion or being misled. Subjects vulnerable to these tactics include the mentally ill, the physically disabled, the elderly, and the economically disadvantaged. In addition, federal and state agencies mandate that IRBs review funding proposals before their submission for consideration by the agency. How a study involves human subjects defines the depth of the review, but the rights of those involved in the study are always a primary concern. Members of IRBs must have expertise in research designs and protocols.

In addition to the ethics committees, large healthcare facilities sometimes employ an ethicist as a consultant or on a full-time basis. An ethicist usually has a doctorate in ethics, bioethics, religion, or a related area and serves in both policy development and patient case review. In addition, ethicists can be a resource for the ethics committee by providing continuing education on ethics topics. He or she can guide the decision-making process of the IRB using models and facilitation techniques (Darr, 2011).

Regardless of the group's title, ethics committee members have an important role in addressing the ethics practices of healthcare organizations. Therefore, members of the O Team and the clinical staff should respect their status and wisdom. To maintain accountability, there should be an annual evaluation of ethics committees to ensure their effectiveness. When healthcare administrators treat ethics committees the same way as they would any other important administrative body in the facility, they send a strong message about the value the organization places on making sound ethical decisions.

As health care continues to evolve, the issues faced by ethics committees will become increasingly complicated. Committees will need to become more diverse by combining professionals with community representatives. Given these circumstances, the solutions to ethics issues will not be simple to derive. Committees will require tools to make decisions in the most effective and efficient manner. Ethics decision models can assist with this process by providing a structure to deal with difficult situations that can be emotionally volatile. It is important to try to minimize this volatility by using a sound decision-making model.

The first step, then, is for the ethics committee to have a selection of models from which to choose or adapt. Beginning with an agreed-on model ensures that the committee will work from a position of information and not from one of opinion alone. Knowledge of the existing models helps the committee choose the one that best meets its needs.

The American College of Healthcare Executive (ACHE, 2013) provides healthcare administrators with an Ethics Tool Kit that includes a model adapted from Nelson (2005). This model suggests that ethics committees follow a seven-step process:

1. Determine the basis of the ethical conflict.
2. Determine the affected parties and their values.
3. Research the circumstances for the ethical conflict.
4. Determine the ethics thinking related to the conflict.
5. Determine the options for action using ethical reasoning.
6. After evaluation, select the best option for resolving the conflict.
7. Communicate and implement the chosen option.

McNamara's (2013) *Complete Guide to Ethics Management: An Ethics Toolkit for Managers* provides resources for addressing business-related ethics issues. This author also presents a 10-step business ethics model for applying ethics in the workplace using the questions paraphrased here:

1. What are the facts?
2. Who are the stakeholders and what do they value?
3. What are the drivers?
4. Which ethical principles or values are appropriate for the situation (in priority order)?

5. Who should be part of the decision making?
6. Which actions will prevent harm, maintain principles, and provide a good solution?
7. How would the best solution affect the stakeholders?
8. How can one prevent this situation in the future (i.e., check the drivers in step 3)?
9. What is the best method for implementing the solution?
10. How can one evaluate the solution?

This model allows the ethics committee to identify those who are affected by the decision and those who should be a part of making it. It also provides a structure for evaluating possible solutions against criteria of ethics and practicality. In addition, it includes consideration of preventive ethics so that the situation is less likely to reoccur in the future. Evaluation and monitoring of the plan are also included to determine the success of the decision's implementation. The structure of this model is intended to bring a degree of rationality or practical wisdom to ethics decision making.

Darr (2011) suggests a schematic model for decision making that uses a decision-tree format. The decision-making process begins with the participants gathering information to clarify the problem. Next, the committee discusses and assesses its assumptions about the problem. When it fully understands these areas, the committee can formulate alternative responses. At that point, the committee members can evaluate these potential responses based on criteria that include the reality of implementation and a cost/benefit analysis. The committee chooses the best response and makes its recommendations. Darr's model also includes a step in which the organization compares the desired outcomes and the actual outcomes of the implementation. This evaluation provides needed feedback concerning the effectiveness of the committee's decisions. In addition, administrators can use checklists to remind the committee of the full picture of the situation before discussing the solution. Such a reminder can slow down the decision-making process, thereby avoiding the temptation to "jump to solution" before all of the information is assessed.

Models are effective only when they are used, and they are used well only committees understand them. Therefore, ethics committees must be thoroughly familiar with whatever model is chosen or adapted. It is important to refresh the committee's knowledge of the model through frequent reviews and training of new ethics committee members as part of their orientation. In addition, there should be a review of the model itself to determine if it is still meeting the needs of the organization and the committee.

■ ADMINISTRATORS' ROLE IN THE CULTURE OF ETHICS

What is the effect of healthcare administrators in establishing organizational culture? Just like other healthcare professionals, HCAs have their own language, stories, and values that are specific to their discipline. In addition, their particular version of administration culture is a factor in how they view the organization and make decisions. HCAs' positions in the organization also give them the power to influence the overall culture of the organization. For example, Lee (2004) suggests that administrators use their influence to create a culture of caring. Such a culture better meets the patients' need for a positive experience with the healthcare system. Employees who are competent and courteous, and who actively and consistently practice compassion exemplify caring cultures. Healthcare administrators can direct this caring culture through their hiring practices, through policies and procedures, and by example.

Although HCAs have the power to make a difference, they also face ethical temptations because of this power. For example, HCAs must deal with both new and ongoing ethical dilemmas during times of great change when the healthcare organization's fiscal responsibilities may trump patient care or employee concerns. The variety and depth of these potential temptations make a case for ethical vigilance and for including the application of utilitarian and deontological ethics theory and ethics principles into the HCA's decision-making process. When dealing with ethical dilemmas in the current dynamic environment, Health administrators need to ask questions such as "How will this decision benefit the mission of quality patient care"? and "Will this decision respect patients, employees, and the community"? In addition, they will need to use decision-making models that include ethics as a component and consult with ethics committees on policies that affect patients, the organization, and the community. Of course, personal integrity and moral maturity must also be present as HCAs make their daily decisions for the good of the organization.

Failure to practice ethics-based administration can have profound effects on both the administrator and the organization. For example, Collis (1998, p. 9) uses the term "managerial malpractice" to describe what happens when administrators cross the ethics line. His work was based on a national study of academics, chief executive officers, union presidents, and others. Collis found many areas of performance weakness in terms of attitudes, knowledge, and skills that can lead to malpractice among leaders. Such weaknesses contribute to what he calls "fatal management sins" (p. 53). Many of these areas relate to organizational culture, including loss of trust, impersonal attitudes toward employees (seen as an expense not an investment), lack of focus, and lack of accountability.

Adams and Balfour (1998), in their powerful book *Unmasking Administrative Evil*, use history to illustrate the negative influence that administration can have over culture. This influence can lead to cultures that encourage malevolent behaviors. The authors cite the example of the civil service administration during the German Third Reich. They found that in this system, ethics was valued less than technology was, and bureaucracy was valued less than people were. Therefore, it became easier to create and implement policies that were evil, yet very efficient. The authors caution that effective HCAs need more than management theory to do their work. To be an ethics-based administrator, one needs to be always aware of the potential for evil caused by failure to consider the consequences of the use of power and lack of an ethical perspective. HCAs, especially those who are part of the ACA era, must consistently take action to avoid situations where their actions become "managerial evil."

The administrative culture of an organization greatly influences whether ethics is valued, and how it is used (or not used) in making decisions on both the corporate level and the daily level. In an environment characterized by multiple subcultures, often with conflicting loyalties, establishing an ethics-centered culture is not an easy task. However, administrators are in a position to influence healthcare organizational culture in a positive way through rituals, stories, policies, and procedures. In addition, administrators can be the voice of ethics when they make decisions that affect those who rely on healthcare organizations for their health or livelihood. In this way, HCAs show that health care is more than just the "bottom line."

Summary

Health care is truly multicultural, which makes the healthcare system a challenging work environment. Because so many cultures work together in often stressful situations, this environment is susceptible to culture clashes. Part of healthcare administrators' responsibility is to become aware of the differences in the cultures in their organizations and use their knowledge and skills to prevent culturally based problems. In addition, healthcare administrators need to be cognizant of the influence they have on the overall culture of their organizations. Behaviors may speak much louder than any policy that administrators create. Therefore, healthcare administrators must not only make sound decisions, but also think about the perceptions created by those decisions.

Within their organizations, healthcare administrators will encounter several types of ethics committees. While HCAs may not be directly involved with all of them, it is important to understand these committees' functions and to appreciate how they assist healthcare organizations in meeting their ethics obligations. Administrators should remember the importance of having a decision-making model that everyone can understand. An ethics decision-making model can also become part of the effective HCA's ethics toolbox.

Cases for Your Consideration

The Case of the White Coat Code

Think about the chapter information and consider the following questions. Sample responses and commentary follow the case.

1. How does this case illustrate the impact of internal healthcare culture on behavior?

2. How did the administration choose to handle the cultural conflict?

3. What was the result of having a policy and program that does not tolerate abuse?

Case Information

Josh O'Shaun, newly appointed CEO of Morris County Hospital (MCH), faced many problems in his 200-bed facility. One of the most pressing, in terms of patient service, was a nurse retention rate that continually caused understaffing. His root-cause strategic plan included hiring a chief nursing officer (CNO) who would have equal status on the O Team. He was fortunate to hire Nicole Franz, a well-respected RN, for the position.

During the first staff meeting, Mr. O'Shaun asked for ideas on how to deal with the nurse retention issue. Ms. Franz presented research that showed that lack of respect for nurses contributed to this problem. With the support of their O Teams, other hospitals had instituted a policy of zero tolerance for physical, sexual, and verbal abuse. Specifically, they had implemented a program policy called Code White Coat. In this program, whenever a physician or other health professional acted in an abusive way, the nurse could call a "code white coat." This action would bring available nurses to stand as witnesses to the event and, if possible, intervene in the immediate situation. Research results in other facilities showed this policy led to a significant reduction of abuse incidents.

Her suggestion led to a lively discussion about differences in perceptions of the nurse retention problem and lack of respect for nurses. The chief of medical services (CMS) said that physicians were there to save lives and had a right to get angry if nurses did not perform according to their standards. He believed that tales of nurse abuse at MCH were just gossip. The chief financial officer pointed out how much the current turnover rate cost the hospital but did not have an opinion about its cause.

After much debate, the O Team decided to try a new policy that did not tolerate abuse in any form and then instituted their version of the Code White Coat program on a trial basis. They decided to evaluate the program one year after its implementation to see if it had made a difference in both turnover and morale. The CMS, although he thought the program was laughable, agreed to support it.

After the MCH staff training, there was an increased consciousness of the lack of respect for nurses, and that factor, in and of itself, seemed to decrease the incidence of nurse abuse. However, after three months, Mr. O'Shaun heard a "code white coat" called. He quickly responded and found Dr. Peters, his only neurosurgeon, still screaming at a nurse. Two other nurses were present as witnesses to this action, but their presence did not stop the physician. Through colorful language, he accused the nurse of being insubordinate and unprofessional.

Mr. O'Shaun asked Dr. Peters to come to his office immediately and contacted the CMS for a conference. He also called the CNO and asked her to meet with the nurse and her witnesses. He needed Ms. Franz's report before considering final action on the situation. By the time the CMS arrived, Dr. Peters was calmer and explained what had made him so angry. Many personal factors besides the nurse's behavior contributed to his outburst. However, he felt that the nurse did not act quickly enough to his order. He also stated that, since he was a neurosurgeon, he had the right to treat nurses any way he chose. After all, he held patients' lives in his hands. He was aware of the hospital's policy of zero tolerance for abuse, but he did not think he was abusive: All he did was raise his voice.

The CMS explained that there were other ways to deal with the situation other than public outbursts and abusive language. He emphasized that the zero tolerance policy applied to physicians as well as the staff at MCH. The CMS warned Dr. Peters that continuing such behavior could lead to sanctions, including loss of privileges if necessary. He also asked Dr. Peters if he would like to have assistance with anger management or other counseling. Seeing that the new policy was not just a joke, Dr. Peters said that he would apologize and watch his temper in the future. The CMS then said that Dr. Peters would receive notice if the hospital decided to take further actions.

After Dr. Peters left, Mr. O'Shaun, the CNO, and the CMS met to discuss the situation. The CMS expressed surprise that this incident happened. He knew that physicians were demanding, but he had never thought the issue of nurse abuse was real. The CNO said that she was not at all surprised. The incident was in keeping with some of her observations of physician–nurse interactions at the facility. After much discussion, the team decided that the appropriate ethics response required some action on this incident. Dr. Peters received a warning letter to document the incident and drive home the seriousness of the matter. The letter also mandated that Dr. Peters attend an information session on the zero tolerance policy and anger management counseling.

Responses and Commentary on Questions

1. How does this case illustrate the impact of internal healthcare cultures on behavior?

   Bullying and abuse are not ethical behavior, no matter who is doing it. However, because of the physician cultural norms, Dr. Peters clearly did not see his behavior as unacceptable. He had been educated to believe that his status as a neurosurgeon entitled him to an instant response from any nurse. His actions were beyond question, he thought. While he was aware of the zero tolerance policy, he believed that it applied only if he physically abused a nurse; yelling, he thought, was acceptable practice.

   The CMS was also part of the physician culture. Initially, he dismissed the whole idea of nurse abuse as just gossip. After all, he was not aware of any physician who had assaulted a nurse. Even though he thought this policy was frivolous, if the new CNO wanted to try it, he would go along. He was completely surprised when a nurse actually had the guts to call a "code." After this incident, he understood that abuse could be verbal as well as physical.

   At this point, one might well ask, "If the problem was so bad that nurses quit their jobs, how could the hospital not know about it?" One should consider that the nursing culture is also a factor in this situation. Nurses' education in the past included the cultural message that nurses were to serve as the "handmaidens of the physician." Nurses viewed verbal and even some levels of physical abuse as just part of the burden they had to bear in their service to patients. They did not question abusive behavior; they just learned to take it or resign. These actions resolved the problem for the individual but did not provide any information to the organization.

   Recent graduates of nursing schools, while still influenced by this thinking to some degree, tended to regard themselves as partners with other clinical staff. These nurses received a different cultural message. They learned to question (in a respectful manner) any actions that did not seem congruent with patient care. This "new nurse" paradigm can lead to a culture clash, especially if there is a perception that it is insubordination.

2. How did the administration choose to handle the cultural conflict?

   First, HCAs must recognize that the basis for the action—that is, instituting the new policy—was not entirely altruistic. Mr. O'Shaun was aware that the turnover rate among nurses was causing potential problems in quality of care, morale, and costs. He was educated to seek the root cause of a problem and had the authority to work with the O Team to find solutions. Notice that he chose an innovative solution that included the input of the CNO.

In addition, Mr. O'Shaun created the position of CNO, which had equal status on the O Team. Because nursing did not always have equal status with medical services, this decision went against some administrative culture norms. In fact, in their early days, hospitals considered nursing services to be part of the bed charge (like linens and disposables). Creating the new position was a risk, but Mr. O'Shaun knew that he needed the expertise of nurses and the support of nursing services. Putting a chief nurse on the O Team helped make the necessary cultural change.

Consider the courage of the O Team to create and support a policy that featured zero tolerance for all forms of abuse. While it is very easy to endorse a policy that declares it inappropriate to abuse someone physically or sexually, including verbal abuse is more controversial. The O Team had to be willing to apply sanctions for words as well as physical actions. This willingness could have had some financial risks. For example, the abuser could be someone who helped to create revenue for the facility. To remain an ethics-based facility and demonstrate justice, the O Team had to risk taking actions that might jeopardize this financial asset. In light of these and other concerns, Mr. O'Shaun had to encourage lively discussion of this innovative policy and gain the support of all O Team members. In the end, even the CMS expressed support for the new policy's implementation.

Consider also the Code White Coat Program. Making the decision to implement it was even more courageous. O Team members were willing to counter deeply held cultural norms. While they were armed with research that showed the program worked at other hospitals, they had no way of predicting its reception at MCH. They risked a backlash from physicians, who might resent such a program, and who might even view it as an encroachment on their power and authority within the hospital.

Despite the fact that the program was for the benefit of the nurses' rights and safety, the O Team had no guarantee that other nurses would respond to a code as witnesses. Perhaps there would be no support for the nurse who had the courage to call a code. This lack of support could create even greater morale issues. In addition, the CMS was not convinced the program was necessary and said so. The whole team hoped that they would never hear a code called but implemented the program despite the risks.

Once there was a code in place, Mr. O'Shaun had to resolve the issue in an appropriate way. Notice that he involved the CNO and the CMS in data collection and problem solution. He needed all sides of the story to be able to make a just decision. The solution that was formulated demonstrated justice for both the physician and the nurse because it worked to change culturally ingrained behavior and was not intended to be solely a form of punishment.

The CMS also showed some ethics courage here. Despite his reservations about the program, he was willing to confront Dr. Peters about his behavior and let him know that it was not acceptable. In doing so, the CMS made an ethics-based decision. He had to risk alienating his only neurosurgeon, who might resign. This would affect the revenue stream of the hospital. However, if he did nothing, after agreeing to support the program, the CMS risked being perceived as a hypocrite. After weighing all the elements of the problem, he used a reasonable approach that would prevent any further incidents. His decision to take the matter seriously also sent a clear message to other physicians and to the nursing staff that the policy was more than just a piece of paper.

3. What was the result of having a policy that did not tolerate abuse?

Creation of a CNO position was a part of the solution for the nurse turnover problem in Mr. O'Shaun's view. However, this decision required an allocation of funds for salary and benefits that came from an already frugal budget. In addition, he had to respect the person whom he hired enough to hear her ideas and expend the resources to act on them. This involved an investment in policy development and training for the entire staff. From a business standpoint, Mr. O'Shaun had to be willing to make these fiscal decisions based on the potential benefits for the organization.

Although the case does not give the results of the annual evaluation of the policy and program, one can make some assumptions based on knowledge of ethics and the business of health care. First, in keeping with deontology, MCH sent a message to its nurses that they were valued. When a verbal abuse situation occurred, nurses had the authority to call a code to stop the behavior. In addition, there was policy support for the program that made it clear that there was no tolerance for all forms of abuse. When a code was called, the nursing staff saw that hospital management made a serious response to the code. Even though the physician involved was a major revenue contributor, there was no cover-up or glossing over of his actions. The response created a better working environment for the nursing staff and had the potential to affect retention and patient care in a positive way.

Consider the physician culture. This new policy and program was particularly difficult for them to embrace. Even the younger physicians did not see nurses as partners and found it difficult to deal with what they perceived as a blow to their authority. However, they also learned that their chief of medicine took this issue seriously. After the first incident with Dr. Peters, they tended to be more careful about their verbal outbursts. The overall work environment became more pleasant for everyone and fewer and fewer "code white coat" calls were heard at MCH.

The Case of the Compassionate Committee

Think about the chapter information and consider the following questions. Sample responses and commentary follow the case.

1. Which ethics principles were included in the actions in this case?
2. How did the action of the Caneyville Hospital Ethics Committee benefit the hospital?
3. How did the action of the Caneyville Hospital Ethics Committee benefit Mrs. Smith?

Case Information

The April meeting of the Caneyville Hospital Ethics Committee in Peace City, Florida, was a particularly unusual one. The eight volunteers on the committee had tackled many difficult issues in the past, but the case before them this month was notably different. A member of the Caneyville community, who was not even a patient at the hospital, had asked for a consultation. This was highly unusual for starters. In addition, the nature of the situation and the problems that it caused for the family warranted a departure from hospital protocol.

Presenting Situation

Mrs. Judy Smith's father, Bill Medford, had suffered a closed head injury when he fell off a ladder at his home in New Mexico. His condition declined into a permanently vegetative state, and he was put on life support and transferred to a long-term care facility. Knowing that her father would not want to have such poor quality of life, Mrs. Smith did all she could to give him a death with dignity. She reviewed his do not resuscitate (DNR) orders and assumed power of attorney.

Because Mrs. Smith and her three children lived in Peace City, she could not visit her father on a daily basis. Her distance from the facility was causing her grave difficulty. Each time her father coded, the staff resuscitated him and contacted her after he was stable. When she asked them why they took these actions, they told her that the administration required a family member to be present before honoring DNR orders. The administrator told Mrs. Smith that the policy ensured that the facility met the true wishes of the resident. In addition, it protected the facility from a potential lawsuit.

This situation was causing Mrs. Smith severe distress. She could not go to New Mexico, sit by her father's bedside, and wait until he coded again. Her vacation days and sick leave were exhausted. Resigning from her job was not an option because she was the sole support for her children. In addition, she was her father's only next of kin. She was frustrated because it appeared that, while she had done all the right things, no one was considering her wishes at the New Mexico long-term care facility. She came to the Caneyville Hospital ethics committee for advice.

Committee Response

The entire Caneyville Hospital Ethics Committee meeting was devoted to the discussion of this one case. The committee used the expertise of its members (who included a lawyer, an ethicist, and a physician), and its knowledge of ethics and law to discuss Mrs. Smith's case. The CEO's representative contributed some insight about the policy of the long-term care facility. He said the policy had merit because it protected the facility from a potential lawsuit. He could understand why the administrators at the facility wanted a family member present before honoring the DNR orders.

The ethicist pointed out that, while the policy was in the best interests of the facility, it neglected to honor the wishes of the patient and his family. The facility should be true to its mission of service to patients. Perhaps it might be willing to consider the application of the policy on a case-by-case basis instead of a blanket procedure (in other words, act with utilitarianism and deontology). The committee used a decision-making model to evaluate several options and prepared a list of recommendations for Mrs. Smith. The recommendations were not binding on the part of Caneyville Hospital, but she could use them in her next discussion with the New Mexico administration.

Mrs. Smith was grateful for the time and effort the committee spent on her case. She made a trip to New Mexico to speak with the long-term care facility's administrator and found that the facility no longer employed him. The new administrator met with her and reviewed the recommendations from the Caneyville Hospital Ethics Committee. Although he did not want to change the entire policy, he agreed to consider the circumstances of her case and make a reasonable accommodation to her circumstances. He instructed the staff not to automatically resuscitate Mr. Medford. Instead, they were to call Mrs. Smith when a code occurred. They were to inform her of the specifics, and get her verbal affirmation of the DNR order. Two weeks later, she received their call. Her father was then at peace.

Responses and Commentary on Questions

   1. Which ethics principles were included in the actions in this case?

   This is a complex case involving end-of-life issues and the reality of DNR orders. To understand all of the ethics involved here, the HCA needs to analyze the situation and the actions of the committee. First, the situation on the surface seems to be a violation of the patient's right of autonomy. Mrs. Smith knew that her father would not recover. Knowing his wishes, she made every effort to secure all of the paperwork to protect his right to a dignified death. However, because of her personal circumstances, she could not be present to be an advocate for those rights and the legal documents seemed worthless.

   Taking the viewpoint of the long-term care facility leads to a different way of thinking about this situation. Given their history of being part of one of the most heavily regulated industries in the United States, long-term care facilities need to go the extra mile to protect their residents. The administrator was aware that sometimes a family wishes to hasten the death of a resident for financial gain or some other unethical reason. In addition, families can change their minds once the DNR order becomes a reality. The facility wanted to protect its assets and its employees by making sure that a family member was present during a patient's death so that legal problems would not ensue.

   Consider the actions of the Caneyville Hospital Ethics Committee. It had no obligation to consider Mrs. Smith's request for a consultation. After all, she was not even a patient in the hospital. However, this committee had a reputation of compassion for the whole community and decided to provide Mrs. Smith with well-considered recommendations. They had to base their discussion on the situation presented to them by Mrs. Smith. Notice that they tried to discuss the situation from more than just her view by listening to the input of the CEO's representative. Given more time, they could have contacted the administrator in New Mexico to get his opinion of the situation.

   In deciding which recommendations to give Mrs. Smith, the ethics committee used the process that had assisted members on other occasions. It included the use of a decision-making model and open discussion among all committee members. Knowledge of the ethical and legal ramifications of the situation was also part of this discussion. While this process was time consuming, the committee was able to develop a set of recommendations that might resolve the situation.

   2. How did the action of the Caneyville Hospital Ethics Committee benefit the hospital?

The decision of the committee to consult on the Medford case did not appear to have any direct benefit to the hospital in terms of increasing revenue or census. However, the committee's reputation of compassion reflected positively on the hospital and added to its status in the community. By deciding to volunteer their time to address a community member's needs, the committee members let the community see that profit was not the only motivation for Caneyville Hospital—the community mattered to them.

3. How did the action of the Caneyville Hospital Ethics Committee benefit Mrs. Smith?

The ethics committee consultation provided several benefits for Mrs. Smith. First, she felt that her situation was important and that people with ethics expertise addressed it. Being able to talk about her case to such a compassionate body gave her a voice and helped to decrease her stress level. In addition, she felt that their recommendations provided her with some tools for a meeting with the administrator in New Mexico. She could present her viewpoint in a cogent manner and feel confident about her position. Fortunately, the new administrator of the facility was more open to patients' rights and Mrs. Smith's unique situation than the previous one and listened to her with an open mind. The long-term care administrator was able to make a reasonable accommodation in this case and Mr. Medford ended his life with dignity.

Web Resources

American College of Healthcare Executives, Ethics Resources Center
http://www.ethics.org/

The Mayo Clinic
www.mayoclinic.com/

The Tuskegee Experiment
http://www.cdc.gov/tuskegee/timeline.htm

WebMD
http://www.webmd.com/

References

Adams, G. B., & Balfour, D. L. (1998). *Unmasking administrative evil*. Thousand Oaks, CA: Sage.

American College of Healthcare Executives. (2013). *Ethics tool kit*. Retrieved from https://www.ache.org/abt_ache/EthicsToolkit/ethicsTOC.cfm

Centers for Disease Control and Prevention (CDC). (2013). *The Tuskegee timeline* [Fact sheet]. Retrieved from http://www.cdc.gov/tuskegee/timeline.htm

Collis, J. W. (1998). *The seven fatal management sins: Understanding and avoiding managerial malpractice.* Boca Raton, FL: St. Lucia Press.

Daft, R. L. (2012). *Organizational theory and design* (11th ed.). Independence, KY: Cengage Learning.

Darr, K. (2011). *Ethics in health services management* (5th ed.). Baltimore, MD: Health Professions Press.

Ginter, P. M., Duncan, W. J., & Swayne, L. E. (2013). *Strategic management of health care organizations* (7th ed.). San Francisco, CA: Jossey-Bass.

Groopman, J. (2007). *How doctors think.* New York, NY: Houghton Mifflin.

Kalina, K., Pew, S., & Bourgeois, D. (2004). *Don't go there alone!: A guide to hospitals for patients and their advocates.* Kansas City, MO: 33-44-55 Publishing.

Lee, F. (2004). *If Disney ran your hospital: 9 1/2 things you would do differently.* Bozeman, MT: Second River Healthcare Press.

McNamara, C. (2013). *Complete guide to ethics management: An ethics toolkit for managers.* Authenticity Consulting. http://www.managementhelp.org/ethics/ethxgde.htm

Nelson, W. A. (2005, July/August). An organizational ethics decision-making model. *Healthcare Executive, 20*(4) 8-14.

Office of Minority Health. (2013). National standards for culturally and linguistically appropriate services in health and health care [Fact sheet]. Retrieved from https://www.thinkculturalhealth.hhs.gov/pdfs/NationalCLASStandardsFactSheet

Roizen, M. E., & Oz, M. C. (2006). *You: The smart patient: An insider's handbook for getting the best treatment.* New York, NY: Simon and Schuster.

Schyve, P. M. (2009). *Leadership in healthcare organizations: A guide to Joint Commission leadership standards.* San Diego, CA: Governance Institute.

Seuss, D. (1986). *You're only old once! A book for obsolete children,* New York, NY: Random House.

Shi, L., & Singh, D. A. (2015). *Delivering health care in America: A systems approach* (6th ed.). Burlington, MA: Jones & Bartlett Learning.

Spector, R. E. (2013). Cultural diversity in health and illness (8th ed.). Upper Saddle River, NJ: Pearson.

West, M. P., & Morrison, E. E. (2014). Hospital ethics committees: Roles, memberships, structure, and difficulties. In Morrison, E. E. & Furlong, B. (Eds.). *Health care ethics: Critical issues for the 21st century* (3rd ed., pp. 251–266). Burlington, MA: Jones & Bartlett Learning.

© file404/Shutterstock

CHAPTER
11

The Ethics of Quality

How can a healthcare administrator create a culture of quality?

Points to Ponder

....

1. What is quality health care?
2. How does health care assure quality?
3. How does ethics relate to the quality assurance in health care?

Key Terms

....

The following is a list of key words for this chapter. Look for them in bold.

Agency for Healthcare Research
and Quality (AHRQ)
Centers for Medicare and
Medicaid Services (CMS)
Donabedian model

Institute for Healthcare
Improvement (IHI)
Lean system
ORYX® system

■ INTRODUCTION AND DEFINITIONS

Quality is an issue in all businesses and services in the United States. For example, parents, teachers, administrators, and legislators are concerned about the quality of education that students receive. Consumers of goods and services want quality for the money that they spend on those goods and services. In health care, of course, the idea of quality carries an even greater weight. Because members of the healthcare system literally hold the power of life or death in their hands, the community is compelled to find protection for itself from this system through regulations, licensures, and sanctions enforced by a myriad of organizations. These regulatory organizations attempt to assure the whole community, including employers, that they hold healthcare organizations to a set of standards. While these measures do not provide an absolute guarantee of quality, community members have some assurance that they will receive competent and safe care from healthcare providers.

However, healthcare facilities often have a different view of regulations and standards. With the emphasis on quality associated with the ACA and tightening revenue streams, healthcare organizations must address areas that might potentially reduce quality, add costs, and diminish profits. Quality efforts have become a top priority for the success of health care. This chapter presents the idea of compliance with external standards from the organization's view. It also addresses how administrators influence compliance through their behaviors. The chapter then goes beyond compliance with externally imposed standards to examine efforts to provide patient-centered quality. Is quality assurance an ethics action? An analysis of the connection between quality and ethics principles and theories answers this question.

■ WHAT IS QUALITY?

The classic model of effective health care, originally developed by Kissick in 1994, is now called the Iron Triangle (Johnson, 2009). This model includes cost, access, and quality as the angles of a equilateral triangle, demonstrating that each area affects the others and that all areas must be addressed to maintain balance. It also suggests that if one area is increased, the other two areas must decrease. For example, increasing quality increases cost. In turn, the increase in cost decreases access. The Iron Triangle model is limited in its ability to address external demands such as legislation and patient demand, but it does serve as a starting point for understanding how important quality is for healthcare organizations.

According to Shi and Singh (2015), achieving quality in health care involves increasing desired health outcomes for populations. Both the individual and the community outcomes should be the focus of quality assessments. Professionals should develop standards for measuring quality in their areas. In addition, quality should include clinical areas such as small-area variations and adverse events. In addition, there should be an assessment of interpersonal aspects of care as well as quality of life. From a societal point of view, quality of care is identified through an evaluation of population health including mortality rates, incidence and prevalence of disease, and access to health care.

Quality in health care often varies depending on who is addressing the issue. For example, for a healthcare administrator, quality may mean hiring the most credentialed professionals, avoiding "never events," lowering uncompensated care expenses, and reducing patient complaints. For a legislator or insurance company, it may mean demonstrating compliance with billing codes, documenting compliance with standards, and providing care within funding levels. For staff members, quality may be achieved when they have the appropriate resources to provide care, are appropriately paid, and receive respect for the work that they do.

For patients, especially those who are treated on an inpatient basis, the definition of quality is more personal and specific. Patients and their families expect care to be appropriate and safe. Therefore, their perception of quality encompasses specifics like food (hot when it should be hot; cold when it should be cold) and call buttons (answered in a reasonable amount of time). In addition, patients assess quality based on their perception of the beneficence of staff members and the window of their own emotions and experiences.

Healthcare organizations face the challenge of addressing quality according to both regulatory and patient-centered standards. In addition, the ACA places new emphasis on quality and cost-effective care for populations. However, health care is still a business—which means that healthcare organizations must turn a profit if they are to make payroll and keep their doors open to the community. Quality assessment, assurance, and improvement will challenge healthcare administrators now and in the future. Cutler (2014) addresses complex issues of quality in health care by focusing on costs and specifically on creating value for funds that are expended. In addition, he presents interventions that can lead to the "quality cure" (p. xvi). Cutler's strategies include examples that demonstrate quality efforts involving direct patient care, process systems, and employee interactions. It is clear that quality improvement is a multilayered process, and one that takes time and effort to play out in healthcare organizations.

How can healthcare organizations address quality when the definitions of this concept vary so widely? Is there any common ground? Donabedian (in Shi & Singh, 2015) identified three major components of quality that can serve to provide this common ground. The **Donabedian model** is based on structure, process, and outcomes; hence it is also called the SPO model. In this model, one can measure quality by looking at the structure of an organization, including licensing, accreditation, staffing, equipment, and systems of delivery. In addition, the process of providing care can be evaluated. This evaluation would include the provision of care and patient outcomes, but can also include interpersonal relationships and the patient experience.

Finally, Donabedian (in Shi & Singh, 2015) suggests inclusion of the outcomes of patient care or results in his model. The outcomes component of his classic model includes patient satisfaction, rehospitalization rates, health status improvement, and mortality rates. Each of the three components—structure, process, and outcomes—is necessary for quality and complements the others. Therefore, this model can serve as a starting point for formulating a definition of quality that could be adapted to a specific aspect of the healthcare delivery system.

■ A HISTORICAL VIEW

Issues concerning the quality of healthcare practice are not new. For example, over the centuries, the American healthcare system evolved from an apprentice structure to its current level of sophistication. This evolution occurred in a market-based rather than social-based context, making the United States unique among other industrialized nations in terms of development of the country's healthcare system. In its early stages, professionals exclusively controlled the U.S. healthcare system and external regulation or community accountability was not part of its structure (Shi & Singh, 2015). Therefore, physicians practiced as they thought best and patients were grateful for whatever care they received. The idea of a second opinion or even a question was not even a consideration.

Over the years, factors such as the development of insurance, increased government involvement, the advent of advanced technology, and increased costs of care brought about a greater need to demonstrate accountability. These factors spawned more widespread external regulation in various forms including "voluntary" accreditation. Even though there was not a legal mandate for accreditation, such an expectation became part of financial and even state licensure requirements. For example, beginning in 1965, reimbursement from U.S. government programs was linked to accreditation of hospitals by The Joint Commission on Accreditation of Healthcare Organizations, now called simply The Joint Commission (TJC, 2013). However, many in the healthcare system deeply resented government encroachment on their autonomy; this resentment persists today. Despite these qualms on the part of healthcare organizations and providers, The Joint Commission continues its work to support collaboration among healthcare organizations to ensure quality health care and value for the public.

TJC is not only involved in the accreditation process for a variety of healthcare organizations, ranging from hospitals to clinics, but also works to improve the quality of health care. In 1995, TJC began a new survey format when it introduced the **ORYX system** of documenting performance outcomes. During its 50th anniversary year (in 2001), TLC announced an emphasis on patient safety and decreasing medical errors, which continues to be an area of assessment (TJC, 2013). In addition, the organization works to improve all of the standards used to evaluate healthcare organizations, including hospitals, home health care, and behavioral medicine services. To keep up with changes in technology, it created electronic-edition manuals, mobile-friendly notification schedules, and electronic portals so that accreditation customers can have easier access to updated information and yearly standard changes.

The Joint Commission continues its efforts to improve the quality of health care in the United States through its yearly updates on standards for healthcare organizations. In addition, its online Quality Check program provides the public with access to information about community facilities. TJC also provides information to healthcare facilities and the community through its Speak Up program and The Joint Commission Quality Check (TJC, 2013).

A major TJC program for improving patient safety, called The Joint Commission Center for Transforming Healthcare, has engaged partner facilities all over the United States. These organizations are working to improve quality through better compliance with hand washing guidelines and more effective hand-off communications. In addition, they are trying to reduce the incidence of wrong-site surgery, surgical-site infections, avoidable heart failure, and falls. TJC's Target Solution Tool (TST) also offers a process for measuring performance and finding solutions to overcome barriers to achieving patient safety goals. The Joint Commission Center for Transforming Healthcare partnership seeks to create organizational cultures where patient safety is of primary concern (The Joint Commission Center for Transforming Healthcare, 2013).

The quality of health care is certainly a part of the Affordable Care Act of 2010. In particular, Medicare payments to hospitals are now connected to quality and value. For example, in 2012, hospitals that ranked in the top quartile in terms of rate of hospital-acquired infections (HAIs) saw a 1% reduction in their Medicare payments. Hospitals will also see reductions in their Medicare payments if they are found to have excessive readmissions of covered patients. In addition, Medicare's Value Based Purchasing Program, which was launched in 2013, pays hospitals based on attainment of or improvement in certain quality measures, including those based on patient satisfaction data. Given that Medicare is a major payment source for many hospitals, a reduction in payments from this source could be a serious blow to a facility's bottom line (Association of American Medical Colleges, 2013; Kaiser Family Foundation, 2013).

Organizations like the Institute of Medicine (IOM, 2001) also cover quality issues on an ongoing basis. For example, the IOM's focus on this topic became clear with the publication of its classic report, *Crossing the Quality Chasm: A New Healthcare System for the 21st Century*. Through forums, workshops, and research projects, the IOM engages in a wide variety of activities designed to improve the quality of health care for individuals and populations. Its mandate is to provide individuals and government agencies with reliable evidence for making the best possible healthcare quality decisions.

■ THE QUALITY RESPONSE FROM ORGANIZATIONS

How do healthcare organizations respond to the need for quality assurance and improvement? In today's healthcare environment, quality assessment and improvement efforts are part of everyday business practice. In earlier times, healthcare professionals and organizations could say, "Trust us; we will give you the care that you need" and expect payment for that care. Now, if they want payment for their services, healthcare providers and organizations must demonstrate that they have provided safe and effective care. However, this minimum quality level is not enough; they must also demonstrate the quality and value of that care. Providers and organizations do so by meeting accreditation standards, complying with regulations developed by state and federal agencies, and satisfying requirements from third-party payers.

Often, however, healthcare organizations face conflicting demands for accountability. Healthcare administrators (HCAs), in turn, feel as if they are drowning in a sea of regulations, paperwork, and site visits. Even though technology provides assistance in meeting the demands made by external organizations, HCAs' reading load has increased dramatically in recent years. Not only must HCAs read this detailed content, but they must also demonstrate an understanding that allows them to explain it to their staff members. Some HCAs view the need for accountability as excessive and unjust. They spend many hours dealing with data entry and electronic submissions to meet various agencies' demands. In addition, their staff members must be concerned with record accuracy, dealing with what they might see as minutia. The time devoted to this work takes personnel away from making quality improvements in patient care. Although the intention is that healthcare facilities should always be accreditation ready, the possibility of unannounced site visits by TJC inspectors also creates stress for healthcare organizations and their administrators.

Regardless of the time and effort necessary to be accountable for quality healthcare services, providers and organizations need to make quality care an inherent part of their culture. With patient populations that are increasingly more aware of their rights and quality standards, healthcare providers can no longer ignore quality on all of its levels. In addition, there is a link between branding, payment, and the organization's reputation for quality as a result of meeting and exceeding standards. Of course, striving to provide the best health care at a reasonable cost is also part of the ethics of patient-centered health care.

■ BEYOND COMPLIANCE

The evolution of communications technology—for example, the world opened up by the Internet, smartphones, Twitter, and television—has changed the public's attitude toward health care. While most of the public still assumes that healthcare organizations are providing high-quality service, many patients have experienced unacceptable treatment from their providers, hospital staff, or insurance companies. Overall, today's consumers are more knowledgeable about the healthcare system and their rights as patients. They want to be partners in their treatment rather than sycophants who blindly follow caregivers' orders. This change, coupled with the responsibility for health and healing inherent in the healthcare system, makes the need for quality assurance paramount.

For the healthcare system, quality improvement is an ongoing process that affects all aspects of a healthcare organization. Quality improvement includes both quality assessment and quality assurance. Quality assessment involves comparing the actions taken within an organization with a standard. Such a comparison relies on data collection, analysis, and interpretation (Shi & Singh, 2015). Whereas assessment focuses on deviations from the standard and seeks to correct these unwanted results, quality assurance involves more sophisticated means of analysis such as presentation of data via dashboards, scorecards, and landscapes. Information technology has improved data collection and analysis so that quality improvement teams can effectively examine medical practice variance, the use of evidence-based medicine, patient experience data, and drivers of quality (Ransom, Joshi, Nash, & Ransom, 2008).

Because of the complexity of the U.S. healthcare system, many agencies have an interest in its quality assurance. For example, the **Centers for Medicare and Medicaid Services (CMS)** is a major payer for healthcare services in the United States (Shi & Singh, 2015). Not surprisingly, given this fact, the CMS has also become a leader in quality care assurance. This organization addressed the quality data needed for implementation of the ACA by creating the Health Insurance Marketplace Quality Initiative, which includes survey tools and assessment systems to measure employer and consumer satisfaction with healthcare marketplaces.

The CMS also created the Center for Clinical Standards and Quality, whose mission is to improve the quality of patient outcomes, experiences, and overall health (CMS, 2013). The CMS engages physicians in voluntary reporting of quality data for Medicare-covered patients through its Physician Quality Reporting System (PQRI). CMS is also active in developing assessment approaches to improve patient transitions to post-acute settings, standardized quality measures, and indicators for Medicare and Medicaid providers.

The **Agency for Healthcare Research and Quality (AHRQ)** is another federal agency that places a major emphasis on quality in health care. The AHRQ works with the U.S. Department of Health and Human Services to support research into evidenced-based health care, quality efforts, access to health care, and costs. Quality improvement programs such as research studies focused on patient safety are among its many funded projects. A recent addition to its mission includes evaluating the impact of the ACA's Medicaid and healthcare marketplaces in terms of access, reduction of health disparities, use and cost of health care, and outcomes. This important task will enhance the amount of information available to decision makers as they consider the ACA's impact and improve their ability to make appropriate decisions about the act's implementation (AHRQ, 2013).

Founded more than 25 years ago, the **Institute for Healthcare Improvement (IHI)** is a not-for-profit organization with a mission of improving the health of patients and communities in the United States (IHI, 2013a). IHI works through collaboration with major hospitals and foundations, and cites the 100,000 Lives and the 5 Million Lives campaigns as among its successes. It also works to improve healthcare practices and implementation of evidence-based medicine through collaboration with the Veterans Health Administration and the Robert Wood Johnson Foundation. In addition to working to improve healthcare outcomes, IHI provides resources to health professionals including its Open School. This program offers online education in patient safety, quality improvement, and patient-centered care. In addition to courses, the Open School provides tools, online communities, and blogs to assist clinicians and administrators in providing quality care (IHI, 2013b).

One of the best resources dealing with implementing patient-focused quality is the book *If Disney Ran Your Hospital* by Lee (2004). This book presents ideas about how to build a patient-centered quality culture by attending to areas that are significant to the patient. It applies Disney thinking to healthcare settings, including attention to areas such as patient respect, compassion, and attention to patients' needs. Lee demonstrates how the patient's experience and the patient's view of that experience lead to loyalty to the hospital. In an era when patient satisfaction scores are linked with reimbursement, Lee's book should be part of every healthcare administrator's library.

In addition to resources provided by organizations that support quality efforts, healthcare administrators have a full set of tools at their disposal for quality assessment and quality process improvement. For example, the **Lean system**, which was developed by the Massachusetts Institute of Technology, has become a useful tool in health care. It relies on the back-to-basics approach of the plan–do–check–act cycle as popularized by Deming (Ransom et al., 2008). This cycle allows participants to analyze their organization's performance and make improvements that increase quality. Various quality assessment tools are part of the Lean model, including cause-and-effect or fishbone diagrams, control charts, storyboards, and checklists. In addition, the Lean model allows organizations to use complementary principles like Kaizen (to address tactical problems) and Six Sigma (to reduce variation in processes) (Dunn, 2010).

Whatever systems or tools are used, it is important that administrators train staff members on their use and that they show commitment to applying the tools and programs. In addition, when the quality programs produce results, those results must be integrated into daily practices. If results identify areas for improvement instead of areas already characterized by quality, efforts must continue to achieve the quality goals. Quality improvement is continuous and must be part of every organization's and healthcare administrator's culture.

■ THE ETHICS OF QUALITY

Quality is important for reasons beyond meeting the standards of government and funding agencies and having a profitable business: It is also a Kantian duty. Providing safe, effective, and quality health care that benefits the patient would certainly pass the categorical imperative. In addition, providing quality care to all patients regardless of their ability to pay correlates with Kant's theory that all humans have value. In fact, many healthcare organizations feature the term "quality" in their mission statements. A mission statement that promotes shoddy quality where the health and lives of individuals are concerned would be nonsensical. However, in this time of great change in the healthcare system and the fiscal restraints imposed on caregivers, the problematic issue does not lie in stating that one's mission is quality care, but rather in having the ethical courage to take steps to assure that quality is present.

The utilitarians would actually agree with the Kantians here, albeit for a different reason. Providing quality healthcare services can achieve the greatest good for the greatest number of persons affected and avoid the greatest harm to the greatest number. Utilitarians weigh the consequences of a decision against its harm or benefit. In health care, the consequences of not providing quality care could adversely affect individuals and the viability of the healthcare organization. For example, failure to provide quality care can add to the pain and suffering of patients and increase their costs of treatment. A lack of quality care could cause harm to the organization through poor patient satisfaction rates or lawsuits. In the ACA era, failure to meet quality standards can also result in a reduction in payments, which in turn may negatively affect the organization's bottom line. Reductions in revenues may then lead to reductions in the workforce and a lesser capacity to serve patient needs. Thinking about the utilitarian ramifications of quality assurance leads to the conclusion that quality assurance is just plain good business.

Rawls would also support the provision of quality service because it is in the self-interest of both the community and the organization. In accordance with Rawls's theory, healthcare organizations should want to protect those persons in a lesser position (patients) because anyone in the community could ultimately be in that position. Interestingly, when members of the healthcare professions are in the patient role, they expect quality care and often report nonquality practices to the appropriate authorities.

What if quality assurance was an essential element in all management decision-making processes? Certainly, this inclusion would affect the business of health care and the public's trust in the system itself. Annison and Wilford (1998) remind healthcare professionals that trust in the healthcare system engendered by practitioners and organizations matters: "Like water, we take it for granted until it begins to slip away" (p. ix). Healthcare administrators should also remember that the Rawlsian concept of justice requires that all patients receive the best possible quality care. Harm to an organization's image and business may ensue when there is a compromise in quality and this action becomes public knowledge.

The principles of ethics also apply to the ethics of quality assurance. Consider the principle of nonmaleficence. Violating this principle by providing poor quality service and making medication and patient identification errors can do harm to patients and affect the careers of caregivers. While necessary, the costs of having to create policies, procedures, training events, and monitoring to assure quality practices add costs to the provision of care as well. The application of the sister principle of beneficence can be seen when healthcare professionals act with patient-centered care and compassion. Additionally, healthcare administrators demonstrate beneficence for employees through policies that protect their rights and dignity and assist with their development as both people and professionals. For example, by investing in a well-managed employee assistance program, an organization exhibits beneficence toward all employees and sends a message that employees are valued.

How do the principles of ethics relate to the actions of the healthcare administrator? First, administrators, as representatives of the healthcare organization, are responsible for upholding the mission of providing quality care. When administrators do not uphold this mission, there is a failure of truth telling and promise keeping, which are part of autonomy. Quality assurance also involves justice. Does the administrator have the duty to provide quality service to everyone or just to those who have insurance or deep pockets? Does the administrator have a duty to employees to assure that they have the resources and training necessary to provide quality patient care? These questions should be answered in the affirmative, of course, but the reality of meeting these duties can be difficult, especially in times of tumultuous change. Even so, the community and patients served by the healthcare organization would find it highly unethical if an organization provided different services to patients who have the same or similar conditions but different financial resources.

Justice, beneficence, nonmaleficence, and autonomy must be applied to the organization as well as to patients. For example, one organizational issue related to quality assurance involves the ethics of competing resources. Healthcare administrators often view the extensive resource commitment in money and time needed for TJC, ACA, and other mandated quality assurance efforts as a drain on the organization's limited resources. Competition for these scarce resources is typically even greater in smaller and rural hospitals where budgets are especially tight. Numerous questions arise concerning the ethics of spending money on data collection and analysis, computers, electronic systems, and reporting when there is a competing need for those resources in improving or providing patient care.

Still other organizations think that they are already engaged in providing quality service and find it difficult to justify all of the expense and paperwork involved in proving that fact to an outside evaluator. They also resent the incursion of even more government regulations that appear to be punitive and threatening to their reimbursement. In addition, they question whether the measures are really a reflection of quality as the community sees it. They even question evidence-based medicine and management standards based on the nature of the studies used for the evidence. Opponents of applying evidence-based practices may, for example, refute the basis for the evidence by asking, "Were the original studies valid and reliable?" "Do they really measure patient-care quality?" or "Would patient interviews or administrative rounds (similar to medical rounds) be better measures of patient care quality?"

Government agencies and third-party payers represent large revenue streams for healthcare organizations and practices, yet some administrators resent these outsiders' intrusion into their businesses. They view the mandated quality improvement programs as an infringement on their autonomy to practice healthcare management. Some of the milder comments heard from healthcare administrators are "Big Brother government is taking over health care" and "We have to practice cookbook medicine and management." Other healthcare practitioners find third-party restriction on practices and procedures to be a violation of their professional autonomy. They insist they should be free to choose what is best for the patient based on their years of education and experience, rather than based on the mandates established by an outside bureaucracy, or on "bean counters'" ideas of quality. Healthcare administrators will have to explain why oversight is necessary and why practitioner support is required for organizational success. While garnering this support is not an easy task, it is critical to success for the healthcare administrator and for healthcare organizations.

Ultimately, quality assurance programs will not be successful unless everyone in the organization makes the ethical choice to take them seriously. While requirements of the ACA and TJC certainly may affect the financial outcomes of an organization, they may not translate to changes in practice among professionals unless they make a commitment to the plan. Healthcare administrators also need to make an ethical decision to prepare all levels of staff to be proactive in providing safe and quality health care and to monitor quality practices. Providing recognition and reward for quality-enhancing practices should be part of the joy in administration. However, administrators must also have the ethical courage to correct practices that reduce patient safety and quality of care, even if that requires termination of employees.

Summary

Providing quality care is not just good ethics; it is good business. However, achieving quality goals requires that organizations comply with both the intent and spirit of the regulations imposed by external evaluators. It also requires that organizations exercise their ability to self-police so that quality practices become part of the culture of the healthcare organization. Quality assurance policies and programs, while requiring organizational resources, assist in maintaining the foundation of trust that is the basis of health care.

This chapter also addressed the ethics behind quality programs, including the application of ethics theories. In addition, it provided insight into the application of ethics principles to quality assurance policies and practices. If the healthcare administrator understands that quality is a sound business practice, it should make his or her role as an educator and monitor of quality practices easier. Moreover, healthcare administrators should remember that in an age of high expectations for patient safety and quality, they must act on Michelangelo's wisdom of "Ancora Imparo": "I am still learning" (Michelangelo Quotes, 2014, para 12).

Cases for Your Consideration

....

The Case of the Obstinate Orthopedist

Think about the chapter information and consider the following questions. Sample responses and commentary follow the case.

1. What was the ethics foundation for adding quality measures to the CMS Hospital Quality Project?

2. Which ethical arguments did Vice President Gormal make in asking for staff cooperation?

3. Which ethical argument did Dr. Cathal make in response to her request?

4. How would you handle this situation?

Case Information

Although the medical staff at Dagma Memorial Hospital (DMH) grudgingly conformed to the annual CMS Hospital Quality Initiative, the new additions to this year's indicators posed some serious concerns for Erin Gormal, Vice President of Operations. DMH was a 100-bed facility with a strong commitment to meeting the needs of its community, even with its limited staff of specialists. The additional indicators based on surgical infection prevention (SIP) made sense from a quality standpoint. In fact, the facility was already complying with most of the new indicators. However, Ms. Gormal knew that collecting the additional data would stretch the resources of her clinical and administrative staff even thinner. She believed in providing the best possible care and in "living the mission" of DMH. Still, she dreaded the upcoming informational meeting with her medical staff.

In keeping with her personal mission to be always learning, Vice President Gormal carefully prepared for the session. In the meeting, she presented the indicators and explained their rationale. However, when she got to the section on knee surgery and the evidence-based quality indicator suggestions for presurgical medications, the orthopedic surgeon, Dr. Sean Cathal, reacted with high emotion. He slammed his fist on the mahogany table and said, "How dare CMS tell me how to practice medicine. What right do they have to dictate which medications I give to my patients?"

At that point, it felt as if someone had opened Pandora's box. Many of the physicians agreed with Dr. Cathal's view and expressed frustration with yet another government mandate. They demanded to know why the administration did not fight this outrage. The climate in the room went from discontented acquiescence to outright hostility.

Although Ms. Gormal was prepared for some displeasure, she was somewhat surprised by the hostile reactions. The chief of medicine intervened and brought the meeting back to order. Ms. Gormal then calmly explained that the list of medications was not mandated but was included as a suggestion to assist in documenting the quality measures. Of course, there must be consideration of the patient's medical history and comorbidities when prescribing drugs. She also pointed out that the data identified in the guidelines were similar to those already collected by TJC. Therefore, these new data points should not be a significant addition to the data collection process. Ms. Gormal also provided each physician with information about the quality measures, including the studies used for determining their evidence-based medicine status. Finally, she pointed out that if DMH wanted to maintain its certification for Medicare reimbursement and avoid fines for noncompliance, it had to document these measures.

After another lengthy discussion, the physicians agreed that, while still hating the "Big Brother" approach from CMS, they did not want to lose certification. However, they hoped that such infringements on their expertise as professionals would not increase. Vice President Gormal breathed a sigh of relief as she returned to her office.

Responses and Commentary on Questions

1. What was the ethics foundation for adding these quality measures to the DMH CMS Hospital Quality Project?

   Vice President Gormal viewed the new requirements from a broad ethics framework that included DMH and the larger community. First, she knew that DMH was already participating in the CMS system for data collection as part of its commitment to maintaining certification. TJC had already asked for similar data, so the burden of additional staff time would not be too great. She had no desire to create more problems for staff members. She was proud of their commitment to the mission of caring for patients even in times of change. In taking this approach, she exhibited what Buber would call an "I-YOU" ethical relationship, because she valued the staff as people, not as just the means to achieve the end of data collection.

   Ms. Gormal was also able to view the situation from CMS's viewpoint. This organization was not concerned with punishing DMH but rather with working toward the utilitarian principle of the greatest good for the greatest number. By trying to ensure that all CMS-certified facilities used evidenced-based practices, the agency was hoping to achieve consistent quality. From the hospital's view, this could mean better patient outcomes, shorter lengths of stay, less use of resources, and higher patient satisfaction. Providing the greatest good for the greatest number would be a winning combination for both the community and the business.

Ms. Gormal could also see some Kantian ethics in the CMS decision. Each patient—not just those who were Medicare-eligible—could be included in the data collection. This meant that all patients were important even if Medicare did not pay for their services. Buber and Frankl would also agree with this position. Although a new set of measurements might bring up issues of conflicting resources, Ms. Gormal could see that it would serve to protect those patients in a lesser position by making sure they received the same quality services as those patients who were better off economically and socially. Her critical issue would be to convince physicians and others of the merit of this addition.

2. Which ethical arguments did Vice President Gormal make in asking for staff cooperation?

   At first, Vice President Gormal tried to appeal to the rational nature of her physician group. Rational people would see that it is in everyone's best interest to provide care based on the latest evidence of good practice. After all, if any one of them were a patient at DMH, he or she would want the gold standard of care. In addition, she tried to appeal to their science-based nature by providing copies of the studies used to justify each measure. She hoped the Rawlsian ethics might prevail, but did not anticipate the emotional aspects of this addition to the CMS requirements.

   What Ms. Gormal did not understand was how this change could be viewed through different "ethics eyes." Even though TJC had already required the collection of similar data, Dr. Cathal saw the new measures as an attack on his expertise and right to autonomous practice. His education as a scientist had taught him to question the reliability and validity of studies and to express a healthy skepticism. Perhaps he just felt overwhelmed by the increase in external regulations, which seemed to be growing almost daily. His colleagues echoed his dissatisfaction. They found the idea of control of their practice autonomy by nonphysicians and external regulators to be an infringement on their authority.

   Perhaps Ms. Gormal should have discussed her ethics rationale with the chief of medicine to get his input and assistance before the meeting. She might have been able to have greater anticipatory insight and to prepare an ethics and financial argument that would have avoided some of the emotional response. In the end, she was able to use ethics and fiscal data to obtain some level of support.

3. Which ethical argument did Dr. Cathal make in response to the physicians?

   Another side of the autonomy issue comes into view when considering Dr. Cathal's response. There is often a conflict of autonomy in health care. Questions occur concerning whose authority is more important. Is it more important for the practitioner to be able to use his or her professional judgment, or should the autonomy of the patient be primary? Remember that when people make the commitment to become members of health professions, they understand that in all things, the patient comes first. While it is true that these measures limit Dr. Cathal's complete autonomy in practice, his first obligation is to his patients. Thus his primary responsibility is to determine if the evidence-based practices are medically appropriate for the patient. If they are not, he must be prepared to provide justification for his decisions. However, if he fails to support the requirements of CMS in total, the organization could lose its ability to admit Medicare-covered patients. Whose autonomy would suffer in that case?

4. How would you handle this situation?

To answer this question, remember that you have the benefit of hindsight. Although the meeting was tense, Ms. Gormal was able to achieve her goal in the end. How would you have handled this meeting? You can see the benefit of continuous learning in this case. The more you can anticipate concerns about an issue and prepare a response, the more likely you are to obtain consensus. It is also a good idea to get support from a respected champion before trying to influence a group of people. In Ms. Gormal's case, she could have approached the chief of medicine ahead of the meeting time to obtain his buy-in. They might have even shared in the presentation of the information to indicate a united approach.

Think of a positive approach when preparing to deliver challenging news. Of course, physicians want to view themselves as practitioners of quality medicine. You can even reinforce how they are already using some of the practices included in the policy that you need to implement. Remember that you are more likely to get support if you ask for implementation by using a velvet glove rather than an iron hand. Finally, you must always be in charge of your emotions. If you lose your composure in such situations, you add to the problem instead of solving it. Since you are also human, you will need to hone your emotional control skills through practice and study.

The Case of the Self-Assured Employee Assistance Program

Think about the chapter information and consider the following questions. Sample responses and commentary follow the case.

1. What did Rampaire Manufacturing assume about the quality of Work/Life Associates (WLA)?

2. Which actions did Mr. Rampaire take to ensure quality?

3. What was his ethics reasoning for taking these actions?

4. What was the result of his actions?

Case Information

This case deals with how corporations respond to employees' mental health issues. Addressing these issues in an appropriate manner affects the organization's mission and profitability. The owner and human resources director of the company featured in the case were concerned about the ethics of quality. The owner also chose to go the extra mile on behalf of employees and their families. His action led to important decisions for quality assurance.

Rampaire Manufacturing was a 2000-employee company, internationally known for its manufacture of self-cleaning lavatories. The owner, Frank Rampaire, prided himself on his Buber-centered ethics and demonstrated caring concern for the employees in a number of ways. Recently, with the assistance of his human resources director, Ruth Washington, he negotiated a contract with a firm for an employee assistance program (EAP).

The contract with Work/Life Associates (WLA) guaranteed certain quality assurance features. For example, licensed counselors or master's-level social workers (MSWs) would do all telephone triage. WLA would also maintain records on current licensure for all staff and keep up-to-date directories for appropriate referral to practitioners in the local area. It promised that reports on referrals would include identifiers to protect the privacy of the employees and their families. The EAP also agreed to annual on-site visits from Rampaire or its designee for quality assurance purposes. Mr. Rampaire believed he had negotiated the best-quality EAP for his employees.

After the program had been in place for seven months, Mr. Rampaire was satisfied with the utilization reports he received but wanted some assurance about the quality of WLA's daily operations. He consulted with the human resources director about a site visit to the WLA facility. She suggested that the best way to obtain information would be to contract with a licensed professional counselor who could judge both the quality measurements and the actual performance of the EAP functions. Mr. Rampaire, seeing the merit of an expert outside evaluator, consented to pay a consultant's fees and travel expenses for a two-day assessment.

When the consultant returned, her findings surprised Mr. Rampaire. WLA had one MSW on duty during the observed telephone triage sessions, but the rest of the intake personnel were students from a local university. The records for licensure and credentialing of counselors and MSWs were not current. In addition, lists of practitioners who were available for referral were not up-to-date and contained incorrect telephone numbers and e-mail addresses. Mr. Rampaire contacted WLA's president about this situation. In his view, the situation, as reported to him, was a violation of WLA's contract and constituted unethical practice. Mr. Rampaire was assured that this was not WLA's usual way of doing business and that the situation would be remedied. However, when the WLA contract came up for renewal, Mr. Rampaire did not feel comfortable with the ethics of this EAP firm and declined to renew the agreement.

Responses and Commentary on Questions

1. What did Rampaire Manufacturing assume about the quality of Work/Life Associates (WLA)?

   Mr. Rampaire assumed that a business based on helping those who are experiencing problems in work or in life would have a high-level commitment to both professional and business ethics. He believed that WLA would exercise fidelity and be self-policing in its quality assurance efforts. By stressing features such as group data reporting, using well-prepared practitioners for triage, maintaining credentialing records, and being open to on-site visits, WLA gave the impression that it was an ethics-based organization. Mr. Rampaire assumed that truth-telling would be critical to WLA's business and that this organization would share in his respect and concern for employees. He entered into the contract based on these assumptions.

2. Which actions did Mr. Rampaire take to ensure quality?

   Because there was no external evaluator for this organization, Mr. Rampaire decided to go the extra mile to make sure that his employees were getting the services that they needed and that he had funded. He knew that neither his human resources director nor he had sufficient expertise to assess the actual performance of the intake staff and the quality of the recordkeeping. Therefore, he was willing to spend extra funds to have a qualified person make the site visit and assess the situation. In addition, he knew that a licensed professional counselor would not divulge any information she heard while observing the intake process. Therefore, he protected his employees' autonomy and privacy.

3. What was his ethics reasoning for taking these actions?

   Mr. Rampaire was working on many ethical levels here. He wanted to make sure that his employees were treated appropriately, using the best quality care. His quality assurance efforts applied Kantian ethics in that he wanted each person to be valued. He also wanted there to be a categorical imperative that the services provided would be of good quality for all employees. You can also see some utilitarian ethics here in that he was trying to avoid the greatest harm to the greatest number. If an EAP does not provide quality services, it has the potential to cause even more distress for employees and their families. Imagine if an inexperienced student gave a distraught employee inappropriate information or made an incorrect referral. The potential for harm was great.

From a business standpoint, Mr. Rampaire had a fiduciary obligation to his organization to make sure that he was spending funds appropriately. Paying for unrendered services could violate his own business ethic of fidelity to his company. Because there was no outside evaluator for this organization, he felt ethically bound to spend funds to get a more accurate, hands-on report of the performance quality.

4. What was the result of his actions?

The first result was that he learned that WLA was not honoring its contract. This information allowed him to contact its president and voice his concerns from a position of information. His immediate response triggered action to remedy the situation. However, the breach of trust left Mr. Rampaire with an unsettled feeling about WLA, and he was careful to question all of its reports. In the end, he decided to discontinue business with the company because he did not trust WLA to be involved with the mental health needs of his valuable employees.

Web Resources

Agency for Healthcare Research and Quality
http://www.ahrq.gov/

American Society for Quality
http://asq.org/index.aspx

Centers for Medicare and Medicaid Services
http://www.cms.hhs.gov/default.asp?

Institute for Healthcare Improvement
http://www.ihi.org/ihi

Institute of Medicine
http://iom.edu/

The Joint Commission
http://www.jointcommission.org/

References

Agency for Healthcare Research and Quality (AHRQ). (2013). AHRQ profile: Quality research for quality healthcare. Retrieved from http://www.ahrq.gov/about/mission/glance/profile.html

Annison, M. H., & Wilford, D. S. (1998). *Trust matters: New directions in health care leadership*. San Francisco, CA: Jossey-Bass.

Association of American Medical Colleges. (2013). Selected Medicare quality provisions under ACA. Retrieved from https://www.aamc.org/advocacy/medicare/153882/selected_medicare_hospital_quality_provisions_under_the_aca.html

Centers for Medicare and Medicaid Services (CMS). (2013). Quality initiatives: General information. Retrieved from http://www.cms.gov/Medicare/Quality-Initiatives-Patient-Assessment-Instruments/QualityInitiativesGenInfo/index.html?redirect=/QualityInitiativesGenInfo/

Cutler, D. (2014). *The quality cure*. Berkeley, CA: University of California Press.

Dunn, R. T. (2010). *Dunn & Haimann's healthcare management* (9th ed.). Chicago, IL: Health Administration Press.

Institute for Healthcare Improvement (IHI). (2013a). History of IHI. Retrieved from http://www.ihi.org/about/pages/default.aspx

Institute for Healthcare Improvement (IHI). (2013b). Open schools. Retrieved from Retrieved from http://www.ihi.org/offerings/IHIOpenSchool/Pages/default.aspx

Institute of Medicine (IOM). (2001). *Crossing the quality chasm: A new healthcare system for the 21st century*. Washington, DC: National Academy Press.

Johnson, J. A. (2009). *Health organizations: Theory, behavior, and development*. Sudbury, MA: Jones and Bartlett.

The Joint Commission (TJC). (2013). History of The Joint Commission. Retrieved from http://www.jointcommission.org/about_us/history.aspx

The Joint Commission Center for Transforming Healthcare. (2013) Creating solutions for high reliability health care. Retrieved from http://www.centerfortransforminghealthcare.org/projects/projects.aspx

Kaiser Family Foundation. (2013). Focus on health reform: Summary of the Affordable Care Act. Retrieved from http://kaiserfamilyfoundation.files.wordpress.com/2011/04/8061-021.pdf

Lee, F. (2004). *If Disney ran your hospital: 9½ things you would do differently*. Bozeman, MT: Second River Healthcare Press.

Michelangelo Quotes. (2014). Retrieved from http://www.brainyquote.com/quotes/authors/m/michelangelo.html

Ransom, E. R., Joshi, M. S., Nash, D. B., & Ransom, S. B. (Eds.). (2008). *The healthcare quality book* (2nd ed.). Chicago, IL: Health Administration Press.

Shi, L., & Singh, D. A. (2015). *Delivering health care in America: A systems approach* (6th ed.). Burlington, MA: Jones & Bartlett Learning.

CHAPTER 12

Patient Issues and Ethics

Why does the patient experience create ethics issues for health care?

Points to Ponder

1. How does the patient culture affect the ethics of health care?
2. How does paternalism affect the organization's view of the patient?
3. How does society's view of illness and health affect the organization's attitude toward patients?
4. What are the ethical issues involved in measuring patient satisfaction?
5. How can the healthcare system improve patient-centered care?
6. What are the ethics of patient-centered care?

Key Terms

The following is a list of key words for this chapter. Look for them in bold.

compliant-patient culture
human interaction
noncompliant-patient culture
paternalism
patient-centered care

patient-partner culture
Planetree Model
self-treatment
sick role
way finding

■ INTRODUCTION AND DEFINITIONS

Understanding the patient experience requires a brief examination of the historical roots of the U.S. healthcare system. Traditionally, professionals—most specifically physicians—have dominated this system. Early in its history, only the wealthy had access to what was then considered physician-provided quality health care. Because of the rarity of access and the status of physicians, patient showed a great deference when presented with their diagnoses and treatments. Patients did not question; they did what "the doctor says." This attitude toward physician practice held strong even when the first U.S. president, George Washington, was the patient. According to historians, physicians may have contributed to his death because of their insistence on bleeding as a clinical procedure (Shi & Singh, 2015). However, even in the early days of clinical practice, patients also sought medical advice from non-physician practitioners. Because of economic and access issues, elders and local healers often provided treatment advice, including the use of herbal remedies.

After World War I, the power and prestige of the medical profession became so great that it controlled both the supply of medical care and the demand for its services. Society did little to control the power of these "medical gods." In addition, physicians were able to restrict those who entered their ranks through medical school admission standards and licensure laws. This power base enhanced the physician group's ethos of "We know what is best for you" as well as the idea of patient compliance as a part of medical practice. Healthcare professionals expected hospitalized patients in particular to comply with the schedules of busy healthcare providers and demonstrate gratitude for their care (Sultz & Young, 2014). This pattern of physician attitudes and patient responses help to establish **paternalism** as the norm in health care (Shi & Singh, 2015).

As part of the ethics of paternalism, the education of health practitioners included their moral duty to avoid doing harm to their patients (nonmaleficence). This emphasis was significant because many of the procedures used, including those practiced today, had the potential to produce harm. For example, even today, surgery has both the power to cure and the power to kill. Therefore, professional judgment is required to make decisions about the risks versus the benefits of this or any treatment. In response to this expert judgment, patients in postwar America continued to trust the wisdom of the practitioner, exhibiting almost blind acceptance of medical practitioners' pronouncements. The physician knew best because he (the male pronoun is used deliberately here) had the knowledge to protect patients from further harm and heal them.

Practicing nonmaleficence also involved professional decision making concerning the amount of knowledge the patient could have and the timing of knowing. For example, physicians withheld information from dying patients so that they could minimize suffering. The rationale was that if patients knew that they were close to death, they would suffer more harm than if they remained ignorant about their condition. Of course, family members also appealed to practitioners not to inform their loved ones about the seriousness of their conditions so that those facing death would not lose hope or suffer. Loving concern was the impetus for "don't tell Grandma," but no one asked Grandma what she wanted.

The sister principle of beneficence was also a part of paternalism in health care. In the beneficence-based view, practitioners have a moral obligation to use their knowledge for the reduction of pain and suffering for individuals and the community. While no one should minimize their superior knowledge of disease and treatment regimens, practitioners often remained ignorant about the patient's view of his or her own illness. This resulted in the paternalistic definition of "doing good" without consideration of whether that action was seen as "good" by the patient. Again, there was a conflict of paternalism versus autonomy, and paternalism seemed to be the winner.

What happened to change the U.S. healthcare system's paternalistic view, and how does it connect to ethics? Multiple factors came into play here. First, the increase in the number of people covered by insurance shifted the source of control over demand of care. Because of their expertise, physicians still diagnose and treat disease, but the other parties, including the federal government and insurance companies, now control payment for services. Once they gained this power, those who controlled the money demanded accountability and fair value for their payments. Increasingly, payers are defining what quality medicine is, right down to which drugs are prescribed and when. This strange business relationship leads to what some physicians see as their loss of control over the practice of medicine. They lament the fact that, to be paid, they have to practice medicine "by the book." They also feel that they have less authority in this model. Bureaucrats who never went to medical school, they argue, are keeping them from practicing the art and science of medicine (Shi & Singh, 2015).

In addition, the greater role played by technology in health care has been a force in reducing paternalism. Increasing use of the Internet has led to a dramatic increase in the medical sophistication of the public, payers, and regulators alike. The arcane knowledge of physicians and other healthcare providers is becoming accessible to many, a fact that is changing the patient–physician relationship. Some groups of patients wish to be treated as "consumers of health care," who are more in charge of their healthcare decisions. In addition, increased knowledge about the healthcare system, physician practices, and medical errors has eroded the public's absolute trust in the system.

The consumer-driven phenomenon of integrated medicine (IM) has also played a role in the change from paternalism to consumerism and patient-centered care (Micozzi, 2011). Because IM emphasizes prevention, holistic healing, and partnerships between practitioners and clients, those who use this model are more active in their treatment. These individuals tend to assume more responsibility for their own health and listen to the wisdom of their bodies. In turn, these clients expect to have a similar experience in the healthcare system and try to share their involvement with their physicians. Although many physicians are coming to accept and even use IM approaches, many do not welcome this change. Some still view IM as a threat to their medical sovereignty and to paternalism. As a result, some physicians either do not listen to their patients or ridicule IM practices (the word "quack" may even be used). When such messages are sent, a "do but don't tell" practice becomes the norm, often with disastrous results.

Regardless of the source of the challenge, paternalism, while certainly not dead, is changing because of healthcare consumerism. In the ACA era, the U.S. healthcare system is expected to undergo a shift from an emphasis on professional control and paternalism to a model characterized by collaboration among physicians, administrators, payers, and patients. This strange set of bedfellows will make delivery of health care interesting and ethically challenging in the future as healthcare organizations attempt to meet the health needs of patients in a rapidly changing healthcare environment.

■ PATIENT CULTURAL EVOLUTION

To understand the concept of patient cultural evolution, one should begin with patients. First, people do not become patients until a health professional gives them that title by identifying their diagnosis. Sometimes, individuals may experience symptoms that are not indicators of a disease or condition, but rather are only temporary. However, if symptoms reoccur or are severe, a person goes beyond self-diagnosis to treatment seeking. This is especially true when efforts directed toward **self-treatment** such as taking over-the-counter medications, changing lifestyle behaviors, or consulting a trusted family healer (Mom works well here), do not correct the problem.

When people seek help from healthcare professionals, that action puts them into what medical anthropologists identify as the **sick role** (Press, 2002; Shi & Singh, 2015). Families and society provide special benefits to those in the sick role, but they also have responsibilities. For example, the sick are to stay home so that they do not infect others. In addition, those around them might give them special treatment to assist in their recovery. In turn, those who are ill have the responsibility to remain true to the expectations about their sickness. For example, if they have a migraine headache, they do not recover in 20 minutes and then go to the mall. Family, friends, and employers would view this behavior as faking illness and being dishonest. The ill are also supposed to be compliant, participate in activities to promote their speedy recovery, and seek appropriate professional help for their condition. Culture and family relationships and, to some extent, gender influence specifics of interactions in the sick role.

A patient's overall responsibility in this sick role is to get well as soon as possible and return to being a productive member in his or her family and workplace or school setting. Notice that this responsibility includes seeking out assistance from an appropriate professional and then complying with the treatment provided. Seeking professional assistance means that a person must be willing to enter the alien world of medical care, with its strange language and rituals, and become part of the patient culture. Professionals run this system and have many levels of power. They also have certain expectations for patients who enter their system.

Today's patients are vastly different from those in the past and have different expectations of the patient role. Through the media, Internet, and other sources of information, patients have the capacity to obtain far more information about the healthcare system and its workings than was available to patients in earlier times. If they choose to do so and have the appropriate technology available, they can watch surgeries as surgeons perform them and listen in on patient care discussions. While this information may be helpful to some, not all patients share the same level of understanding. In addition, the presentation of information without context may lead to mistrust and fear of the healthcare system.

For example, there is a difference between reading information on the Internet about a condition and having a personal level of health literacy about that condition (Office of Disease Prevention and Health Promotion, n.d.). Health literacy involves processing and understanding health facts and services so that patients can make the best decisions regarding their care. While patients may be educated in other areas, it does not mean that they have a high level of health literacy. Culture, language, and the existence of overwhelming and conflicting information can affect the decree of health literacy and a person's ability to make the best decisions about his or her health. In addition, there is connection between patients' lack of health literacy and the concerns addressed by healthcare administrators—for example, patients' ignorance of prevention practices, effective disease management, increased hospital utilization, and healthcare costs.

In addition to including knowledge about the healthcare system, health literacy means that patients understand the complexities of health insurance (Roizen & Oz, 2006). Not only must they understand the financial and medical implications of point-of-service plans versus indemnity plans, but they must also choose coverage from a company that reimburses their healthcare professionals. They must understand all aspects of that coverage and the costs of their premiums, deductibles, and copayments. In addition, they must be able to read and interpret pages of fine print that describes everything from financial requirements to Health Insurance Portability and Accountability Act (HIPAA) rules. If individuals are older than age 65, they must also be fluent in "Medicarese" so they can receive the benefits to which they are entitled and avoid fraud.

The healthcare system changes introduced by the ACA have affected both health literacy and the patient culture. While profound changes in financing and regulating health care have created concerns about providers and organizations, current and future patients are also worried about the amount and quality of care available. As early as 2009, *Consumer Reports* found that patients feared a government takeover of health care, along with rationing of drugs and services. They also worried about increased costs for every aspect of health care and a loss of quality health insurance coverage at affordable prices. Anti-reform agencies and worried patients are using the Internet and other media to voice their fears as the implementation of the ACA continues to affect the U.S. healthcare system. For patients on Medicare and those with lifelong disabilities, the fear of loss of care, increased pain, and earlier death because of ACA changes may decrease their trust in the entire healthcare system.

The complexity of technology, the changing healthcare system, and the patient role leads to distinct patient subcultures. Currently, three such subcultures can be identified: the **patient-partner culture**, the **compliant-patient culture**, and the **noncompliant patient culture**. Each of these patient culture groups demonstrates different behaviors, but all will be entitled to ethics-based treatment by members of the healthcare system.

The patient-partner culture involves individuals and family members who wish to be a part of their health care. Patient-partners tend to have high levels of health literacy and often view healthcare professionals as "quasi-detectives" (Roizen & Oz, 2006, p. 3) who work to diagnose and treat their health conditions. These patients ask questions to clarify their knowledge about their conditions and treatments. They also protect their health by engaging in preventive lifestyles and come prepared for appointments with healthcare professionals. They take medications as directed.

One would think that healthcare professionals would laud the activities of patient-partners and treat them well. In reality, some professionals view their questions as threatening their autonomy and authority or, at the least, as being annoying and time consuming. These patients can upset the delicate balance inherent in a practice's daily schedule and lead to a longer day for healthcare providers. In hospitals, their questions may annoy the nurses and other staff who are already busy with their many duties.

Professionals need a strong commitment to patient-centered care and to healthcare ethics when working with patient-partners. This means that they recognize all aspects of patient autonomy—not just informed consent. Healthcare professionals must also act with beneficence by answering patients' questions effectively, efficiently, and with appropriate concern. They should view these questions as a means to practice nonmaleficence by preventing harm caused by misunderstanding and misinformation.

Compliant patients may be subject to cultural influences that require that they do not question those in authority. For example, people from certain age groups still exhibit "doctor as god" thinking. However, they may be uncomfortable or embarrassed telling their private information to an authority figure, so their diagnoses may not be as accurate as possible. In addition, if they have questions about their diagnosis or about taking their medications, they will not ask the "busy doctor" or the "busy nurse." This over-compliance and lack of questioning may actually cause harm to the patient. In this case, professional ethics also require respect for patient autonomy, beneficence, and nonmaleficence. The busy professional will have to assure that these patients understand their conditions and treatments. Achieving this level of understanding may require the services of a translator, the support of a family member, or a patient advocate (Roizen & Oz, 2006).

Noncompliant patients often wait until the last possible moment to seek care for their condition (Roizen & Oz, 2006). Not seeking care may be the result of financial issues, distrust of healthcare professionals, or cultural norms. As a consequence of their delay in seeking care, these patients may be more severely ill and frequent emergency departments at a higher than average rate. They tend to have greater acuity and may be in greater pain when they present for treatment. Because of their circumstances, they also tend to communicate in negative and hostile ways. Additionally, noncompliant patients may resist necessary treatment or refuse consent. Despite the difficulty they pose to healthcare providers, this group of patients requires excellent and compassionate communication skills.

With the ACA's emphasis on quality and lower readmission rates, healthcare professionals must use their ethics skills to respect patient autonomy, while still providing accurate and understandable information. They must inform noncompliant patients about the consequences of their decisions and obtain needed documentation for refusal of treatment. In addition, healthcare professionals need to remember to act with beneficence even if these patients are not respectful or pleasant. As Kant would suggest, while noncompliant patients may try the ethics sensibilities of healthcare professionals, they are due respect owing to their status as fellow human beings.

From an ethics viewpoint, healthcare administrators should remember that regardless of health literacy, patient culture, or financial status, patients tend to share some common experiences. When they are in pain, have intense fear, or are in a strange place, they require healthcare providers' ethical best. Their level of vulnerability and suffering make patients dependent not only on providers' competence, but also on their compassion, patience, justice, and nonmaleficence. The practice of patient care is often emotionally and physically difficult. Therefore, healthcare administrators must do all that they can to provide the resources and support needed so that clinically appropriate and ethically sound patient care can be given.

■ UNDERSTANDING AND MEASURING THE PATIENT EXPERIENCE

One way to serve various patient cultures is to understand their experience. In the ACA era, it makes good business sense to have a record of satisfaction for all patients. This credential can lead to better status in the community and increased patient referrals to help practices attract a financially sound patient census. Press (2002) also links patient satisfaction to employee satisfaction. High levels of patient satisfaction can actually lead to decreased turnover and absenteeism among employees, which in turn can create a better bottom line. Of course, patient satisfaction numbers are a significant area of review for external evaluators (e.g., the Centers for Medicare and Medicaid Services [CMS] and The Joint Commission [TJC]). In fact, these organizations translate patient satisfaction data into "report cards" that provide patient-focused information about the status of healthcare organizations. These report cards are publicly available on various websites, and both individuals and businesses can use them to make judgments when choosing providers and seeking referrals.

How do organizations measure patient satisfaction? Although there are many ways to do this, a survey or questionnaire is the most commonly used method. Organizations can use instruments prescribed by an agency, purchase instruments through a company that specializes in measuring patient satisfaction, or create their own instrument in-house. Regardless of the format used, all such tools are subject to limitations that can also create ethics concerns. First, measurement tools do not measure actual real-time patient satisfaction (Press, 2002). Because organizations conduct surveys weeks or even months after the actual encounter, they actually acquire data about perception and memories. In addition, sample bias may occur if only patients who were very pleased or very unhappy choose to respond to the survey. The use of biased data in incentive plans could also create as an issue of staff justice.

Several other ethical issues must be considered when using survey data alone for measuring patient satisfaction. Organizations must take into account statistical concerns such as sample size, random sampling techniques, population representation, and data manipulation.

Knowledgeable and less-than-ethical staff can word surveys or conduct them so that the surveys obtain only positive responses. The organization can then use this "good news" for CMS, TJC, and other reports. However, they also run the risk of having their ethics deceptions uncovered by audits, attentive patients, or curious media reporters.

Of course, questionnaires are not the only way, or even the best way, to identify the root cause of patient satisfaction issues. Press (2002) and others encourage using survey data as a spark for discussion and for beginning the process of root-cause analysis. In addition, data from other sources can make a real difference when an organization is trying to improve patient satisfaction levels. For example, administrators can gain valuable insight into the real patient issues by practicing "management by walking around." Observation is a powerful tool, even if it does not yield quantitative results. Healthcare administrators (HCAs) should consider talking with patients, staff, and practitioners to get a better sense of how things happen in real time. In fact, many administrators now conduct administrative rounds where they sit in the emergency department waiting room or visit patient rooms. With this approach, they get a much better sense of the patient experience by becoming a part of it. For additional insight, other administrators actually become mock patients and go through the admissions and work-up process. Administrators also make it a point to talk to the housekeeping staff because they are often a source for real information about operations.

Press (2002, p. 36) emphasizes that "measurement is not management." Regardless of the source, data alone will not change anything. Healthcare professionals on all levels will have to be fully engaged in problem analysis and problem-solving strategies to make a real difference in the patient experience. In the ACA age, when patient satisfaction is considered an element of quality, it is prudent to include the internal experts (the people who really do the job) as part of the quality improvement team so that the improvement of patient experience becomes a reality and not just another piece of paper.

■ HOW DOES MEASUREMENT RELATE TO ETHICS?

Using patient satisfaction data is good for business, but is it good ethics? From a Kantian view, administrators have a moral duty to assure that patients are treated with respect because they are fellow human beings. In fact, this duty passes the categorical imperative test because it should be a universal feature of healthcare practice. It also fits the Golden Rule, in that administrators would want respect if they were patients. For administrators to be true to this Kantian imperative, they must evaluate patient care practices even if an external reviewer does not mandate such a review. How else will HCAs know if they are acting in accordance with the Kantian mandate?

From a utilitarian view, healthcare organizations must provide the greatest good to the greatest number of people affected or cause the least amount of harm. Healthcare administrators' actions have consequences that they must measure to determine if their organizations are providing the greatest good. Policies are created (rule utilitarianism) to ensure that treatment of patients provides this greatest good or serves to prevent harm. Collection of data from multiple sources assists in obtaining a more accurate picture of what is really happening in the patient's care experience and how to improve this experience.

Rawls would also agree that gathering data on the patient's experience and satisfaction enhances an administrator's ability to provide ethics-based care. Despite their different diagnoses, patients are all in the same position: They want the best possible outcome from their medical experience. This is always true, even when the outcome is death. Patients wish to have death with dignity and without overwhelming pain. They trust that healthcare professionals will be able to provide this outcome. The Rawlsian principle of protecting the least well-off also relates to the need for assessment and improvement of the patient experience. Healthcare organizations and professionals want to be known for their compassionate care and not just for their profit margins. Therefore, both ethics and self-interest suggest that continuous assessment and improvement of the patient experience is a healthcare imperative.

When administrators consider the founding healthcare ethical principles, they can also see a connection to measuring patients' experience and satisfaction. For example, the principle of autonomy stresses the patient's ability to own his or her body and make decisions about what happens to it. Infringement of this principle should occur only when it is necessary for the best interests of the patient (e.g., life-saving treatment even when no consent is given). Measuring the patient's view of autonomy and the HCA's impact on it should help the organization provide appropriate care and respect the patient's boundaries. If the organization understands the patient's view, it should also be able to move from paternalistic, professionally driven care to patient-centered care with greater ease.

Consider the sister principles of nonmaleficence and beneficence and their relationship to patient satisfaction. Perhaps health care causes harm unintentionally because the patient does not understand its procedures or intent. Understanding the patient's experience may help prevent harm by leading to better patient education and communication. Healthcare administrators also have a moral obligation to provide benefit, which should be easier to accomplish if they understand what the patient sees as beneficial. There are, of course, different definitions of benefit depending on who is defining it.

Finally, consider the principle of justice. How do administrators know if they are being fair and just to patients if they have no qualitative information or data? Patient satisfaction data and information from multiple sources help to assess fairness and assist in making any necessary policy and procedure changes that affect patient experiences and the bottom line.

■ PATIENT-CENTERED CARE AND ETHICS

Influences including access to information, an educated and involvement-oriented patient base, ACA implementation, and mandates from external agencies have created a new focus on **patient-centered care** in the U.S. healthcare system. Healthcare organizations including hospitals, clinics, and long-term care centers are reexamining their missions in light of this interest. In addition, owing to the fiscal implications of patient satisfaction and safety, there is an increased interest in patient-centered care. Should this interest be surprising? When HCAs give the matter some thought, they should surmise that all healthcare organizations should be patient centered. After all, if there were no patients, would there even be a need for healthcare facilities and professionals?

In today's healthcare world, the challenge is to provide patient-centered care, maintain a profit margin, and meet standards. For HCAs, this translates into a challenge to change a paternalistic environment into a patient-centric one. How does this action relate to ethics?

Fortunately, means to help HCAs find answers to this question have been developed, beginning with the **Planetree Model** (Frampton & Charmel, 2009). Elements of this model can also be found in later studies conducted by the Institute of Medicine on improving bedside care and suggestions for changing patient care (Steiger & Balog, 2010; Taylor & Rutherford, 2010).

The Planetree Model had its beginnings in the patient care experience of one woman, Angela Thieriot. Her hospital experience was one of "[a]lienation, fear, hopelessness, loneliness, and dehumanization" that led her to feel that "I would never get out alive" (Frampton & Charmel, 2009, p. xxviii). After this experience, Thieriot began extensive qualitative research through literature searches and interviews to determine what could make the patient's experience more humane and healing.

Through her research and experiences, Thieriot identified nine major areas to bring health care back to its roots of holistic patient-centered care. Using this information, she founded a nonprofit organization named Planetree in honor of Hippocrates. In 1985, Thieriot opened the first Planetree Model hospital unit with the assistance of the Kaiser Foundation and other grants (Frampton & Charmel, 2009). Physicians, nurses, and other staff participated in this unit and agreed to function within the Planetree philosophy. An architect also assisted in the physical design and created a space to provide patient-centered, holistic care.

Thieriot's original model has since evolved into a patient-focused care delivery plan that includes her nine key areas (Frampton & Charmel, 2009). These areas include a focus on human interactions, emphasis on information, inclusion of social support networks, and an emphasis on nutrition as part of healing. In addition, the Planetree Model addresses the spiritual needs of patients, includes integrative medicine as part of the healing process, and recognizes the role of the arts in healing. Finally, the model considers the environment and the community as part of the patient care experience. The following is a brief summary of these key areas.

Human interaction is a key area in the Planetree Model because it reflects the essence of the patient care experience. Patients admitted to the hospital enter an alien culture where someone can take away their life functions and dignity. They are expected to assume the compliant and noncomplaining sick role and behave in a way that is convenient for the caregiver. However, in the Planetree Model, human interaction involves the relationships between the practitioner and the patient, and between the practitioner and other practitioners. It should center on kindness, concern for patient needs and comfort, and inclusion of patients in their own care. Human interaction builds patient trust, and satisfaction increases when quality interaction occurs. In addition, even staff satisfaction increases because they make a difference for the patients and their families (Frampton & Charmel, 2009).

Providing health information has always been a focus of the Planetree Model. In fact, one of the first accomplishments of this model was the provision of information to patients who were often limited in their ability to obtain accurate and unbiased data about their own health. Today, with the increase in Internet usage, patients seem to be subject to information overload, yet there is still a need to have trustworthy sources. The Planetree Model includes a policy for open access to the patient chart. This is a way to inform patients about their treatment and status. While this feature of the model has been somewhat uncomfortable for staff, it increases trust. Some patients even add their own comments to the record. In addition, the Planetree Model suggests hourly nursing rounds—an action that provides for compassionate care and addressing patient concerns in a timely manner. It also increases efficiency and effectiveness because healthcare professionals can provide appropriate patient care before issues become problems.

The concept of a healing partnership is important in the Planetree Model. The family is part of the healing process in this model of patient-centered care. A family member does not always have to be a direct relative, but rather can be someone else who is important in the patient's life. Many Planetree strategies involve healing partners, including care partner programs and unrestricted visitation. Some facilities also choose to share clinical guidelines for treatment with these care partners. This action enables care partners to serve as an extra pair of eyes and alert the staff about potential problems. Facilities have also made room for family members by providing for overnight stays in the patient's room or at a nearby facility (Frampton & Charmel, 2009).

Food and nutrition are also part of the healing process in the Planetree Model. Diet ties into health outcomes and the model considers food service personnel to be caregivers. These staff members are empowered to assist in improving the patient experience with food and nutrition. The patient food experience includes having the correct menu items arrive at the correct temperature and at the correct time. Because food is more than just fuel, innovations such as pantries on nursing units, improved cafeteria design and service, nutrition education, and personalized menus have become part of this model. In addition, some facilities use aromatherapy by baking cookies or bread on the floor to decrease the "hospital smell" and increase the comfort level of the patients and their families (Frampton & Charmel, 2009).

The power of the spirit is also included in the Planetree Model. Despite the increase in double-blind studies focusing on the power of prayer and spirituality, many healthcare facilities still cling to the notion of separation of body and spirit. However, the Planetree Model agrees with Frankl and others that humans are more than their bodies. The model addresses the differences between religion and spirituality and includes both in patient-centered care. To implement this feature, Planetree-based facilities actively involve hospital chaplains, conduct spiritual assessments, provide counseling, and honor rituals. Some have included interfaith chapels where patients and their families can go for solitude and prayer. Where Native American healing traditions are part of the culture, Planetree facilities make efforts to respect and include these practices in healing (Frampton & Charmel, 2009).

In addition, the model acknowledges the benefits of integrative medicine. Therefore, Planetree facilities offer modalities such as massage, aromatherapy, and acupuncture as ways to personalize the hospital environment. For example, hospitals include infant massage programs and others even offer massage to employees. Including integrative medicine services leads to an improved patient care experience, which relates to improved healing and reduced length of stay (Frampton & Charmel, 2009).

The healing arts are also included in the Planetree Model as a holistic way to increase the patient experience. In modern times, Florence Nightingale endorsed the power of beauty as part of healing. The

Planetree Model reflects the importance of the arts when facilities select healing-support paintings and sculptures for public areas such as lobbies and activity rooms. In addition, some Planetree facilities allow patients to select art for their rooms from "art carts" or to participate in art therapy programs. Arts programs are not a negative for the bottom line of healthcare organizations because they often use volunteers. Most important, they provide a "time-out" from the stress of illness for patients and their families. Examples include artists-in-residence for the visual and music arts, concerts by local groups, pianos in the lobby, and portable DVD players (Frampton & Charmel, 2009).

Attention to the total healing environment is also a feature of Planetree Model facilities. Details in facility design and construction are not merely cosmetic; they are rooted in the concepts of holistic healing. Through careful choices in design, the hospital becomes a place where practitioners and patients work together for healing. The facility design makes this process easier and adds a more positive element to the patient care experience. The hospital becomes less sterile and foreboding and is instead perceived as a healing place. Attention to patient safety, noise controls, lighting, and use of space contribute to a design for patient-centered care. In addition, the Planetree Model addresses the idea of **way finding** so that patients, families, and visitors have a greater sense of control and less stress (Frampton & Charmel, 2009).

Finally, the Planetree Model includes an emphasis on healthy communities (Frampton & Charmel, 2009). It encourages organizations to address the biologic, social, intellectual, environmental, and spiritual health needs of the communities that they serve. Working to improve community health is not just an ethical thing to do; it has business benefits. First, if the organization is a nonprofit entity, it must demonstrate benefit to justify its tax-exempt status. Actively engaging in community health improvement can assist in this justification. Second, in this age of competition, healthcare organizations need to maintain a strong positive image in their communities. If organizations genuinely care about the health of the communities that they serve, their image can be enhanced if the community recognizes this orientation. Finally, it makes financial sense to improve the overall health of a community. Since healthcare resources are limited, it is a fiscally sound move to prevent as much illness as possible. Using community input and creativity, healthcare organizations can take the lead in improving the community's health.

Since its foundation in 1978, Planetree has grown into a national and international organization that works to assist healthcare organizations with their cultural change to patient-centered care. It collaborates with facilities including the Department of Veterans Affairs' Office of Patient-Centered Care and Transformation (Planetree Organization, n.d.). Using the nine components of the Planetree Model, this organization has established a program that awards the title of Planetree

Designated Hospital. To achieve this status, hospitals must go through a validation process that includes a self-assessment, site visits, reviews of measurement data, and focus groups with staff, patients, and families.

Hospitals that achieve the Planetree designation report a solid business case and potential for positive return on investment from this effort, particularly when the ramifications of the ACA are a business concern. Financial incentives and disincentives around patient satisfaction and safety make Planetree-type programs for patient-centered care more attractive from a business viewpoint. While these programs involve a leadership commitment, staff education, and improvements in communication, Planetree Designated Hospitals show higher than the CMS average rates in many areas of patient need; for example, they are rated higher in 9 of the 10 HCAHPS categories of patient satisfaction (Charmel, 2010).

Other healthcare facilities have developed their own models of patient-centered care and patient partnerships (Taylor & Rutherford, 2010). In these models, patients receive customized care, have open visitation from family members, and establish daily goals for their recovery. These models give patients greater control over their care through information, food choices, and patient-generated help codes. In some facilities, family members are included on hourly rounds and on change-of-shift reports.

■ THE ROLE OF THE HEALTHCARE ADMINISTRATOR

The cultural change required for patient-centered care to become the norm cannot be successful unless it receives the full support of healthcare administrators and their associates. Taylor and Rutherford (2010) suggest that HCAs' role is "to shape the views, perspectives, and behaviors of the individuals throughout the organization to achieve patient- and family centered care" (p. 3). Using the Institute of Medicine aims, the authors stress the need for care that is "(1) safe, (2) effective, (3) patient-centered, (4) timely, (5) efficient, and (6) equitable" (Taylor & Rutherford, 2010; p. 4). To meet these aims, healthcare administrators must become models for the process by partnering with patients and hearing their stories. They must be willing to shadow patients and take an active role in administrative rounds. Administrators should also encourage clinical and other staff to make changes that improve the patient experience. Data and observations about the patient experience should also be part of the change process.

Taylor and Rutherford (2010) and Steiger and Balog (2010) encourage healthcare administrators to use their commitment to ethics-based management and put the patient at the center of health care. This cultural change will also enhance business outcomes by providing quality care from the patient's viewpoint and increasing patient satisfaction. While the change to an increased focus on the patient requires additional effort from healthcare providers in times that are already challenging, it promises to create organizations that go beyond surviving and actually begin thriving. Such organizations will center on the real customer of health care—the patient. Putting the patient first is also an ethically sound practice because it respects the autonomy of patients, provides beneficent care, reduces harm, and treats each patient with justice.

Summary

This chapter describes the various views of the patient in a healthcare facility. At the negative end of the continuum, staff and administrators may see patients as whining interruptions to the flow of their day. If patients do not remain in a state of quiet suffering and cooperation, then they receive the label of noncompliant and staff may avoid them whenever possible. At the other end of the continuum, patients are viewed as partners in their own care. When this perspective is adopted, patients are included in care decisions whenever possible and have greater control over their circumstances and environment.

The healthcare administrator's role is essential to making a culture shift from professional-centered health care to patient-centered care. This role includes the measurement of patient satisfaction. Just like any other business, the healthcare organization needs information about what is working for patient care and what is not. It cannot improve the patient experience unless it knows what that experience is. Therefore, it makes good business and ethical sense for healthcare administrators to acquire as much accurate data about patient care experiences as possible. However, just collecting data is not enough. Healthcare administrators have to determine the best way to use these data for ongoing improvement of practices in patient-centered care. Failure to use the data collected creates an ethics issue of wasting funds for useless surveys that could otherwise be applied for patient, employee, or business benefit.

Issues on financial, staffing, technology, regulatory, and consumer fronts all challenge the healthcare organization of today. If it is to remain competitive and fiscally sound, the organization must put greater emphasis on its mission of patient care. This will require healthcare administrators to work toward a shared vision, provide hands-on leadership, and practice excellent communication skills. They must also show the creativity necessary to move beyond what is to what should be. Not only will these challenges require greater leadership skills, but they will also create ethics challenges. In times of change, healthcare leadership requires a solid core of ethics coupled with a vision to guide healthcare facilities that put the patient first.

Cases for Your Consideration

The Case of Kelly Beth's Mother

Think about the chapter information and consider the following questions. Sample responses and commentary follow the case.

1. Which factors contributed to Kelly Beth and Caitlin's experience?
2. Which ethics principles does this case illustrate?
3. If you were the administrator at Dagma Memorial Hospital, how would you handle this situation?

Case Information

Caitlin brought her three-year-old daughter Kelly Beth O'Brian into the emergency department (ED) at Dagma Memorial Hospital (DMH). Radiographs revealed a lateral fracture of the left femur that would require several weeks of traction before the application of a cast. Naturally, Caitlin was beside herself with worry. The information about Kelly Beth's prognosis and treatment was frightening in itself, but she had other troubling concerns. Caitlin was a single mother who needed to keep her job to support her family. She knew that her employer did not allow any time off for family illness, and she had no one to help her with this situation. What was she going to do?

Somehow, Caitlin worked out a schedule that allowed her to spend maximum time with her daughter. She went to the hospital early enough in the morning so that Kelly saw her when she woke up. She took her lunch hour to check on her daughter and returned immediately after work. At night, she left only when Kelly was asleep. This schedule became a way of life and, although exhausting, helped Caitlin to keep her job and be there for her daughter.

Several days into this routine, Caitlin arrived at the hospital a little late, after personnel had served lunch. When she kissed Kelly Beth and adjusted her bed, she found that Kelly was lying in food. It was in her hair, which was matted and filthy. When she asked Kelly Beth about this, the child said, "Mommy, I tried to eat my lunch but it was too high and everything kept falling," and then she began to cry.

Of course, Caitlin was extremely concerned about this event. Therefore, after comforting her daughter, she went to speak to the nurses. Although she was upset about her daughter's treatment, she made a conscious effort to control her feelings and speak calmly. The nurse who responded to her said, "We don't have time to feed your child; that is your job. If you are not here, we just leave the tray. You are also responsible for washing your own child's hair. You should bring the supplies and figure out how to do it. That's what good mothers do."

Caitlin was stunned. Not only was this a rude response, but no one had told her about all of these rules. She knew she was being a good mother by juggling her schedule to be present at every possible moment, but now the nurse accused her of neglect. She just assumed that because nutrition was important to Kelly Beth's healing, someone would make sure that the child could eat. She also assumed that the nursing staff would help to maintain hygiene as well as changing the sheets. How was she supposed to know that her assumptions were wrong? Caitlin called one of her nurse friends to find out which supplies she needed to wash Kelly Beth's hair. She also made sure that she never missed a meal again to ensure that her daughter did not go hungry.

After Kelly Beth's discharge in her body cast, Caitlin had mixed feelings about DMH. While she was pleased with the technical care her daughter received there, she was not at all happy with the quality of the support care. In fact, she considered sending DMH a bill for patient care services.

Responses and Commentary on Questions

1. Which factors contributed to Kelly Beth and Caitlin's experience?

   In this case, consider the situation from two viewpoints. First, consider what was happening for Kelly Beth and Caitlin. Kelly Beth was only three years old and had no experience with what she was supposed to do in a hospital. Her mother had not arrived yet and she was hungry. Being a resourceful child, she tried to feed herself but because she was so little, and in traction, her efforts created a mess. Had she been an adult or even an older child, she might have known to ring the call button and get help. However, the nurses had not taught her how to do this.

   Imagine Caitlin's experience. She was trying her best to be there for her daughter and to keep her job so she could pay her bills. She happened to be a bit late for the lunch service and found her daughter lying in her lunch. When she inquired about the situation, she received a rude response that increased her "mother guilt." Now she felt like everyone knew the rules but her. While she was annoyed at the nursing staff, on some level she felt guilty because she was not holding up her part of the care burden. She did not know this was her role in the process. She even made the effort to learn how to wash her daughter's hair. Once her daughter was recovering at home, she became angry at the lack of support from those whom she trusted with the care of the most precious one in her life. She wanted to do something about this but felt that nothing she could do would make a difference.

   How did the staff view this situation? The nursing staff felt overwhelmed by the serious tasks of caring for ill children. They had to complete all of the physician's orders, document their notes on the computer, and take care of their own sanity. There was no room for "patient-centered care"; they needed to get tasks done. Here was a "Nervous Nelly" mother who was complaining about food in her child's hair and one missed lunch. The nurses thought somebody should tell Caitlin how she was supposed to take care of her own daughter, and one of the nurses did just that.

There might been some other messages going on in the nurse's response. Because she had "seen it all," she might have assumed that Caitlin was just another one of those uncaring mothers who are not at their children's bedside. After all, how important could Kelly Beth be to this woman if she just popped in and out all day? If she really cared so much, she would take off from work and be there 24/7 for her daughter. The nurse had no idea about the difficulty of Caitlin's situation. Perhaps the nurse just assumed that good mothers were with their children in the hospital at all times.

Regardless of the view, there was a serious lack of communication and beneficence in this situation. Rules regarding the responsibilities for Caitlin and the nursing staff may have existed, but Caitlin had no knowledge of them. In addition, there were no simple acts of kindness. All the nurse had to do was to explain the rules to Caitlin in a nonjudgmental way. She could have taken a brief moment to instruct Caitlin on how to care for her daughter's needs and which supplies she needed to purchase. With even greater compassion, she could have assisted with the first shampooing of the child's hair with the understanding that Caitlin was responsible for this care in the future. Such an action would have led to a much different patient care experience for both Kelly Beth and Caitlin.

2. Which ethics principles does this case illustrate?

It is easy to see issues with all of the major principles of ethics in this case. First, consider the idea of nonmaleficence. The hospital staff's obligation in treating Kelly Beth was to do no harm. Certainly, a missed meal and dirty hair were not as harmful as a medical error, but the lack of attention to the needs of the child and mother did cause some damage. Kelly Beth suffered by not being able to feed herself and making a mess. She was worried because her mother was late. She was also hungry. None of this enhanced her ability to heal.

When a child is the patient, the family is also part of the picture. Did the staff cause harm to Caitlin? Again, this is a matter of degree. While no physical harm occurred, the response to her questions caused psychological damage to the conscientious mother. The tone of the nurse's message implied that Caitlin was not following the rules and, therefore, was not being a good mother. Perhaps the harm was not intentional, but certainly Caitlin was emotionally and spiritually harmed.

How does the sister principle of beneficence fit here? Did the staff act with kindness and compassion in this situation? Obviously, they did not. It is true that they were extraordinarily busy, but placing a lunch tray where a three-year-old child in traction has to struggle to reach it borders on cruelty. In addition, the staff nurse's actions toward Caitlin did not even resemble beneficence or respect for her autonomy. The nurse might have been acting from "compassion fatigue" and not from a lack of kindness, but the effect was certainly negative.

There was also a violation of justice in this situation because the hospital experience did not provide appropriate care in the views of both mother and daughter. It was unjust to expect a parent to care for her child's hygiene when she received no information about her responsibilities or education on how to act on them. In addition, the staff left a little girl alone to feed herself, just because her harried mother was late. She did not deserve this treatment; she was only three years old.

3. If you were the administrator at Dagma Memorial Hospital, how would you handle this situation?

This seems like a facility that could benefit from the Planetree Model or other patient-centered care education and from some lessons in communication. The HCA has the obligation to consider this situation from both sides before taking action to prevent further incidents of this kind. In addition, gathering information for process improvement requires that the HCA look at all aspects of the situation.

What could you as a healthcare administrator have done to increase Caitlin and Kelly Beth's comfort level within the alien culture of DMH? As a first step, it might be helpful to include both written and oral communication about the expectations and responsibilities of staff and parents when admitting a child to the facility. For better communication, a brief conference might be coupled with an appropriate handout or pamphlet to assure that understanding is present.

You could also employ the principles of the Planetree Model to learn more about Caitlin's experience and her struggle to meet her daughter's needs before passing judgment. After assessing the situation, you could try to provide appropriate support services. To do this, you could involve social services, pastoral care, or even a family support group. Perhaps there is a way to provide respite services for Caitlin when she has to be late and nursing services are too busy. The Planetree Model and other patient-centered efforts include volunteer care partners for patients who are alone. Perhaps this option could be adapted to Caitlin's situation. The driver for your efforts would be to secure the best healing environment for Kelly Beth.

The nontangibles offered through the Planetree Model would also have enhanced this patient-care experience for mother and daughter. Kelly Beth and Caitlin needed a mechanism for asking questions and voicing needs without fear of staff retaliation. For example, showing Kelly Beth how and when to use the call button would have made a major difference in her care experience. It could also alter her mother's negative perception of the facility.

Other nontangibles like spirituality, touch, and the healing arts could be useful in improving this care experience. Perhaps the use of some integrative medicine such as pet therapy or aromatherapy would improve Kelly Beth's healing process. Other healing arts like storytellers, clowns, or play therapy might also decrease Kelly Beth's discomfort and assist in her healing.

In considering the patient's viewpoint, you must also include the Planetree Model's emphasis on empowering the patient. There might have been a different outcome had Caitlin been educated about the rights and responsibilities of a parent of a hospitalized child. The lack of education and good communication meant that Caitlin left the facility with a deep resentment of DMH's treatment of both daughter and mother. She felt that the treatment of her child showed indifference and disrespect when she deserved so much better. Unless the facility provided a mechanism for listening to Caitlin's concerns, there was a high potential that she would voice her negative impressions to the outside community.

Consider the staff in your decision making. Surely, their intent was not to cause harm to a helpless three-year-old. However, they may have been in a situation that stretched them beyond their limits, such that compassion fatigue became normal. Planetree principles, which also apply to staff, might have been useful in preventing this situation. The model stresses the way staff are treated and the way that they treat one another. For example, employees need to receive care and support, just as the patients do. This might be as simple as increasing the number of volunteers so that "extra hands" are available during busy patient care times. Caring for staff might include creating a physical environment that supports their health along with that of the patient. The model also includes areas where staff can go to regenerate their spirit and enjoy a respite.

Healthcare professionals need to understand that they are valued and respected. The Planetree Model stresses that staff members also have a need for touch and a spiritual connection. As a way to demonstrate this, you could listen to clinical staff and determine the best way to relieve their stress. For example, staff members can enjoy the same music and art that you provide for patient healing.

Finally, good staff–patient communication cannot be overemphasized. You could begin this process by conducting a policy audit regarding proper communication methods. Perhaps it is time for a change or reinterpretation. If the policy is appropriate, you need to stress the ethical principle of "first do no harm" as part of patient communications. Acting with kindness and compassion could also go a long way toward preventing situations like that faced by Caitlin in the future. In other words, the same message conveyed with empathy might have had a very different result.

The Case of the Ardent Administrator

Think about the chapter information and consider the following questions. Sample responses and commentary follow the case.

1. Why did Dorothy Dee find the Planetree Model attractive for implementation at DMH?

2. What was the CEO's reaction to Dorothy's proposal?

3. Which ethical principles were involved in the implementation decision?

Case Information

Dorothy Dee, RN and vice president of nursing services at Dagma Memorial Hospital (DMH), read something extraordinary in her latest nursing journal. A hospital had adopted something called the Planetree Model, where patients were the center of its business. Dorothy read, at first with disbelief, about the changes this facility made based on the principles of the model. After reading about a hospital where there was patient-centered care and an environment dedicated to healing, she wondered how the organization was able to make such a complete change.

Becoming more curious, she found the facility's website and located the name and number of her counterpart who wrote the article. She called and had a long conversation about the accomplishment of the Planetree effort. She also learned that workshops were available at the Planetree Annual Conference. There were even manuals to assist organizations that wanted to try this patient-centered model. Dorothy wanted to know more, including whether this model might work for DMH.

Fortunately, she had a chief executive officer (CEO), Christopher Higgins, who was open-minded. In fact, he prided himself on being community centered and patient centered. When Dorothy told him about the Planetree Model and the documented increase in patient satisfaction scores and employee retention rates, he agreed to support her attendance at the conference and workshops.

Dorothy was amazed at what she learned at the workshop sessions. She purchased the manuals and stayed up many nights reading them. She began to consider how to use the model to make DMH a more patient-friendly environment and one that would enhance healing. Because this model made sense to her on many levels, she used her nights and weekends to develop a proposal for submission to Mr. Higgins. It included everything from changing the color of the wall paint to different modes of lighting. There were ideas for integrating music and art throughout the facility. She even had a plan to update the nursery using local art talent and staff assistance. She researched the budget to make these changes and attached it to her proposal. True, her plan included some costs, but they seemed minimal when compared to the potential benefits.

Dorothy submitted her ideas to Mr. Higgins and made an appointment to discuss the document. Because she knew about his history of innovation and community service, she had high hopes that he would accept her ideas. Mr. Higgins told her that he had read the proposal carefully and that it did contain some promising ideas. However, it was just too radical and he worried about the reaction of the physicians and other staff. This much change might just be too much for DMH.

Dorothy was disappointed but, having learned to have a Plan B, she asked if she could take alternative action. What if she put together a team and created a feasibility study using the short-stay unit only? She would keep the budget to bare bones and provide documentation that the changes produced a positive result. Would Mr. Higgins "green light" such an effort?

Knowing that Dorothy had the knowledge and skills to deliver on her plan, Mr. Higgins consented. She assembled a team, making sure to include a physician champion. Other members included representatives from housekeeping, materials management, dietary, nursing, patient services, and other involved staff. After providing an information session, she said, "What if we changed the short-stay unit into a patient-centered environment? What would it be like?"

The group became enthusiastic about the chance to change things for the better. They came up with a way to get the rooms painted, add bedspreads and drapes to each room, and even provided aromatherapy by having cookies baked on the floor on Friday afternoons. The team asked local artists to donate healing art for the halls. The biggest change was in the family waiting room. It now housed a small resource center with a computer, a fish tank, and plants. It also included a "Kids Nook" with bright-colored walls and children-sized furniture. With the team's support, the transformation was nothing short of amazing and was finished on a very limited budget.

Almost immediately, Dorothy noticed a change in the routine of the short-stay unit. Patients appreciated the nonhospital environment. Instead of being negative about the change, staff seemed to embrace it and want it to work. Their attitude seemed to be more positive with patients and each other. In fact, they seemed to want to be scheduled for short-stay rather than traditional floors. Family members were also pleased to be able to learn more about how to care for their loved ones through the computer programs offered in the waiting room. The children used their own area and were less of a distraction.

Somehow, the local paper found out about this patient-centered care effort and featured Mr. Higgins in an article as a community-caring administrator. The print article sparked the interest of the local TV station, which ran a human-interest piece. It gave DMH the title of "A Hospital That Cares." Mr. Higgins was so pleased with the results that he gave the "green light" to Dorothy's next innovation idea. Onward to the nursery and bunnies on the walls!

Responses and Commentary on Questions

1. Why did Dorothy Dee find the Planetree Model attractive for implementation at DMH?

   The first question to ask is why Dorothy chose nursing as her profession. Even in her student days, she wanted to make a difference in the health of her patients. She understood that healing was a process that occurred between the patient and the professional. Her current position at DMH seemed so far removed from her original vision of nursing. She struggled with scheduling, TJC reports, staff complaints, physician complaints, and community issues. Where was the healing environment she had hoped to create? She was experiencing quiet discontent when she found the journal article about Planetree and its philosophy.

   Being a realist, she knew that this would be a major change for the physicians, her nursing staff, and the other professionals. Yet she believed that if she were able to communicate the model well enough, most of the professionals would at least want to try it. She knew that patients and their families would appreciate respectful treatment and the ability to be part of their own care decisions.

While Mr. Higgins did not accept her initial proposal because it was too far reaching, tackling the change in small steps and demonstrating positive results seemed to work. Her data showed that staff morale increased, as did patient satisfaction. An added bonus came when the press and TV media found the change newsworthy. DMH received priceless marketing through its improved community image.

2. What was the CEO's reaction to Dorothy's proposal?

Mr. Higgins's response was almost predictable. Although Dorothy had done a good job in showing cost-effectiveness for the change, Mr. Higgins had to consider the political elements. The last thing he wanted was a revolt because staff members had to move too far from their comfort zones. He also worried that if the physicians were not supportive of this radical change to patient-centered care, a disaster might result.

Still, the idea had merit. Therefore, when Dorothy asked to pilot a more limited version of the Planetree Model with a fixed budget, he gave it the green light. As it turned out, she was right. The staff seemed to rally around the project, and the patients and their families were full of praise for it. The press coverage was excellent and several board members called to congratulate Mr. Higgins on his foresight.

3. Which ethical principles were involved in the implementation decision?

There are many ethical principles at work here. From the patient side, autonomy is central to the entire Planetree Model. When DMH made its changes, patients received treatment as valued individuals instead of as noncompliant nuisances. As a result, there were actually fewer patient complaints on the unit. Certainly one can see beneficence and the sister principle, nonmaleficence at work in this model. Everything from the physical environment to the staff interactions demonstrated the ability to provide compassionate care that produced an optimal healing environment.

This model also provided justice both for staff and patients. While improving the physical environment for the patients was a clear goal, the process and the results improved the environment for the staff as well. They were enthusiastic about work again because they were engaged in a process that respected their knowledge and allowed them to make a visible difference. In fact, the short-stay unit became the place to be among the hospital staff. Dorothy felt certain she would have their support for other Planetree-type changes.

Web Resources

Institute of Medicine
http://iom.edu/

Planetree Organization
http://www.planetree.org/

References

Charmel, P. A. (2010). Defining and evaluating excellence in patient-centered care. *Frontiers of Health Services Management, 26*(4), 27–34.

Consumer Reports. (2009, August). 5 common fears about health reform. Retrieved from http://www.consumerreports.org/cro/magazine-archive/august-2009/viewpoint/5-common-fears-about-health-reform/reform-5-common-fears.htm

Frampton, S. B., & Charmel, P. A. (2009). *Putting patients first: Best practices in patient-centered care* (2nd ed.). San Francisco, CA: Jossey-Bass.

Micozzi, M. S. (Ed.). (2011). *Fundamentals of complementary and alternative medicine* (4th ed.). Atlanta, GA: Elsevier.

Office of Disease Prevention and Health Promotion. (n.d.) *Quick guide to health literacy* [Fact sheet]. Retrieved from Retrieved from http://www.health.gov/communication/literacy/quickguide/default

Planetree Organization. (n.d.). *About us* [Fact sheet]. Retrieved from http://planetree.org/about-planetree/

Press, I. (2002). *Patient satisfaction: Defining, measuring, and improving the experience of care*. Chicago, IL: Health Administration Press.

Roizen, M. F., & Oz, M. C. (2006). *You the smart patient: An insider's handbook for getting the best treatment*. New York, NY: Free Press.

Shi, L., & Singh, D. A. (2015). *Delivering health care in America: A systems approach* (6th ed.). Burlington, MA: Jones & Bartlett Learning.

Steiger, N. J., & Balog, A. (2010). Realizing patient-centered care: Putting patients in the center, not the middle. *Frontiers of Health Services Management, 26*(4), 15–26.

Sultz, H. A., & Young, K. M. (2014). *Health care USA*. Burlington, MA: Jones & Bartlett Learning.

Taylor, J., & Rutherford, P. (2010). The pursuit of genuine partnerships with patients and family members: The challenge and opportunity for executive leaders. *Frontiers of Health Services Management, 26*(4), 3–14.

CHAPTER
13

Public Health and Ethics

What is the ethical basis for the public health system?

Points to Ponder

1. What is the relationship between public health and individual health?
2. How does the ethics foundation of public health differ from that of clinical medicine?
3. Which ethics issues do public health administrators face?
4. How does the ACA affect public health?

Key Terms

The following are this chapter's key terms. Look for them in bold.

bioterrorism
disease surveillance
environmental specialists
epidemiologists
health disparities
health educators

Healthy People 2020
mortality rates
public health
public health administrators
social beneficence

■ INTRODUCTION AND DEFINITIONS

Public health has many definitions depending on one's view. Winslow created the classic definition of public health in 1923, which included "preventing disease, prolonging life, and promoting physical health through organized community efforts" (as cited in Schneider, 2000, p. 5). According to Turnock (2012), public health is a healthcare system that uses an interdisciplinary approach to address the health of populations in positive ways. It is also can be defined as the profession that deals with population health. Others define public health as a set of activities such as immunization clinics, water treatment, restaurant inspection, and epidemiological studies. These activities often require community action, so public health is also political and involves local, state, and national government. Public health can be perceived as a form of warfare as well (Bernheim, Childress, Bonnie, & Melnick, 2015) because its systems and personnel fight against factors that lead to disease and premature death. For example, when contagious diseases threaten populations, public health systems and personnel lead the effort to contain factors that contribute to the spread of disease.

When considering the system of public health, one can begin with its mission and functions. The Institute of Medicine offers a definition of public health's mission that includes "The science and art of preventing disease, prolonging life, and promoting health and efficiency through organized community effort" (as cited in Turnock, 2012, p. 10). This broad definition of its mission provides an understanding of the scope and functions of the public health system. Within the mission is an expanding agenda that goes beyond prevention of the flu or food poisoning. Today, for example, public health is involved in preventing **bioterrorism** and population health issues such as teen pregnancy, epidemics of violence, and mental health.

Public health differs from clinical medicine in that it bases its goals on population health and not on individual health. Brülde (as cited in Dawson, 2011) explains these goals by dividing them into priority areas. For example, a goal of public health is to "improve the average level of health" (p. 21), which includes benefits both for individuals and for the population as a whole. For example, if large-enough groups of individuals chose to reduce their processed-food intake, their decision would lead to improvement in the population's health. Other goals for public health involve reducing health inequities, promoting health practices, and prolonging life through disease and injury prevention.

Because of these goals, the scope of practice for public health is extensive and engages local, state, and federal resources. In addition, these goals require partnerships with clinical medicine, healthcare facilities, laboratories, epidemiologists, schools, and businesses. Public health functions include **disease surveillance**; screening, testing, and contact investigation; immunization; and communicable disease investigation and control. Its functions also include health communication through means including mass media, and development and implementation of a variety of environmental policies and practices. In fact, public health touches the lives of all Americans in ways that often go unnoticed. For example, people assume that their water, food, and housing are safe: They can thank the public health system and its employees for making this assumption a valid one.

The public health system also requires organizations, each with its own structures and purposes, to accomplish its purposes. Typically, the community views public health as the local health department, which is responsible for functions such as immunizations and restaurant, swimming pool, and water treatment inspections. However, public health organizations also include state departments of health, which are responsible for planning and carrying out programs that protect and promote the health of a state's citizens. In addition, multitudes of federal organizations—such as the Institutes of Medicine, Centers for Disease Control and Prevention, Food and Drug Administration, and Homeland Security Agency—have a role in protecting and promoting the health of Americans. While government agencies are major players in public health, one should not ignore the efforts of voluntary organizations such as the Red Cross, Catholic Charities, and the United Way. When considering the scope of the mission of public health and the organizations that play a role in its mission, it is easy to see that everyone has the potential to interact with and benefit from public health organizations.

By examining the variables that contribute to the health and well-being of individuals and communities, Turnock (2012) demonstrates public health's value. For example, public health efforts account for 25 of the 30 years by which life expectancy increased from 1900 to the present. Specifically, this increase in longevity is a result of prevention of infectious diseases and improvements in sanitation. In addition, public health campaigns geared toward the prevention, control, and treatment of polio, smallpox, measles, and whooping cough have greatly reduced infant and child **mortality rates**. Recent public health achievements that contribute to the public's health include safer workplaces, use of seat belts, safer foods, fluoridated drinking water, and anti-tobacco campaigns. While public health has much more to accomplish in terms of reducing **health disparities** and improving overall health, it also has demonstrated the worth of its efforts through better health and longer lives for Americans.

■ PUBLIC HEALTH PROFESSIONALS

Public health requires a workforce of professionals who are both multidisciplinary and highly skilled. Turnock (2012) estimates that more than 586,000 people work in the public health sector, representing more than 30 different job categories. Professionals in the public health workforce have education both in their areas of specialty and in public health. They may be nurses, physicians, pharmacists, or laboratory personnel. In addition to their professional education, they receive additional training that fits their positions in the public health system. For example, they may be educated in essential public health services such as developing regulations, coordinating services, monitoring health status, and promoting healthy behaviors. There are also professionals whose education and experience is unique to the public health arena. Examples of these professionals include epidemiologists, environmental specialists, health educators, and public health administrators.

Epidemiologists work in both state and federal public health organizations and study the origin and spread of disease. These public health "detectives" are valued for their research skills and for their fieldwork during epidemics. They collect information from the environment and from those persons affected to determine the source of the outbreak. This information assists the public health team in controlling or eliminating the source of the epidemic. Epidemiologists are scientists and have a master's degree in public health. Many of them also have a PhD or MD (Bureau of Labor Statistics, 2012a).

Environmental specialists work to protect the public from hazards caused by natural and human-created environments. Using their backgrounds in biology, chemistry, or hydrology, these specialists collect and analyze samples from food, water, air, and soil to determine the presence of health hazards. They also measure the impact of industry on the environment and create plans to address current or potential health problems (Bureau of Labor Statistics, 2012b).

Health educators serve a major role in addressing the core functions of public health for the community and individuals (Turnock, 2012). They are educated in schools of public health and similar programs, and design and implement programs to promote healthy behaviors and respond to health threats from disasters and epidemics. In addition, these educators conduct needs assessments, plan community and school health programs, and evaluate the effectiveness of educational efforts. Health educators now have the opportunity for certification based on national standards and can become a Certified Health Education Specialist (CHES) or Master Certified Health Education Specialist (MCHES). The basis for certification is national standards and a rigorous examination process (National Commission for Health Education Credentialing, 2008).

Public health administrators (PHAs) must be able to work in both government and private organizations and manage a divergent workforce. Because their budgets are often limited and influenced by political considerations, they must have a vision for health improvement and provide efficiency and effectiveness in organizational management. Therefore, their education goes beyond management science to include an understanding of the functions of the public health system and the various roles filled by the public health workforce. Public health administrators share some of the same ethical challenges as their traditional healthcare system counterparts, but also face some unique issues.

■ PUBLIC HEALTH AND *HEALTHY PEOPLE 2020*

A discussion of the background of public health and its ethics issues would not be complete without an introduction to *Healthy People 2020*. This document serves as a model for public health planning and programming in both federal and state settings. Its history began in the 1970s with the efforts of the U.S. Surgeon General to assess the status of the U.S. population and mechanisms for health improvement (Turnock, 2012). The foundation of *Healthy People 2020* is the goals and assessment data from the earlier versions of this program, *Healthy People 2000* and *Healthy People 2010*.

The *Healthy People 2020* document forms the basis for health improvement in the United States through national healthcare objectives. Its goals and objectives drive policies and interventions that address health issues in the physical, social, and individual environment. The *Healthy People 2020* plan has several main goals, including those that address preventable disease and premature death. In addition, it seeks to improve the health of all Americans by eliminating healthcare disparities. The plan is to measure progress toward meeting these goals by measuring 38 focus areas such as oral health, obesity, tobacco use, immunizations, injury and violence, environmental health, and access to healthcare services (Turnock, 2012). Bernheim, Childress, Bonnie, and Melnick (2015) stress that public health deals with healthcare problems that require ethics decision-making and long-term commitments. They cite *Healthy People 2020* as an example of this type of commitment.

■ ETHICS AND PUBLIC HEALTH

Dawson (2011) makes a case that the ethics thinking for clinical medicine is not adequate for public health. His premise is that the very nature of public health presents different moral theory and practice issues from those evident in the traditional healthcare system. The work of public health is population based and seeks to prevent—not cure—disease. It also requires collective effort facilitated by the public health workforce. Each of these elements of public health poses different ethical issues from those found in traditional medicine. For example, efforts to prevent disease require health promotion and health education. These efforts may increase anxiety for individuals. While this increased anxiety can be harmful, public health officials must weigh these risks against the potential harm to a population if there is no prevention of a disease.

Because of the nature of public health, Dawson (2011) begins his theory of ethics by identifying the population, and not the individual, as the primary value. Community- or population-based ethics requires what Dawson calls "an approach to ethics based around a substantive notion of the good" (p. 13). The ethics of public health includes ideas of consequentialism, based on goodness of outcomes rather than goodness of intentions. For public health, goodness is concerned with the effort to improve health and prolong life.

Dawson (2011) also explains that social justice forms the foundation for public health activities. For example, healthcare inequalities among populations cause harm to both the population as a whole and individuals within that population. Justice would require that public health workers make every effort to decrease inequities and increase access to health care. However, for public health entities to achieve such a goal, individuals may have to give up some of their autonomy. For example, when federal or state governments require immunizations, they impede the autonomy of individuals. However, this imposition can lead to the higher good of protection against a disease or condition for populations in the community, state, or nation.

Bernheim, Childress, Bonnie, and Melnick (2015) also present a foundation for ethics in public health. They stress the prevalent considerations for moral actions in public health. Examples of these considerations include trust, benefit, harm, privacy, and promise keeping. Bernheim et al. use the theory of utilitarianism as a basis for their ethical framework of public health. For example, public health officials must consider appropriate actions to provide the greatest good for the greatest number or to prevent the greatest harm. In addition, public health professionals must base their policies on cost/benefit and cost-effectiveness analyses that incorporate quality of life, risks, and benefits into the evaluations. This is especially true when budgets are limited and demand for services is high. Bernheim et al. even provide a triage model to assist healthcare professionals in making ethics-based decisions for the allocation of scarce medical resources.

Bernheim et al. (2015) also discuss the idea of justice as part of the ethical foundation for public health. These authors consider justice to be a significant principle in public health ethics and explain why a primary goal of public health is not just health care. Distributive justice—the way in which healthcare is provided by a society—is also important to public health, particularly because it deals with persons who are vulnerable or disadvantaged. The authors present various views of justice in their discussion of this element of ethics. For example, Bernheim et al. cite John Rawls' ideas about the justice of fairness and the duty of the society to remove obstacles for opportunity. These concepts are especially important in public health care because many of the populations served are in a lesser position where healthcare access is concerned.

Principles of Ethics in Public Health

The foundation of public health ethics also includes the principles of autonomy, beneficence, and nonmaleficence. Perhaps the most obvious of these three principles is the concern for individual autonomy as it relates to the health of the population or community. When a health crisis exists or when there is a need to prevent a disease or disability, conflicts may arise between public health action and individual autonomy. For example, when dealing with communicable diseases, public health officials may have to violate an individual's right to confidentiality or even the individual's civil rights. While public health avoids such violations whenever possible, it may be necessary to make trade-offs between the rights of the individual and the protection of the community itself. In addition, there may be a violation of individual autonomy when someone's personal values conflict with the benefit of a choice for the society as a whole. An example of this trade-off of autonomy exists when parents do not believe in immunizations, but are required to have their children immunized before enrolling them in school.

Other issues related to autonomy also exist in public health practice. For example, public health organizations have a duty to protect the privacy of those who utilize their services. This includes ensuring the privacy of information, which in the case of public health can be very sensitive. Agencies must also be careful to violate patients' privacy only when it is necessary for the safety of the population or community. For example, when public health professionals need to collect data on the community's health or to investigate reportable communicable diseases, they must do so in ways that protect individuals' privacy as much as possible. Public health organizations, like organizations in the traditional healthcare system, must also respect autonomy by protecting confidentiality in accordance with HIPAA and policy. Nevertheless, if necessary to protect the health of the community, public health personnel may violate their confidential relationship in cases of reportable diseases and conditions. Examples of legal requirements to report include those applying to wounds caused by firearms, alleged child abuse, and certain contagious diseases (Bernheim et al., 2015).

The principle of nonmaleficence is also a foundation and critical concern for public health actions (Turnock, 2012). It encompasses the entire scope of the public health system, with its mission to prevent disease and to promote health for populations and communities. The consideration of "first do no harm" is an integral part of the entire public health system. For example, when public health efforts attempt to control communicable diseases and address health disparities, the intent is to reduce the harm experienced by both individuals and populations. Efforts to provide safer and healthier foods, prenatal care, health education, and environmental services all have an intention of eliminating or reducing harm.

As a sister principle to nonmaleficence, beneficence is applied to the ethics foundation of public health as well. **Social beneficence** in public health has its roots in the ideal that well-being is morally important and people should have the ability to seek it. Capability theory (Robeyns, 2011) seeks to define the abilities necessary for individuals and populations to avoid poverty and deprivation and achieve well being. Nussbaum (as cited in Robeyns, 2011) describes 10 basic human abilities, which she terms capabilities: "life; bodily health; bodily integrity; senses, imagination and thought; emotions; practical reason; affiliation; other species; play; and control over one's environment" (p. 15). Social beneficence creates a duty for public health organizations and systems to do whatever they can to create opportunities for people to achieve well being. This duty influences public health programs at the local, state, national, and international levels. It includes efforts to collect data, design programs, engage staff and other resources, evaluate existing programs, and create new ones. The emphasis is on eliminating or diminishing areas that inhibit individuals and population from achieving the highest possible quality of life.

Public Health Code of Ethics

The mission of public health is multifaceted and includes protecting and promoting community health, preventing disease, and improving health status for everyone (Turnock, 2012). In addition, these principles stress confidentiality, professional competence, collaboration, and effective use of resources. Public health affects every American from the beginning of life through the end of life. When one considers all of the functions of the public health system and its scope, it is easy to see that this part of the healthcare system faces a variety of ethical issues. In addition, public health professionals serve a multitude of functions in a system that has its place in social justice, but whose reality is characterized by scarce resources and multiple demands. Therefore, public health requires a unique code of ethics to guide its mission and the professionals who serve as its workforce. A group representing multiple professions within the discipline directed the publication of the most recent public health code of ethics (Bernheim at al., 2015).

Of particular interest to public health administrators is the basis for action identified by the Public Health Leadership Society (2002). It stresses that healthcare professionals, including administrators, have a duty to improve their understanding of health issues and the knowledge base needed for effective policymaking. In addition, they are required to use the scientific method, including all of its qualitative and quantitative tools, to provide the best solutions to health problems and disparities. Healthcare professionals must be careful not to take action unless adequate information is available that supports their action. In addition, their actions must respect the dignity of human beings. To meet this standard, public health administrators must balance cost-effectiveness with respect for humanity.

The code of ethics for public health also clarifies ethics standards and responsibilities for public health professionals. Not only do these principles serve as a guide for action by health professionals, but they also link to the essential functions of public health itself. For example, a function of public health is to "research for new insights and innovative solutions to health problems" (Public Health Leadership Society, 2002, p. 9). Items in the public health code of ethics related to providing communities with information and respecting confidentiality form a link to this function.

■ PUBLIC HEALTH AND THE ACA

The ACA does not ignore public health. Changes related to the federal public health system and functions are included under the category of prevention/wellness. The ACA calls for creation of a National Prevention, Health Promotion, and Public Health Council that will coordinate federal efforts in areas of prevention and wellness (Kaiser Family Foundation, 2013). The National Prevention Strategy created by leaders of 17 federal agencies under the aegis of the National Prevention Council provides guidelines and mechanisms for working with the private sector on critical public health issues. These issues include "tobacco-free living, preventing drug abuse and excessive alcohol use, healthy eating, active living, injury and violence free living, reproductive and sexual health, and mental and emotional well-being" (Bernstein et al., 2015, p. 77). The efforts of the National Prevention Strategy, in conjunction with *Healthy People 2020*, could produce improvements in the overall quality of life for Americans, thereby reducing overall health costs in the United States.

Summary

The public health system and its professionals have long been involved in improving the health of Americans through organized efforts for disease prevention, environmental improvements, and early diagnosis and treatment of disease. In fact, many of the health improvements achieved by Americans over the last 100 years largely stem from public health efforts. In the ACA era, there is new emphasis on the idea of "population health." This term has been part of the vocabulary in public health system since its inception. However, in public health, there is an emphasis on community efforts for prevention and treatment, rather an exclusive focus on the individual. This makes public health different from clinical medicine and changes its ethical foundations.

Because of the nature of public health, its ethics foundation draws from ethics theories such as social justice and utilitarianism. The theories espoused by Rawls and others are used to address those in a lesser position because such action serves to the benefit of all. Any American could find himself or herself in a lesser position at some point, and would find it appropriate to receive assistance in such a situation. For example, when a human-made or natural disaster hits, Americans expect public health agencies, whether they are government or private organizations, to assist with rescue, recovery, and rebuilding. Unfortunately, public health never has sufficient funds to provide all the needed services for all Americans. Therefore, it must use the ethical foundation of utilitarianism to make decisions about providing the greatest benefit to the greatest number of people. An example of utilitarianism in action would be public health efforts to provide immunizations to the public at reasonable costs. By immunizing the greatest number of people possible, public health contributes to reducing the greater harm to the population in general.

Public health is not without its ethical dilemmas. For example, a critical issue in public health is respect for individual autonomy versus the protection of the community. Sometimes public health workers are required to violate an individual's civil rights to privacy so as to prevent harm to the community at large. For example, certain sexually transmitted diseases must be reported to public health agencies so that public health workers can determine the source case and treat those who have been exposed to the disease. The action of reporting disease often causes discomfort and embarrassment for the individual, but is necessary to realize the broader community benefit.

The sister principles of beneficence and nonmaleficence are other parts of the ethical framework for public health. Given the diversity and extent of the public health system, it is often difficult to remember that its function is to improve the quality of life for all people, regardless of their economic or social circumstances. In addition, public health efforts serve to prevent harm through educational, research, and surveillance activities. While challenges remain for public health in the ACA era, this system continues to make progress in meeting its mission and staying true to its ethical foundations.

Cases for Your Consideration

The Case of the *Salmonella* Surprise

Think about the chapter information and consider the following questions. Sample responses and commentary follow the case.

1. Before he had to deal with the *Salmonella* surprise, which ethics issues did Joe face?

2. What were the ethics principle violations in this case?

3. Should Joe lose his job?

Case Information

"It's going to be a great day!" thought Joe Ascot, director of environmental services for Peace County Health Department. Even though he struggled with having too few restaurant inspectors for the many restaurants in his growing county, Joe knew that public health workers always soldier on and get things done. Then the telephone rang.

The caller was the Director of Emergency Services at Peace County Hospital. He said that his emergency department (ED) waiting room was full of vomiting patients. He suspected that *Salmonella* poisoning was the reason for this ED rush. The most severe symptoms were occurring in eight children under the age of five and five women older than the age of 70. Two of the children were in serious condition. The ED nurses were able to determine that the patients had all attended the Grandma and Princess Luncheon at Aunt Tandy's Restaurant in Peace City. This catered event featured a menu of a fruit cup, chicken divan, French mashed potatoes, and green beans. Dessert was Aunt Tandy's chocolate cake and ice cream.

The ED director asked Joe to contact the Centers for Disease Control and Prevention (CDC) immediately and to check his records for inspection reports on Aunt Tandy's Restaurant. Joe was surprised about an outbreak of what looked like *Salmonella* poisoning. He knew that poor kitchen hygiene was one of the sources of this problem, but he felt certain that Aunt Tandy's was not to blame. After all, the restaurant had a great reputation in Peace County.

Before Joe called the CDC to report a possible outbreak of *Salmonella* poisoning, he searched his inspection database. "There's nothing here!" he thought as he searched and re-searched the database. There simply was no record of any inspection of Aunt Tandy's Restaurant during the past six months, or even within the past year. Immediately, he telephoned each of his restaurant inspectors. None had a record of inspections for Aunt Tandy's on their lists.

"What should I do now? There is no documentation for an inspection at Aunt Tandy's, and I have to call the CDC. Will I lose my job?" thought Joe. With great anxiety, he picked up the telephone and followed the specified protocol. He dialed the number for the state health department, which would then contact the CDC.

Note: The state health department, working in cooperation with the CDC, conducted an investigation of Aunt Tandy's restaurant based on the data from the patient reports. Investigators found that Aunt Tandy assigned a new employee to food preparation. This employee first cut up the raw chicken for the chicken divan; then wiped the board with a dishcloth and cut up the fruit for the fruit cup. This error allowed transfer of the *Salmonella* bacteria from the uncooked chicken to the fruit. Those who were most susceptible (children and the elderly) had the worst symptoms.

Responses and Commentary on Questions

1. Before he had to deal with the *Salmonella* surprise, which ethics issues did Joe face?

Think about the situation that Joe faced before the telephone call. He knew that he did not have enough staff in the area. This meant that his inspectors had heavy caseloads, and there was a high probability that they were spending too little time in each of the restaurants that they did inspect. The lack of staffing increased the likelihood that there would be a failure in the system and in the potential health problems for the community.

Joe insisted that the Peace County Health Department hire more restaurant inspectors and presented his rationale to the director. However, the director might not even consider his request because the director used utilitarian ethics. For example, he had to weigh the community benefit of hiring more restaurant inspectors against the benefit of hiring more public health nurses. Given a limited budget, which of these hiring decisions provided the greatest benefit to the community, or reduced the potential for the greatest harm? In general, the director favored hiring nurses over hiring restaurant inspectors. Therefore, Joe was likely to remain without a full restaurant inspector staff for some time.

Joe was counting on the ethics of restaurant owners to be concerned with nonmaleficence and, to some degree, justice for their clients. He counted on them to obey the rules and regulations and to make sure that kitchen sanitation was up to code. He hoped that restaurant owners would spend the effort it took to train new employees. After all, it was in their self-interest to make sure that a negative health event never happened. However, given human nature, this was a high risk for Joe and was not in keeping with the code of ethics for public health.

2. What were the ethics principles violations in this case?

To answer this question, one has to consider all of the factors contributing to this situation. The restaurant owner, employee in charge of the preparation, restaurant inspectors, and Joe all violated ethics principles in different ways. In examining these violations, one can see how things that appear to be unimportant can lead to serious healthcare consequences.

Aunt Tandy's restaurant violated the principle of staff justice. Aunt Tandy did not provide the new employee with adequate training concerning kitchen sanitation and correct food preparation. Perhaps the restaurant owner assumed that the new worker knew not to prepare raw chicken on the same cutting surface on which fruits and vegetables are prepared. Perhaps, the owner did not have enough time to provide training for this newly hired employee. Whatever the reason, Aunt Tandy placed the employee in a disadvantaged position. He did not receive training for the job that he was required to do, yet he was accountable for the outcomes of his actions. Certainly, this employee contributed in a major way to the *Salmonella* poisoning outbreak that happened in Peace County, but was he solely to blame?

Aunt Tandy's restaurant also contributed to the harm caused by the *Salmonella* poisoning. The owner's lack of due diligence in protecting the public through training of employees and inspecting their work led to the unsanitary practices and to serving contaminated food to her customers. Although Aunt Tandy did not intend to cause harm, her decisions certainly contributed to harmful events in her community. In addition, the reputation of Aunt Tandy's restaurant could suffer. Negative publicity from the *Salmonella* surprise could cause many Peace County residents to choose another restaurant when dining out. The potential lack of business could lead to staff layoffs or even to the closing of this once well-respected restaurant.

One can also look at the actions of the food preparation employee. Certainly, one can view his actions as violating the ethics principle of nonmaleficence. Perhaps he was in a rush and took the shortcut to speed up his preparation. Maybe he actually thought that wiping the cutting board with a towel would make it sanitary. Whatever the reason for his actions, he was a major contributor to the *Salmonella* outbreak in Peace County and the harm to the children and their grandmothers.

The food preparation employee also violated the intent of the principle of justice. His actions did not demonstrate fairness to the customers, who relied on his integrity to produce safe food for their consumption. In addition, he was not fair to his fellow employees because his actions could cause harm to their collective reputation and to their potential livelihood. Certainly, this person had no negative intent. He was merely careless and did not think beyond the moment. His actions explain why Aristotle asks for practical wisdom in making decisions. Had this individual thought about the best way to prepare food or asked questions about the correct protocol for preparation, no *Salmonella* poisoning would have occurred.

One must also look at the inspectors and their violation of ethics principles. First, one might think that the inspectors honored the principle of autonomy by not conducting inspections at Aunt Tandy's Restaurant. They assumed that the owner would want to protect the restaurant's reputation and, therefore, would conduct her own inspections. They also assumed that the restaurant was up to code and, according to their records, did not conduct an inspection of this site. In their defense, with their busy schedules and their knowledge of Aunt Tandy's positive reputation, they may have decided to use their limited resources to inspect restaurants with a less stellar reputation. One can see this as a form of utilitarianism in that the inspectors assumed that newer restaurants might have more code violations. Therefore, they were trying to realize the greatest benefit with their limited resources.

The inspectors also violated the principle of justice. By not inspecting Aunt Tandy's restaurant in favor of having more time to inspect those restaurants that were new to the community, they did not provide fair treatment for all. For example, the new restaurants received different treatment than Aunt Tandy's because they did not have an established reputation in the community. Although it would be logical to assume that they had more code violations, the element of fairness was not part of this assumption.

In addition, the inspectors were contributors to the harm to Peace County. Their lack of inspection might have given the owner of Aunt Tandy's Restaurant a sense of false security and led to less diligence in health code compliance. Given that the inspectors were not reminding Aunt Tandy of her responsibilities through their evaluations, the she may have become less vigilant in providing proper kitchen sanitation.

What about Joe? In this case, he violated several ethics principles. Joe had the authority of a directorship to supervise all the staff in his department and to meet the goals of the Peace County Health Department. This authority gave him a great deal of autonomy over his actions and those of his staff. However, Joe did not use his autonomy appropriately. For example, when he checked his database, he could not find any record of an inspection for Aunt Tandy's Restaurant. This omission demonstrates a lack of responsibility on his part, as Joe should be checking this system frequently. In addition, Joe contributed to violations of justice. For example, he did not check to see which restaurants his inspectors were evaluating. Had he done so, he would have seen that Aunt Tandy's restaurant was not on their lists. Given this information, he could have followed up to make sure that all restaurants received an inspection, which would have been fair treatment.

Even though Joe was not directly responsible for the actions of the restaurant preparation employee, the owner of Aunt Tandy's Restaurant, or his inspectors, he held a position of responsibility for the safety of all restaurants in Peace County. Therefore, his actions contributed to the *Salmonella* poisoning outbreak that affected citizens in that county and violated the principle of nonmaleficence. His actions not only contributed to the patients' harm, but also potentially harmed the community and its reputation. Media coverage and word of mouth could result in the labeling of Peace County as a place to avoid because of the *Salmonella* outbreak.

3. Should Joe lose his job?

The answer to this question relates to the policies and procedures for Peace County Health Department. In all likelihood, the Health Department director will hold someone accountable for the conditions that led up to the *Salmonella* poisoning outbreak. Even though Joe was facing staffing shortages and had many other problems in his department, he had the authority and autonomy to make decisions with respect to the safety of restaurants in the county. Joe might consider it unjust, but it is likely that he will lose his job because of the *Salmonella* surprise.

The Case of Pox on a Plane

Think about the chapter information and consider the following questions. Sample responses and commentary follow the case.

1. Which ethical principles did Mari and the captain demonstrate?
2. Why did the airline choose to notify the CDC before the plane landed?
3. Which ethical position did the passengers in the first-class cabin demonstrate?

Case Information

Flight 1414 was one hour out of its destination of Newark. It had been already been a seven-hour flight from London; flight attendants Cindy, Mari, Eva, and Jason were tired and ready to land. "No one wants to land more than those kids and their sponsors in second class," thought

Mari as she approached the back of the plane. She knew that the high school students and their three adult sponsors were returning from a missionary trip to Gambia, Africa. When she reached the missionary group section, one of the sponsors, Mrs. Stanley, stopped her.

"Stewardess," said Mrs. Stanley, "I am worried about Patti, LaDonna, and Fred. They are feverish and sweaty. Look at their arms; they have a rash that looks all bumpy. Can you help them? I am afraid that they have monkeypox." Mari went to the galley and brought the students water and a snack. Then she remembered her training on prevention of contagious diseases. Could this be smallpox? What was her responsibility in this situation?

Mari immediately went to alert the captain. She explained that the missionary group was returning from a trip to Gambia, Africa. From her training, Mari knew that Gambia was a source of cases of monkeypox, a disease that is similar to smallpox. Although smallpox vaccinations protect most people from this disease, monkeypox was contagious and could spread to the passengers. It also looked a lot like smallpox. "What should we do?" she asked.

The captain had also received training on controlling contagious diseases and immediately contacted the airport. The authorities at Newark airport took the report seriously and contacted the CDC. Within a few minutes, the captain received instructions to prevent all passengers from leaving the plane after it landed. The CDC had to quarantine all passengers and staff until they investigated the situation and ruled out a more serious disease such as smallpox. Because she knew that these passengers were going to be very unhappy, the captain made the announcement about this process. She made sure to apologize for the inconvenience on behalf of the airline. The captain also explained what would happen as accurately as she could.

Cindy, Mari, Eva, and Jason worked to calm the passengers and assure them that they would be able to leave the plane as soon as possible. They explained that the quarantine was to protect everyone. However, several passengers in the first-class cabin complained that they had important things to do and that airline could not hold them against their will. They had rights! Some of the passengers demanded to talk with the captain and the airport authorities about this matter. Cindy, Mari, Eva, and Jason used patience and respect while explaining the necessary actions. They also asked the captain to confirm that arrangements would be made for those passengers who had continuing flights.

Imagine the surprise when the Flight 1414 passengers saw vehicles from the Newark Emergency Medical Services, Newark Fire Department, and Newark Health Department, and the CDC rolling onto the tarmac. The CDC and Newark Health Department staff went to the back of the plane to evaluate Patti, LaDonna, and Fred and question the rest of the students and their sponsors. Using their iPads, the investigators took pictures of the rash and sent them to the CDC. In about 30 minutes, they received confirmation that the three students had monkeypox, not smallpox, and that they could lift the quarantine for the rest of the passengers. However, they needed to advise all members of the missionary group and those who were seated around them to get immediate medical care.

Before allowing the passengers to deplane, the Health Department staff member informed all of the passengers about the situation. If not vaccinated against smallpox, they needed to seek medical help. Even though they were not a great risk for monkeypox, the Health Department staff also advised that passengers practice healthy habits. As a precaution, the airline would collect detailed contact information for each passenger. Most of the passengers were greatly relieved to be ending their journey. However, many in the first-class section threatened to sue. As for Cindy, Mari, Eva, and Jason, they would never forget this flight.

Responses and Commentary on Questions

1. Which ethical principles did Mari and the captain demonstrate?

   First, Mari used her autonomy and training to make the best decision given the information that she had available. She knew that monkeypox was not as severe as smallpox. However, she also understood that the diseases presented with similar symptoms and that there was a need to differentiate one from the other. Therefore, she felt that she had a duty to protect the passengers on the plane and the community itself by reporting the incident.

   In addition, Mari, along with the other flight attendants, used the principle of beneficence when dealing with the missionary group and the passengers on the plane. The flight attendants also tried to make all of the passengers as comfortable as possible. Mari answered their questions with accurate information and provided justification for the quarantine. In addition, she asked the captain to check with the airline regarding flights for passengers with continuing travel plans.

   The captain also used the autonomy of her position to make a decision. She had to weigh many factors in doing so. For example, there was a chance that she could lose her job if her decision was determined to be inappropriate by the airlines. She also knew that there was a potential for high number of complaints from inconvenienced passengers. However, she trusted Mari's judgment and training. Therefore, she made the call to Newark authorities that led to the CDC order of quarantine.

The captain also practiced nonmaleficence and beneficence in her decision. In taking this action, she prevented what could have been an outbreak of a serious disease. Even though the affected passengers' condition was determined to be monkeypox and not smallpox, she was instrumental in making sure that passengers on the plane received correct information about prevention and treatment of monkeypox. In doing so, the captain decreased the potential harm to passengers. Likewise, her treatment of the situation exhibited beneficence. The captain fully informed the passengers about the need for the quarantine and explained the procedures, as she knew them. In addition, she apologized on behalf of the airline and assured the passengers that the airline would make every effort to accommodate their needs. Providing this information demonstrated kindness as well as good business sense.

2. Why did the airline choose to notify the CDC before the plane landed?

The airline had to consider its duty to the passengers and to the city of Newark itself. To assure the health and safety of the passengers, the CDC and the Newark Health Department had to confirm that the passengers were suffering from monkeypox and not smallpox. In addition, they had to protect the city of Newark from exposure to smallpox, if it was present. In making the decision to call the CDC, the airline took risks. The publicity generated by the incident could produce benefit or harm to the company, depending on how people viewed it. For example, the public could think of the airline as a hero because it made a decision to protect both the passengers and the city of Newark. Alternatively, the public might see the airline as being hyper-reactive to a situation that meant nothing. If this were the case, there could be a reduction of credibility and, perhaps, in the purchase of the airline's tickets. Despite the risks, the airline decided that the most ethical decision would be to contact the CDC and risk the consequences of doing so.

3. Which ethical position did some of the passengers in the first-class cabin demonstrate?

Passengers in the first-class section of the flight from London demonstrated the concept of ethical egoism. They saw themselves as being much more important than other people on the plane are. Therefore, they felt that their rights included protection from inconvenience, even if their inconvenience protected others from exposure to disease. They did not base their ethics decisions on duty toward others or on the greatest benefit for the greatest numbers. Instead, they saw as ethical and fair only those actions that benefited them as individuals. They also planned to voice their displeasure by writing complaint letters to the airline, the CDC, and the Newark Health Department and by calling their lawyers.

Web Resources

American Public Health Association
http://apha.org/

National Commission for Health Education Credentialing
http://www.nchec.org/

Public Health Leadership Society
http://phls.org/home/

References

Bernheim, R. G., Childress, J. F., Bonnie, R. J., & Melnick, A. L. (2015). *Essentials of public health ethics*. Burlington, MA; Jones & Bartlett Learning.

Bureau of Labor Statistics. (2012a). Epidemiologists. *Occupational Outlook Handbook*. Retrieved from http://www.bls.gov/ooh/lifephysical-and-social-science/epidemiologists.htm

Bureau of Labor Statistics. (2012b). Environmental specialists. *Occupational Outlook Handbook*. Retrieved from http://www.bls.gov/ooh/Life-Physical-and-Social-Science/Environmental-scientists-and-specialists.htm

Dawson, A. (2011). *Public health ethics: Key concepts and issues in policy and practice*. New York, NY: Cambridge University Press.

Kaiser Family Foundation. (2013). Summary of the Affordable Care Act. *Focus on Health Reform*. Retrieved from http://kaiserfamilyfoundation.files.wordpress.com/2011/04/8061-021.pdf

National Commission for Health Education Credentialing. (2008). Retrieved from *About us*. http://www.nchec.org/aboutnchec/mission/

Public Health Leadership Society (2002). *Principles of ethical practice of public health, version 2.2*. Retrieved from http://www.apha.org/NR/rdonlyres/1CED3CEA-287E-4185-9CBD-BD405FC60856/0/ethicsbrochure.pdf

Robeyns, I. (2011, Summer). The capability approach, *The Stanford Encyclopedia of Philosophy*, Retrieved from http://plato.stanford.edu/archives/sum2011/entries/capability-approach/

Schneider, M. J. (2000). *Introduction to public health*. Gaithersburg, MD: Aspen.

Turnock, B. J. (2012). *Public health: What is it and how it works* (5th ed.). Burlington, MA: Jones & Bartlett Learning.

SECTION IV

The Inner Circle of Ethics

■ INTRODUCTION

This section completes the circle model introduced at the beginning of this text. In the era of the ACA, there will greater challenges to live ethics and function as an ethics-based healthcare administrator. These challenges originate from the influences of many forces that are part of the outer circles of the model. Given these challenges, the ability to practice eudaimonia and use practical wisdom will not be easy. However, taking action to continue to be a person of virtue can provide a level of integrity that will last for the entirety of one's healthcare administration career.

This last section comprises three chapters that focus on the challenges for the individual healthcare administrator as he or she serves patients, staff members, and the community. The *Moral Integrity* chapter explores what moral administration means in a healthcare environment filled with whitewater change. The chapter begins with definitions of morality and its relationship to ethics. It presents experts' views on practicing morally centered administration in a healthcare environment. It also explains the effects of losing one's moral center and the devastating effects of administrative evil. Finally, some specific challenges are included to help identify one's moral center and practice ethics-based management.

The *Codes of Ethics and Administrative Practice* chapter features professional codes of ethics and their relationship to healthcare administration. There is a detailed discussion of the American College of Healthcare Executives (ACHE) Code of Ethics and its application. Because administrators supervise professionals who have other codes of ethics, this chapter also examines codes from several professional groups and analyzes their themes. By the end of this section, healthcare administrators should understand how a "code clash" can occur and how to deal with it. To provide a balanced view, criticisms of codes are also discussed.

The *Practicing as an Ethical Administrator* chapter presents the core management functions and examines the relationship of ethics to each of those functions. The chapter also includes practical advice about ethics in management practice from writers in business and health care. In addition, it suggests ways to continue learning about applied ethics through everyday sources such as novels, anecdotes, and observations.

CHAPTER
14

Moral Integrity

Why is moral integrity important to the success of healthcare administrators?

Points to Ponder

1. What are morality and moral integrity?
2. Which temptations do healthcare administrators face when choosing moral integrity as a basis for professional actions?
3. What is the best way to maintain moral integrity?

Key Terms

The following are this chapter's key terms. Look for them in bold.

administrative evil
deceit
evil

labeling
moral integrity
personal morality

■ INTRODUCTION AND DEFINITIONS

What does morality mean? How does **moral integrity** affect the practice of healthcare administration? What is the relationship between morality and ethics? If healthcare administrators (HCAs) want to answer these questions, they need understand the many aspects of morality and operational definitions of it.

As seen with other ethics concepts, there is no absolute definition of the term "morality," but experts seem to agree on certain themes. Research by Bloom (2013) indicates that morality is complex. His research demonstrates that the roots of morality can be traced back even as far as the brains of infants and toddlers. Their natural moral sense includes a sense of good and bad. In addition, Bloom's research found that infants and toddlers exhibit forms of empathy and compassion very early in their lives. These basic components of morality expand as human beings mature in knowledge and experience. For example, babies learn to find "joy in the joy of others" (Bloom, 2013, p. 40) and "respond to the pain of others" (p. 47) as they learn and grow. Infants also have a sense of fairness and of otherness early in their lives. These behaviors may relate to instincts rooted in survival, but they form the basis for developing morality.

Purtilo and Doherty (2011) define morality as a set of guidelines that assist individuals and groups in determining what they should do and what they should value. In addition, morality is concerned with how people relate to one another and how they live together successfully. Practicing morality requires that a person consider the context when making decisions. In addition, moral decisions have their basis in traits such as compassion, courage, honesty, respect, and humility. This list also reflects virtues identified by ethics theorists such as St. Thomas Aquinas and Aristotle.

How does morality relate to ethics? Purtilo and Doherty (2011) explain that ethics is a way to study moral problems by using a systematic and theory-based process. By applying philosophy and the social sciences, healthcare administrators can develop a mechanism for ethical reflection and conduct analysis to find answers to ethics dilemmas that they face in the practice of administration. Ethics differs from morality in that it provides tools and guidelines that go beyond what morality provides. For example, in health care, many complex situations require various forms of reasoning and decision making. "Ethics is the discipline that waits in the wings as a health-restoring resource when moral guidelines fail to do the job" (Purtilo & Doherty, 2011, p. 16).

Purtilo and Doherty (2011) further divide morality into personal, societal, and group categories. **Personal morality** includes values, duties, and actions that are independent of work or social groups. For example, if a person says, "I honor myself and give others the same honor," then the person is expressing a value within his or her personal morality.

By comparison, culture, geography, religious foundations, and even legislation influence societal morality. This type of morality includes the values and duties that reasonable people expect of one another and allows for a secure and peaceful society. An example of this morality is the statement, "All people are created equal." Because health care exists within a society, society's definition of morality affects healthcare organizations' practices. Put simply, these organizations' business practices must conform to society's view of a moral organization. For example, there is societal expectation that healthcare organizations will make a profit, but also treat those persons who are least well off with dignity.

Finally, Purtilo and Doherty (2011) include group behavior as part of the definition of morality. As they point out, groups in health care often codify their own set of values and duties. Groups express desirable actions through policies and procedures so that all group members have an understanding of the definition of acceptable behaviors. In addition, healthcare groups formulate codes of ethics that serve to identify appropriate moral behaviors for members of their professions. These codes often have similar moral expectations, such as respect for patients' rights, honesty, and the provision of quality care.

Aristotle (Summers, 2014) also teaches about morality and explains how to apply ethics to daily living. Through his concept of practical wisdom and eudaimonia, he creates an awareness of the need to apply ethics through moral action. In other words, just talking about morality is not enough; rather, a person must act on his or her beliefs. Individual virtue or moral character also allows individuals to decide the best action during challenging situations. Those who live a life congruent with eudaimonia make ethical principles and virtue the center of their lives. Certainly, using practical wisdom and living eudaimonia will be part of the successful lives of healthcare administrators in the ACA era.

Frankl (1971) adds further to the definition of morality. His theory of logotherapy includes the concept that individuals have choice, but with choice comes responsibility. This idea is also in keeping with practicing as a moral agent (Darr, 2011) for the community and organization. In the role of moral agent, a healthcare administrator must be able to make personal and professional choices that have a foundation in ethics. Exercising choice also means that the healthcare administrator takes ethics beyond theory or discussion and into action. Nevertheless, Frankl reminds decision makers that with choice comes responsibility. Therefore, healthcare administrators must not only make the best moral choice for the situation, but must also take responsibility for the choices they make. In a practical sense, ownership of choices means that HCAs cannot blame other employees for their choices. The responsibility for the decision made lies with the person who holds the title and the authority.

It will never be easy to make choices and to assume responsibility for those choices in the ever-changing healthcare world. However, if administrators consistently and actively use theory, principles, and practical wisdom, they will build a reputation as persons of character and integrity.

■ WHAT DO THE EXPERTS SAY ABOUT MORALITY?

After establishing an operational definition of morality, the next step is to study expert views about this topic. This section includes a survey of the extensive literature available on the topic of morality.

The discussion provides a foundation for addressing the real problems that healthcare administrators will encounter in their careers. New research on morality from Bloom (2013) and Turak (2013) provides insights into ways to increase one's knowledge base of concepts of morality. In addition, ideas about combining leadership and morality from Palmer (2000) will aid in expanding the application of morality. The application of morality, presented by Johnson (2009) and Gilbert (2007), will be discussed as well. In addition, Dye (2000), Hofmann (2006), and Gilbert (2007) show the effect of the immoral or amoral actions on health care and other areas of society. Their research provides information on maintaining a moral center in the rapidly changing, ever-challenging healthcare environment.

Bloom's (2013) research focuses on how human beings develop their moral center. As a developmental psychologist, this author discusses some elements of morality that are present in babies and toddlers. Moreover, moral development encompasses family experience and learning. In his final chapter, Bloom (2013) provides information on how to increase one's moral attitudes. He suggests that individuals need to think beyond themselves and their families to include people who are different from them. When they succeed in thinking beyond the personal level, individuals can develop greater empathy and compassion for those who come from different ethnicities and social economic groups. This does not mean that a person has to agree with everyone: Free will is always present. Rather, it suggests that knowing more than the immediate world can build a person's moral character and practices. Bloom also proposes that stories about people's lives and experiences can increase perspective, understanding, empathy, and compassion. In his view, practicing morality requires both reasoning and the ability to understand others' circumstances and ideas.

Turak's (2013) research addressed the question of how a community of Trappist monks could run a highly successful business and remain true to their deeply held moral position. An entrepreneur and corporate executive, Turak sought to understand the moral behaviors of this group. He also wanted to apply their behaviors to his work as a business executive. During the course of his research, he found that the principles of morality actually supported the success of the monks' business. For example, the monks linked their business success to the mission of supporting their monastery. In addition, their concept of service and excellence contributed to both their business success and their moral center. Turak found that the monks lived their principles in everything they did and, therefore, were able to be fiscally successful and morally centered.

Earlier writers have also contributed to understanding of how morality applies to leadership in healthcare settings. For example, Palmer (2000) believes that, to be a respected leader, a person must practice what he calls authentic leadership. This form of leadership stems not from the profit/loss statement, but from the heart. As "co-creators" of the world in which healthcare administration exists, HCAs must make choices that lead to positive moral action. Nowhere can one clearly see the impact of these choices than in healthcare organizations and patient treatment decisions.

Often HCAs are required to make decisions based on producing good and avoiding harm, a scenario that Palmer calls light versus shadow. In other words, as morally centered leaders, HCAs are called upon to "cast less shadow and more light" (Palmer, 2000, p. 85). To accomplish this, they must be willing to explore their inner or spiritual life, including their moral center. While it not always pleasant or easy, this exploration can be conducted through activities such as journaling, allowing time to reflect or meditate, participating in discussions about morality, and praying. Palmer also asks administrators to assess the role of fear in decision making. While all leaders have fear, they should not use fear as a basis for making decisions. Rather, they need to draw on their knowledge, skills, and moral core to lead from a position of strength.

Johnson (2009) devotes an entire chapter in *Meeting the Ethical Challenges of Leadership* to character. The basis for his conclusions is national and international research concerning characteristics of model leaders. Johnson finds that leadership virtues include courage, integrity, humility, reverence, optimism, and justice. The author stresses that these characteristics are more than "talking points"; rather, they are integral parts of a leader's inner life and behavior. For example, courage means that leaders are willing to do the right thing even when it makes them unpopular. Integrity happens when they are consistent in their public statements and their private actions. In addition, humility requires an accurate view of one's strengths and weaknesses (Johnson, 2009). Praise does not seduce morally centered leaders, and its power is not likely to co-opt them. Optimism helps them to expect good things from the future, and justice instills in them a duty to treat people with equality and fairness. In the media-saturated age, one need simply view a news report or talk show to see the effects of leaders who have strong moral centers versus those who do not.

For healthcare leaders, practicing morality requires a commitment to lifelong learning and personal growth. Johnson (2009) suggests that leaders find role models who can be examples of morality in leadership. These exemplary leaders provide wisdom for dealing with situations in which moral challenges arise. Morally centered leaders can also instruct others on making a difference when there is a need for moral action. Reading and reflecting about the actions of these leaders, whether they are fictional or actual, can build moral character.

In addition, Johnson (2009) suggests extending one's moral character by developing the ability to experience and overcome difficult situations. While often uncomfortable, this type of deep learning comes from suffering a personally traumatic event such as an illness or divorce, dealing with difficult employees, or making a business mistake. The way in which a person handles such a situation and learns from it can add to that individual's moral center and personal strengths.

With respect to moral action, this text's author often asks ethics students, "What is your personal bottom line? Over which issue or action would you be willing to quit your job?" When the questions are stated at this basic a level, these students struggle with the reality and fear of unemployment versus what they feel to be morally correct. However, when this author turns the situation around and asks, "What are you worth? Would you be willing to sell your integrity for a paycheck?" a different understanding appears. By going along with something that the students know is morally wrong, they are endorsing the action. This is in agreement with the often-stated maxim, "If you permit it, you condone it." Often students do not consider things morally wrong because the immediate consequences seem to be negligible. However, establishing a pattern of moral compromise for personal or corporate gain can have damaging effects in the long term.

Gilbert (2007) discusses leaders' personal integrity as a function of their legacy, mindfulness, and choices. As administrators, HCAs build their future legacies through both their words and their actions. When serving in leadership positions, leaders do not function in a vacuum. Therefore, their actions and inactions reflect their ethical stand on issues, and employees and superiors notice what they do. Building a positive moral legacy requires a commitment to going beyond discussing ethics. It means that healthcare leaders choose to live in eudaimonia.

Mindfulness is also a part of the healthcare leader's personal integrity (Gilbert, 2007). It involves a person's thought processes and the ability to practice ethical wisdom. Mindfulness allows a healthcare leader to be aware of potential ethical issues and decide what to do about them before situation involving those issues occur. Making decisions about ethics issues requires that healthcare leader evaluate his or her biases, gather information, and use a system to evaluate possible options. It also includes consideration of the feelings that accompany making the appropriate decisions as well as those that accompany making the incorrect decisions. Choice is also a major factor in leadership integrity. Each day healthcare leaders have the choice to make ethical decisions or to avoid them. This is especially true in the current ACA era, where new ethics dilemmas are bound to emerge.

Leadership choices do not always involve major events. On a smaller scale, they can deal with the leader's attitudes, treatment of fellow employees, or creation of the work environment. When HCAs choose to be consistent in the values they incorporate across this spectrum of leadership, they create their own sense of personal peace. In addition, their employees know that they are true to what they say. In other words, such HCAs' actions match their statements. In turn, employees feel they can trust these leaders because they are consistent in what they say and what they do.

Gilbert (2007) offers advice on ways to build personal integrity. For example, if HCAs want to have a positive legacy, he suggests that they make their career matter. Gilbert views work as a way to make a difference, rather than as just something a person has to endure until retirement. Healthcare leaders can choose to be the example of an active ethics-based administrator and not lose faith in the future. In a time of great change, such as the current ACA era, having faith in the future can be a strong moral and leadership characteristic. However, Gilbert (2007) cautions against making decisions that seem right in the short term, but may be disastrous in the future. Again, using practical wisdom that combines reasoning and ethical choice is essential for decision making in the current healthcare environment.

■ MORALITY IGNORED: WHAT HAPPENS WHEN THE COMPASS IS BROKEN?

What happens when healthcare organizations and administrators ignore moral integrity and break their moral compass? Are there any consequences for being an immoral administrator, or is such behavior just what one does to be expedient and profitable? Dye (2000) speaks about the outcomes when normally effective leaders choose behaviors that are destructive and result in poor performance and poor leadership. He calls this phenomenon "managerial derailment" (p. 170). He attributes this management failure to negative or immoral behaviors such as pessimism, dependency, low self-esteem, laziness, lying, and excessive egoism. Unfortunately, one cannot easily detect these traits during the hiring process, but they can seriously affect employee morale and the organization's bottom line.

Dye (2000) also stresses that administrators need to assess future and current employees in terms of their moral integrity. For example, this process requires asking more than just surface-type questions during an interview. Administrators may need to develop ethics-type scenarios, and sometimes they may decide to use group interviews to gain perceptions from more than one person. In addition, it may be cost-effective and morally effective to follow up with a job candidate's references by asking ethics-related questions about the potential new hire. HCAs also need to be aware that a seemingly "good" administrator can be tempted to make less than ethical decisions when faced with fiscal and patient care challenges. To prevent managerial derailment, administrators need to take the morality pulse of their staff from time to time and provide meaningful continuing education on moral choices, ethics, and the true mission of the organization. Most importantly, HCAs cannot forget to monitor their own moral behaviors and decisions.

Hofmann (2006) agrees with Dye (2000), suggesting that healthcare administrators evaluate potential employees for their ethical integrity and ability to fit within the moral environment of the organization. He suggests that administrators need more than reference letters or résumés for discerning a future employee's integrity. For example, Hoffman (2006) suggests that interviews include questions about how candidates have handled ethical situations in the past. HCAs could also ask candidates to review short ethics cases and respond to them. Hoffman stresses that administrators should also assess the potential new hire's compatibility with the healthcare organization through group and individual interviews. The goal is to hire a person who exhibits integrity and can decrease the likelihood of moral derailment within a healthcare department or division.

Gilbert (2007) introduces the idea of "ethical erosion," which he defines as "a pervasive and subtle, negative dynamic to which we are all vulnerable, organizationally and personally" (p. 13). Ethical erosion happens when employees and administrators slowly move away from their positive values. At first, they make only small decisions that are expedient, but may undermine the organization's mission and values. Over time, these practices become part of the procedures and practice of the person, department, or organization. In such a case, healthcare professionals do not think that they are acting immorally; they are just doing "business as usual." Such immoral practices may become acceptable over time, to the point that the professionals no longer view them as unethical.

Gilbert (2007) suggests that the counterbalance for ethical erosion is the application of ethical wisdom to create an alert when there is a compromise of values. Healthcare administrators can also apply ethical wisdom through their culture, structure, leadership, governance, and integrity. For example, when examining the culture of an organization, one can prevent erosion by encouraging employees to voice ethical concerns about specific patients or the business itself. In addition, the organization must work to resolve unethical situations, and provide a legacy of quality that it communicates to employees and the community. Actions to prevent ethical erosion will become increasingly important as patient satisfaction becomes more intertwined with fiscal success in the ACA era.

Johnson (2009) presents a view of the shadow side of leadership and its effect on the leader's moral center. He posits that all leaders have both light and dark sides. Because of this dichotomy, they must struggle to master the darkness and not let it be a dominant force in their leadership. HCAs are particularly at risk of falling prey to this darkness because of their tremendous power and prestige in the community.

Johnson (2009) addresses dark qualities that can make for a bad (ineffective and/or unethical) administrator. He also goes beyond the ineffective or unethical to discuss the concept of **evil**, and the ability to overcome it.

When administrators exhibit certain qualities, they have the ability to create adverse effects for their employees and their organizations. These negative qualities include overriding ambition, inflated ego, and arrogance. For example, if a person is greedy, he or she cannot easily discern right from wrong in certain decisions. If the individual is reckless, he or she can cause great personal and organizational harm. In addition, failure to understand problems and issues, unwillingness to make difficult decisions, and general incompetence can lead to personal and organizational downfall. These destructive behaviors also contribute to violations of employee rights, unethical or illegal actions, creation of scapegoats, promotion of incompetence, and a toxic work environment. It is easy to see how such noxious administrative qualities can spiral into personal and organizational disasters.

How can HCAs keep from becoming bad administrators? Johnson (2009) suggests that they address the administrative shadows of power and privilege. First, healthcare administrators must recognize that they cannot do their jobs without power. As healthcare administration students know from their management courses, power takes many forms, each with its own use. If an administrator uses these many forms of power inappropriately or excessively, there is a potential for abuse.

How do healthcare administrators avoid the shadow of abuse of power? Johnson (2009) suggests that HCAs should make sure to balance their own power with the power they delegate. In addition, becoming impressed with one's own power can cause a loss of perspective. This loss can lead to behaviors that can harm the HCA and others. In reality, HCAs do not have actual power unless people choose to give it to them and comply with their plans and direction.

Because healthcare administrators assume leadership positions, there is also a link between their power and certain privileges. For example, they may receive more money, benefits, and status than others in the organization do. These privileges are intended as compensation for the extra responsibility and accountability that HCAs bear. But how much privilege is fair? Can administrators misuse privilege? Are they guilty of hoarding wealth and status, or feeling that they are better than others are? Introspection to answer these questions can help administrators surmount the shadow cast by privilege (Johnson, 2009).

Fidelity is also an important part of autonomy and one's moral center as a healthcare administrator. However, Johnson (2009) warns that the dark-side behavior of **deceit** is a risk for healthcare administrators. For example, HCAs have may access to greater sources and levels of information than many other members of their organizations.

This access is appropriate because they must be "in the know" to do their job, but the knowledge power that derives from this insider's position can also add to their ethical burdens. For example, HCAs may be privy to information that could adversely affect their staff, but may not choose to disclose it. Deceit does not have to be as direct as lying. Healthcare administrators can also practice deception by denying that they have particular knowledge, withholding information to sabotage others (as in bullying behaviors), or using information for their own benefit. Deception, once uncovered, undermines the trust of staff members and the community alike. Once healthcare administrators have lost trust, it can take years, if ever, to be restored.

The practice of showing favoritism—known as "in-group/out-group" management—is another possible administrative shadow. Johnson (2009) identifies a lack of consistency as the basis for this designation. Because healthcare administrators are human, they will undoubtedly find some people more appealing than others. However, in the workplace, they must strive for consistency of treatment. Preferential treatment exists in perception as well as in practice. For example, if the healthcare administrator lunches with only employees whom he or she likes, the HCA is selecting an "in-group," even if this is not the intent. To avoid the perception of favoritism, healthcare administrators should have lunch with all staff members as much as possible, or else eat alone. Similarly, administrators should be careful about socializing outside of work, particularly in dating behaviors. Dating subordinates not only sets up the temptations of favoritism, but can also backfire if "love goes bad." In the worst-case analysis, a spurned subordinate might retaliate with claims of sexual harassment that can ruin the healthcare administrator's career. Indeed, it is lonely at the top.

Loyalty and responsibility are other key areas where shadows can overtake light in leadership. Healthcare administrators have multiple loyalties that may often conflict. Their first loyalty should be to patients and the community that they serve. Obviously, healthcare administrators also want to be loyal to their bosses and their staff. However, this loyalty cannot be absolute. For example, HCAs must be willing to take appropriate action if the boss is engaging in behaviors that jeopardize the organization or the community. This type of scenario creates a moral Catch-22 for health administrators: They want to be loyal to their boss, but if they say nothing, they are supporting the boss's unethical behaviors. When healthcare administrators feel compelled to report their bosses, they must always have appropriate documentation and go through the appropriate organizational channels. Whistleblowing, while necessary in certain circumstances, can backfire on the individual who has the moral courage to make such a decision. Therefore, it is important to have a backup plan should the worst-case scenario come to fruition.

There is also a link between responsibility and loyalty. Because of their position, healthcare administrators are accountable for their own actions as well as for the actions of the employees in their department. Therefore, the community, patients, and staff members expect HCAs to act responsibly, and to do everything possible to create successful decisions. HCAs cannot blame staff members or others for their decisions, or expect more from staff than they are willing to do themselves (Johnson, 2009). Again, assessment of level of responsibility and the expected accountability will help healthcare administrators maintain their moral integrity. It is also critical that they hold their staff accountable for their own decisions and behaviors.

Before addressing the challenge of maintaining moral integrity, it is important to examine the most difficult challenge for healthcare administrators—namely, the challenge of administrative evil. Johnson (2009) discusses aspects of this threat to moral integrity and presents ideas on how to combat evil. The first step is to understand that evil exists and to define it from the HCA's viewpoint. According to Johnson (2009), evil is a force that can destroy health, happiness, and community. It causes human suffering on many levels and destroys dignity. For healthcare administrators to understand the impact of evil, Johnson (2009) organizes it into categories including perverse enjoyment, deceit, and bureaucratic-approved injury and destruction. He also provides information on the role of choice and situational factors in the practice of evil. How do these categories relate to evil?

Evil can express itself as perverse enjoyment. For example, boredom can create situations where people seek alternatives that are more exciting or fill voids in their lives. They may seek enjoyment from the power of inflicting pain on others or having lives full of secret practices. Great harm can result if a member of the healthcare profession exhibits this behavior. This characteristic of evil may also be part of what Frankl (1971) calls "filling the existential vacuum." For example, when a person is bored or feels a distinct sense of existential emptiness, he or she is more likely to fill that void with alcohol, drugs, or reckless sexual behavior. These choices produce harm for the individual and for those who are close to him or her. In addition, they increase the cost of health care for everyone.

Self-deception can also lead to evil behavior. For administrators, this could happen if they think of themselves as a higher force: perfect and all-powerful. Controlling others' behavior and bending staff members or patients to the administrator's will reinforces the HCA's inaccurate perception of the appropriate use of power. However, the HCA's self-deception regarding his or her omnipotence may lead to actions that can destroy individuals and even the entire organization.

Bureaucratic or **administrative evil** happens when faith in technology, science, and the power of reason—devoid of compassion or conscience—becomes the driving force for a group, organization, or society. Ultimate faith in technology and science serves to remove HCAs from the human part of their decisions and makes it easier for evil to exist. This belief also allows them to engage in daily operations that produce great pain and suffering for others without any sense of guilt or remorse.

Administrative evil has existed throughout time and explains many destructive actions. The classic example of this practice in modern times is the extermination camps that existed in World War II. Through daily operational functions (e.g., providing on-time transportation, building campsites, collecting taxes, and compiling records), Nazi civil servants supported and enabled the death camps to execute their deadly work. These citizens did not view their role as evil at all. Indeed, they felt pride in doing a job well and did not regard that work as terminating human lives. Instead, these workers perceived that they had found the best technology to solve a problem. In turn, those who ran the camps would argue that they were merely doing their jobs with business as usual and earning money for their cause.

Caplan (1992), in his classic book *When Medicine Went Mad*, brings the role of administrative evil in the Holocaust even closer to home. He presents the case that certain elements of German society went beyond compliance with government policy. The medical community, through its scientists, physicians, and administrators, actually designed and implemented many of the government's destructive programs. The focus of these endeavors was racial hygiene and extinction of undesired populations. The medical community viewed these programs as highly ethical because they were utilitarian in nature. The design of racial cleansing was intended to prevent the degeneration of the human race via genetic contamination from undesirable population groups. Sterilization laws, euthanasia, ghettos, and eventually death camps were all part of this effort. Technology made this evil much more horrific because it increased efficiency. The German workers could kill more people with greater efficiency by administering a research-identified amount of gas, thereby improving the organization's bottom line. In addition, it was found to be cost-effective to use "extermination by labor" to simultaneously remove undesirable people from populations while benefiting from their work. More than 14 million people were subjected to this process, and their captors literally worked them to death (London Grid for Learning, 2014).

Administrative evil can also occur when the healthcare administrators perceive their intent as ethical or do not consider the patient in their decisions. A recent case, chronicled in Skloot's (2011) book, *The Immortal Life of Henrietta Lacks*, deals with actions taken by physicians and administrators at Johns Hopkins Hospital beginning in 1951. Henrietta Lacks, a patient at Johns Hopkins, received a diagnosis of cervical cancer. After the surgeons removed her cancer, the pathologist discovered that these cancer cells reproduced in extraordinary ways. In fact, they formed the basis for new cell line called the HeLa line (HeLa was used to protect Henrietta Lacks's identity). This cell line subsequently became part of research studies conducted in laboratories all over the world and contributed to polio treatment, gene mapping, chemotherapy, and other modern-day healthcare advancements. The HeLa cells not only improved the likelihood of successful research, but also generated high levels of profits for healthcare laboratories and facilities. This line remains essential to scientific research even today.

Henrietta Lacks came from a poor neighborhood near Baltimore. She never had health insurance and regarded Johns Hopkins as the only place where she could receive care. In a time before true informed consent was the norm, she did not understand her treatment or appreciate how researchers would use her cells. Skloot (2011) intensively researched Lacks's case and found that Johns Hopkins and its physicians, while not intentionally doing so, omitted essential information about the use of Lacks' cells. These omissions helped to expedite the accomplishment of research goals, but violated the basic ethical principles of respect for persons, beneficence, nonmaleficence, and justice. While there was great benefit to society from development of the HeLa cell line, there was a lack of respect and harm to Henrietta and later to the Lacks family. One can also view this situation as a clash between Mill's utilitarianism and Kant's deontology.

Henrietta Lacks never provided true informed consent, nor did she receive any benefit from her extraordinary contribution to medical science. Even though Lacks died, her cells live on in the HeLa line. The HeLa line is profitable, but her heirs have been unsuccessful in receiving compensation for the use of her cells. At this point, they hope that "Johns Hopkins and some of those other folks who benefitted off of her cells will do something to honor her and make it right with the family" (Skloot, 2011, p. 328).

Another category of evil defined by Johnson is "evil as sanctioned destruction" (2009, p. 107). In this view, evil occurs when a person in authority gives direct or implied permission to victimize others. This victimization is acceptable when the group or individual in authority does not value the victimized group or individual as members of society. Such action violates all of the ethical principles presented in this text. However, if health administrators are not careful, this practice can be regarded as "business as usual" for health care. This perception occurs because it is not always easy to treat each person with dignity when surrounded by pain and suffering. All too many healthcare professionals experience compassion fatigue and grow angry about the choices that people make that imperil their own health. It is especially frustrating when these choices also adversely affect the bottom line of the healthcare organization or inconvenience staff members.

Without reminders that the healthcare organization's true mission should recognize the worth of all human beings, it would be all too easy to deny compassionate care or treat only those persons whom society decides are the "deserving poor." Johnson (2009) reminds HCAs that even a small dose of this evil as sanctioned destruction, such as **labeling** those found to be undesirable (e.g., GOMER, frequent fliers), can lead to a loss of dignity and undesirable behaviors by healthcare professionals. Even if HCAs never personally use any of these labels, if they laugh at them during conversations with staff members or say nothing when they hear them, they are supporting administrative evil.

Johnson (2009) also notes that evil often occurs through a series of choices rather than just in a single event. Even small choices can have large moral consequences. Therefore, it is imperative that healthcare administrators determine why they are choosing one option over another and think about the consequences of their choices. A rush to a decision can lead to a wrong action that is both morally and fiscally unsound. However, as one builds moral integrity, it becomes easier to discriminate between a good choice and one that can have negative consequences. As in any skill, practice improves the likelihood of making ethical choices.

■ HEALTHCARE ADMINISTRATORS AND PERSONAL MORAL INTEGRITY

As suggested earlier, a person can develop moral integrity through education, experience, self-assessment, and decision making. Healthcare administrators, therefore, must make a lifelong commitment to cultivating and supporting their moral base. The following suggestions, offered by classical writers in the field of healthcare administration, provide practical wisdom concerning this commitment.

Griffith (1993), a well-respected leader in health administration, believes that HCAs can be both moral and successful leaders. This idea of balancing morality and leadership is particularly important in today's era of great change in the healthcare system and its practices. As healthcare administrators advance in their careers, they serve as moral beacons for their employees and community. Their visibility creates a greater need to commit to do what is right and to have strong moral convictions.

Griffith also challenges HCAs to conduct the business of health care in a way that fosters integrity. This action includes designing policies and procedures that encourage employees to do the right thing. The culture of a healthcare organization should make it easy and nonpunitive for staff to identify and report problems, and administrators should give serious attention to such employee reports. In addition, healthcare administrators should build work groups whose members do not jump to the first solution, but rather take the time to ask, "What is the right thing to do?" Administrators need to avoid becoming moral hypocrites and truly put patients first instead of just including these words in a mission statement.

Griffith (1993) encourages healthcare administrators to use true participative management. This means effectively delegating both the task and the responsibility to individuals and teams. While micromanagement might feel like a safe way to lead, it sends the message that employees are neither trusted nor respected. Delegation also requires healthcare administrators to provide rewards to those employees who deserve them and not just to those persons who curry favor. Certainly, Griffith (1993) asks much of HCAs, but following his suggestions can provide benefits to both the organization and HCAs in their individual careers.

Purtilo and Doherty (2011) also provide advice on survival in the healthcare world and retaining moral integrity. For example, the principle of beneficence means that healthcare administrators act with kindness and charity for others. However, beneficence also applies to how administrators treat themselves. This duty entails giving HCAs permission to care for their own needs as well as those of others. While the necessity of taking care of oneself might seem obvious, many administrators find it difficult. Perhaps the professional socialization process has been too effective and they feel guilty when they take time for themselves. In some cases, HCAs may work so much that they become ill or come to work when they are ill. While this sacrifice might seem to be noble, it is not. These seemly selfless professionals are actually increasing the risk of illness for their colleagues and patients. Honoring one's duty toward self-beneficence is morally and fiscally sound practice because balance in life and work can make an individual more efficient, effective and productive.

Purtilo and Doherty (2011) also suggest that HCAs exercise their morality through civil responsibility and being moral agents. They explain that when a person is in a position of authority, he or she cares for the patient, the staff, the organization, and the community. This caring requires HCAs to respond in appropriate ways to organizational and community situations so that their response provides benefit. They should carefully assess their areas of expertise and provide support that is within the scope of their knowledge and experience. In addition, Purtilo and Doherty note that caring about what happens in one's organization or community requires moral courage. They define moral courage as "a readiness for voluntary, purposive action in situations that engender realistic fear and anxiety to uphold something of great moral value" (p. 409). Because the price for one's choice is high, HCAs must use practical wisdom and effective decision making when exercising moral courage. However, taking a stand, despite the consequences, may sometimes be the best choice.

When thinking about morality and the practice of health care, this text's author remembers a remarkable person who came to speak to her students. He was a chaplain in a hospice program and spoke to her class about his work. At the time, his clients ranged in age from 4 to 98, and he spoke about how he supported each of them through the end of life. One of the students asked him, "How do you deal with all of this as a person? How do you keep a sense of balance?" This author still remembers his answer. He said, "When I play, I play. I take time to be away from work physically and emotionally. I use the time to recharge." Healthcare administrators should ask themselves, "When was the last time I played?" Even a small "time-out" can help the HCA gain better balance and maintain moral integrity.

In addition, healthcare administrators should be vigilant about their moral integrity—they should never take it for granted. Self-assessment and acknowledging strengths, weaknesses, and one's moral bottom line should be a frequent activity in the HCA's professional life. This process should help the administrator avoid the delusion of self-deception. Self-deception includes decisions like choosing to be ignorant, ignoring the unpleasant, becoming emotionally distant, and rationalizing one's behavior.

Summary

This chapter provides insight into moral integrity and its maintenance. Healthcare administrators have the power to affect more than the bottom line of their organizations. As has been emphasized throughout this text, the U.S. healthcare system is going through a time of great challenges and changes. Because of this transition, the community may have different attitudes toward health care and some degree of trust may be lost. Because healthcare administrators and others represent the healthcare organization to the community, they can help to restore trust in the healthcare system through their actions. Admittedly, restoring and maintaining trust will not be easy. The work of Annison and Wilford (1998) on trust still applies. When trust is lost, all aspects of health care suffer, from patient care to the bottom line. However, HCAs can make a conscious choice to maintain trust through their moral integrity. They will have to use moral courage to do what is right even if they do not personally benefit from those decisions. They can create a working environment where moral integrity becomes the norm rather than the exception. The challenges and ideas presented here are intended to assist HCAs in maintaining lifelong efforts to serve health care as moral leaders.

Ten Challenges for Maintaining Moral Integrity
....

The following 10 challenges assist HCAs in the process of refining and maintaining their professional moral integrity. Each of the challenges requires introspection to reap positive benefits. In addition, comments under each of the challenges are offered that provide insights and encouragement. The section uses the first person voice so that the author can speak to the reader directly. Revisit this list at different stages of your career and use it to confirm or reestablish your moral center.

1. Answer this question, "Why do I want a career in health administration?"

   Comments
   On the surface, this seems like an easy question. Some of my students would jump to an answer and say, "So I can earn the big money." Obviously, no one chooses a career in health administration to be poor—not even those who serve in public health where salaries are historically low. However, the "material goodies" do not compensate for having a job that does not satisfy you or, at the worst, a job that you hate.

   Your reasons for wanting to be a part of this enormously challenging career are as individual as you are. However, when you get to the essence of most people's decisions to choose and remain in a career, two powerful forces are likely to be apparent: the desire to make a difference through service and the desire to engage in meaningful work.

   We can start with making a difference. What would happen if you chose a different career? Are there things that you can contribute through that career that will make a difference to your staff, your organization, and your community? When I consider these questions, I recall the root of the word "vocation." It actually means having a calling rather than finding a job. If you are called to health administration, it means that you are willing to work even when things are not so pleasant. It also means that you are willing to make a commitment to prepare yourself intellectually and ethically for this challenge. You are willing to go beyond the minimum or "duties as assigned" to accomplish what the patient, staff, and organization need. Your goal is to create a better organization and make a difference.

   Of course, Frankl (1971) would encourage you to consider how your work contributes to your life's meaning. Meaning, he tells us, happens because of what you take from the world, what you give to the world, and what you choose to love. When service becomes a focus of your work, you are more likely to view it as a source of meaning rather than as a grind to endure. In contrast, if your work is meaningless and you consider yourself as just another cog in a great bureaucratic wheel, you can justify poor performance, and disloyalty. When work has no meaning, it is easier to be a shadow leader or even to practice evil.

The key becomes how you find this meaning and a way to make a difference on a daily basis. First, as Frankl (1971) reminds us, you must always remember that you have a choice. You can choose to take even small actions that create a positive work environment. You can choose to be a role model for moral integrity through your actions. You can choose to make a lifelong commitment to moral integrity. It is also helpful to remember how important you are to your staff and your organization. Although the healthcare administration profession may not get its own TV show like the some of the clinical staff does, your actions make saving lives possible. You are the foundation of the work of health care.

2. Conduct a personal moral integrity cost/benefit analysis.

Comments

Does this sound strange to you? First, this is not a cost/benefits analysis in its traditional definition, where you assign dollar values to items. In my version, you assign a career "cost" to a decision to help you decide if it "benefits" your morality. For example, you can draw up a table to help you make a decision whether to accept a job promotion. Then, by filling in the blank cells, you can perform a cost/benefits analysis to help you arrive at the best decision for your moral health. Your table might look like the following example.

Decision: State what you plan to do. Then fill in the blanks on this chart.

Moral Costs of Making the Decision	Benefits of Making the Decision	Moral Costs of **NOT** Making the Decision	Benefits of **NOT** Making the Decision

Notice that this example includes columns for not accepting the promotion. A cost/benefit analysis of *not* choosing an action can be just as beneficial to your moral health as such an analysis of choosing the action, but this option is not always considered.

A simple self-brainstorming technique can help you think about possible benefits and costs. Remember to think about the "big picture" and include your family in the benefits and/or costs. They are often the beneficiaries or bear the emotional and financial burdens of your decisions. You can also use this technique, in addition to fiscal and risk analysis, to assist in making organizational decisions that involve moral issues.

3. Define your "moral bottom line."

Comments

Establish the criteria that, if met, would cause you to resign from your job. This process of defining your moral bottom line asks you to identify what you are worth. Will you compromise when you know that your boss is doing something illegal? What if his or her action is legal but immoral: What would you do? You might struggle with this task for a while, but it is important for you to assess this area for your career. Having a defined moral bottom line can also help you decide whether to take a position in the first place. For example if, after doing your homework and participating in interviews, you detect something that would compromise your moral bottom line, your decision is easy: Do not take the job.

Your moral bottom line does not have to focus solely on things that would cause you to resign. You also need to identify those principles that will cause you to take action or speak out in meetings, even if it makes you unpopular. Because no one wants a reputation as a complainer—or worse, a snitch—this is also a difficult assessment to make. The thing to remember is that failure to speak up or to provide a different view can actually lead to disaster. If you choose silence, you are condoning the behavior. Condoning also implies supporting the behavior. The last thing you want to say when a moral disaster occurs is that "I knew and I should have said something."

4. Engage in directed activities to build and maintain your moral integrity.

Comments

A variety of options are available for taking on this challenge. None of them, however, will have any effect unless you choose to implement them. In your already busy world, it might seem unreasonable to take on yet another "thing to do," but the payback is worth the effort. Remember to start small and simple so you will make this practice a part of your daily life (just like showering or brushing your teeth).

Palmer (2000) suggests several techniques for building moral integrity. First, try keeping a journal. This technique is a variation of "freedom of speech." You are free to write anything without any censors or restrictions. You do not need any special books or tools, just paper and pen or a computer. You do not have to write in your journal every day. However, it is a good idea to set aside time to write an entry at least once a week.

You can use a rhetorical question to gear your journal toward your moral integrity issues. Any question or issue of concern to you will do. You can ask yourself, "What is morality to me?" "What is the moral way of dealing with this situation?" or "Who could be hurt if I make this decision?" Then just write. Keep writing until you have captured all of your thoughts about your question. This author usually sets her journal aside for a day or so, then goes back, and reads it. There is often some practical wisdom in my musings that can really help my decision making. The author also saves her journals and revisits them to read about former areas of concern. This review helps her see how much she has grown as a person.

Reflection is also a way to foster growth in moral integrity. It usually requires a trigger event or source to guide it and gear it toward moral issues. You can use the actions of others as such a trigger and think about what you would have done if faced with that situation. Use events in the news and reflect about the moral issues that relate to them. Certainly, with all of the corporate and personal scandals that have eroded trust in American business, sports, and even churches, you should not lack sources for reflecting on moral integrity.

Remember that reflection sources do not have to come from the work setting. The arts can provide some great opportunities. For example, photography captures a point in time and can lead you to muse about morality and growth. You can look at the photo and ask, "What would I have done or felt at that point in time?" Similarly, movies can illustrate many areas of moral and immoral behavior for consideration. In fact, Johnson (2009) features many movies in his book and provides ethical thematic analyses of them. His suggestions include *Dead Man Walking*, *Twelve Angry Men*, and *Schindler's List*. This author is sure you can find many more examples, including movies that relate specifically to health care such as *Patch Adams*. Regardless of your choice, take time to reflect on which critical moral decisions the characters experienced and what they did. How did the decisions affect the person and the organization? What would you have done in that situation?

Do not neglect the power of literature as a source for reflection. This author particularly likes poetry because it can affect me emotionally as well as intellectually. One of her favorites is *A Brave and Startling Truth* by Maya Angelou. This author also had great conversations about moral integrity that centered on novels and short stories. You can also find book clubs that reflect on the moral issues presented in a specific novel. If you do not have time to read for "fun," use your journal entries to spark this process. The main idea is to think about your moral integrity and its practice. You cannot assume integrity will be there without taking direct action to help it grow.

5. Identify a moral mentor.

Comments

Do you know a person whom you consider a highly moral leader? Is there someone who could serve as your moral mentor or as a role model? You have already heard about the benefits of mentoring in some of your courses. Perhaps you have completed an internship or a residency where you had a mentor. This person taught you the inner workings of the organization and made your transition easier. A moral mentor, however, is someone who is willing to go beyond sharing information about how things work; that is, he or she is willing to hear and understand your deepest professional concerns in confidence and provide guidance without judgment.

Because the healthcare system increases in complexity almost daily, it will be normal for you to have concerns and questions about the right thing to do. It is possible that you might not want to "lose face" by expressing them too publicly. This is where a moral mentor can be invaluable to your career. He or she will let you think through your options and conduct a verbal moral cost/benefit analysis. Your mentor will not solve your problem for you, but rather will guide you in selecting your best plan of action.

How will you find a moral mentor? First, be observant. See how people interact with their staff. Are their behaviors consistent with their words? Can they be trusted? Second, when you identify such a person, take time to get to know him or her. See what he or she is like in a variety of settings. Is this someone you can trust?

If the answer is "yes," make an appointment to talk with this person. Ask if he or she will be your moral mentor, and observe the reaction. If there is any reluctance, do not pursue the matter further. It has been this author's experience that if you choose carefully, mentors are honored by being asked to serve in this role. However, keep in mind that your mentor has many other duties. Do not abuse the privilege of having a personal adviser by engaging in "whine sessions" or "pity parties." Instead, come to your mentor with the tough decisions and listen to his or her wisdom. The advice you receive will be a valuable asset to cultivate and maintain your moral integrity.

6. Examine your life experiences (successes and failures) and find their moral lessons.

Comments

This is a difficult challenge. It is easiest to start with your successes. This author is sure that you have had shining moments when you achieved your goals and made yourself and your family proud. List those accomplishments and next to them write the moral lessons you learned from them. For example, one of this author's shining moments was the first time my major professor called me, "Dr. Morrison." Because this author was working full-time and raising a family, completing her doctorate was not easy—so this moment meant a great deal to her. Her moral lessons were that everything has a price, but the price was worth it. This author also learned to follow her heart, even when she was tempted to give up.

Now look at the areas of which you are not so proud. All of us have actions we wish we had not taken, decisions we wish we had not made, or words we wish we had not said. For this part of the challenge, you need to list at least some of these areas. Because they are in your past, you cannot change any of them. However, some good can still come out of these experiences. Beside each item on your list, think about a lesson that you learned from this experience and write it down.

Finally, go beyond just writing. Use these lessons, regardless of where you learned them. They can help you in the future by assisting as you decide what to do and avoid doing. In taking this last step, you can increase your moral integrity through the analysis of your own experiences.

7. Design a prevention plan to avoid moral derailment.

Comments

As the list of your career successes grows, there will be increased potential for moral derailment or moving closer to the shadow side of leadership. All of us have aspects of our personalities or behaviors that can cause us to derail as administrators. Therefore, you need a plan to avoid derailment and understand its causes. First, think about who you really are as a person. For example, how do you feel about power? Without power, you could not be in an administrative position. But what will happen when your power increases? Will power become the center of your life, or will you maintain your judgment and humility? Will you use your power to help others or to benefit yourself alone? You need to formulate the answers to these questions before power becomes an issue. They should come from introspection, as you look deep into your heart.

What about the privilege that stems from your position? It can be a great temptation if you assign too much value to your privilege. Privilege can also lead to shadow leadership if you see your possessions as a reflection of who you are. How much is enough for you? Are you what you wear and what you drive? While you will no doubt live comfortably as a healthcare administrator, you are part of a culture that puts great emphasis on external appearances. Understanding the responsibility that comes with privileges can keep you from thinking too highly of yourself and forgetting the people whom you serve.

One of the many lessons that the events of September 11, 2001, taught us is that we can lose impressive creations, privileges, and material possessions in an instant. However, as the death toll rose on that tragic day, what turned out to be of utmost importance to both individuals and the nation were the demonstrations of compassion, service, and heroism. These actions lingered in our memory even when buildings were rubble.

Another way to move toward the shadows of leadership is through deceit. Deceit can involve more than just lying to others or covering up the misdeeds of those in higher positions. Sometimes we practice self-deception as leaders. In the ACA era, you will be required to make difficult decisions in which the solutions are not always easy. To be successful, you must be able to stand up to pressure, motivate yourself, and have courage.

Practicing self-honesty instead of self-deception requires taking time to think. Ideally, you should have a minimum of 30 minutes per day to be alone and practice self-reflection. While this can seem like just another demand on your time, it pays off in terms of more effective and morally sound decisions for yourself and your organization.

8. Engage in PQI.

Comments

PQI—that is, personal quality improvement—is my morality version of the quality improvement/continuous quality improvement process. Think of your life beyond the work environment. Do you have a life fully lived? Do you work to live or live to work? Gilbert (2007) offers a mechanism for assessing your moral integrity and makes suggestions on "what we want to minimize and what we want to instill" (p. 194). You can also conduct a health assessment to develop your PQI.

Start with the most obvious factor: your physical health. Because you have only one body, you will want to keep it as healthy as possible for as long as possible. However, your body cannot accomplish this task without your cooperation. In other words, you must do what you counsel others to do: eat in moderation, exercise, take time to rest, and sleep. Yet, all too often, we think of our physical selves as the exception to these rules. We ask our bodies to function without even the minimum of care. The truth is that you cannot take time for moral reasoning (or any kind of reasoning, for that matter) when you are tired, hungry, and ill.

Now consider your mental and emotional health. Are you learning and experiencing new things, or fighting to keep everything the same? In health care, professionals have no choice but to be life-long learners. The changes in the system are happening too fast for healthcare administrators not to be on an active learning curve. The dynamic healthcare environment will make demands on your emotional health as well. Yet, you cannot afford to get too sad, too lonely, or too stressed. Extremes in your emotional health can compromise your effectiveness as a healthcare leader.

To rejuvenate your emotional resources means taking time for recreation. Think about what recreation actually means: You re-create yourself based on your choices. Do you remember the author's story about the chaplain? He took time to renew his mind and his emotional health through play. Hemsath and Yerkes (1997) created an entire book devoted to this idea, called *301 Ways to Have Fun at Work*. Their examples come from highly successful corporations and illustrate the impact of fun on morale and productivity. Remember that, while health care should be a part of your mission, you also have a life beyond work. Which activities can you do to renew yourself? The author's students are always able to create long lists of these activities, but finding time to do these activities and be successful students becomes their challenge.

Social health is also a component for building moral integrity. We all learn from our friends, especially those who know us well enough to be caring and honest. You might not always like what you hear, but when something comes from your friend's heart, it is worth hearing. Friends listen even when they have heard you talk about the same topic many times. Having this empathetic sounding board is critical to your moral development because it lets you process your thoughts in a nonjudgmental and supportive environment.

There is a caution to be sounded here. You cannot have this level of friendship without investing time and energy on your friends. A truly supportive relationship cannot be one-sided. Sometimes this means that you have to be the one who listens, even when you do not feel like it. It can also mean that you have to show up and support someone when you would rather do something else. If true friendships are to thrive, they must be cultivated.

There are so many writings about emotional health and its care that we would need another text to fully cover this topic. Nevertheless, two concepts have proved especially helpful for this author in my roles in health administration. First is a phrase from a Beatles song: "Let it be." Sometimes you just have to let go of whoever or whatever is causing you emotional stress. This is especially true if the cause of the stress happened in the past, because you cannot change its outcome. The author asks herself, "Did I do everything I could about the situation that was so stressful?" If the answer is "yes," then she knows that she should let it go.

Second, the author uses the phrase, "It is not about me," to remember that there are always at least two sides to a situation. This realization helps when you get a reaction that is not expected or when people say things that are rude or hurtful. Maybe the person is having a bad day and the reaction has nothing to do with you. Try not to take it personally; this an axiom often used in business. However, not taking things personally is often easier to say than it is to do. Even so, reminding yourself that you might not be the source of the problem helps to maintain positive emotional health.

9. Have a rich and varied spiritual life.

   Comments

   Spiritual health is also a component of PQI. There is a connection between your spiritual well-being and maintaining your moral integrity. This connection may present its own challenges. Johnson (2009) presents a model for spiritual maturation that is similar in some ways to Kohlberg's model of moral development. Johnson's model, however, gives insights into the process of becoming more spiritually centered. This process includes reflecting on your beliefs, understanding your part in the world, and learning to deal with life's struggles and disappointments,

   You can enhance spirituality practiced in private through contemplation using either the Western tradition (connecting to God) or the Eastern tradition (opening your mind). Prayer or connecting to a higher spiritual center, or what Frankl (1971) calls the ultimate meaning, is a part of this process as well. Prayer helps you to concentrate on your spiritual issues and learn patience. Johnson (2009) also includes study as part of private spirituality. This technique helps you to concentrate and explore various concepts related to spiritual health. Study includes reading and being present in nature as inspirational sources.

   Spirituality that you practice in public can get you back to basics. If you can learn to bypass the glitz and dig deep into what is important, you can have a deeper spiritual experience. For some people, this can mean divesting themselves of things that once seemed so important, but that now feel like burdens. Living more simply allows more time and energy to live more spiritually.

Johnson (2009) suggests that you spend time alone in silence and in service as techniques for spiritual growth. The discipline of solitude is very difficult for most Americans because we live in such a sensory-saturated environment. For example, think about what it would be like to have no cable or other television, radio, Internet access, smartphone, Twitter, Facebook, e-mail, and other media goodies. Some of this author's students would find the silence stressful. Yet making the effort to find time for solitude can reward one with insight and ways to maintain spiritual balance. Service is also a major component of public spirituality. Johnson (2009) defines it as putting others first when you are not rewarded for doing so. Your motivation in this case is not recognition; instead, you practice altruism in the fullest sense of that word. When you are engaged in service just because there is a need, you will find gratitude in the experience and humility in what you learn.

10. Work to create a climate of moral integrity.

Comments

This last challenge asks you to go beyond yourself and provide an opportunity for others to experience their own moral growth. You can provide a workplace where moral action is normal.

Such a workplace might be counter to the current culture, because some think that people who strive for morality are trying to be superior or "holier-than-thou." Conversely, such people can be considered naïve because "everybody acts in their own interests" and takes advantage of their power. Sometimes people mistake cheating, dishonesty, and other moral flaws for good behaviors because they seem to create "winners." Can you imagine trying to be a healthcare administrator in a department where everyone is out to get everyone else? Where would patient-centered care and service be in such a department?

Part of the creation of a morally centered workplace starts with you as the healthcare administrator. As the leader, you model the actions that you expect from others. In fact, your behavior sets the tone for what is acceptable and what is not. For example, if you say you believe in diversity, then you must put together teams that represent differing opinions and not just your own. While you might not get much ego stroking by making this choice, you could get answers to problems that really work. In addition, if you say that patient care is your mission, then you must do all you can to make quality patient care a reality. This includes getting out of your comfort zone and becoming visible to patients and caregivers.

Johnson (2009) advocates using practice-based "servant leadership" as a way to increase moral integrity in your department. With this approach, although you are a leader, you are simultaneously a servant to your staff in that you care, listen, accept, grow, and build community. Viewing staff as an asset instead of a liability can go a long way toward creating the trust needed to assure a morally centered workplace. Some bosses will criticize you for being a servant leader because they think you are weak and will lose control over "your people." These leaders prefer to use intimidation and fear to keep their staff in line. However, force and fear tend to be productive for only a limited time and as a tactic do not work for all employees. The best way to lead is to understand the people with whom you work. Then you can choose the best way to cooperate to meet goals for the benefit of patients and the organization as a whole.

These 10 challenges are not easy ones; they will take time and thought to address. This author hopes that you will continuously work on them after you complete your education and enter the workplace. Remember that change and growth are a process, so be patient with yourself and with others. The rewards for making this journey can be life affirming and life giving.

Web Resources

A Brave and Startling Truth, by Maya Angelou
http://www.inspirationpeak.com/poetry/bravetruth.html

Henrietta Lacks
http://rebeccaskloot.com/the-immortal-life/

The Holocaust and administrative evil
http://www.ushmm.org/

The Holocaust Explained
http://www.theholocaustexplained.org/

References

Annison, M. H. & Wilford, D. S. (1998). *Trust matters: New directions in health care leadership*. San Francisco, CA: Jossey Bass.
Bloom, P. (2013). *Just babies: The origins of good and evil*. New York, NY: Crown.

Caplan, A. L. (Ed.). (1992). *When medicine went mad: Bioethics and the holocaust.* Totowa, NJ: Humana.

Darr, K. (2011). *Ethics in health services management* (5th ed.). Baltimore, MD: Health Professions Press.

Dye, C. F. (2000). *Leadership in healthcare: Values at the top.* Chicago, IL: Health Administration Press.

Frankl, V. (1971). *Man's search for meaning: An introduction to logotherapy.* New York, NY: Pocket Books.

Gilbert, J. A. (2007). *Strengthening ethical wisdom: Tools for transforming your health care organization.* Chicago, IL: Health Administration Press.

Griffith, J. R. (1993). *The moral challenges of health care management.* Ann Arbor, MI: Health Professions Press.

Hemsath, D., & Yerkes, L. (1997). *301 ways to have fun at work.* San Francisco, CA: Berrett-Koehler.

Hofmann, P. B. (2006). Evaluating ethical fitness. *Healthcare Executive, 21*(3), 34–35.

Johnson, C. E. (2009). *Meeting the ethical challenges of leadership: Casting light or shadow* (3rd ed.). Thousand Oaks, CA: Sage.

London Grid for Learning. (2014). The Holocaust explained. Retrieved from http://www.theholocaustexplained.org/

Palmer, P. J. (2000). *Let your life speak.* San Francisco, CA: Jossey-Bass.

Purtilo, R. B., & Doherty, R. F. (2011). *Ethical dimensions in the health professions* (5th ed.). Philadelphia, PA: Elsevier Saunders.

Skloot, R. (2011). *The immortal life of Henrietta Lacks.* New York, NY: Broadway Paperbacks.

Summers, J. (2014). Theory of healthcare ethics. In E. E. Morrison & B. Furlong (Eds.), *Health care ethics: Critical issues for the 21st century* (3rd ed., pp. 3–46). Burlington, MA: Jones & Bartlett Learning.

Turak, A. (2013). *Business secrets of the Trappist monks: One CEO's quest for meaning and authenticity.* New York, NY: Columbia University Press.

CHAPTER
15

Codes of Ethics and Administrative Practice

How does a code of ethics assist healthcare administrators in becoming better leaders?

Points to Ponder

1. Why do professional groups and associations create codes of ethics?
2. What are the key features of a professional code of ethics for health administrators?
3. Why should administrators care about codes of ethics of other health professionals?
4. What are the limitations of codes of ethics?
5. How can healthcare administrators use their professional code of ethics in their administration practice?

Key Terms

The following is a list this chapter's key terms. Look for them in bold.

ACHE Code of Ethics   self-regulating

■ INTRODUCTION AND DEFINITIONS

The word *code* has a variety of meanings that relate to computer programming, medicine, genetics, and even spycraft. Derived from the Latin *codex*, meaning "tree trunk," in ethics this term refers to a collection of rules that describe acceptable ethical behavior ("Code", n.d.).

Scholars and other experts developed ethics codes for groups in societies, organizations, and professions.

The concept of determining acceptable ethical behaviors for individuals is not new. Indeed, it has been studied and discussed for thousands of years. Using one's imagination, one can envision a small group of Neanderthals sitting around the fire before the hunt. They know that their world is difficult and survival is often threatened. Therefore, they discuss what will happen after their successful hunt and develop an agreement (code) about their actions. For example, they may decide that women and children must receive a share of the meat before others. While this action may seem beneficent, it is actually a decision affecting the continuation of the tribe. If only the men receive meat, future generations of the tribe may not survive. Using this example, one can see that society needs guidelines to protect both individual and group interests. Religions provide this protection because they present guidelines for acceptable moral behaviors for groups and individuals. However, societies often also develop laws that serve to determine acceptable behaviors and punishments for violations of these actions (Purtilo & Doherty, 2011).

When moral decisions affect the practice of professionals and those whom they serve, a professional code of ethics needs to be developed. Why are these codes necessary? Owing to the vulnerability of patients and the community, healthcare professionals possess great power. Because of the imbalanced relationship created by this power, definitions of appropriate professional conduct and moral responsibility are needed. These codes do not just focus on regulating behaviors, but must also explain appropriate moral character and practice.

In general, professional codes of ethics include some form of introduction, an explanation, and a set of conduct rules and information on how to implement the code. Conduct rules often give specific information about common ethical issues that the professional might face. For example, there may be sections on conflict of interest, respect for patients, duties to the profession, and even professional appearance. Professional codes of ethics also include expectations for reporting violations of the code and sanctions that can apply in cases of such violations.

An early example of a professional code of ethics is the Hippocratic Oath, which was written in the fourth century BCE. This document guided the practice of physicians over the centuries and influenced their patient care and personal behavior. This document, which includes instructions to avoid harming patients, continues to be used by today's physicians as a guide (US Legal, 2014).

Codes of ethics also exist for healthcare administrators (HCAs), though they vary depending on a particular individual's professional role. For example, the American College of Healthcare Executives (ACHE) developed the code of ethics for healthcare administrators' practice and defined expectations for ethical conduct. If healthcare administrators serve as nursing facility administrators, they have a slightly different code of ethics. Likewise, a code from the American Public Health Association guides the professional behavior of public health administrators (Darr, 2011).

■ RATIONALE FOR HEALTHCARE CODES OF ETHICS

Healthcare personnel continually face situations where an ethical course of action is not always clear. In fact, these gray areas can be disturbing and cause sleepless nights for a person with an active conscience. Because of the ethical challenges inherent in health care, both organizations and professions have developed standards in the form of codes to provide greater guidance and wisdom in decision making. The bases for these codes are the theories and principles of ethics and the experience of other professionals. One could consider a code of ethics to be a sort of prevention tool or "ethics vitamin" that sets boundaries for acceptable behaviors for organizations and professionals. Of course, this understanding assumes that individuals know their codes and try to live their lives according to the codes' tenets.

Codes of ethics also connect to the development of professionals. How do people become professionals? First, they must understand what it means to be a professional. The community assumes that, if they are professionals, they are highly competent, well educated, and highly ethical. The process of creating professionals is called professional socialization and requires study, role modeling, and practice experiences. Becoming a professional often requires years of study to master a body of knowledge that is germane to a particular field. It may also require that an individual pass a comprehensive examination that demonstrates his or her basic understanding of the profession's knowledge. In addition, being a professional may include meeting the requirements for licensure and functioning under a practice act that limits one's actions. Another major component of being a professional is adhering to a code of ethics. This code, which is typically developed by professional associations, spells out the ethical expectations for a member of the profession.

Sansom (2013) suggests that professionals may ignore their codes of ethics when the basis for these codes is rules and regulations. In health care, however, such codes can serve as a guide to virtues or the characteristics needed to serve the larger community. In this sense, codes of ethics take professionals beyond the monetary side of health care to the provision of the best possible patient care. Medical codes of ethics also assist professionals to understand medical care as a blending of patient care, technology, and scientific knowledge. Codes also assist in understanding both the ethical responsibilities and the limitations of patient care in a complex environment.

Even with their limitations, codes are the most commonly used ethical device for professionals (Johnson, 2009). They can define a person's position on ethical issues and provide an expectation for those who interact with healthcare professionals. In addition, when applied appropriately, codes protect professionals from lawsuits and increasing external regulation. In fact, health professionals should strive to be **self-regulating**. This means that they make the choice to maintain high standards of practice because it is the right thing to do. Practicing a code of ethics, therefore, requires that professionals obey the law, but also work within the spirit of the law. Why is self-regulation so important? Healthcare professionals must always remember that the public puts an extraordinary amount of trust in them. In turn, they must honor this trust through their thoughts and actions. When this expectation is honored, codes can be a useful tool for practicing patient-centered ethics and maintaining community trust.

Codes of ethics help healthcare professionals resist behaviors that can lead toward the shadow side of administration (Johnson, 2009). However, to be effective, such codes must contain certain features. First, they must explain the minimal standard of acceptable behavior rather than make global statements. For example, the **ACHE Code of Ethics** (ACHE, 2011) addresses specific areas concerning professional behavior. These statements delineate the organization's recommended actions. The American College of Healthcare Executives reviews and revises the ACHE Code of Ethics frequently, with the most recent changes being completed in 2011.

In addition, the basis for codes should be identified; that is, the moral principles, theories, and virtues underlying the code should be made explicit (Sansom, 2013). Codes provide a basis for taking action and explaining the rationale behind the action. Because they can be useful in decision making, codes should be living documents that are integral parts of healthcare practice. Finally, codes should be relevant and useful for addressing new challenges such as those created by the implementation of the Affordable Care Act of 2010 (ACA) and other healthcare laws and policies.

The presence of a code of ethics is not sufficient to ensure professional self-regulation. Darr (2011) stresses that, even with enforcement, "codes of ethics can only guide the behavior and decisions of individuals who want to do the right thing but need help determining what it is" (p. 78). In addition, professionals must maintain currency with respect to their codes of ethics. To accomplish this goal, Darr and other authors stress the necessity of continuing education and discussion about ethics codes, challenges, and decisions.

In summary, no document is perfect, but the knowledge and use of an ethics code can assist healthcare administrators to determine the appropriate standards and expectations for their conduct. Following this path allows them to use their titles with the full understanding of what the title means. A code also protects healthcare administrators against others who choose not to abide by professional standards and helps them to "know them by their deeds." The choice to avoid association with non-code-compliant healthcare administrators can protect one's reputation and the reputation of one's organization. Codes of ethics also challenge administrators to practice self-regulation by not hiring those persons who practice unethically and by not condoning their actions by practicing inaction. Finally, codes make it easier for healthcare administrators to avoid the shadow areas of leadership by giving them a fallback position and a way to avoid future difficulties.

■ CODES OF ETHICS FOR ORGANIZATIONS

Darr (2011) suggests that the culture of health care is different from that of general business. Because of the nature of health care, private actions of both administrators and practitioners have a greater impact on the industry itself. In addition, healthcare organizations must maintain a special bond of trust with their patients. This fiduciary relationship requires a clear identification of acceptable and unacceptable behaviors. Therefore, healthcare institutions must carefully define these behaviors and practices to avoid negative actions. Healthcare organizations also expect all of their employees to maintain high ethical standards.

Given the importance of ethical behavior to healthcare organizations, they often develop codes of ethics to delineate expectations for their employees. The basis for such organizational codes consists of both principles and theories of ethics. In addition, many codes stress respect, beneficence, nonmaleficence, and justice as organizational priorities. Purtilo and Doherty (2011) also suggest that ethics needs to be applied to the policies and customs found in healthcare organizations. Martin (2013) discusses the need for ethics code in healthcare organizations to address issues of cost, quality, and access. He specifies that organizations need to use The Joint Commission and other resources to design codes of conduct. The resulting codes should specify acceptable behaviors for professionals who have contact with patients. This specificity, in turn, should explain the behaviors of an organizational citizen, define expectations for stewardship, and reduce risk.

Martin (2013) and Niles (2013) provide information concerning the design process for organizational codes of ethics. Martin (2013) encourages alignment with the organization's mission and values when constructing such a code. In addition, organizations need to undertake a collaborative approach to design that includes healthcare professionals, and to provide training for those who will use a code or enforce it. Martin suggests that a retreat may be an effective way to accomplish organizational code design and facilitation. Niles (2013) also offers ideas on developing codes of ethics. She suggests that code developers review current laws and regulations before beginning the process. It is also important that they write codes in clear language and represent the core values of the organization. In addition, an extensive training program should be included as part of the code development process.

■ CODES OF ETHICS FOR HEALTHCARE ADMINISTRATORS

The field of healthcare administration holds a unique position in the healthcare industry. Professionals who serve in this capacity must balance the mission of health care, including delivery of quality patient service, with the business requirements of organizational profitability. This challenge alone presents many ethical challenges for healthcare administrators. In addition, numerous changes in the healthcare environment, such as the implementation of the ACA, ICD-10 coding system, and new HIPAA laws, may lead to future concerns. Therefore, it is not surprising that healthcare administrators must be aware of and practice their code of ethics.

Healthcare administrators may have different codes depending on their specific career field. For example, many healthcare administrators use the American College of Healthcare Executives Code of Ethics. In contrast, healthcare administrators in nursing homes follow the American College of Healthcare Administrators Code of Ethics. For their part, administrators in public health settings follow the code of ethics established by the American Public Health Association. A brief discussion of each of these codes follows.

American College of Healthcare Executives Code of Ethics

The online sites for the ACHE Code of Ethics, Ethics Toolkit, and Ethical Policy Statements are identified in the Web Resources for this chapter. These documents provide tools for busy administrators and are subject to frequent review.

According to the ACHE Code of Ethics, healthcare administrators' primary ethical duty is to serve those who seek health care. They fulfill this duty by working to create a better healthcare system. In creating this system, healthcare administrators must consider more than the financial aspects of health care. In addition, the community's rights and needs must be part of the decision-making process because healthcare administrators serve as "moral advocates" for the community (ACHE, 2011, para. 6).

The Code of Ethics (ACHE, 2011) divides responsibilities into eight areas involving the needs of the profession, patients, organization, employees, and community. Further clarification of the HCA's responsibilities and behaviors is included under each area. For example, administrators have a duty to their profession to act in a manner that honors it. Administrators must also be careful not to use their power and knowledge to further their own finances or betray professional confidences. Avoidance of conflicts of interest is also expected.

As part of HCAs' duty to the patient, they are supposed to protect individual rights and resolve the conflicts that arise when patients' and staff values differ. Protecting patients' rights also means that they preserve autonomy, protect confidentiality, and do not tolerate abuse. Quality assurance is another part of HCAs' duty to patients, because it serves to provide an environment where the best patient care is possible. Healthcare administrators also owe a duty to their organizations. This duty involves being truthful in communications, implementing a code of ethics for the organization, and providing appropriate resources for staff when ethics issues arise. When considering employees, HCAs have an obligation to create a place where ethics is the norm. They must also protect employees from harassment and create a safe environment where employees can use their talents to benefit patient care. In addition, HCAs are expected to be vigilant about their accounting practices to avoid fraud and abuse.

Finally, the Code of Ethics (ACHE, 2011) provides examples of duty to the community. Healthcare administrators are to provide information that allows the community to make informed decisions about healthcare services. There is also an obligation to assess the community's healthcare needs and work to provide access to needed services. While maintaining a strong fiscal position, healthcare organizations must advocate actions that improve community health.

The ACHE Code of Ethics demands much from healthcare administrators. It makes these demands because HCAs have a great deal of influence and power and represent both their profession and their organization to the public. Individuals can file ethics complaints against an ACHE member, and the ACHE has a detailed process for dealing with any such complaints. The ACHE Ethics Committee has several actions it can take in response to a complaint, including censure and expulsion from the organization. While these actions do not carry the same weight as a loss of licensure, they can have a negative effect on the HCA's career. For example, a person might not receive positive consideration for new positions, particularly those in higher levels, if he or she is not in good standing with the ACHE. In addition, the field of healthcare administration is still one where many peers can be aware of a particular HCA's reputation. For all these reasons, maintaining compliance with the Code of Ethics makes good professional and personal sense.

ACHE goes beyond the Code of Ethics to provide healthcare administrators with ethical policy statements. These statements serve as "mini-white papers" on issues that affect personal and organizational ethics. They define the ACHE's position on each issue and give recommendations for action. One example that is especially interesting is the statement about ethical decision making (ACHE, 2013a). This document reinforces the expectation that healthcare administrators are leaders who practice eudaimonia and ethical wisdom. It encourages HCAs to foster ethical decision making in their healthcare settings and offers suggestions for practice. These recommendations include offering educational programs on ethical practice and decision making, maintaining an ethics committee populated with members who have diverse views, and evaluating processes for addressing ethics issues.

In addition to the Code and Policy Statements, ACHE offers several other ethics resources through its website (ACHE, 2013b). These resources, called the Ethics Toolkit, include a self-assessment instrument. This document measures the frequency with which healthcare administrators engage in behaviors that reflect compliance with the Code of Ethics. Healthcare administrators should pay special attention to any answer that falls below the "usually frequent" category. Of course, as with any other self-assessment, this instrument is only valid to the extent that the HCA answers its items honestly.

The ACHE website also provides a list of resources to assist HCAs with ethics concerns. Among these resources is a copy of Nelson's (2005) article on ethics decision making. This article is particularly useful because it contains an eight-step process for making sound ethics decisions. The first three steps focus on clarifying the situation, identifying the affected stakeholders, and researching the circumstances. Next, HCAs are asked to determine the ethics principles involved, consider possible options, and select the best possible decision. Finally, Nelson suggests that healthcare administrators communicate the ethics decision and use it in their organizations with appropriate evaluation.

What should healthcare administrators do with the ACHE Code of Ethics? Darr (2011) suggests that HCAs' role is to safeguard the public against potential abuse from the healthcare system. To accomplish this mission, healthcare administrators need well-identified, professional standards and the ability to act on those standards. Therefore, they must use the Code of Ethics as a tool for self-regulation, even if they are not members of ACHE. Darr also encourages use of the ACHE Code because professional integrity is essential for healthcare administrators' career progress. Adherence to the Code's basic principles will also help maintain employee and community trust. Finally, using a set of standards should assist healthcare administrators to be persons of integrity even when there is no financial reward for doing so. Darr considers this to be "the right thing to do—it is a principle for life and the profession" (p. 93).

Nursing Home Administrators Code of Ethics

Long-term care administrators (LTCAs) are responsible for the care of the most vulnerable members of the community: the elderly and the disabled. Given this fact, residents, families, and the community hold them to a high level of ethical conduct. The American College of Healthcare Administrators (ACHCA) provides a code of ethics that features four major expectations for integrity for long-term care administrators. The ACHCA Code of Ethics also outlines other expectations, including that LTCAs maintain high standards of personal competence, place a priority on the interests of their facility, and maintain their duties to the public and other professionals (ACHCA, 2010; Darr, 2011).

Each of the expectations in the ACHCA Code of Ethics features prescriptions and proscriptions that provide guidance for the LTCA. For example, there is a prescription for LTCAs to maintain competency and enhance knowledge through continuing their education. The proscriptions state that LTCAs should not misrepresent themselves or provide services for which they are not qualified to do so. In addition, there is an expectation that long-term care administrators will be self-regulating and report ethics violations to the Standards and Ethics Committee (ACHCA, 2010; Darr, 2011).

Public Health Administrators Code of Ethics

Administrators who are part of the various fields that represent public health are also required to maintain high ethical standards. Public health administrators' responsibilities for protecting community health, preventing disease, and prolonging life mean that they face ethics challenges on an almost daily basis (Turnock, 2012). Therefore, they, like other healthcare administrators, need guidance on expectations for their practice. One source for this information is *Principles of the Ethical Practice of Public Health*, developed by the Public Health Leadership Society in 2002. Expectations specific to public health administrators include that they will act as advocates for those persons who are in lesser positions in a community, will be respectful of the rights of individuals while achieving community health, and will be well informed before making policies that affect the community. In addition, they should respect and protect confidentiality, ensure competency of their employees, and collaborate with other healthcare professionals. The Public Health Leadership Society (2002) also explains that its ethics document is a living work and encourages feedback for updating.

■ LEARNING FROM CAREGIVER CODES

Healthcare administrators can also be "bicodal." This term means that they can be members of clinical professions as well as healthcare administrators. For example, bicodal professionals are educated on the code of their caring profession. When they assume administrative roles, an administration code of ethics then becomes part of their practice. The good news is that there is often congruence between the codes, which may make their simultaneous application easier. For examples, areas like integrity, honesty, appropriate communication, respect for others, and confidentiality are common features found in virtually all ethics codes. When caregivers serve in an administrative role, they must also honor their ethical responsibilities as an administrator including fidelity, stewardship of resources, and implementation of policies that respect the organization and the employee.

Darr (2011) suggests that healthcare administrators can enhance their careers by familiarizing themselves with the ethics codes of the many other professionals who work under the aegis of the same organization. The rationale for this suggestion is that HCAs need a deeper understanding of these professional groups' ethics standards so that they assist in creating effective healthcare teams. An excellent resource for codes of ethics is the Center for the Study of Ethics in the Professions (CSEP, 2014). Its website includes examples of ethics codes from hundreds of occupations, including more than 50 from the field of health care. While it would be educational to examine all 50 codes, the discussion here focuses on examples from health professions that are often part of the healthcare workforce and the supervision responsibility of healthcare administrators. The selected examples may serve as lessons for the healthcare administrator who is seeking to foster an organization that is ethical to patients, clinical staff, and the community.

Codes of Ethics for Physicians

Codes of ethics for physicians have their origins in the Code of Hammurabi (18th century BCE) and in the teachings of Hippocrates (460–370 BCE). These works established guidelines for the practice of medicine and the relationship between physicians and their patients. In modern times, many types of physician practices exist, each of which is subject to its own guidelines for ethical practice. However, the American Medical Association (AMA) provides a code that can apply to physicians in general (AMA, 2014; Darr, 2011).

The AMA Code of Medical Ethics (AMA, 2014) includes seven sections, which in turn encompass numerous subsections. The Code goes beyond describing the relationship between law and ethics by addressing interpersonal and hospital relations, confidentiality, fees, medical records, and practice management. The longest section in the Code is on social policy; it includes 66 subsections. This section offers advice on social policies including abortion, futile care, and torture. It also addresses a broad range of issues associated with research, including issues related to genomic research and end-of-life care. The social policy subsection offers physicians a mechanism for determining ethical practices to address these many issues.

Section 8: Opinions on Practice Matters (AMA, 2014), for example, addresses ethical issues of concern in practice management. It provides practical information on areas ranging from charging for missed appointments to self-referrals and consultations. In addition, there is advice on pay-for-performance programs, practices for prescribing drugs and devices, and even accepting gifts from healthcare industries.

The AMA Code of Medical Ethics (AMA, 2014) is one example of a practical ethics code that provides professionals with detailed information and examples to assist in applying practical wisdom to decisions. In today's complex healthcare environment, physicians can benefit from this detailed code of ethics. They can rely on its advice to avoid practices and decisions that can jeopardize their patient relationships and their practice solvency.

Lessons from the Code

The following lessons come from an examination of the AMA's (2014) Code of Medical Ethics. Application of these concepts should assist HCAs in becoming better administrators.

1. Health care presents ethical issue that go beyond one's immediate scope of practice. It is important to keep current on issues that relate to one's position, but are not always in daily practice.
2. Healthcare administrators can use the AMA Code as an example when preparing codes of practice for direct reports and others under their supervision. Notice the level of detail and the provision of examples for clarification.
3. Becoming familiar with the AMA Code can provide administrators with a greater understanding of the depth and scope of physician practice. This understanding can enhance administrator–physician communications and relationships.
4. Remember that physicians, like administrators, are charged with the responsibility of self-regulation, but they also have licensure at stake when ethical practices are violated.

Codes of Ethics for Nurses

Healthcare administrators work with members of the nursing professionals who represent all levels of care delivery. For this reason alone, it is recommended that HCAs become familiar with the nursing code of ethics. Just as with physicians, there are codes of ethics for specialists in nursing. However, the American Nurses Association (ANA, 2010) offers a *Code of Ethics for Nurses with Interpretative Statements* that provides a general understanding of the nursing profession's positions on ethics and the issues it faces.

The *Code of Ethics* has nine provisions, each with detailed subsections that provide examples of acceptable behavior on ethical issues ranging from health advocacy, to duty to the nursing profession, to duty to the health environment. Of interest is how the ANA places particular emphasis on patients and their needs. In fact, almost every provision ties back to the patients and their needs.

For example, Provisions 1 and 2 (ANA, 2010) stress the need for nurses to respect patients' humanity and dignity under all circumstances. Nurses must treat patients with the same level of respect and dignity regardless of their income, social status, lifestyle, or disease. They must also make the patients' interest the primary focus of their care and settle any conflicts of interest by putting the patient first. In addition, nurses must be willing to collaborate if this collaboration will benefit patients. Other provisions in the *Nursing Code of Ethics* (ANA, 2010) relate to being an advocate and addressing questionable nursing practices or impaired colleagues (Provision 3). Nurses must also be accountable for their delegation of tasks and their clinical judgments. In addition, they are responsible for maintaining competency and continuing to grow as professionals.

Lessons from the Code

The following lessons come from an examination of the *Nursing Code of Ethics with Interpretive Statements* (ANA, 2010). The application of these concepts should HCAs assist in becoming better administrators.

1. The first lesson from the *Nursing Code of Ethics* is that health care is about the patient. When a person is busy running the business of health care, it is easy to forget its mission. Patients are not just present to give healthcare professionals work to do. They are the center of health care and deserve the considerations stressed in the *Nursing Code*.
2. A foundation in theory or business practice is not enough to be an ethics-based healthcare administrator. Just as described in the *Nursing Code* for nurses, there might be times when administrators have to be willing to delegate and collaborate with others to achieve the best care for patients.
3. Like nurses, healthcare administrators must commit to lifelong learning. They must, on their initiative, take steps to ensure

competency by being up-to-date on information and taking continuing education classes. In the ACA era, change in health care is both rapid and profound. Failure to maintain competency is more than unethical; it can be career suicide.

Code of Ethics for Acupuncture and Oriental Medicine Practitioners

Healthcare administrators do not always work in hospitals, clinics, or other traditional settings. There are an increasing number of Americans who are seeking alternative forms of health care, including wellness programs, integrative medicine (complementary and alternative medicine [CAM]), and other providers. Therefore an example of a code of ethics from a different form of health care is included here.

The code of ethics of the National Certification Commission for Acupuncture and Oriental Medicine (NCCAOM) can serve as an example. The NCCAOM Code (2014) uses the format of a pledge to the patient, profession, and public. With respect to the patient, professionals pledge to respect privacy and dignity, and to provide high-quality service within the scope of their practice. They also promise to keep accurate records. In addition, the code prohibits sexual contact with patients while they are being treated. This prohibition exists because of the nature of the treatment and the need to maintain patient trust.

In addition, acupuncturists promise to honor their profession by maintaining high standards in their practice. They pledge to give the community accurate information about their education and training, advertise only accurate information, and comply with all public health agency regulations. Acupuncturists also assure the public that they will respect and collaborate with other forms of health care. The patient is the center of practitioner's actions and the NCCAOM's ethical code (NCCAOM, 2014).

Lessons from the Code

Healthcare administrators can adapt information from the code of ethics of NCCAOM (2014). These lessons for HCAs include the following:

1. The NCCAOM Code requires making promises to patients, the community, and the profession. Using the format of a promise strengthens the power of the statements. When healthcare administrators state that they will do something, fidelity requires that they do it. Therefore, administrators need to consider what they promise to patients, staff, and the community.

2. The NCCAOM Code also includes statements about honest business practices and quality of care in its commitment to both the patient and the community. Certainly, ethically sound business

practices should also be a part of healthcare administrators' professional commitment.

3. This code also promises that NCCAOM members will respect other healthcare professions and work with them to ensure the best care for patients. This promise should also be a part of the ethics considerations of practicing healthcare administrators. Being respectful of all professions should go a long way toward attaining quality care for patients and the community.

■ LIMITATIONS AND CRITICISMS OF CODES OF ETHICS

This chapter makes an argument for knowing and using professional codes of ethics. However, it would not be fair and balanced without presenting the limitations of such codes. Sansom (2013) discusses a crisis relating to codes of ethics because of their ineffectiveness. He found that practitioners are still interested in seeking answers to practical ethical questions, but do not always find these answers in codes of ethics. This is because many codes of ethics are too simple and are based on a series of rules. They speak more about what one should *not* do rather than provide guidance about what one *should* do. Samson (2013) suggests that, to be successful, codes of ethics need to have their basis in moral virtues and the covenant that healthcare professionals have with the community they serve.

Darr (2011) emphasizes that a code of ethics is only a guide for behavior. Those who choose to be immoral can use codes as a way to do what they wish and avoid sanction. In addition, if codes enter into legalities, they become too difficult to apply. Therefore, all codes have to walk the line between vagueness and constriction. Even without a professional code, the principles of respect, justice, beneficence, and nonmaleficence should guide professional behavior.

A classic work by Eriksson, Höglund, and Helgesson (2008) identifies three main problems with respect to ethical codes. First, there is a problem in interpretation because of the difference between the statements in the code and actual practice. That is, the person who must interpret the code needs an understanding of ethical theory to fathom its intent. Second, there is a problem of multiplicity; this problem occurs because there so many codes and guidelines under which professionals operate (the author's term is "bicodal"). This situation requires professionals to find the commonalities of their codes and determine how to handle situations and stay within them. Third, there is a legalization problem. According to Eriksson, Höglund, and Helgesson (2008), practitioners might potentially view ethical problems as legal situations. If this happens, those affected may see the situation in terms of how to stay within the law and not as a moral duty.

Summary

As Darr (2011) stated, a professional code of ethics helps healthcare administrators know the right thing to do. Certainly, such a code is not a panacea for all the ethics problems faced by healthcare administrators. In fact, codes of ethics can even assist those who choose the shadow side of administration to continue skating on thin ice without falling in. Unless there is a tie to licensure, codes of ethics are also very difficult to enforce.

So why bother? A code provides healthcare administrators with a way to understand their professional obligations and expected behaviors. In some codes, these behaviors are carefully delineated. When they are, they assist HCAs with resolving serious ethical and even legal problems. In any case, healthcare administrators can use the information provided in their ethics codes as starting points when making professional and personal decisions.

If administrators and other health professionals read and use codes of ethics, these codes will have a positive impact on their behavior. Therefore, keeping a copy of one's professional code readily available, reading it, and using it as part of the decision-making process lowers the potential for lawsuits and career failures. Darr (2011) also stresses that using codes of ethics can lead to greater success in one's career. This is because codes of ethics help to maintain integrity and public trust. Even if a code of ethics had nothing to do with personal wealth or status, Darr (2011) encourages healthcare administrators to live by a code because it is the right thing to do.

Five Challenges for Living in Code

The five challenges presented here can assist future healthcare administrators in using codes of ethics effectively. The author chooses to use first person voice in discussing these challenges so as to speak to the reader directly. In addition to considering the challenges, it is recommended that future healthcare administrators research the ACHE Code of Ethics and examine at least one other professional code for comparison. Discussing the ACHE Code with other administrators should also help the HCA to form a concept of how to use this code of ethics in decision making. Finally, this author challenges future healthcare administrators to include the ACHE Code in their operational decisions. They should also it as a starting point for developing a personal code of ethics.

1. Learn your professional code.

   Comments

   In this challenge, locate a copy of the ACHE Code of Ethics and all of its support documents and read them in-depth. Do not just scan the words on the page. Instead, thoughtfully peruse the material and answer the question, "What do they mean by that?" You can get helpful insights just by slowing down as you read the document. It is supposed to define who you are as a professional.

After reading the code, ask, "Do I believe this, and can I support it?" This will allow you to formulate your position on the ACHE Code. Finally, ask, "How can I use this in practice?" The answers to this question will help you identify ways to apply this code of ethics to your daily operation as a healthcare administrator.

2. Investigate codes from other professions.

Comments

This challenge can be met in a number of ways. First, you can use the CSEP website to identify a code that is interesting to you. You might select one from a professional group with whose members you work. If you are bicodal, you can investigate a code of ethics from your co-profession. Try to determine just what this code is asking of its professionals. Read the section on limitations again and see if you can identify some of those mentioned in your study code. Finally, ask yourself, "What can I learn from this code?"

Second, after you have learned about the code, have an informal conversation with a member of the profession represented in the code. Find out if this person uses the code. If the individual does, how does it assist the professional in his or her practice? If the individual does not, why does the professional not find it useful?

3. Ask key administrators about the challenges of living by a professional code.

Comments

This will be an easy challenge if you have already identified your moral mentor. If not, take time to find an administrator who will give you some discussion time. Next, discuss what the ACHE Code means. Why does the administrator think that you need a professional code? Does he or she find particular features helpful? You can also ask for cases where the ACHE Code has made a difference to this person. This information will give you insight into the practical application of the ACHE Code and assist you with Challenge 5.

4. Live the code in your daily operations.

Comments

Pick a decision that you must make in your daily operations as a healthcare administrator. If you have not begun your career, think of a hypothetical case for this challenge or ask your professors for an example. Next, obtain the ACHE Code or the appropriate Policy Statement. Along with financial and any other data you are using, review the Code and add a question to the decision process—for example, "Would this decision fit with the ACHE's recommendations?" What did you discover?

5. Design your own personal code starting with the ACHE Code as a foundation.

Comments

This challenge is by far the largest of the five. Think about what is expected of you by the profession as presented by the ACHE Code and what you have learned so far. Next, take your time and put your perceptions into your own words. Make sure that you are willing to stand by what you write. This process should not be done lightly; make each word count.

You can also design what some authors call a personal mission statement, or what this author calls a personal ethics code. It will combine your foundation beliefs about moral behavior, professional codes of ethics, and the application of ethics to practice. This statement should be something that you could frame and put on your office wall. In fact, some of this author's braver students have done just that. They also review this ethics statement at least once a year to see if they are staying true to their personal morality and their professional obligations.

Web Resources

American College of Health Care Administrators
http://www.achca.org/

American College of Healthcare Executives
http://www.ache.org/

American Medical Association
http://www.ama-assn.org/ama

American Nurses Association
http://nursingworld.org/

Center for the Study of Ethics in the Professions
http://ethics.iit.edu/

National Certification Commission for Acupuncture and Oriental Medicine
http://www.nccaom.org/consumers/acupuncture-certification

References

American College of Health Care Administrators (ACHCA). (2010). Code of ethics. Retrieved from http://www.achca.org/content/pdf/ Code%20of%20Ethics_non%20member_111019.pdf

American College of Healthcare Executives (ACHE). (2011). *American College of Healthcare Executives code of ethics*. Chicago, IL: Author. Retrieved from http://www.ache.org/abt_ache/code.cfm

American College of Healthcare Executives (ACHE). (2013a). Ethics policy statements. Retrieved from http://www.ache.org/policy/index_ethics.cfm

American College of Healthcare Executives (ACHE). (2013b). Ethics toolkit. Retrieved from http://www.ache.org/abt_ache/EthicsToolkit/ethicsTOC.cfm

American Medical Association (AMA). (2014). AMA's code of medical ethics. Retrieved from http://www.ama-assn.org/ama/pub/physician-resources/medical-ethics/code-medical-ethics.page?

American Nurses Association (ANA). (2010). Code of ethics for nurses with interpretative statements. Retrieved from http://www.nursingworld.org/MainMenuCategories/EthicsStandards/CodeofEthicsforNurses/Code-of-Ethics.pdf

Center for the Study of Ethics in the Professions (CSEP). (2014). Codes of ethics collection. http://ethics.iit.edu/research/codes-ethics-collection

Code. (n.d.). *Merriam-Webster's online dictionary*. Retrieved from http://www.merriam-webster.com/dictionary/code

Darr, K. (2011). *Ethics in health services management* (5th ed.). Baltimore, MD: Health Professions Press.

Erikson, S., Höglund, A. T., & Helgesson, G. (2008). Do ethical guidelines give guidance? A critical examination of eight ethics regulations. *Cambridge Quarterly of Healthcare Ethics*, 17(1), 15–30.

Johnson, C. E. (2009). *Meeting the ethical challenges of leadership: Casting light or shadow* (3rd ed.). Thousand Oaks, CA: Sage.

Martin, W. (2013). Beyond the Hippocratic Oath: Developing codes of conduct in healthcare organizations. *OD Practitioner*, 45(2), 26-30.

National Certification Commission for Acupuncture and Oriental Medicine (NCCAOM). (2014). Code of ethics. Available at: http://www.nccaom.org/

Nelson, W. A. (2005). An organizational ethics decision-making process. *Healthcare Executive*, 20(4), 8–14.

Niles, N. J. (2013). *Basic concepts of health care human resource management*. Burlington, MA: Jones and Bartlett Learning.

Purtilo, R. B., & Doherty, R. F. (2011). *Ethical dimensions in health professions* (5th ed.). St. Louis, MO: Elsevier.

Sansom, D. (2013, Summer). Codes of ethics in health care: Virtues versus rules. *Ethics & Medicine*, 29(2), 95–105.

Public Health Leadership Society (2002). *Principles of ethical practice of public health, version 2.2*. Retrieved from http://www.apha.org/

NR/rdonlyres/1CED3CEA-287E-4185-9CBD-BD405FC60856/0/
ethicsbrochure.pdf

Turnock, B. J. (2012). *Public health: What is it and how does it work.*
Burlington, MA: Jones & Bartlett Learning.

US Legal. (2014). Code of ethics law & legal definition. Retrieved from
http://definitions.uslegal.com/c/code-of-ethics/

© file404/Shutterstock

CHAPTER
16

Practicing as an Ethical Administrator

Do ethics matter in the ACA era?

Points to Ponder

1. Why is it important to apply ethics to the daily practice of health administration?
2. How does ethics apply to the functions of healthcare administration?
3. How can healthcare administrators better prepare themselves to be ethics-based practitioners?

Key Terms

The following is a list of key words for this chapter. Look for them in bold.

ethical hypocrisy   ethics of "bossdom"

■ INTRODUCTION

Aristotle and other theorists would support the concept that ethics without action has no value. Healthcare administrators (HCAs) who profess to be ethical, yet are never courageous enough to put their ethics into practice, run the risk of **ethical hypocrisy**. In today's era of health care, however, they should be asking themselves, "Do I have the integrity to make the changes that must be made while still remaining true to ethics principles?" If administrators do only what is expedient, they may cause harm to the patients whom they serve and to the staff whom they lead. In addition, they may be successful in the short run but harm their careers in the future. For example, staff members notice when there is dissonance between the administrator's words and actions. Ethical hypocrisy can go a long way toward undermining their trust. Without trust, administrators will find it difficult, if not impossible, to be successful. The question becomes how to integrate ethics into daily operations during this time of acute changes in the U.S. healthcare system.

This chapter addresses the issue of practicing ethics as an administrator. To maintain administrative integrity, administrators need to go back to their roots in the classic functions of healthcare management. This chapter presents examples of the application of ethics practices for each function. In addition, wisdom from scholars and anecdotal information from practicing healthcare administrators is included to assist the reader in developing a strategic plan for ethically sound administrative practice. There also is a section on acquiring ethics wisdom from "everyday" events and the arts (movies, music, and fiction). Finally, the reader is presented with three challenges to assist the HCA with balancing accountability, fiscal responsibility, and integrity in this period of major change.

■ ETHICS IN THE KEY PROCESSES OF HEALTH ADMINISTRATION

Many texts define the essential functions of healthcare administration. In general, the classifications include planning, organizing, staffing, influencing, and controlling (Dunn, 2012). This section presents a definition and three examples of applied ethics for each function. The examples should assist HCAs in applying practical wisdom in their day-to-day administrative practice.

Planning

The planning function sets the future direction of organizations and departments and includes the ability to meet community needs. Planning also includes establishing mission, vision, goals, and objectives for an organization or department (Dunn, 2012). These steps lead to the development of policies and procedures, rules, budgets, and other operational actions to achieve the desired plan. While some think of planning as solely an upper management function, all healthcare administrators must engage in this process. Whether they are CEOs or supervisors, effective planning allows administrative professionals to keep a competitive edge, maintain a strong bottom line, and serve those who use healthcare services. How can ethics apply?

Ethics Applications

Considering the complexity of the planning function, one can identify several areas where the practice of ethics makes a difference. The ethics of data integrity, information presentation, and overall communication are just a few examples that should be considered. With respect to data integrity, it is important to remember that planning decisions rest on the quality of the data used to make them. If administrators collect data appropriately, record data honestly, and consider those data fully, they have a greater chance of making appropriate, successful decisions.

Ethics also has a major influence on the quality and integrity of any data set. This quality begins with the ethics of those who are responsible for data collection. If these individuals do not see data collection as important, they might be tempted to collect such data in a haphazard manner. Too much speed and a lack of attention to detail can lead to errors and omissions, producing poor-quality data. In addition, employees who do not exhibit high ethical standards might be tempted to fabricate data. Healthcare administrators have a duty to educate staff concerning the importance of the data they collect and the need for integrity. They must also design work schedules to allow for adequate and accurate collection. Finally, organizations or departments should have a published policy that allows checks for data integrity so that HCAs can comfortably "stand on the data."

The manner in which HCAs conduct their analyses also influences data integrity. Choosing the correct format is the first step in preserving the quality of data. While statistical packages assist greatly with creating information, they are not perfect. For example, it can be tempting to omit those numbers that appear to be negative, especially when HCAs receive bonuses based on their numbers. In the end, poor decisions made with faulty data can cost more than a bonus.

It is also important to remember that not all data are quantitative in nature. Collecting qualitative data can also challenge the ethics of HCAs. Administrators can gather such data through interviews, surveys, and data mining efforts.

To ensure that all data—quantitative and qualitative—are of high quality, healthcare administrators should design appropriate protocols, conduct data collection in an ethical manner, and design accurate codes. To assure validity of the information collected, it is helpful to have an outside reviewer assess the data collection procedures. Aside from the need for procedural accuracy, HCAs must be aware of the many ethical temptations to "fudge" data when the results do not reveal what administrators hope to see. Protecting data integrity means that healthcare administrators need to use practical wisdom and foresight to avoid tampering with results.

The ethics of presentation is also important in the planning process. Because of their educational background, healthcare administrators know that numbers can say almost anything. The temptation may be to present information only in a positive way so that administrators and their departments can shine. Providing an unbalanced account of achievements by neglecting the whole picture (the sin of omission) can serve the HCA well in the short run. However, decisions made on incomplete data can produce negative results for departments and organizations in the long term. In addition, readers of healthcare information are becoming more sophisticated in terms of their ability to interpret data. Therefore, if administrators try "stacking the deck" or hiding data, their unethical practice can be uncovered through readers' scrutiny of those data. At a minimum, those HCAs who use this technique will look foolish and dishonest, and they might even jeopardize their careers. Ultimately, the need to present a balanced picture means that HCAs do not just provide the bad news and neglect their accomplishments. Rather, it means that along with successes, they diplomatically address unreached goals. This honest assessment allows for process improvement, better quality of care, and greater fiscal responsibility.

Presentation encompasses clarity of information as well, which can also lead to ethics issues. For example, to avoid addressing the real issues, some healthcare administrators choose to obviate them through data dazzle and presentation confusion. They resort to these tactics because they know that the human brain can absorb only so many numbers. In addition, unethical HCAs may include a large number of PowerPoint slides in their presentations, which causes the audience to tune out (take a mental vacation) and miss the key points (a phenomenon sometimes called "death by PowerPoint"). While it can be tempting to use a data fog to avoid criticism, healthcare administrators are not providing good stewardship of resources if they choose to go this route. Instead, practical ethics means that administrators make every effort to be clear, concise, and accurate in their presentations. As they design presentations, they need to ask themselves, "Do I understand this, and will my boss get it?"

Applying ethics to communication also facilitates successful planning. Administrators can develop the most beautifully designed strategic plan, but if no one uses it, such a plan is worthless from a practical standpoint. To avoid this fate, HCAs must support the plan themselves and communicate their support for it. Administrators also have an ethical obligation to educate their staff about the plan's purpose and implementation. For this implementation to succeed, HCAs must create an environment where staff members feel that they can communicate honestly. In the absence of this climate, "group-think" (employees who think only what someone tells them to think) is likely to rule. In such a case, administrators will learn only what their staff members think they want to hear. The result can be disastrous for a strategic plan.

Health administrators also need to be careful about "group-speak" (i.e., saying only what people want to hear) in their communications with superiors. While diplomacy and a spirit of cooperation are important in effective communication, HCAs should not be afraid to express concerns. Because it is not possible for everyone to understand all sides of a decision, the courage to speak up can actually assist one's employer in making correct decisions. In the ever-changing healthcare environment of the ACA era, communication needs to be both top-down and bottom-up if a strategic plan is to be successful.

Organizing

The organizing function of healthcare administration includes deciding what it takes to accomplish the goals of the organization (Dunn, 2012). It also includes the correct placement of activities, materials, and staff to accomplish the goals and objectives of the strategic plan. In addition, the organizing function involves designing specific jobs and educating staff about how to do those jobs. Delegation of authority and assigning accountability are part of the organizing function as well. Healthcare administrators must provide the structure that facilitates the work of their departments and leads to the staffing function. Organizing also involves many areas of human resources and finance and engages much of the time of the busy healthcare administrator.

Ethics Applications

There is great potential for ethics challenges within the organizing function. Examples of these challenges include the ethics of design, matching, and delegation. Job design and redesign are important steps in the organizing function. These steps may lead to either success or failure of healthcare organizations. Specifically, designing jobs to be both effective and efficient conserves scarce resources by avoiding unnecessary use and waste. If the task of job design and redesign is to be done well, healthcare administrators need an accurate picture of what is to be done and the best way to do it.

One ethics issue in job design is the rush to creation. In a time of great change, such as the ACA era, it is all too easy to obtain a job description or a set of practice guidelines from another facility or website and simply plunk it into a document. This quasi-plagiarism may be expedient, but can cause problems for the organization. This situation arises because there are no clones among organizations; all job designs must be adapted to the individual organization. Achieving effective adaptation of a template job design, or creation of a new one, requires consultation with those individuals who actually do the job. These experts can review a draft job description for accuracy and omissions. Taking this step provides HCAs with two benefits. First, HCAs can capture a better picture of how the job is actually done in their organizations. Second, HCAs honor their employees and the knowledge they have by including them in the design process. Moreover, implementation of the design tends to flow more smoothly because the design is not just a top-down effort; that is, when staff members are included in its development, they take ownership of the end result.

Once job design is complete, health administrators have to engage in the ethics of matching. Part of the art of administration is the ability to match the best person to the job. In today's time of great change, matching is especially critical in healthcare organizations because of the need for higher levels of professional knowledge and skills. To make a decision regarding the best fit between a professional and a job design, healthcare administrators need to know the strengths and weaknesses of each staff member. They need to ask, "Who is interested or educated in this area?" In addition, they must ask, "Who would have the shortest learning curve if assigned this task?"

Healthcare administrators also need to take the workload of each staff member into consideration. It has been this author's experience that when certain staff members demonstrate job excellence, their reward is often more work to do. Having a full and varied workload can make a staff member's day interesting, but overload can lead to burnout and resignation. Ethics requires that healthcare administrators avoid delegating everything to "old faithfuls" and take the opportunity to challenge a staff member who might be a "coaster."

Healthcare administrators must also consider that the ethical matching of staff members to jobs requires training. They should not assume that selected staff members will always fully understand the assignment. Instead, to meet the organization's strategic objectives, HCAs have a responsibility to ensure that all staff members are appropriately prepared for their positions. However, in providing this education, HCAs should recognize employees' reluctance to ask questions or request help. It may be a better strategy to assume that everyone needs orientation for successful implementation of tasks connected to organizational strategies and goals.

Finally, HCAs must encourage employees who receive additional tasks. This encouragement is important to implementation of tasks, but it does not have to be time consuming or expensive. It is often enough for HCAs to just informally check in with the employee and ask, "How is everything going?" If the administrator has established a climate of trust, management by walking around will prevent problems before they happen.

Once healthcare administrators make job assignments, they face the challenge of the ethics of delegation. The delegation process is often misunderstood; it is not just giving the "dirty work" to the "worker bees." Delegation is a decision of trust, through which administrators grant the implementation and authority for essential tasks to another person. The key word here is "authority." Delegation will not be effective if a person is made responsible for an outcome but does not have the authority to make it happen.

From an ethics standpoint, the basis for delegation is common trust. Healthcare administrators trust staff members to do their jobs and to communicate when they need assistance. Staff members must also trust that health administrators will allow them the autonomy to do their jobs without micromanagement. They also expect that HCAs will recognize and acknowledge their efforts toward accomplishing the department's objectives.

This process sounds very easy on paper, but it is often difficult to implement in practice. Early in their careers, HCAs often wrestle with trust issues. As a consequence, they do not always delegate effectively. For example, if HCAs do not trust their staff members or believe that they are competent, delegation will be troublesome. Healthcare administrators will wear themselves out by checking and redoing their staff's jobs. To avoid the temptation of false delegation, health administrators should first get to know their staff members. They should ask themselves, "Can I work with this staff member? If not, why not?" It may be necessary for administrators to assess their attitudes toward delegation and accept the fact that they are not omnipotent. For the jobs to be completed and the plan achieved, they must be able to rely on staff members to carry out their responsibilities.

Recognition is another part of the delegation function. A staff member who is working well will make the administrator look like an organizational star. However, this does not mean that the administrator absorbs all of the starlight. Ethical and effective administrators know the basis for their success and acknowledge it. They celebrate progress toward goals and thank their staff members with humility and appreciation. Making this step part of delegation is not only ethical, but also goes a long way toward making work meaningful. In addition, staff members who are engaged in meaningful work and receive appreciation are less likely to create turnover problems for the healthcare administrator.

Staffing

Dunn (2012) lists staffing as a separate function of management. This function considers both recruitment and hiring efforts to assure quality employees. It requires a balance between the need for quality employees and labor costs. In addition, the staffing function includes documentation of current licensure and training for maintaining staff competence. Performance evaluations and improvement planning are included in this management function as well. In many organizations, the staffing function is a critical area for human resources departments.

Ethics Applications

The staffing function involves numerous challenges to ethical administrative practice. Three examples arise in conjunction with autonomy, justice, and responsibility for competence. Autonomy issues begin with the hiring process. Healthcare administrators will have access to candidates' transcripts, talk to their references, and conduct personal interviews. Because of these activities, HCAs will have information about future employees that they should hold in confidence or on a need-to-know basis. However, there is often a temptation to talk about the future employee's personal information with those who do not have a "need to know." The "juicy gossip factor" may be tempting, but engaging in this activity may endanger trust. After all, the person hearing this information may wonder, if the administrator is telling confidential information about a candidate, what else would he or she divulge?

Justice issues are also frequently encountered within the staffing function. To be ethical, HCAs must treat everyone fairly and in compliance with department policies. However, healthcare administrators are compassionate, and this compassion sometimes challenges fairness. For example, if a healthcare administrator has an employee who is just returning from maternity leave, the HCA might be more lenient when this employee is late for work. Those employees who come on time every day, however, will not view this apparent favoritism as just. Therefore, effective HCAs practice rule utility and strive to treat all employees in the same way. While this may not make administrators popular, they will receive respect for exhibiting fairness.

Healthcare administrators must also practice justice when it comes to conducting performance evaluations and recommending raises. There is often a temptation to be less than just in this area, especially when standards are not clear. For example, suppose the administrator has an employee whose personality clashes with his or her own personality. The employee does excellent work, but grates on the administrator's nerves. The temptation would be to reduce the employee's performance evaluation score based on an "obnoxious personality." Inviting as it might be to do so, succumbing to this temptation would not be just. It can also lead to major discord and trust issues with employees.

Healthcare administrators are trusted by their organizations to hire and maintain competent staff. As part of this responsibility, they must provide documentation of licensure and continuing education. An ethics challenge occurs when there is not a clear policy on who is responsible for monitoring staff members' currency on these fronts. For example, some organizations consider continuing education to be the individual's responsibility and do not pay for any courses. Others offer on-site courses to facilitate currency and control for the costs of staff member absences. Healthcare administrators must know their organization's policies regarding continuing education benefits and communicate them to their staff members. Clear communication should reduce issues related to financial responsibility for competency assurance and discontent among staff members.

Influencing

Influencing or directing is the process of getting the work done (Dunn, 2012). It uses the tools of communication, motivation, and education to influence staff to achieve organizational goals and objectives. In other words, HCAs get the job done through their staff members. This area involves ethical challenges such as those related to morale, motivation, productivity, and turnover. HCAs must demonstrate an ability to influence the behaviors of others and create productive and successful workplaces. The function of influencing is one of the main reasons for hiring healthcare administrators and is a source of their organizational value.

Ethics Applications

While many areas of ethics are connected with the influencing function of management, this section addresses three areas of ethics practice: the **ethics of "bossdom,"** staff motivation, and effective teamwork. The ethics of "bossdom" is not just focused on one's competence in the technical areas of management, but also includes one's attitudes toward those employees over whom one has authority. As part of this ethics practice, healthcare administrators must consider their personal definition of the role of the boss. In formulating this definition, HCAs can ask questions such as, "Do the best bosses respect their employees and demonstrate at least an 'I-YOU' relationship?" "How would I feel if I have to terminate an employee?" and "What makes me want to go to work in the morning?"

Administrators need to consider that the benefits of increased salary and status come with the responsibility of using power astutely. However, they have no real power unless those whom they supervise grant it. Free will is always present, such that staff members have the option to work toward organizational goals, do their jobs well or poorly, or leave the organization. The HCA's function is to influence staff members to provide their best efforts to meet goals and contribute to organizational quality. In fulfilling this function, HCAs should also consider the appropriate leadership style and consider that power based on respect, honesty, and fairness is more effective than power based on coercion and fear.

The responsibility of influencing also includes employee motivation. To motivate other members of the healthcare organization in times of great change, HCAs must go beyond being organizational cheerleaders. It is more effective to influence employees' desire to make the organization's goals their own and find pride in completing them successfully.

Many administrators believe that the best way to motivate employees is to pay them. If you pay staff enough, they reason, staff will do anything. While money is a motivator when people cannot pay their bills, this factor loses its influence as they become more secure. In fact, healthcare employees are often more strongly motivated by the concept of providing service to patients and by loyalty to their organizations.

What do employees want as motivation? One somewhat radical way to determine this is to ask them. Instead of forging ahead and designing programs that the administrator thinks will be motivational, HCAs should consider management by walking around or sending e-mails to ask employees for their ideas. Then administrators can build their strategies based on activities that have a better chance of accomplishing their goal of instilling a sense of purpose in staff members. In addition, administrators can read current literature for ideas. For example, research shows that recognition; interesting, meaningful work; and loyalty are stronger motivators than cash. From an ethics view, employee motivation begins with an "I-YOU" relationship between the administrator and the staff. Once this climate of trust and respect exists, it becomes easier to keep the mission and goals in the forefront.

In the ACA era, many administrative tasks are performed by teams rather than separate individuals. A good example of an effective team can usually be found in the emergency department (ED). In ED teams, each team member knows his or her job and all members work together for the good of the patient. Teams also exist in the nonclinical aspects of health care and need to work equally well. Healthcare administrators' responsibility is to practice ethics when establishing and leading teams so that each team member will work well with the others.

The first step in meeting this responsibility is to consider whether a team is needed and who should be on it. To avoid the appearance of busywork, administrators should be careful to use teams for important tasks that single individuals cannot accomplish. In addition, HCAs need to select team members based on their knowledge and ability to contribute to the solution, rather than simply based on their titles. When an administrator asks people to serve on a team, he or she should inform those individuals of their value to the team and their reason for selection.

Once administrators have assembled teams, they need to remember key ethics principles related to team management. For example, administrators should respect the team's time and autonomy by making sure team members understand the tasks, organize efficient meetings, and provide follow-up information. Meetings should foster open and honest communication so that the best solution can be derived. As moderators, administrators must assure that there is a place for all ideas and that one or two members do not dominate the process. In addition, they should not schedule meetings if there is no real reason for holding them. Doing so can be perceived as a lack of respect for employees.

Teams, like individual employees, need recognition for their work. Ethics-based means of recognizing accomplishments include making sure that team members' names are on the final product or document. This acknowledges that the product was not the work of one person, but rather represented the best thinking of the team. The names on the document also provide a source for information when outside staff members have questions; that is, team members become champions for the plan that they helped to develop.

Controlling

The controlling function monitors activities and ensures that organizational goals and objectives are met. This process includes developing performance measures, evaluating those measures, and taking necessary corrective action. Financial controls are also part of this function, including budgets, cost/benefit analyses, and inventory controls. Information systems can provide valuable tools to assist with the controlling process if they are used ethically and effectively (Dunn, 2012). Ethics issues related to the controlling function include stewardship, patient and employee satisfaction, and justice.

Making sure that resources are optimized and not wasted is part of HCAs' responsibility as stewards for the organization's assets. Controlling waste in healthcare inventory is a serious challenge, however, because a large part of the annual budget in any facility is devoted to supplies and equipment. In addition, controlling inventory can be a challenge because of the sheer number and variety of products and supplies that are used. Of course, there are also problems with shrinkage (another word for theft) that administrators must address. Likewise, HCAs need to determine the best way to conserve resources and still provide quality care. Technologies such as computer systems that help to monitor the use of inventory are often part of the HCA's resource-balancing act.

To be good stewards, health administrators must pay attention to their balance sheets and other financial data. Such attention is especially important when there is the potential for lower revenues, as may occur with implementation of the ACA. No matter what level of administrative responsibility they bear, healthcare administrators should learn to question accounting data, especially when entries do not make sense. In addition, HCAs must be accurate and honest in documenting the expenditures and inventory within their departments or organizations. In the ACA era, "creative accounting" might solve an immediate problem, but such a quick fix can come with a high long-term price that administrators will not want to pay.

Controlling also includes documenting treatment outcomes and progress toward organizational goals. This aspect requires the analysis and evaluation of mandated and proprietary data sets, including those related to patient satisfaction. In the ACA era, patient satisfaction data will be even more important because of their formal connections to reimbursement. In addition, external evaluators often analyze these reports to assess for compliance with regulations or reimbursement rules. Therefore, administrators need to pay special attention to the accuracy and frequency of data collection.

Ethics Applications

Because of its connection to funding and accreditation, patient satisfaction can become a source of temptation in regard to ethics. Research reveals that there are a number of unethical ways to obtain favorable data.

First, if administrators limit the size of their mailings, they will get a smaller return. This tactic may allow administrators to claim higher levels of patient satisfaction based on only a small sample. This sample bias, however, is both inaccurate and unethical. For example, if an administrator uses a small sample or has only a 5% to 10% return rate for a patient satisfaction survey, the data collected do not have important and statistically sound meaning. However, these data may show the organization in a positive light, and the administrator might be tempted to use them in reporting information and in marketing campaigns.

Second, timing affects survey data. If the administrator does infrequent surveying, some of the patients who receive surveys long after their experience ended will not remember whether they received good treatment. Therefore, patient satisfaction data can be highly inaccurate.

Third, the length of the questionnaire makes a difference. If it is too long, it will be tossed rather than completed, giving the administrator lower return numbers. Administrators can also word questions in a way that encourages more positive responses than negative ones.

To avoid ethical temptations related to data collection, healthcare facilities are beginning to use a triangulation method for gathering patient satisfaction data. To improve data integrity, they use multiple methods such as telephone surveys, focus groups, and visits with patients who are still in the facility. While this method of data collection might be more expensive, it yields useful information that can be used to improve patient care and positively affect reimbursement. With respect to patient satisfaction, knowledge is power; that is, once administrators become aware of a problem, they can fix it.

There is also an ethical temptation to "cook the books" to show favorable numbers on patient satisfaction surveys. Healthcare administrators might ask themselves, "Who would ever know?" This temptation is particularly enticing when written comments are included on surveys. If someone takes the time to write a comment, he or she wants the facility to have this information. However, it takes time to organize comments into categories and to match specific comments with these categories. In addition, not all of the comments are likely to be favorable. When there are too many negative comments, HCAs could show their organizations in a more positive light by omitting comments or showing only those that include positive feedback. In addition to being unethical, this decision robs healthcare administrators and facilities of important information for improving patient services.

HCAs also need to consider the ethics of employee satisfaction under the controlling function. What can an ethics-based organization do to provide an environment where employees can engage in meaningful work? Is it important to measure employee satisfaction? Some organizations think measuring employee satisfaction is not important. They take the "You are lucky to have a job" attitude, while still expecting staff to treat patients and families with care and compassion. This dissonance can lead to poor morale and soaring turnover rates. Employees, like patients, want to have at least an "I-YOU" relationship in the workplace. As leaders within their organizations, healthcare administrators have the ability to demonstrate respect and value for their staff members. This is not just sound ethical practice; it is also good for business.

Part of the controlling function in management may involve employee discipline and termination. Therefore, these decisions are also part of the job of healthcare administrators. While these tasks are unpleasant at best, they can be handled ethically and respect the dignity of the persons involved. For example, corrective steps should always be taken in private and agreements pertaining to necessary improvements should be provided to the employee in writing. Even though it is a frequently used tactic, it is not ethical to drive out an undesirable employee by making that person's experience in the workplace so miserable that he or she resigns. Even if administrators succeed in getting the desired resignation, they leave themselves vulnerable to legal action and send a powerful message of fear to the remaining staff.

This section examined a few of the ethics challenges involved in the five processes of administration. HCAs will experience many others in the course of their careers. The key to dealing with challenges is to combine a sense of ethics with sound business practices, which requires a strong emphasis on practical wisdom. Healthcare administrators might have to risk being unpopular to be ethical. However, their consciences will be clear if they consistently balance the right thing to do with what is best for the business. In addition, HCAs will be able to pass the "sleep at night test" when they base their decisions on the needs of patients and employees, rather than solely on profitability.

■ PRACTICAL ETHICS IDENTIFIED BY BUSINESS AND HEALTHCARE WRITERS

Where does a busy healthcare administrator find advice on how to practice ethics in the ever-changing healthcare environment? Fortunately, the issue of ethics in business and in health care has become of increasing interest. This next section provides ideas for consideration by summarizing key elements addressed by selected writers. These authors, who represent both the business community and the healthcare industry, provide suggestions that should inspire healthcare administrators to apply ethics in their daily practice.

Aburdene (2007) has been involved in a series of books concerning megatrends in American culture. A megatrend is a phenomenon that has the potential to affect a culture profoundly for a decade or more. In her latest book *Megatrends 2010*, Aburdene explains that recession, healthcare costs, media exposés, and other factors affect capitalism. Business is finding that the top-down model of leadership is not working and is seeking a different model to support capitalism. This new model includes ethics-type areas such as social responsibility, spirituality, organizational healing, and increased involvement of middle managers.

Aburdene (2007, p. 134) finds that health care is a "bellwether for business." She suggests this is true not only because of the healthcare industry's mission, but also because healthcare organizations consider research to be part of their operation. Aburdene's findings concerning megatrends in 2010 and beyond are helpful in understanding how ethics will be an increasing part of health care. For example, she regards the quest for spirituality and a concern for ethics as one of the greatest megatrends. Businesses are seeking opportunities to incorporate social justice as part of their corporate models, in efforts that Aburdene describes as "conscious capitalism" (p. 22).

Another example of a megatrend that may affect HCAs is the trend of increasing involvement of middle managers in organizational affairs. Aburdene (2007) suggests that businesses are seeking greater creativity and understanding of how things actually work within the organization. In turn, they are paying much more attention to middle managers, who are closer to the front line and serve as grassroots leaders. Using middle management in this way allows businesses to accomplish their goals more effectively and maintain their corporate values.

Another megatrend stems from the consumer side of business. Consumers, especially those involved in health care, are examining the practices of corporations and not just their prices. In light of this phenomenon, businesses are trying to embrace social responsibility in their practices. They are also using metrics to understand how employees' values mirror those of the corporation. In one healthcare example,

Aburdene (2007) notes that when the healthcare staff values are comparable to those of the organization, there is an increase in both patient and employee satisfaction scores, along with a decrease in turnover rates. This would indicate that values are important areas of consideration in health care, as well as general business.

Finally, Aburdene (2007) suggests that capitalism is transforming itself to reflect the position of its shareholders in its need for profitability. While "the greed factor" (p. 162) appeared to be a center of capitalism in the past, the attitude in today's market reflects a type of capitalism that goes beyond "What's in it for me?" In an era characterized by cost cutting, staff reductions, and increased scrutiny, all businesses, including health care, are required to maintain profitability. How will organizations do this? The answer may lie in creating organizations that focus on creativity, passion for work, altruism, and social responsibility.

A writer who is part of an ethics dynasty, Steven A. Covey, includes ethics in his books *The 7 Habits of Highly Effective People* (1989) and *Principle Centered Leadership* (1992). While not specific to health care, these works are often taught in workshops on healthcare leadership and are included on ethical practice reading lists. In 2006, Steven A. Covey's son, Steven M. R. Covey, followed his father's path and published a book that also offers ethics wisdom: *The Speed of Trust: The One Thing That Changes Everything.*

In this book, Covey (2006) discusses the concept of trust and its influence on leadership. Trust is the core of interaction, but low levels of trust exist in many aspects of life and business. Covey believes that the ability to establish and grow trust is the most critical element to success in a global economy. He presents five waves of trust: self, relational, organizational, market, and societal. His first wave of trust starts with administrators. The essence of this wave of trust is one's credibility as a leader and a person. How do leaders build this credibility? Covey suggests that they concentrate on four core areas.

The first area of concentration in building credibility is personal integrity. Covey (2006) suggests that integrity involves more than just talking about ethics; it means acting on values and practicing humility. Credibility also includes doing what one says and being willing to stand by one's principles. Certainly, Aristotle would agree with this version of eudaimonia.

In addition to credibility, healthcare administrators need to be clear about their motives and their personal agenda. They need to ask themselves, "What do you support, and why do you support it?" The answers to these questions should translate into behaviors. In other words, healthcare administrators should consider the beneficiaries of their actions. To increase trust, HCAs should act for the benefit of others as well as for themselves. Taking this position means that they are willing to know and communicate their intent, and have the courage to act on it.

Elements of character are not enough to build trust as a leader: Healthcare administrators also need to build their capabilities (Covey, 2006). Capabilities can be described in terms of the "acronym 'TASKS' or Talents, Attitudes, Skills, Knowledge, and Style" (p. 94). Covey encourages administrators to know their strengths in each of these areas and use these strengths appropriately. They must maintain currency by mastering the knowledge and skills in their field and continuing their education beyond graduation. In today's healthcare environment, the need to build capabilities and maintain them is an absolute must for leadership growth and success.

Finally, to build credibility and trust as a leader, HCAs need to have a record of performance. Covey (2006) states that the ability to make things happen matters in the overall assessment of credibility. Administrators need to keep thinking about achieved results and future results. As Frankl (1971) points out, everyone (including HCAs) has choices, but must take responsibility for those choices. In addition, HCAs must be willing to stick with their plans and not give up when things are difficult. Quitting does not build credibility and trust.

The information presented in Covey's (2006) first wave of trust can provides solid advice for healthcare administrators. If administrators are people of personal integrity and act on their values, they will add to their status as leaders. If HCAs gear their actions toward the benefit of their patients, their employees, and their organizations, they will establish themselves as trusted leaders. Finally, if HCAs use their capabilities to produce results, they will not only gain trust, but also be valuable to both the patients they serve and the organizations they represent.

In practicing ethics-based leadership, healthcare administrators must consider what it means to be authentic and use both head and heart in practice (Palmer, 2000). While money and measurable results are important to operational success, intangibles also matter. HCAs must balance the concrete (data, reports, and financial information) with these intangibles (integrity and fairness) to be effective. Achieving this balance requires contemplation, conversation, courage, and conviction. Healthcare administrators are encouraged to find time for solitude, overcome their fears, and learn to lead from strength. Palmer (2000) believes that when one has a calling to the profession of healthcare administration, he or she must be able to balance the elements of life; achieving this balance makes ethics-based practice possible.

Writers from the healthcare field also offer advice on practicing as ethics-based administrators. Studer is a prolific writer in the field of healthcare leadership. His books include *Hardwiring Excellence* (2004) and *Straight A Leadership* (2009). In his most recent book, *A Culture of High Performance* (2013), Studer, while not discussing ethics directly, presents information to assist healthcare administrators in realizing ethical practice. He views the current healthcare system as being subject to almost constant change. Variables such as the need to remain current in technology, requirements for transparency, and research practices all combine to produce change in the healthcare field. In addition to being responsive to such changes, the healthcare culture is called upon to remember its roots in compassion, resilience, inner strength, and the ability to make a difference.

To address all these changing demands, Studer (2013) suggests that healthcare administrators foster accountability and respond to data in positive ways. This means that they must own their data, and not deny or find scapegoats for negative results. Elements of justice exist when administrators use data to make their organizations deliver quality care that is responsive to both patients and profitability. In addition, Studer encourages leaders to foster value-driven employees who are self-motivated and passionate about their work. He offers practical tools to assist with evaluation systems, improvement plans, and other leadership responsibilities.

Studer (2013) encourages administrators to connect to the work environment with their minds through effective leadership techniques and use of data. However, connection to the mind is not enough to ensure effective leadership. Healthcare administrators must also connect with their hearts, which includes having a passion for the work of health care. This author encourages HCAs to recognize that patients likewise need connections of the mind and heart. For example, educating patients about their diagnoses and treatment plans requires a connection to the mind. At the same time, healthcare practitioners must go beyond the mind connection to look for a patient's needs at the heart level—for example, by providing comfort, compassion, empathy, and hope.

Finally, Studer (2013) provides recommendations for effective leadership in a time of change. Many of these recommendations are linked to the application of sound ethical practices, including use of ethics theory and principles when making decisions. For example, the best leaders in health care are in touch with their own values, including the need for empathy and compassion. Such HCAs exhibit the ability to make decisions for implementing change. In addition, they are able to connect change and necessary management functions to the mission, vision, and values of the organization. With this approach, health care is not just about making a profit from sickness or suffering, but rather focuses on creating quality care that incorporates elements of social and fiscal responsibility.

Adams (1993) offers ethics advice for the healthcare administrator from the patient's view. He believes that service, joy, and humor should be part of the practice of health care. He also suggests that administrators should always be thinking about the patient as they conduct their daily operations. Patients should never become an inconvenience or a data point on a profit/loss statement; rather, they should be the core of an administrator's career.

Adams (1993) asks administrators to make a decision to be happy when the world seems to reward them for being unhappy. Choosing happiness means that they grow friendships, remember when to let go, build community in their workplaces, and choose wellness. Healthcare administrators also need to increase the level of humor, laughter, and silliness in their lives. HCAs do not often view humor and silliness as effective health administration, yet these forces can assist in healing, maintaining morale, and decreasing burnout. Adams offers advice on how to increase humor levels, such as finding silliness from reading, watching television and films, laughing, and playing. If administrators are happy, in Adams's definition, they should find it easier to practice ethically.

Purtilo and Doherty (2011) also give advice on using ethics in administration practice. According to these authors, healthcare administrators should begin their practice by reading and understanding the organization's mission statement. This knowledge provides an understanding of how the organization views its purpose and allows HCAs to evaluate whether they can support this purpose. Assuming that administrators want to be part of the organization's mission, they must next read and assess its policies and procedures. They need to use the key principles of ethics (i.e., justice, beneficence, nonmaleficence, autonomy) to assess the ethical foundation of the policies that they must administer. If this analysis indicates the need for alterations or changes, HCAs must work to support policies that are rooted in ethics and not just in profit or convenience.

Dye (2000) asks healthcare administrators to begin their practical application of ethics with the American College of Healthcare Executives (ACHE) Code of Ethics. This code should be part of administrators' daily operations. He also advocates that HCAs develop a personal code and create a written ethics statement. This statement serves as another tool in effective management.

Dye (2000) also suggests that when making a decision, healthcare administrators should analyze the costs of not being ethical. To do so, they can ask, "What would happen if someone finds out?" If the consequences of this knowledge are not acceptable for their organizations, their community, or themselves, they should think again, conduct more research, and make another choice. In addition, HCAs should avoid playing with the truth (stretching, padding, or bending it) and honor their promises. Dye also advises that healthcare administrators demonstrate care in using their power, take responsibility for their mistakes, and be vigilant in their personal financial management. By this, he means that HCAs need to be good stewards of their expense accounts, perquisites, and benefits.

■ PRACTICAL ETHICS IN THE EVERYDAY WORLD

Areas beyond research and professional sources can be valuable sources of ethics lessons for healthcare administrators. Anecdotes, novels, theater, movies, and even television programs give insight into the application of ethics in everyday life. This insight can increase the knowledge and experience of healthcare administrators. However, achieving the full benefit of these lessons requires that HCAs be open to receiving these lessons and to applying them to healthcare practice.

For example, the novel *The Book Thief* (Zusak, 2005) provides the reader with an extraordinarily well-written example of ethics in action. Set in Nazi Germany in 1939, this novel explores the ethical issues of everyday people living under extraordinarily challenging times. Zusak gives the reader an understanding of the costs of behaving in ethical ways and the severity of ethical dilemmas faced by the German people. While healthcare administrators will likely never experience ethics issues as deep as those found in this novel, the writer amply demonstrates the ability to see more than one side of an ethics situation. In addition, readers (and HCAs) are able to develop empathy for people who are not sympathetic characters.

Anecdotes can also bring insight into practicing ethics in healthcare situations. Although anecdotal information does not constitute science-based research, this author has found that conversations with practicing administrators often highlight some real-world ethical issues. One recurring issue from these conversations involves balancing money and mission. With the need to trim budgets and manage the challenges of the ACA, there are real concerns about providing necessary services at the appropriate level of quality. One administrator expressed the frustration that the best interests of the patient are becoming lost when the message of the system sounds like "Show me the money." This ethics issue becomes even more problematic in times of recession, staffing shortages, and changes connected to the ACA. Certainly, being a healthcare administrator in current times is not for the ethically faint of heart!

Balancing money and mission will always be a part of the healthcare administrator's challenge, no matter what his or her specific position. Each administrator must be sure that he or she acts as a good steward of organizational resources, In addition, HCAs should read financial statements carefully and ensure the accuracy of their own records. Given the changes and challenges of the current era, healthcare administrators are also likely to face challenges that might make them forget the reason that they chose this career. However, if service is not the basis for staying in the profession, ethical HCAs need to consider other career options. Being a healthcare administrator is a prestigious, powerful, and even lucrative adventure, but a foundation in service is the only thing that will enable the HCA to enjoy career longevity and happiness.

Coupled with the ongoing monetary pressure faced by healthcare organizations is the growing awareness of healthcare consumers and their demand for quality care. For example, when consumers see a new procedure or technology on television, healthcare providers' phones seem to ring incessantly with requests for this new miracle. Administrators are also gravely concerned about the overuse of their emergency department (ED) services. Patients seem to be using the ED as a clinic with greater frequency, and the problems with which they present there are becoming ever more complicated to treat. It is hoped that the ACA, when fully implemented, will reduce inappropriate use of ED services.

Conversations with administrators often yield examples of behaviors that can kill an administrator's career. These examples form a list of what this author calls the *Suicide Twelve*:

1. Getting drunk at organizational functions
2. Dating a subordinate
3. Telling ethnic or other inappropriate jokes
4. Sending offensive e-mails
5. Repeatedly violating corporate culture
6. Getting arrested
7. Getting into a physical fight
8. Falsifying records
9. Violating patient or employee confidentiality
10. Invading staff members' privacy
11. Taking kickbacks from vendors
12. Giving away proprietary information to competitors

While these 12 behaviors would seem to be obvious career killers, they all have occurred in healthcare settings.

Healthcare administrators should remember that their behavior is noted by their colleagues. All too often, however, healthcare administration students feel that they should be able to do whatever they want in their private lives while working as healthcare administrators. They may feel that they should have the freedom to date whomever they want or to drink when and where they wish. In theory, these actions might be part of personnel autonomy, but students frequently do not see the need to balance their actions with responsibility. In addition, with higher levels of technology sophistication, such as that provided through cell phone cameras, Twitter, Instagram, and Facebook, private actions often become public without the individual's desire to make them public. In turn, private behaviors may have serious consequences for the HCA's career.

Healthcare administrators also need to remember that the healthcare administration community is a small world. Knowledge of unethical behavior may precede the administrator as he or she builds a career in the field. Although ancient, Aristotle's concept of practical wisdom and St. Thomas Aquinas's idea of control over one's impulses have merit for healthcare administrators who wish to make ethics a vital part of their lives and careers.

Summary

Health care, with its emphasis on service and compassionate patient care, should be the easiest environment in which to practice ethics. However, the unfortunate truth is that practicing ethics in health care involves balancing business and compassion. Pressures related to finance, technology advances, personnel needs, and external evaluators all add to the burdens of HCAs who are struggling to find this balance. Ensuring that ethics remains at the center of the business of health care will never be easy, but patients and the community expect nothing less. They understand that the healthcare system is a business, but they trust that the primary focus of this business is their needs, rather than just profitability.

As an introduction to the Challenges section, reflect on the following quote attributed to Ralph Waldo Emerson (Quoteworld, 2014). It will help define a meaningful, ethics-based life for a healthcare administrator:

> To laugh often and much;
> To win the respect of intelligent people and the affection of children;
> To earn the appreciation of honest critics and endure the betrayal of false friends;
> To appreciate beauty, to find the best in others;
> To leave the world a bit better, whether by a healthy child, a garden patch, or a redeemed social condition;
> To know even one life has breathed easier because you have lived.
> This is to have succeeded.

Challenges

This section include three challenges for ethics-based HCAs. They should assist health administrators in finding their own sources of wisdom to meet ethics challenges now and in the future. Administrator should always remember that they have a choice. The key to ethics success is to make choices that are true to one's conscience and that benefit patients, the organization, family, and self.

1. Ask.

   Comments

   Repeat the author's informal study. Contact three or more health-care administrators and ask them the question, "What are your top three ethics challenges?" Listen to their responses and learn from them. This information can also assist with deciding what you would do if faced by similar situation. Thinking about how to behave ethically is the first step in acting ethically when a situation arises.

2. Evaluate.

   Comments

   Conduct an ethics assessment and analysis in a department or organization. Look at the policies that most strongly affect services and their implementation. After reviewing the policies, identify any ethics gaps. If they exist, create a team to clarify existing policies and practices so that they reflect the mission, vision, and values of the department in the organization.

3. Go within.

   Comments

   Health administrators should evaluate their own practices with respect to ethics. A strategy for doing so would be to gather a notebook and pen and find a quiet place. Then list all the activities that are part of the HCA's daily operations. The HCA could then decide whether these activities were practiced with an ethics basis. If the answer is "no or maybe," he or she could brainstorm ways to use a more ethics-based approach. The challenge for the administrator would be to take the list and actually make the changes in his or her daily activities.

   The most important challenge in this section is to create a personal ethics statement. This statement can be a powerful resource for practicing ethics-based healthcare management. Students of this author are required to create this statement on one page, suitable for framing. They begin with the question, "For what do you want to be known?" Brave students frame their document and put it in their offices. At a minimum, they keep their personal ethics statement as a reference for their beliefs and definition of ethical practice. Although some students find the development of an ethics statement to be a difficult assignment, they all report change in their views on ethics in the management of health care.

Web Resources

Patch Adams

http://www.patchadams.org/

Parker Palmer Center for Courage and Renewal

http://www.couragerenewal.org/parker

Studer Group

https://www.studergroup.com/learninglab/

References

Aburdene, P. (2007). *Megatrends 2010: The rise of conscious capitalism.* Charlottesville, VA: Hampton Roads.

Adams, P. (1993). *Gesundheit!* Rochester, VT: Healing Arts Press.

Covey, S. M. R. (2006). *The speed of trust: The one thing that changes everything.* New York, NY: Free Press.

Covey, S. R. (1989). *The 7 habits of highly effective people.* New York, NY: Simon & Schuster.

Covey, S. R. (1992). *Principle centered leadership.* New York, NY: Free Press.

Dunn, R. T. (2012). *Haimann's healthcare management* (9th ed.). Chicago. IL: Health Administration Press.

Dye, C. F. (2000). *Leadership in healthcare: Values at the top.* Chicago, IL: Health Administration Press.

Frankl, V. (1971). *Man's search for meaning: An introduction to logotherapy.* New York, NY: Pocket Books.

Palmer, P. J. (2000). *Let your life speak.* San Francisco, CA: Jossey-Bass.

Purtilo, R. B., & Doherty, R. F. (2011). *Ethical dimensions in the health professions* (5th ed.). Philadelphia. PA: Elsevier Saunders.

Quoteworld. (2014). Ralph Waldo Emerson. Retrieved from http://www.quoteworld.org/quotes/4405 will

Studer, Q. (2004). *Hardwiring excellence: Purpose, worthwhile work, making a difference.* Gulf Breeze, FL: Fire Starter.

Studer, Q. (2009). *Straight A leadership: Alignment-action-accountability.* Gulf Breeze, FL: Fire Starter.

Studer, Q. (2013). *A culture of high performance: Achieving higher quality at a lower cost.* Gulf Breeze, FL: Fire Starter.

Zusak, M. (2005). *The book thief.* New York, NY: Alfred A. Knopf.

Glossary

ACHE: (7) American College of Healthcare Executives; one of the professional organizations for healthcare administrators.

ACHE Code of Ethics: (15) A document that serves as guide for health administrators for practicing ethics in their profession.

Administrative evil: (14) Actions of perverse enjoyment, deceit, and bureaucratic-approved injury and destruction. These actions cause harm to individuals, organizations, and society.

Affordable Care Act of 2010 (ACA): (5) More formally, the Patient Protection and Affordable Care Act of 2010; federal legislation designed to increase the number of insured Americans and positively affect the quality and cost of health care. It was signed into law in March 2010.

Agency for Healthcare Research and Quality (AHRQ): (11) A federal agency that emphasizes quality. It supports research on evidence-based medicine and quality efforts.

AHA: (7) American Hospital Association; an organization that represents the interests of hospitals.

APHA: (7) APHA stands for the American Public Health Association which is the professional association for members of the health professions who have careers in public health fields.

Authorization: (2) The final part of informed consent, during which the patient or his or her designee gives permission for a procedure or treatment. Authorization allows the practitioner to do what is necessary according to the patient's permission.

Beneficence: (3) Acting in charity and kindness. This principle of ethics applies to patients, staff members, and the community as a whole.

BFOQs: (7) Bona fide occupational qualifications; specific requirements for a position. An example is the ability to see.

Bioterrorism: (13) The act of using biological substances to cause harm to groups or populations.

Case management: (6) A mechanism used in managed care to evaluate appropriate use of resources for patient care.

Categorical imperative: (1) A test developed by Kant to determine ethical duty. If a duty exists, moral action becomes universal.

Centers for Medicare and Medicaid Services (CMS): (11) A federal agency that is a leader in quality assurance. It addresses some components of quality requirements under ACA.

Competence: (2) In a medical context, the ability of a person to understand the procedure or treatment to be provided and be able to authorize it.

Compliant-patient culture: (12) A culture in which people try to act on what they are told by authority figures in the healthcare system. Compliant patients tend not to question treatment or outcomes.

Consequentialism: (1) The basis for Mill's theory. Ethics is based on consequences and not on intent.

Conventional: (1) The stage in Kohlberg's moral development theory in which people make moral decisions based on the need to please people.

Culture: (10) The values, beliefs, and practices of members of a society. Their culture shows how they think about their lives and the world in which they live.

Culture clash: (10) The situation in which cultures interact and there is a potential for misunderstandings that can lead to conflict.

Deceit: (14) Behaviors that try to hide the truth by omitting information, altering facts, or lying. One can also practice self-deceit, which can lead to management errors and malpractice.

Deontology: (1) Kant's theory of ethics. It is based on determining moral duty and acting on that duty.

Disclosure: (2) In a medical context, a patient's receipt of information about a procedure or treatment in a way the he or she can understand. Disclosure is part of informed consent.

Disease management: (6) The mechanisms used to control the acuity of chronic diseases and reduce acute care episodes.

Disease surveillance: (13) The processes of collecting and analyzing large amounts of information so as to identify high-risk populations, evaluate programs, or assist with health planning.

Distributive justice: (4) A form of justice based on decisions about dividing resources among members of a society or group. Fair decisions must be made about who gets what and when they get it.

Donabedian model: (11) A leader in the field of quality assessment, who developed the SPO model.

Electronic medical record: (8) The use of technology to capture patient information via computer systems.

Emerging technology: (8) Innovations in the use of technology for medical and other applications.

Environmental specialists: (13) Public health professionals who are responsible for collection and analysis of samples from various environmental sources. Their work helps to prevent future health problems and address current ones.

Epidemiologist: (13) A public health professional who conducts research related to the nature and spread of disease. Epidemiologists' work is especially important when preventing or controlling the spread of epidemics.

Ethical egoism: (1) A type of ethics view in which what is considered right or wrong is what best benefits the individual. It is not acceptable in healthcare practice.

Ethical hypocrisy: (16) The practice of saying that one is ethical, but not practicing ethics on a daily basis. It erodes trust and negatively affects one's reputation.

Ethicist: (4) A person who specializes in the study and application of ethics. These professionals often serve as consultants or as members of an ethics committee in a large facility.

Ethics of "bossdom": (16) Attitudes and practices that involve having power over other people.

Ethics policy statements: (15) Suggested policy statements provided by ACHE. The sample statement can guide health administrators in developing organization-specific documents.

Eudaimonia: (1) Part of Aristotle's theory of ethics, which is based in the Greek concept of excellence. It means happiness or flourishing by living a virtuous life.

Evil: (14) Intentional or unintentional actions that cause human suffering and destroy dignity.

Fidelity: (2) The willingness of healthcare personnel to keep their word. It can relate to both clinical and business interactions.

Gatekeeper: (6) A feature of managed care in which the primary provider authorizes referrals to specialists and other services. Authorization is needed for the plan to cover the services.

Health benefit exchange: (5) A mechanism to assist Americans in purchasing healthcare insurance that is provided through the state or federal government.

Health disparities: (13) Differences in access and the quality of health and health care faced by racial, ethnic, and socioeconomic groups.

Health educators: (13) Public health professionals educators who conduct needs assessments, plan community and school health programs, and evaluate the effectiveness of educational efforts.

Health information technology (HIT): (8) A generic term that describes the use of computers and other technologies to capture health data for patients and organizations.

Healthy People 2020: (13) A national plan for improving the health of all Americans. It contains objectives and guidelines for addressing health disparities, preventing premature death, and preventing disease.

HEDIS: (6) Healthcare Effectiveness Data and Information Set; the quality assessment data set used by the National Committee for Quality Assurance. The data gathered for HEDIS assist with quality control and provide quality indicators for managed care organizations.

HIPAA: (7) Health Insurance Portability and Accountability Act; federal legislation that deals with the protection of confidentiality with electronic records.

Hospital Consumer Assessment of Health Care Providers and Systems Survey (HCAHPS): (9) A hospital survey developed through the federal government that includes information to measure improvements in customer services and quality.

Hospital Value-Based Purchasing Program (Hospital VBP): (9) A tool to reward health care organizations, such as health plans and other purchasers, when they improve access, costs, quality, and efficiency.

Human interaction: (12) Part of the Planetree Model; it forms the basis for health care.

Independent Payment Advisory Board (IPAB): (9) An agency that was created under ACA 2010 and charged with saving Medicare costs without affecting quality or coverage.

Individual mandate: (5) A provision of the ACA that requires all nonexempt American citizens to have health insurance or pay a fine.

Informed consent: (2) In a medical context, the situation in which the patient understands the procedure or treatment to be given and gives permission for its implementation. Informed consent includes educating the patient on all aspects of the procedure or treatment in terms that he or she can understand.

Institute for Healthcare Improvement (IHI): (11) A nonprofit organization that collaborates with hospitals and other healthcare institutions to improve the quality of patient care.

Institutional ethics committee: (10) A group that exists to address general ethics issues for a healthcare organization. It advises on ethics issues, reviews policy, and provides education.

Institutional review board (IRB): (10) A committee that deals with ethics issues related to research, such as informed consent and protection of research subjects.

Integrative medicine: (6) Sometimes called complementary and alternative medicine; an area of medicine that includes services not traditionally covered in medical schools. Examples include massage and acupuncture.

I-THOU: (1) In Buber's theory, the highest moral relationship between people. It means that one chooses to make another beloved.

Justice: (4) A principle of ethics that addresses what is fair or what is deserved.

Labeling: (14) The practice of assigning names to people based on their disease, personal characteristics, or behaviors.

Lean system: (11) A tool for assessing and improving the quality of healthcare processes and services.

Liberty principle: (1) In Rawls's theory, the principle that all people should have the same rights as others in the society.

Managed care: (6) A generic term for a number of healthcare insurance options whose mission is to provide quality and cost-effective health care.

Mandate: (5) An official order to do something, such as to purchase health insurance.

Market justice: (4) A form of justice that is based on principles of capitalism. The ability to pay for goods and services is part of market justice.

Maximum principle: (1) In Rawls's theory, the principle that, in a just society, the needs of those in a lesser position must be addressed.

Medically necessary: (9) A descriptor for treatments that are appropriate for patient care.

MGMA: (7) Medical Group Management Association; an organization that represents the interests of group practice managers.

Moral awareness: (8) The process of discerning the potential ethical issues surrounding technology use or in other healthcare situations.

Moral development: (1) The concept in Kohlberg's theory that describes how individuals grow morally.

Moral hazard: (9) This term is used to explain the increase in the use of the healthcare system when individuals are insured. They chose to avoid health risks and therefore, see healthcare professionals more frequently.

Moral integrity: (14) The process of consistently applying virtue and practical wisdom to make ethical decisions.

Mortality rate: (13) A numerical way to measure the number of deaths in a population.

Natural law: (1) St. Thomas Aquinas's theory of ethics, which emphasizes God's gift of rationality and humans' ability to choose good over evil.

NCQA: (7) National Committee for Quality Assurance; an organization that accredits managed care organizations and assesses quality through its data sets and programs.

Noncompliant-patient culture: (12) A culture in which people wait to get treatment or resist compliance when they are treated. Such actions often worsen individuals' health conditions.

Nonmaleficence: (3) The principle of "First do no harm." In health care, the term also means to avoid unnecessary harm.

Normative ethics: (1) A type of ethics concerned with how ethics is used. It applies to both individual and organizational ethics practices.

Original position: (1) The hypothetical proposition created by Rawls to explain his ethics theory; it assumes that all people are equal.

ORYX® system: (11) A tool developed by The Joint Commission for assessing quality in healthcare organizations.

O Team: (9) The top leaders of a hospital or other organization. Examples are the chief executive officer (CEO), chief information officer (CIO), chief nursing officer (CNO), and chief financial officer (CFO).

Paternalism: (12) In health care, the situation in which an authority figure believes that he or she should make decisions in the patient's best interest because of his or her superior knowledge.

Patient-centered care: (12) A form of health care that considers the patient to be the primary concern for the professional or organization.

Patient justice: (4) A form of justice based on decisions concerning what is fair or deserved when treating clients or patients. Patients often have a different perception of justice from that of providers or administrators.

Patient-partner culture: (12) A culture in which people practice prevention and wish to be partners in their own health care.

Pediatric ethics committee: (10) A hospital committee that deals with ethics issues related to the care of infants and children. Members of this committee are often on 24-hour call.

Personal morality: (14) An individual's personal moral compass, which the person uses to make decisions about his or her interaction with others and in society.

Planetree Model: (12) A way of delivering health care that emphasizes areas that support health and healing.

Practical wisdom: (1) A key component of Aristotle's theory. It means that one can make the best moral decision by using learning and experience and then act on that decision.

Practice profiling: (6) A mechanism used in managed care to evaluate the use or overuse of services within a medical practice that is under contract with the managed care system.

Preconventional: (1) In Kohlberg's moral development theory, the stage that precedes a person's ability to make moral decisions.

Premoral: (1) Another term for the preconventional stage of Kohlberg's moral development theory.

Principled moral reasoning: (1) In Kohlberg's moral development theory, the use of moral ideas or principles to make decisions.

Professional socialization: (10) A process used to educate individuals on the knowledge, beliefs, standards, ethics, and obligations of being a member of a certain group. This process involves education, practice, and identification with the profession.

Protected patient information: (8) Sensitive patient data that need extra attention for confidentiality protection.

Public health: (13) A healthcare system whose focus is on using community-based efforts to prevent disease and prolong life.

Public health administrators: (13) Public health professionals who are responsible for conducting the business of public health using sound business practices. They also must be able to collaborate with community agencies and facilitate the work of a diverse workforce.

Reasonable person standard: (2) In healthcare law, the level of information that a patient must have to be considered competent to make decisions. It means that there is sufficient information for the average person to make a healthcare decision.

Self-insured: (9) A descriptor for employers who assume the risk of health insurance coverage for their employees.

Self-interest: (1) The idea of addressing what is in the individual's own best interest. In ethics, it can be seen in ethics egoism, in which a person's interests define his or her behaviors.

Self-regulating: (15) The expectation the professionals will police their own behaviors and their peers' behaviors. It includes acceptable practice and ethics behaviors.

Self-treatment: (12) The practices that people use to care for their health before consulting a healthcare professional.

Sense of meaning: (1) A concept that is part of Frankl's theory and forms the core of who we are as people.

Sick role: (12) In a social context, the actions one would take when diagnosed as being ill. There are responsibilities associated with these actions.

Social beneficence: (13) An ethics principle based on the position that well-being is morally important and people should have the ability to seek it.

Social justice: (1) The basis of Rawls's theory of ethics; it is concerned with the ethical practices in a just society and the rights of members of society.

Staff justice: (4) A form of justice that deals with the fair or deserved treatment of staff members.

State sovereignty: (5) The right of a state to do what is needed to govern itself. It includes the right to make and enforce laws and levy taxes.

Stewardship: (9) The management of resources for others. It implies that stewards use care when taking care of property, resources, and financial assets that are not their own.

Technology diffusion: (8) The prevalence of technology within a group or society.

Technology imperative: (8) The assumption that when technology is diffused within a society, it must be used by healthcare organizations and other segments of society.

Telehealth: (8) A form of health technology that uses cameras, computers, and the Internet to support healthcare providers in diagnosing and treating patients from remote sites.

The Joint Commission (TJC): (7) An organization that serves as the major accrediting body for healthcare organizations. It sets standards for acceptable performance, conducts site visits, and works on national programs for improving quality of care.

Upcoding (coding creep): (9) The practice of assigning a billing code that is higher than the actual procedure in order to obtain greater reimbursement.

Utilitarianism: (1) Mill's ethics theory. It is concerned with the consequences of actions and producing the greatest good for the greatest number affected. It also includes preventing the greatest harm.

Utilization review: (6) The process for measuring the effective prescription and use of health care. Reviews can examine use of care by authorization, concurrently with use, or after use.

Veracity: (2) A component of autonomy that deals with telling the truth.

Virtue: (1) Attributes and characteristics that make up moral excellence. People are willing to act on these characteristics, and they form the core of their person. Examples include honesty, fairness, and courage.

Voluntariness: (2) The state in which the patient is not forced into making a decision when providing informed consent.

Way finding: (12) A strategy to assist patients and others in navigating within a healthcare setting.

Index

Note: Page numbers followed by *f* indicate material in figures.